TRANSFORMING INDIA

TRANSFORMING INDIA GAMECHANGER IN ACTION

SUDESH VERMA

Vitasta

Published by
Renu Kaul Verma
Vitasta Publishing Pvt Ltd
4348/4C, Ansari Road, Daryaganj
New Delhi - 110 002
info@vitastapublishing.com

ISBN: 978-81-19670-44-4

First Edition 2024
MRP ₹ 495

Edited by Vichitra Goel
Typeset by Rohit Gautam
Cover Design by Somesh Kumar MISHRA
Printed by Chaman Enterprises, New Delhi

To my mother, Smt Hemant Bala Verma,
whom I lost during Covid.

I realised my helplessness and desperation that I could not provide her with hospitalisation when she needed it the most. I wish she had lived some more years, allowing me the opportunity to care for her as a devoted son, especially after her relocation to Delhi.

To my 86-year-old father, Shri Vijoy Kumar Verma, who lives in his own make-believe world that his son is one of the most educated persons in this country, and chastises me for choosing politics over intellectual pursuits.

Contents

Foreword

1986 was perhaps the most eventful year in the history of independent India. In the month of January, the government decided to reverse the judgement of the Supreme Court of India delivered in 1985, in the Shah Bano case upholding the right of every Indian woman, including divorced women, to receive subsistence allowance under section 125 of the CrPC which was enacted to prevent social vagrancy and destitution.

The Muslim Personal Law Board had strongly protested against this judgment and dubbed it as 'interference in religion' and a 'threat to the Muslim community identity's (Milli Tashakhkhus)'.

A member of Parliament belonging to the Muslim League brought a Private Members Bill in Lok Sabha seeking to reverse the Supreme Court verdict and exclude Muslims from the jurisdiction of section 125 of the CrPC.

At that time, I was Minister of State in the Ministry of Home Affairs, which officially dealt with this subject. Since the controversy was gaining momentum, a meeting was taken by the Prime Minister attended by Home Minister Sri S B Chavan, myself and other officials. In this meeting, I said that the SC verdict has nothing to do with personal laws, instead it has been given under section 125 of CrPC, which deals with prevention of vagrancy and destitution.

I further explained that the object of section 125 of the CrPC is grant of subsistence allowance to the wife or former wife who after desertion or divorce is not in a position to keep her body and soul together, which means that she has no personal income and nobody to support her. This is a measure of social welfare and it provides a speedy remedy for ensuring bare minimum for her survival.

The Prime Minister asked me to explain it in Parliament and accordingly I spoke in Lok Sabha on 23 August 1985 for 57 minutes and tried to clear the misgivings of the critics of the SC verdict. The point I underlined was that most of these cases are result of the obnoxious practice of instant divorce where three arbitrary oral pronouncements are enough to effect divorce. This method of divorce finds no sanction in *Quran*, and the history of Muslim jurisprudence shows that those who resorted to triple divorce were subjected to physical punishment.

Therefore, I argued that instead of opposing the SC verdict, the Board should consider measures to reform the practices which are not only against the clear provisions of *Quran* but morally repugnant as well.

Next day, I was pleasantly surprised to receive a letter from the Prime Minister in which he had said that he is happy to see the widespread appreciation that my speech in Parliament has elicited.

But in next three months, the Personal Law Board and their supporters in the government and the ruling party succeeded in building pressure before which the Prime Minister meekly surrendered, and on 15 January, 1986 he announced that the government and Personal Law Board have reached an understanding and a bill to reverse the SC verdict will be passed in the coming winter session of Parliament.

One can understand that a government has to be sensitive to public grievances but to submit to violent and threatening language is difficult to digest. The Personal Law Board in its campaign had not only used communal slogans but reportedly threatened to break the legs of Muslim MPs who opposed their stand.

The supporters of the Board inside Parliament used highly derogatory language for the honourable Judges of the Supreme Court. Instead of rebuking them, the government accepted their demand and gave credibility and respectability to the politics of communalism. This abject surrender left me with no option but to resign from the government.

This issue came to the fore again in 2017, when the Hon'ble

Supreme Court declared the practice of triple divorce as arbitrary and hence unconstitutional. The Court further observed that it found no mention in the scripture and said that how something that is bad in religion can be good in law. So finally the highest court of the land declared triple divorce as unlawful.

Again the Personal Law Board gave expression to their dissatisfaction with the SC verdict and some of their members said that notwithstanding the verdict the practice will continue. In one month period after the verdict more than 300 cases of triple divorce were reported. One case happened in my former constituency Bahraich. For a month I did all I could do to make the parties understand that this divorce is no more valid and lawful and the husband has no option but to take back the wife. Finally the husband's side agreed but insisted that the girl should go for Halala and then only they would accept her. I was happy that the proposal was outrightly rejected by the girl.

It was at this stage that I wrote a long letter to the Prime Minister Sri Narendra Modi and requested him to make a law to make triple divorce, an unlawful act and a punishable offence otherwise the verdict of the Supreme Court will be as good as dead letter.

To my surprise, next day, I was given time to meet the Prime Minister. We discussed the issue for about an hour and the Prime Minister agreed that a new law is needed to give effect to the verdict of the Supreme Court and save the dignity of Muslim women and future of the children who become real victims in the wake of such unfortunate situations.

Right from 1986, I was involved with individuals and organisations who were campaigning for banning of triple divorce but I had not even imagined that one meeting with Narendra Modi Ji would produce positive result so quickly. I could hardly believe my ears when an officer of Parliament informed me a week later that the draft bill has reached Parliament Secretariat.

Within few days the bill was passed and Congress MPs walked out of the house at the time of passage. But they blocked it in Rajya Sabha and it took almost two years for the government to manage the majority therein and then it became a law in August 2019.

Iraq was the first country to ban triple divorce in 1920 and subsequently all Muslim countries did the same. Even Pakistan, including Bangladesh, legally banned this practice in 1962. So India was the only country where this obnoxious practice continued legally till 2019.

The official data shows that after the banning of this particular mode of divorce, the rate of divorce in Muslim society has declined by more than 96 per cent. Do we realise that this one measure has liberated the Muslim women from the perpetual fear in which they lived and saved the future of many innocent children?

The political biases and prejudices do not allow us to take an objective view of the importance of this brave step taken by our Prime Minister in the face of same kind of opposition which was demonstrated after the Shah Bano verdict. But I am confident that history will judge him as the greatest benefactor of Indian Muslim women for putting an end to a custom which was no less worse than Sati. This one measure has immensely empowered Muslim women and has strengthened the Indian quest for gender equity.

Prime Minister Modi's focus has been on bringing people above poverty line and making their life more meaningful by integrating them into the larger economic life of the country. His government has uplifted more than 25 crore people from the curse of poverty and it has been recognised the world over. The money allocated for pro-poor schemes is directly reaching the beneficiaries. All the welfare schemes have benefitted all poor people without any kind of distinction.

This book brilliantly captures the country's transition from a group of 'fragile five' to the 'fabulous few' and the massive infrastructural investment that has been done. Modi has given the vision to develop India by 2047 and has laid the foundation for this exciting journey guided by the spirit of *Atmanirbhar Bharat.*

Narendra Modi has taken special steps to encourage India's cultural renaissance based on ancient tradition of acceptance and universal brotherhood. He has especially underlined the universal vision of Indian culture enshrined in the concept of *Vasudhaiva Kutumbakam*. He made every Indian proud by taking yoga to the world stage not only as a recipe for good health but also for peace of mind.

When Sudesh Ji wrote his first book *Narendra Modi: The GameChanger*, he had studied Gujarat and its unparalleled transformation into a state contributing maximum to the country's GDP.

The question he raised then, was whether Modi ji would be able to achieve similar feats for the country after becoming the Prime Minister.

The way Sudesh Ji has described Prime Minister in action is a tribute to Sri Narendra Modi's untiring energy, zeal and commitment to transform India into a super power, whose resources will be used not only for the good of Indians but the whole mankind. This moving description reminds me of a verse of *Bhagavad Gita* :

सक्ताः कर्मणि अविद्वांसः यथा कुर्वन्ति भारत
कुर्यात विद्वान तथा असक्तः चिकीर्षु लोकसंग्रहम्

As the ignorant men work actuated by selfish desires, O Bharata (Arjuna), so should the wise work actuated by the desire to do the welfare of the world.

I wish that the book reaches the hands of many people so that they can appreciate the tremendous work done by the Modi government in the last ten years.

Arif Mohammed Khan
Governor of Kerala and former Union Minister

Preface

My publisher wanted me to revise the book *Narendra Modi: The GameChanger*. However, I found that a mere revision would not do justice to the evolving narrative surrounding Narendra Modi's tenure. The landscape has shifted significantly since the book was last written in 2013 before Modi became the Prime Minister. A hastily revised book came in 2014 after he became the Prime Minister, capturing developments up to his first Independence Day address that year. Yet, the queries from my readers persisted, questioning whether I still deemed him gamechanger.

I stood among the very few who called him the gamechanger early on, having witnessed Gujarat's transformation across development metrics. A befitting thing was to assess how he had performed during his last two terms in office, spanning from 2014-24, encapsulating a nine-year period, from 2014-23.

My friends had wanted me to write a book on Modi when he had completed five years in office. However, I observed that those initial years were primarily focussed on setting things right and laying the groundwork for a big set-off. While some key initiatives had been launched during that time, it seemed premature to assess their impact without allowing sufficient time for implementation. The book would lack depth and fairness unless the initiatives were given a chance to be translated into action.

Nation-building is a continuous process that goes on without a stop. The leaders try to shape the nation as per their vision, but the true measure of their success lies in the assessment by analysts. The strength or weakness of a nation's emergence becomes apparent in various indicators, including the sense of pride in belonging to the country. This can be reflected in both our internal perception of being Indian and external perceptions of others regarding the country and its citizens.

Narendra Modi proved to the world that the development and aspirations of people can indeed become an electoral plank and defeat all divisive issues of religion and caste. The Bharatiya Janata Party (BJP) came to power riding on promises of development and on the plank of checking corruption. The prophets of doom were proved wrong; people aligned with the Modi's dream of making India strong. The BJP-led National Democratic Alliance (NDA) won 336 Lok Sabha seats on its own–a feat that was second only to the electoral performance of the Congress in 1984. Riding a sympathy wave in the wake of the assassination of the then Prime Minister, Smt Indira Gandhi, her son Rajiv Gandhi won a landslide for the Congress and won 404 of the 514 Lok Sabha seats.

Thus, it was after 30 years that a political party had come to majority on its own, winning 282 Lok Sabha seats. It was incredible since critics always held that the BJP would begin with a handicap of minus 15 per cent votes since Muslims are considered to have a pathological hatred for the BJP, and they vote for any party other than the BJP.

The victory in the 2019 Lok Sabha elections proved that the victory in 2014 was not a fluke. Not only did the BJP win from 303 Lok Sabha seats, but the NDA alliance also won from 353 Lok Sabha seats. The victory was attributed primarily to the beneficiary class that benefitted from the Modi's vision of caring for the underprivileged.

My interactions with Narendra Modi while writing the previous book allowed me to delve deep into his emotions and grasp the narrative of transformation first-hand.

The Book *Narendra Modi: The GameChanger* was written much before anyone had imagined that Narendra Modi would become the Prime Minister with such a massive majority. The book offers readers a glimpse into Modi's psyche and his resolve to serve the nation, unfazed by either praise or criticism.

It was rated as bestseller by my publisher and was also identified as one of the most authentic books on Narendra Modi. For a comprehensive understanding of the intricacies and nuances discussed in this book, I encourage readers to also explore *Narendra Modi: The GameChanger,* as some details cannot be reiterated here due to space constraints.

Narendra Modi: The GameChanger resulted in a big dilemma for me. I was so massively impressed by Narendra Modi that I realised I could not maintain a neutral stance any further, and that it would be best to support my subject rather than protect my neutrality.

Should I continue as a journalist and make money, basking in the new-found glory of being the Prime Minister's unauthorised but authentic biographer? Or, should I follow my heart's calling and become a part of the system to bring change? A closer understanding of the Modi phenomenon convinced me he was the country's best bet. Eventually, I made the decision to join the BJP's media relations department. It was the new team formed by the then party President Amit Shah that comprised veteran journalist M J Akbar and others. My interactions with Prime Minister Modi reinforced his message of diligence and perseverance motivating me to defend the party's stance on various platforms.

Recognising the need for a comprehensive evaluation of Modi's tenure, I started writing *Transforming India: Gamechanger in Action.* The performance assessment of the nine-plus years aims to provide readers with an informed perspective on Modi's leadership. While acknowledging the hurdles and shortcomings, it underscores the monumental task of dismantling entrenched systems and vested interests hindering progress.

A comprehensive analysis of the government's performance over the past nine years would help understand the situation. *Transforming India: Gamechanger in Action* empowers readers to make informed decisions and uphold the mandate for change.

Understanding the Leader and His Vision

They alone live, who live for others.
–Swami Vivekananda

To appreciate the impact of Narendra Modi's leadership on India's development since 2014, we need to know some facts about him as we proceed to examine his role as the gamechanger. By knowing his personality and his way of thinking, we can understand how he has implemented his vision through a series of actions.

He never shows off his power ostentatiously. He comes from a small town, Vadnagar, and never acts like the most significant person in the country. He prefers to call himself a *Pradhan Sevak* (main worker). His simplicity and attention to detail impresses everyone who meets him. He has made many new friends because of this quality. People do not feel intimidated or awed upon meeting him, even though he is the most powerful person in the country.

He has a realistic and practical vision for the country's development, influenced by his exposure–his travels, interactions with people at different levels, and his experience as an administrator. Once, when he was the Chief Minister of Gujarat, a young girl from an NGO requested him to allow her organisation to adopt villages for their comprehensive development; he asked her how many villages the organisation wanted to adopt. When the girl timidly said 'One', Modi told her, 'Ask your NGO to adopt as many villages as possible for a larger impact. India is a big country, and to make a difference, the impact has to be large.'[1]

Such is the vision of the Indian Prime Minister for the country's development. He believes that the scale of action in India has to be large to achieve success and make a difference. He looks for this vision in the young entrepreneurs or solution providers interacting with him. He also uses this criterion to make any public decision. It is consistent with the Gandhian Talisman, under which Mahatma Gandhi advises any policymaker to consider the impact of their decision on the underprivileged.

When Modi became the Prime Minister, his task was before him. He had to lead the country's development and governance amidst various challenges and opportunities. He had to balance the interests and aspirations of 1.3 billion people with diverse cultures, languages, religions, and regions. He had to deal with the threats and pressures from external and internal enemies of the nation. He had to implement the reforms and policies he had promised to the people and deliver the results and benefits to them. He had to maintain the stability and unity of his government and his party and manage relations with the allies and the Opposition. He had to represent India on a global stage and work on its image and influence on the world. He had to fulfil his vision of making India a strong, prosperous, and self-reliant nation.

He realised that India, being a huge country, did not have a single easy solution for its development. Each region or area had its own issues and challenges and needed a different development plan. What worked for Gujarat might not work for Bihar or Jharkhand. Understanding the regional differences was key to the development strategy. However, the method of finding a solution was the same. The principles of good governance were the same.

India required a leader who could set an example for others and was honest and upright. His thirteen-year stint as the Chief Minister of Gujarat and his ten-year stint as the Prime Minister of India have shown that he is uncorrupted by authority. He has not used his position to benefit his family or friends. He has contradicted Lord Acton's famous quote, 'Power tends to corrupt, and absolute power corrupts absolutely.' Perhaps this is because, in the West, power is an end in itself, but in the true Indian tradition, power is a means to achieve the common good of the people. In ancient times, kings were judged not by their authority but by the way they used it to protect their subjects.

He does not favour anyone, though it has sometimes cost him the friendship of those who expected rewards for helping him ascend to power. He follows the rules and expects others to do the same. He knows he has to promote merit and equality for everyone so he cannot be biased towards anyone. He prefers to have institutional checks and balances. A case in point is his decision in 2015 that interviews would no longer be a criterion for non-gazetted government jobs.

He developed a model of development as the Chief Minister of Gujarat, providing solutions to governance issues. He would first create a prototype for a small population and then apply the model in other places based on the feedback. Modi has implemented the best practices from Gujarat across the country since becoming the Prime Minister in 2014. His imprint has been visible in the functioning of not only the Union government but also the State governments and the local bodies. He has brought governance reforms by simplifying processes and using IT to improve the interaction between the government and the public.

In October 2021, Modi completed 20 years of being in power, during which he successfully tried to improve good governance. And the results have been astounding. Reform has been the hallmark of his regime, and there is no field of governance where improvement has not taken place. The entire rank and file of the BJP celebrated Modi's governance reforms of the last 20 years.

The celebration was a fitting tribute to rolling out a new culture in government and administration. The Home Minister Amit Shah aptly described it as 'kickstarting the country's journey of good governance and development'. Translated into action, these found expressions in finding solutions to vexatious issues facing the country, according to the BJP President J P Nadda.

'Be it abrogation of Article 370, law against "triple talaq", Rama Temple in Ayodhya, CAA (Citizenship Amendment Act), constitutional status to OBC commission, the GST (Goods and Service Tax), and reservation for economically backward sections, PM Modi has resolved issues that ailed country for last 70 years and implemented decisions (that) will lay the foundation of a strong nation', Nadda said.[2]

Celebration in the BJP was not a boisterous affair. People did not dance on the streets. The cadre undertook the task of service to people during the 20-day *Seva aur Samarpan Abhiyan*. BJP workers participated in creating awareness about the cleaning of rivers, various welfare schemes of the Union government, organising blood donation camps, creating consciousness about protecting the environment and offering prayers in temples and Gurdwaras between 17 September and 7 October. On Modi's birthday, 17 September, the country achieved the rare distinction of vaccinating close to 2.25 crore people in one day. Such a feat was not possible without a firm resolve and commitment. It filled Indians with confidence and raised our heads high, on what we could if we decided to.

Commenting on the feat, Modi said, 'I had never imagined that I would rise from the post of Chief Minister to the post of Prime Minister (but) on this day, 20 years ago, I got a new responsibility to serve the public. My journey of serving the people...living among the people... had been ongoing for many decades earlier, but 20 years ago, I got a new responsibility–as the Chief Minister of Gujarat.'[3]

Modi's life has been an example for most Indians of what one can achieve with sheer determination and effort. When he became the Chief Minister of Gujarat, he had no administrative or legislative experience. The task was daunting, and it was a crown of thorns since the state was devastated following the earthquake of 26 January 2001. Rebuilding the state amidst chaos was a Herculean task. Modi, being a workaholic, undertook efforts and leadership to mobilise the society and organise the largest relief and rehabilitation exercises the country had ever seen. One needs to visit Kutch–completely destroyed by the earthquake–to understand the task undertaken to transform Bhuj into a modern city.

Another trait of Modi is he does not compromise on his principles. His tenure in Gujarat saw many challenges because he did not compromise. I remember the story of two media giants in the state approaching him and the late Arun Jaitley, the then party in-charge for Gujarat. The representatives of these two media organisations had asked for a price for better image management. Modi and Jaitley had a one-to-one meeting and then declined the offer. While the media continued with efforts to tarnish his image, Modi kept carving space in people's hearts by working for their betterment. No matter how much the media houses predicted doom for Modi, he always emerged triumphed.

But this does not mean he is not flexible. He is ready to improvise if it helps in achieving the larger goal. For instance, he did not withdraw the demonetisation decision in 2016, instead, he adjusted the government's steps according to the changing situations. His intention was not to trouble the commoners but to curb the role of black money in the economy.

Only a leader confident of his decisions and commitment to the nation can take such a bold step as demonetisation. While critics would continue to pick loopholes, those who know the system are aware that this bold step saved the country from falling into the trap of a black economy. Also, this helped to bring greater transparency in the system besides keeping the prices of various sectors under control. Housing has become more affordable. It increased the premium of hard-earned money and, accompanied by many other legislations, launched a frontal attack on *benami* transactions. Earn money transparently, pay taxes and live happily–became the new mantra.

There are many instances of the government pulling back due to intense public pressure. One would recollect the farmers' agitation demanding a repeal of the three farm laws passed by the Parliament in 2020. The government brought these laws to modernise agriculture and increase private sector participation in agriculture without compromising on the interests of the farmers. Vested interests to mobilise public opinion against the Modi government, supported the agitation where emotion ruled over logical reasoning and furore dictated democracy.

The affluent farmers created doubts in the minds of ordinary farmers regarding the possibility of the government abolishing the Minimum Support Price (MSP) regime, and the northern part of the country witnessed massive agitation. The agitation had also become a security threat, as highlighted by the then Chief Minister of Punjab, Captain Amarinder Singh.[4] Anti-India interests across the world had started ganging up, making their best attempts to undermine the country's democratic credentials.

The government tried its best to persuade the farmers to see reason, but the task was too daunting. Finally, without losing logic or argument, Modi decided to withdraw the three farm laws. The words of the Prime Minister while announcing the decision to withdraw after almost a year of the farmers' agitation were profound. On the occasion of the Guru Nanak Jayanti, on 19 November 2021, he addressed the nation while announcing the withdrawal:

> While apologising to the nation, I want to say with a sincere and pure heart that maybe something was lacking in our *tapasya* (dedication) that we could not explain the truth, which was as clear as the light of the diya, to some of our farmer brothers. But today is *Prakash Parv*, not the time to blame anyone. Today, I want to tell the country that we have decided to repeal the three farm laws.

The Prime Minister insisted that the three farm laws were beneficial to the farmers, but he took the onus when he said that the government had failed to convince a section of the farming community despite its best efforts. He did not harbour ill will or a feeling of insult. It is because he had worked sincerely and had good intentions to work for the farmers. While the Opposition assumed that the farmers' agitation would damage the BJP electorally, the BJP's decisive victory at the assembly elections in Uttar Pradesh in March 2022 proved them wrong.

Modi can make tough decisions without affecting his popularity because he has no ulterior motives. He follows the philosophy of *Nishkaam Yogi*, taught in the *Bhagavad Gita*. It means a person must work selflessly, with dedication, without any attachment or expectations of results. Modi's life journey is an example of this attitude, and this is the message he wants to give to the younger generation. Roadblocks will come, but if you stay steadfast and do not succumb to the pressure, you will come out with flying colours. All his interactions with students or people carry this underlying message.

Smarting under the insult of not being able to blame Modi for the Gujarat riots, the miffed media tried harder to bring him down and portrayed a negative image of him. The entire establishment of the United Progressive Alliance (UPA) targeted him because they knew that he could throw them out of power. The UPA government launched a witch-hunt against both Modi and Amit Shah (the then Home Minister of Gujarat) and unleashed Central agencies to implicate them. Modi faced all the inquiries, and none found anything worth incriminating him. People loved him for his honesty and integrity, and when the right time came, they rewarded him by voting him to power at the Centre in 2014, giving the BJP the largest-ever victory.

His character has helped him overcome difficulties, even as the Prime Minister for two terms. The Opposition, hurt upon losing out to him, did not stop and heaped personal abuses on him. But he stood steadfast and worked tirelessly for people's welfare. He has built a strong bond of trust with the masses.

Narendra Modi has been a wanderer and loner. It has kept him looking for new meanings in life, finding spirituality while interacting with children and finding solutions. His loneliness and selflessness help him to connect with the ordinary man. 'Service to man is service to God', said Swami Vivekananda. Modi is bringing this vision into reality.

I have often witnessed my middle-class friends hold a grudge against his efforts to empower the poor and the deprived. I have often heard them complain that the Prime Minister is not doing much for the middle class and is splurging resources only on the deprived. However, this is not true. Many of his initiatives, such as developing good infrastructure, creating a conducive environment for entrepreneurship, and enhancing the ease of doing business, will create new opportunities for the middle class.

The underprivileged of the country deserve attention. Our Prime Minister has himself experienced poverty, and he understands the problems of such families when they face illness or lack of money for food or education. Sometimes, they even struggle to feed their family a nutritious meal. It is a challenging task to provide education and top-class medical care to everyone. Nonetheless, he is doing his best even amidst the constraints.

He has launched the free ration scheme, also known as Pradhan Mantri Garib Kalyan Anna Yojana, which provides 5 kg of food grains and 1 kg of pulses per month to 80 crore people since the COVID-19 outbreak. The scheme will continue till December 2028. He has also launched the Ayushman Bharat Scheme, also known as Pradhan Mantri Jan Arogya Yojana, which provides health insurance coverage of up to Rs 5 lakh per year to 50 crore people from the underprivileged and vulnerable section of society. It is the world's largest health insurance scheme.

Modi's life journey inspires an average Indian who sees his rise to the top as his own achievement. A child who had sold tea in trains plying to and fro Vadnagar Railway Station had become the country's Prime Minister. It is aspirational India, where the lineage of the family or caste does not count on parameters of success. Modi is following his dreams, and demolishing ascription-based order to usher in true democracy.

Modi is a fast learner–be it technology or governance, or even ways to use technology for good governance. As a greenhorn political administrator, he allowed the bureaucrats to become his torch-bearers. After getting a grip on the administration, the entire bureaucracy followed his lead. It is because his vision was clear, and once he had honed the instrument of implementation, the task of providing good governance became much easier.

He is an organisational man and understands human behaviour quite well. He was trained in the Rashtriya Swayamsevak Sangh (RSS), where he learned the values of ideology, discipline, and organisation. He is a good listener who always encourages his officials to suggest practical solutions. He is a leader who knows what he wants for his people. He continued the same approach even after becoming the Prime Minister. There are many stories about a person who had a five-minute appointment with the Prime Minister whom he ended up meeting for hours. This is because he is interested in solution-oriented presentations and pays attention to details. Hence, even his cabinet colleagues are always alert while discussing issues about their ministries.

He encourages the younger generation of high-tech professionals to provide easy and quick solutions to the problems faced by India. He quickly adapts to new technologies and uses the same to empower people. He is dismantling orthodox thinking and making decisions faster, but the superstructure is too strong, and it needs time to respond to the changing hemlines.

Change is faster than one can imagine. The youth of the country dreams big. The young are not affected by feudalism; they treat everyone equally and seek to be treated with respect. Bringing them together and leading them in the right direction is the main task. The country's 65 per cent population is in the category of youth. Modi has championed the New Education Policy to bring flexibility to education so that youths can acquire skills that would enable them to make a decent living. The way start up companies are mushrooming, India is likely to become the start up capital of the world.

His spirituality, rooted in the cultural moorings of the country, encourages him to promote human values, rule-based order and the philosophy of *vasudhaiva kutumbakam* (the world is one family). However, he is also aware of the harsh realities of the evil forces that work to destroy humanity. Closer home, he is aware that some of the ambitious neighbours of India are jealous of the country's progress and would do everything to undermine peace and stability.

He knows that the country's territorial integrity is significant for people to realise their highest potential. Therefore, he does not hesitate to make decisions that strengthen the armed forces. India's military capabilities have tremendously strengthened under his leadership. India will no longer be passive if someone tries to strike at its sovereignty. He is the leader of the new India, keen to assert itself and demonstrate that it should not be taken for granted.

In addition to energising the country on a faster growth trajectory, he is consistently working towards uplifting India's image internationally. He happens to be the first Prime Minister born in independent India (1950). He had, thus, no colonial baggage. Moreover, he has been representing the largest population in the world. No Indian Prime Minister had such massive support of the people as he enjoys today. This confidence is evident during his interaction with various global leaders. The Indian diaspora is elated that brand India has gained prominence since Modi became the Prime Minister.

Narendra Modi has been working hard to transform the country and change its political discourse. He has nothing to do for himself. He is like a person who does not need anything for himself but one who is trying to remove fetters and empower people using the instrument of the state to deliver the goods. What should be the motive of an elected government? To work for every citizen without discrimination. The country has been trying to move away from the politics of caste and religion to the politics of development.

The last mile delivery has become much better because of the introduction of JAM (Jan Dhan Yojana Accounts, Aadhaar as identity for benefit transfer and Mobile for sending messages once the payment gets credited to accounts of beneficiaries). Late Prime Minister Rajiv Gandhi had stated that due to leakages in the system, only 15 paisa of the 100 in a Rupee reaches the intended beneficiaries of various government schemes. He would have been a happy man today after seeing that the entire 100 per cent reaches them now because of electronic transfer. The beneficiary class seems happy, too.

The trinity of JAM has helped save Rs 1.78 lakh crore by plugging loopholes and removing the names of fake beneficiaries. One can only speculate who was pocketing the money and who had vested interests in keeping such a system moving.

There are close to 440 schemes of the Union government where subsidies are transferred directly into the account of the intended beneficiaries. There are more than 104 crore beneficiaries of various government schemes. The Direct Benefit Transfer (DBT) is disbursed through the Public Financial Management System (PFMS) which facilitates digital transfers and tracks fund transfers from the government accounts into the bank accounts of intended beneficiaries. There are approximately 1,016 schemes, including state schemes, where payments are made through PFMS.

Modi is a tech-savvy politician who knows the significance of digital technology and its effective use in ordering transparency and better governance. The faith of the common man, particularly the youth, in the system has increased manifold. Registration of companies and tax compliances have become easier and more transparent. Systems of claims and refunds have become more transparent and accountable in the tax departments. Most services are available online, including the issuance of passports and various licences. Many institutes of excellence have been developed, including multiple AIIMS, IITs and IIMs. More opportunities have been made available in IT-enabled services.

One of my friends who is a businessman, while commenting on the Modi government's policies, said, 'The business has suffered a loss due to lack of understanding of various schemes by our vendors. People used to old ways find it difficult to work, and the transition is torturous. But, I am happy that the system is trying to bring transparency and accountability. My son will not face the problems I faced. He will not need to wait before a non-descript bureaucrat just to meet and get his problems resolved. The country will benefit.'

Many things have improved since he told me this at the time of the launch of the GST regime when confusion prevailed due to a lack of clarity or failure of understanding on the part of businessmen. Many people agree that the ease of doing business has promoted a start up environment like never before. A transition takes time. But the country has moved swiftly towards more compliance. That most people now prefer to pay through cards rather than cash is a testimony to the Modi vision. Even in the real estate, the use of cash has diminished considerably.

What distinguishes Modi from others is the immense trust he has in people. He has introduced IT so extensively that even for a labourer working in the field, his smartphone is his priority. He may be illiterate but he wants to stay connected with the world. CoWIN has won the hearts and trust of people. The rapid rate of vaccination has saved people's lives.

The world has produced many leaders constrained by the fear of how the world would judge them. It limited their abilities to make difficult decisions even when needed in the interest of the country. This decision-making is what defines the leader. And one can make bold decisions only if one is sure of the vision, the goal and the need to venture into uncharted territory.

One has to overcome fear to make bold decisions that can shape the country's future. It is like building dikes of courage to hold back the flood of fear that Martin Luther King Jr spoke about. It comes from spiritualism. It comes from understanding what people desire from their leader. Politics is like a baton race. Finally, you pass the baton after running your part to the best of your abilities. If one's conscience is clear, one can take decisive steps without fear or favour. And Modi has been working with a clear conscience.

Martin Luther King Jr said, 'There comes a time when one must take a position that is neither safe, nor politic, nor popular, but he must take it because his conscience tells him it is right.'

Prime Minister Modi

Some are born great, some achieve greatness,
and some have greatness thrust upon them.
–William Shakespeare, Twelfth Night.

It would be interesting to analyse some of the prominent Indian Prime Ministers on this parameter. The same would help us understand Narendra Modi better.

Jawaharlal Nehru, India's first Prime Minister, was born with a silver spoon. He was foreign-educated, foreign-bred and lived a life of luxuries. The more eligible leaders during the pre-Independence movement were sidelined while Nehru became the Prime Minister. His idea of a command economy was borrowed from the socialistic philosophy of the then Soviet Union.

Lal Bahadur Shastri, who succeeded him, was the son of the soil, and his popularity increased by leaps and bounds when he gave the slogan of *Jai Jawan, Jai Kisan*. If it were not for his untimely death, he would have become an iconic Prime Minister with his simplicity and inner strength. But he died under suspicious circumstances in Tashkent after signing a peace treaty with Pakistan.

Indira Gandhi became the Prime Minister due to her father's legacy. However, she worked hard to consolidate her position in a male-dominated world. India's decisive victory over Pakistan in 1971 and the formation of Bangladesh proved that she was a leader made of steel. Though the Emergency brought her political fortunes down, she bounced back. She was further increasing and strengthening her political influence when she was assassinated by her bodyguards.

The forces that opposed the Emergency came to power in 1977. There were many contenders for the top job but the baton came to Morarji Desai as JP supported him. One must recall that there were many contenders for the post. Hence, it cannot be said that Desai worked hard to provide leadership or had public endorsement.

Rajiv Gandhi owed his post to his mother's sad demise, but he raised the hopes of the average Indian when he spoke against corruption and tried to acquire the image of being Mr Clean. However, the case of Bofors Kickbacks and the revolt by V P Singh, the then defence minister, tarnished his image. Singh had worked hard to create a movement against corruption and the entire country seemed to rise under his leadership.

The combined Opposition launched a massive agitation, and Singh became the Prime Minister. However, he acquired the magical wand of caste polarisation to create his own constituency. Though it did not benefit him, his disciples Lalu Prasad Yadav and Mulayam Singh Yadav weaved the caste narrative better to stay in power in Bihar and Uttar Pradesh, respectively.

P V Narasimha Rao became the Prime Minister after the assassination of the late Rajiv Gandhi, who left the Congress leaderless. He was chosen because he was considered meek and pliable. Chandra Shekhar, H D Deve Gowda, and I K Gujral became Prime Ministers by circumstances. Dr Manmohan Singh got the top job because Sonia Gandhi calculated him to be meek, weak, and docile. They all had one thing in common–they had not worked hard or had a public mandate to be the Prime Minister, even if they had other qualities that helped them to deliver as per their roles.

Atal Bihari Vajpayee and Narendra Modi do not fall into any of the categories explained above. So good was his understanding of the society and the oratory as Nehru had predicted that Vajpayee would become Prime Minister one day. Vajpayee, along with L K Advani and Dr Murli Manohar Joshi, worked hard to take the BJP to every Indian heart. Anyone who has heard him speak or met him personally would be mesmerised by his persona.

After Advani announced in 1995 in Mumbai that Vajpayee would be the Prime Ministerial candidate from the BJP, it was just a matter of time before the entire country waited to see him as the Prime Minister. The BJP emerged as the single largest party in the 1996 Lok Sabha elections but could not get a majority. Vajpayee became the Prime Minister for 13 days, after which he resigned since he did not get the support of other parties.

During the 1998 Lok Sabha elections, the main issue was stability since no party other than the Congress could complete a full term in office. The experiments of coalition governments in 1977, 1989, and 1996 were not encouraging, and this evoked a feeling that no party other than the Congress could provide political stability.

In the 1998 Lok Sabha polls, the BJP under Vajpayee won more Lok Sabha seats than earlier, but it was still short of the majority. But the party had now weaved a coalition of other parties, and Vajpayee became the Prime Minister for the second time. However, he lost confidence in the Lok Sabha in April 1999 after being in power for 13 months. Pakistan waged the Kargil war in May, and Vajpayee, the Prime Minister, had to deal with the situation. The entire country witnessed the war on their television screens and lauded Vajpayee's deft handling of the situation.

Vajpayee became the Prime Minister for the third time in 1999 with the full majority of the National Democratic Alliance that promised an agenda-based stable coalition. The alliance won 303 seats even though the BJP could not improve its numbers. The coalition lasted its term of a full five years.

After Vajpayee, it was Narendra Modi who proved to the world that he could work hard and achieve greatness. The journey from serving tea to passengers in trains at Vadnagar as a kid to becoming the Prime Minister of India was almost impossible. After years of sleepless nights, the struggle and the desire to do something meaningful propelled him to the top post.

Narendra Modi's fate has been such that he always creates history. A sadhu had once predicted that he would become the King. However, the prediction was forgotten in the chapters of his struggle, where the family barely managed even two meals a day. God finally showered his blessings on him when he became the Chief Minister of Gujarat even when he was not a member of either House of the State Legislature. Before that, he had not even contested an electoral post ever. He took oath as the Chief Minister of Gujarat four times and stayed as Chief Minister until he moved to the Centre to take oath as the Prime Minister of India.

When you work hard and shape your destiny, the entire world comes calling. None could miss the grand show at the Sardar Vallabhbhai Patel in 2012, where he took the oath (fourth time) as the Chief Minister. The ceremony was viewed across 83 nations, including the USA, the UK, Australia, and Canada. Modi took a victory lap in the packed stadium.

People in Gujarat lovingly called him *Chhote* Sardar (after Sardar Vallabhbhai Patel), and they knew that their leader would soon move to Delhi to lead the country from the front. He had proved his skills as an able administrator and a leader of the masses.

When Narendra Modi took oath as the Prime Minister of India on 26 May 2014, he had already become the most popular leader India had ever seen. He represented a vast sea of humanity and was the first Prime Minister of India not born in British India. It was not an easy task. Modi had worked very hard to get this mandate.

His marathon campaign helped the BJP to an unprecedented victory–no single party since 1984 had secured a majority. The BJP won 282 Lok Sabha seats whereas the BJP-led National Democratic Alliance won 336 Lok Sabha seats.

Modi had already emerged as the country's hope for rejuvenation. The sweeping victory was prompted by the hope people saw in Narendra Modi and his idea of India–the strength of a cultural renaissance with modern values. People knew that the country was in safe hands.

The five years (from 2014-19) of the Modi government have been a period of intense action and fast decision-making. No government before this seemed to be in so much hurry to change things. This sense of urgency was missing after India gained Independence. When Nehru became the first Prime Minister of India after the General Elections in 1951-52, he was a tad too guided by Western worldview and liberalism. While we had no problems fighting a war with Pakistan, our inadequate military preparedness lay exposed when we faced war with China. Nehru could not fathom that China could attack India, and the Indian defence forces were immensely ill-equipped to fight the war. It inflicted a lethal blow to our morale as a strong nation.

The unrestrained energy that defined India's golden age, the wealth that attracted foreign invaders to India and India that sustained the mighty British Empire were chained in bureaucracy and babudom. Entrepreneurship that had got hooked to government patronage needed to be unshackled. However, Nehru did not seem interested in dismantling the British legacy and the thought process that worked for the continuation of the system.

The same police used by the British masters to arouse fear in the masses to facilitate better tax collection, were retained. Patel laid the foundation for All India Civil Services as a unifying force. However, the corrections that could make it more effective for good governance were ignored. Alas, Patel died in 1950, much before the formation of the first democratically elected government under free India. Had he been alive, he would have certainly applied quick correctives.

Mahatma Gandhi spoke about strengthening the villages and wanted power to flow upwards like a pyramid. His idea of Village Republics was a suitable model for a big country like India that had so much diversity. Nehru chose just the opposite. He believed in the trickle-down approach. Under him, the government became all-powerful, and individuals got habituated to looking towards the government for everything. The *mai-baap* approach that defined the British government continued.

Nehru did nothing to break this nexus. A strong leader was needed, who could redefine India and where individuals could dream big and script their destinies. The government should have been merely a facilitator. The legacy of the past made successive governments the biggest purchasers of goods and services and the biggest distributors of the largesse. It bred corruption. Access to those in power meant access to finance, licences, and even jobs. It created a different mentality that persuaded everyone to try for a government job first.

Prime Minister Jawaharlal Nehru envisioned a command economy for the country's economic growth. But Modi's vision says that the trickle-down theory would not work for a country as huge as India.

The arteries of human capabilities must be unclogged by liberating individuals from governmental controls and enabling them to achieve excellence and write India's success stories. The government would play the role of the facilitator of economic growth and encourage private players to participate in economic development.

P V Narasimha Rao gave a death blow to this approach in the 1990s. He tried to free the economy from the various bondages and encouraged entrepreneurship. The wave of liberalisation integrated the economy with the outside world, and India started dreaming of growing fast into an economic superpower. However, the opening of the superstructure was not supported by a matching infrastructure and institutional reforms.

The structure of bureaucracy that trained individuals to assume they were the Kings of the yesteryears continued. A matching reform in bureaucracy and strong institutional checks and balances were lacking. This mismatch created unheard-of opportunities to indulge in corruption at unprecedented levels. The era after that, except the period of the NDA regime under Atal Bihari Vajpayee, was marked with corruption and nepotism of the worst kind. The regime of United Progressive Alliance (2004-14) under the then Prime Minister Dr Manmohan Singh witnessed scams one after the other. The 2G scam, the mines allocation scam, defence scams etc. became the talk of the country. This period also witnessed agitation against corruption as seen in the Anna agitation.

In the various seminars and conferences all across the country, people started talking about black money and how siphoning off wealth to the tax haven countries had negatively impacted India's image and, subsequently, its potential to become a superpower. Nothing moved in the corridors of power without greasing the palms of decision-makers, and people seemed to be losing faith in the system. Different forces and personalities worked, either separately or together, to highlight the issues faced by the country. The Anna movement articulated this frustration, and people across the country came on the streets. Something must be done to stop the rot.

It was during this time that Narendra Modi rose like a Phoenix from the ashes of controversies surrounding his first term as Chief Minister of Gujarat. He had become Chief Minister in October 2001, and Gujarat witnessed the burning of *karsevaks* in Sabarmati Express at Godhra Railway Station on 27 February 2002. Fifty-nine people, mostly women and children, died. This was followed by riots that took away many innocent lives from both the communities–Muslims and Hindus. The official figures said 1,044 people were killed and 2,500 were injured. Close to 223 people were missing. Of the dead, 790 were Muslim and 254 Hindu.

Hence, began a fight between a biased pseudo-secular media and Modi. While this media tried to blame the riots squarely on the Chief Minister, Modi focused his attention on developing the country and dismantling the institutions inhibiting economic growth and progress. The entire UPA establishment had given *supari* (bribe) to this media to defame Modi and the BJP. Facts have now come out that the CBI used cigarette butts on the hand of senior Intelligence Bureau (IB) official R S Mani to force him to implicate Amit Shah in an encounter that killed terrorists, including Ishrat Jahan.

Now it has become clear that Teesta Setalvad and her NGO, funded by Congress and other agencies, were given the task of attacking Modi and spoiling his image. However, the Congress, NGO, and media triad failed to achieve their design. The Special Investigation Team (SIT) set up to look into the Gujarat riots did not find any authenticity in the blame this section tried to put on Modi. The court gave a clean chit to Modi. Amit Shah, too, walked out honourably, and the charges against him in the case of a fake encounter with terrorists were dropped. Imagine what damage a party in power can do if it acts in vengeance and forces its agencies to fabricate evidence. Modi continued in power in Gujarat for more than 12 years, but he defeated those trying to damage his image. It is still surprising how he was framed as the villain when he tried his best to control the riots.[1]

Ignoring the witch-hunt by the then ruling Congress government at the Centre and a tirade by the vested interests, Narendra Modi refused to be perturbed and stayed focused on his development agenda. He knew he was trying to achieve growth and prosperity for Gujarat and he had no qualms in saying so. When the Sachar Committee visited him and sought to know what he was doing for the welfare of minorities, he said he was not doing anything. When asked what he meant, he said he was working for six crore Gujaratis, including Muslims. The *sabka saath, sabka vikas* agenda took birth in this belief that what is good for one, is good for the other too. Why should the government talk in terms of Hindus or Muslims?

Unprepared for such a reply, the Sachar committee was dumbfounded. The facts from the state testified to the improved status of Muslims. Muslims had more representation in government jobs than their proportionate population. Maximum *Zakat* came from Gujarat, showing the economic empowerment of the community. Modi used to say that if he had built better roads, those were for every citizen of the country. The media that sought to find discrimination was proved wrong.

Under the leadership of Narendra Modi, Gujarat clocked a double-digit growth, and the Indian growth story owed a lot to the Gujarat story. The state attracted maximum foreign investment from Non-Resident Gujaratis (NRGs). 'Sow a Rupee and reap a Dollar' was his slogan. The state became the model state of development in all parameters. In place of drought, the state had enough water. The dried aquifers were easily recharged with the innovative schemes implemented by the state government.[2]

Modi successfully implemented his development vision as Chief Minister of Gujarat for 13 years from 2001 to 2014. His task after becoming the Prime Minister in 2014 was to replicate the good practices from Gujarat all over the country. People have liked his approach to addressing the problems. The slogan of *sabka sath, sabka vikas* (support from all, development of all) was coined during this phase.

His abilities to put the plan into action and being a doer and deliverer caught the attention of all countrymen, particularly the youths desperate for a change. They were not bothered about what the people with vested interests were saying. They were not bothered about the past. They wanted a new beginning for a new India that would witness economic prosperity and make India the Superpower that it deserved to be.

They wanted economic empowerment and the country to move faster than ever. Modi had emerged as their best bet. He seemed to be filling the void created by the Anna movement. In the 2014 Lok Sabha elections, the BJP under his leadership became the single largest majority party–a feat that any party has achieved after 30 years. Along with the allies, the NDA presented a formidable alliance. India had voted decisively for Modi and the change that he represented.

Modi tried to live up to the expectations from day one. He launched many pro-poor schemes the country had not heard of. He took momentous decisions to set things right internally and create a level playing field. He showcased India to the world and brought new international recognition to the country. He took steps to unleash the creative energy of the youths, as we will see in the subsequent chapters.

Five years later, when he faced the polls again, people rejected the Opposition's tirade and gave him a bigger mandate than ever before. He became India's most popular and loved leader. When Congress made a baseless charge of '*Chowkidar chor hai*', Modi gave a befitting reply by changing his Display Picture (DP) to '*Mai bhi chowkidar*'.

Modi secured an unprecedented victory for the BJP in the 2019 Lok Sabha elections. The party won 303 seats, and the NDA won 353. The BJP also witnessed a substantial increase in its vote share. The Opposition Congress won only 52 seats, which was not enough to give Rahul Gandhi the status of the Opposition leader.

Narendra Modi took oath as the Prime Minister of India for a second time on 30 May 2019. People wanted to give him enough time to consolidate his unfinished agenda of developing and transforming India. If his first tenure was for reaping the seeds and achieving institutional changes, the second tenure was the time to see the seeds growing into trees and bearing fruits. Both the tenures must be taken together to analyse what the country has achieved under his leadership.

His popularity is ever on the rise, even as he is the world's most popular leader. *The Economist* headlined one of its articles in June 2023 as 'Narendra Modi is the world's most popular leader'. It said Modi has been more popular than his party, the BJP. 'With an approval rating of 77 per cent, the Prime Minister is more than twice as popular as his party. He is by far the world's most popular elected leader.'[3]

A few months ago, it had pronounced Modi the most popular leader and with a popularity rating of 76 per cent, he was ahead of US President Joe Biden and UK Prime Minister Rishi Sunak.

New Cultural Awakening, Removing Vestiges

Just as a man would not cherish living in a body other than his own,
so do nations not like to live under other nations,
however noble and great the latter may be.
–Mahatma Gandhi

While India gained independence in 1947, vestiges of the British legacy and governance refused to die and were carried over by new India's democratically elected leaders. Despite the cosmetic changes, the structures remained essentially colonial, perpetuating the British legacy.

The British discarded everything Indian, and the Macaulay education system replaced the Indian system that produced human beings rooted in Indian culture and tradition, preaching universal brotherhood and community living.

Lord Thomas Babington Macaulay introduced the English system of education to produce Indians who were British in taste, habits and orientation. Macaulay's Minute premised that English education is superior in not just 'science' but also inculcates higher morals, etc. He believed this was what made the English superior.[1] He envisaged creating 'a class of persons, Indian in blood and colour, but English in taste, in opinions, in morals, and in intellect'.[2]

He came to India as a law member of the Governor General's Executive Council and was soon appointed President of the Committee of Public Instruction. Even after 75 years, a lot needs to be changed.

The British system produced 'brown sahibs' who looked at their own culture with contempt and sought solutions through the Western model. These brown sahibs produced the Command economy and trickle-down theory and jettisoned Mahatma Gandhi's model of grass root democracy where Panchayats act as the building blocks of democracy. The pyramid of democracy was inverted where the Central government at the top made decisions for implementation at the grass roots.

Response to this colonial hegemony came during the late nineteenth and early twentieth century. Aurobindo Ghose, who began his life as a revolutionary, awakened the beauty of spiritual Hinduism as a way of divine path. Swami Dayananda Saraswati founded the Arya Samaj as a response to the ideological challenge to the Hindu faith. Swami Vivekananda worked to spread the strength of Hinduism and founded the Ramkrishna Paramhans Society to spread the philosophy.

They all lived and worked around the same time, inspired by the *Vedas*. They were able to inculcate a sense of pride in their own culture and tradition, but these were not enough to respond to the economic exploitation that was going on in the name of civilising the natives.

The first intellectual response to British Colonialism came from Dadabhai Naoroji. He was elected to the British Parliament in 1892. He spoke for Indian interest and criticised the British for exploiting India. He brought out the theory of economic drain (Drain of Wealth theory) of India in his book *Poverty and un-British Rule in India*. Through his documentary evidence, he proved that the British plundered India to fund British industries and contribute to the prosperity of the United Kingdom in general.

Naoroji calculated that yearly there was a loss of approximately £ 30-40 million with only £ 2,50,000 worth of capital injected back into India[3]. Other scholars such as William Digby (1849-1904), British author and journalist, also gave a similar figure. In contemporary times, renowned economist Utsa Patnaik's research suggests a drain of USD 45 trillion between 1765 and 1938[4].

This reveal of the British loot gave an ideological spine to those who described the British Raj as a symbol of exploitation. Bal Gangadhar Tilak, Gopal Krishna Gokhale and Mahatma Gandhi were immensely impressed with the work of Naoroji. Gandhi's book *The Hind Swaraj* was a harsh critique of British rule and was subsequently banned.

After Independence, many ordinary Indians desired a system suitable to their own needs and aspirations. But, it was not easy to bid goodbye to the British system that had taken deep roots, particularly in education and bureaucracy. The colonial structure erected to ensure forceful revenue collection and keep a distance between the ruler and the ruled continued as before. The police had become a symbol of terror during the Daroga raj, and it continued to hold sway even after Independence.

Rulers changed, but the system did not. The problem was figuring out how and where to start. A communist-like revolution was impossible as the society would witness bloodshed, and a complete transformation to a different system would cause disruption that would take centuries to settle.

In a democracy, the issues need to be discussed and debated, and corrections applied. Incremental changes are preferred over revolutionary transformation. It explains the amendments made to the Indian constitution, the biggest and the most elaborate constitution in the world. The desire to change the system was not seen amongst the new rulers.

The first hope of change came when the Janata Party formed its government in 1977 after defeating Congress. The leaders in power spoke against the British legacy and the need to bring a comprehensive change. However, the fledgling government could not achieve much because it failed to take up major reforms or set the system on the right course. The government eventually lost power within three years.

The most significant transformative step was taken by the then Prime Minister P V Narasimha Rao, who launched economic reforms and tried to rework the institutions and processes that had stifled economic growth. The economic liberalisation policy was a drift from the past and allowed a larger role for private participation in economic growth. The Hindu rate of growth, around 4 per cent, needed to change if India had to become a big economy and tackle its problems of poverty and international dependence.

Rao's economic liberalisation, however, created a system that strengthened corruption. Economic liberalisation was not complemented by matching reforms in the existing systems. It led to a system where government favours could be procured through bribes.

Most of the sensational cases of corruption happened during the period following liberalisation.

The BJP coalition government under Prime Minister Atal Bihari Vajpayee came to power in 1996 for 13 days, in 1998 for 13 months and for a full five-year term in 1999. It tried to create a system of transparency and give a big push to infrastructural development and poverty alleviation. However, it could not make major liberalising decisions due to coalition compulsions.

The United Progressive Alliance (UPA) government that stayed in power (2004-14) brought in the Right to Information (RTI), but it did not seem to bother much about corruption. Despite having a majority, the government appeared weak during the ten years and suffered due to various acts of omission and commission. There were scams everywhere, and this led to people coming on the streets. The Anna movement became a symbol of the fight to stop the rot.

Modi came to power in 2014 as a symbol of hope. His experience of governance in Gujarat empowered him to make bold decisions. He knew and understood his public and was tutored in an ideology that abhorred British colonial rule. He started dismantling rules that inhibited individual liberty and economic growth and removed thousands of laws that had outlived their utilities. We will try to analyse some steps that have led to a new cultural awakening.

Modi gave a new thrust to the movement he started by announcing Panch Pran (five vows every Indian should undertake) from the ramparts of the Red Fort during his Independence Day speech in 2022. These were to be the guiding spirit during the Amrit Kaal of 25 years that began when India completed 75 years of Independence in 2022.

These five vows were to ensure a full-fledged development in India by the time the country completes 100 years of its Independence in 2047[5]. These were:

- A resolve of developed India
- Removing any trace of the colonial mindset
- Taking pride in our legacy
- Our strength of unity, and
- Fulfilling the duties of citizens with honesty.

The task to remove colonial legacy and vestiges of the past should be seen in this context, too. In doing so, the government is also promoting a new cultural awakening of every citizen for a strong Bharat.

No Need for Attestation by a Gazetted Officer

One of the ways the British Raj existed in the minds of an average Indian was the need for attestations of certificates/documents by a Gazetted Officer or holders of similar posts. If one had to apply for a government job or seek admission in any educational institution, one had to get his or her certificates attested by a Gazetted Officer.

While this gave a symbolic power to the occupants of such posts, it sought to humiliate those who had to keep moving from pillar to post to get these attestations done. One would often look for family connections or friends to get help. It also encouraged corruption since people would rather pay than go from one location to another.

In June 2014, Narendra Modi stressed that there should be a minimum use of affidavits, and self-certification should be encouraged. After working out the modalities of the new system he wanted to implement, the Prime Minister's Office (PMO) instructed all ministries and departments of the Union government and State governments to allow self-certification of documents in place of affidavits.[6]

With this one decision, the government resolved the problems faced by millions of students, job seekers and citizens interacting with the government. It was Modi's way of saying that the government trusted the citizens. You sign your own documents, and the authorities would trust you. If later you are found to be making false claims, action will be taken against you.

It also made economic sense since it was immensely difficult and costly for a poor person to submit these affidavits. The Department of Administrative Reforms and Public Grievances, in its letter to the State governments and Union Ministries, said, 'Obtaining either an attested copy or affidavit not only costs money to the poor citizen but also involves wastage of time of the citizens as well as of the government officials.'[7]

Considering that millions of people apply for government jobs or admissions in schools and colleges, attestations from a Gazetted Officer were futile to ask for. Only a few would succeed, and it would make better sense to vet their certificates later. Though it impacted every citizen, it was not much thought about.

Scrapping Red Beacon Lights from VIP Cars:
The Shift from VIP (Very Important Person) to EPI (Every Person is Important)

A symbol of the British Raj and the governmental authority and power has been the red beacon light used indiscriminately by anyone who was even remotely connected to power and authority. Rather than facilitating the movement of VIPs (Very Important Persons), these became public nuisance. These lights had become show-off tools for higher officials and ministers and came to be a part of the VIP culture.

Modi gave a death blow to this VIP culture when, on 19 April 2017, the Union government decided to end the use of red or any coloured beacon lights by all, including the President, Vice President and the Prime Minister of India. 'Every Indian is special. Every Indian is a VIP', Prime Minister Narendra Modi tweeted soon after[8].

'The government is of the considered opinion that beacons on vehicles are perceived symbols of VIP Culture, and have no place in a democratic country. They have no relevance whatsoever. Beacons, however, will be allowed on vehicles concerned with emergency and relief services relief services such as ambulance, fire service, etc.', a government release said[9].

Citizens cheered excitedly as the news came about announcements by Union Cabinet Ministers, state Chief Ministers and Judges of the Supreme Court and High Courts, saying they had removed *lal battis* from their respective cars. Chief Justice of India was allowed to use the red beacon as an exception, but then Chief Justice J S Khehar got it removed from his car.

At the monthly *Mann Ki Baat* on 30 April, Modi postulated his concept of an average Indian. 'The concept behind the "New India" is that EPI should replace VIP. EPI means Every Person is Important. We should accept the importance of 125 crore Indians. Then we will have the collective power to fulfil our dreams and aspirations.'

'There is a sort of hatred for VIP culture in our country but I realised the hatred was so deep only when the government decided to do away with red beacons on cars of the officials, no matter how important he is', he added.

Planning Commission Scrapped:
Replaced by Niti Aayog

Some institutions outlive their utility, so they must change to reflect the fast-changing realities in society. While these institutions may not be a colonial hangover, the idea behind setting them up was shaped by a colonial mindset.

One such institution was the Planning Commission, set up in 1950 by India's first Prime Minister, Pandit Jawaharlal Nehru. Nehru believed in a command economy and decided to set the public expenditure as per the planned economy. Rather than planning as per local needs, the Planning Commission believed in giving one model for the whole country.

The idea was proposed by a bunch of socialists within Congress in 1938. They were freedom fighters, and their credentials could not be questioned. Meghnad Saha persuaded Netaji Subhas Chandra Bose (the then Congress president), Atul Tiwari and Jawaharlal Nehru to establish a 'National Planning Committee'.

The originator of the idea was Sir M Visvesvaraya. In 1934, he wrote a book called *A Planned Economy for India*, outlining his idea of how India should grow. He wanted to set up car and aeroplane factories in India.

Visvesvaraya was elected its first head. But, Saha persuaded him to step down in favour of Nehru so that it could usher in an era of better coordination between science and politics. It shaped the mind frame of Nehru for the command economy.

Politicians in Congress believed that the prototype of the Planning Commission would suffice to bridge the gap between the Gandhian push for village-centric governance and a starry-eyed urban Nehru[10].

Nehru became the first Chairman of the Planning Commission, and the institution started acting like an arm of the Union government.

Nehru was the planner, the legislator and the executive. The Leftists not in the government could easily influence Nehru on the Planning Commission, and the role of the private sector in the country's development was severely undermined.

Within a few five-year plans, the shortcomings of the communist way of managing the affairs of the country became evident. The second Five-Year Plan witnessed a 63 per cent increase in the prices of goods. The Reserve Bank of India found it difficult to keep inflation below the psychological 6 per cent mark. The Indian economy was growing at a snail's pace. No government, whether the Union or the State, was in a position to fight poverty. Unemployment was rampant, as only a handful of jobs were available in the public sector.

The Planning Commission spent more money in the states of western India, making them more prosperous. As a result, states in the East, such as Bihar, West Bengal and Odisha, along with states in the North East, lagged on developmental parameters. It clearly shows that India missed balanced economic growth.

While some states emerged as centres of economic activity, others lagged behind even when they were densely populated and elected more members to Parliament. These states came to be known as sick states following the acronym BIMARU, representing Bihar, Madhya Pradesh, Rajasthan and Uttar Pradesh. These states were low in most economic and development parameters.

By the time Modi resumed office, the Planning Commission had outlived its utility, yet it continued to hold sway over government priorities. The country needed transformation, and the Commission was not flexible enough to address immediate concerns. The Independent Evaluation Office (IEO), set up under the UPA regime to review the functioning and relevance of the Planning Commission, had suggested scrapping the Planning Commission. It recommended setting up a Reform and Solution Commission as a government think tank.

The recommendations of the IEO came to Prime Minister Modi on 29 May 2014, three days after he had taken oath. On 13 August, the government decided to dismantle the Planning Commission and replace it with an ad hoc body that temporarily functioned like the

National Advisory Council. A new body called the National Institution for Transforming India (NITI), replaced it on 1 January 2015. It finally came to be known as the NITI Aayog. The first meeting of this Aayog was chaired by the Prime Minister on 8 February 2015.

Unlike the Planning Commission, the Niti Aayog is an advisory body that keeps itself abreast with the latest happenings and tries to give solutions when states approach it with problems concerning good governance. Also, it keeps looking at the functioning of the government and suggests ways to bring efficiency. The suggestions are institutional and not people-centric. It promotes competitive federalism.

Unlike the Planning Commission, the Niti Aayog (or NITI) is a consultant-like service by the Union government. It does not allocate sums, arbitrarily or otherwise, to respective states, telling them what to do with the money as *fait accompli*. It serves only upon being solicited by a state. When invited, a group of experts meet their counterparts in the state to advise them on how they can accomplish the governance targets they have set.

One of the most significant things Niti Aayog has accomplished since its inception is discarding British-era laws and recommending new ways to tackle human survival issues. The Niti Aayog came up with a Three-Year Action Agenda in April 2017. During this period, it also came up with policy changes for a harmonious existence and better coordination amongst various ministries and departments of the Union governments and their interface with the State governments.

The Niti Aayog has emerged as a strong advisory arm of the Prime Minister and is rightly termed a Government Think Tank for improving governance and meeting the demands of the aspirational India that wants the government to act and react speedily. The Niti Aayog also studies institutions across the world and tries to contextualise these to the Indian condition rather than ape it and add to the chaos.

Be it waste management or new education policy, setting up universities of international standards or designing the future of dispute resolution, there is a heavy imprint of the Aayog recommendations. The Aayog commissions researchers to identify problems, find solutions and make recommendations after intense deliberations. One should not be surprised that Niti Aayog was the first to recommend scrapping the practice of presenting a separate railway budget.

Repealing Obsolete Laws/Practices:

British Legacy of Separate Railways Budget Scrapped

The British legacy of presenting a separate railway budget was discarded in 2017, and the demands for grants for the Ministry of Railways were presented as a part of the General Budget. Those still hooked to the past and impressed with the British legacy criticised the move, whereas those willing to rewrite a new chapter for fast-growing India welcomed it.

In 2016, the Niti Aayog strongly recommended removing this legacy and prepared an integration plan on instructions of the Prime Minister. Even in the past, the idea was mooted but not implemented due to stiff opposition from the Railways and a lack of determination from political leaders.

The Niti Aayog Report said, 'The Constitution does not mandate the government to lay a separate Railway Budget'. Doing away with the annual practice could help depoliticise operations and create room for the government to make commercial decisions which could be unpopular, it added.

'Phasing out the rail budget could be the foundation for transforming the public transporter', the Niti Aayog panel said. It suggested that it could usher in commercial accounting practices, clean up finances, establish a framework for sharing social costs between departments and reinstate the commercial character of Railways[11].

The Report suggested that the Railway Budget would be easily dealt with in annual reports, outcome reports and vision documents. The Railways could be like any other department of the Union government.

On 21 September 2016, the Modi government approved the merger of the Railway Budget and the General Budget. Hence, when Arun Jaitley presented the first combined budget of independent India in 2017, he described this as a historic step. 'We have discontinued the colonial practice prevalent since 1924. This decision brings the Railways to the centre stage of the government's fiscal policy and would facilitate multi-modal transport planning between Railways, Highways and Inland Waterways', he said while delivering his budget speech in the Parliament in 2017.

Since then, the Railways have witnessed a complete transformation in terms of passenger experience, safety and modernisation. There is a complete makeover, and the stations are being expanded, and modernised to take the load of the ever-increasing population.

The Acworth Committee (1920-21), headed by British railway economist William Acworth[12], had recommended reorganising the railways and separating the department's finances from the general government finances in 1924. India was the only country in the world to have a separate budget for the Railways.

The size of the Railway Budget had started shrinking compared with the General Budget. It shrunk from 85 per cent during the British Raj to 15 per cent during 2016. The Niti Aayog strongly argued that presenting a separate budget for the Railways was no longer required due to its reduced size.

The merger offered more elbow room to the finance ministry for better allocation of resources. It also facilitated planning transportation in multiple modes like railways, roadways and waterways.

The Railways suffered due to politics and populism. Every Railway Minister preferred catering to their state's demands over the demands from other states. They announced newer trains without bothering about the already overcrowded tracks. The Railway Ministry was considered a worthy slot to grab by any leader when alliance politics started dominating governance.

With politics dominating commercial sense and passenger fares not rising due to political reasons, the burden came on the freight. However, increasing freight would mean a loss of business to road transporters. The net result was a loss to the ministry. This, in turn, resulted in an extra load on the roads by heavy vehicles (trucks), reducing their lifespan, besides adding to the environmental pollution.

Since the merger of the Railways Budget with the General Budget, this sector has witnessed unprecedented modernisation which should be discussed in detail in the chapter on infrastructural development.

A New Financial Year: January to December

The merger of the Railway Budget with the General Budget must be seen as a part of the exercise to have the Indian financial year in sync with the Gregorian calendar. The odd practice of beginning the financial year after a quarter of the year (1 April), began under the East India Company in 1751. Later, the British moved to the Gregorian calendar.

In India, the imperial rulers found the Hindu year's first month, *Chaitra*, convenient since it coincided with March, which marks an end to the annual cycle of harvest festivities. It was linked to the economic activity that was primarily agricultural.

The financial year ending on 31 March helps avoid a clash in the schedule with Navratri, Diwali, Christmas and New Year, as markets see heightened economic activity.

As the economy is increasingly getting integrated into the global economy, there is a demand to match the economic cycle followed by most countries. It makes for better accountability and business planning. The Modi government has already advanced the budget presentation from 1 March to 1 February. The shift cannot be sudden since it would disrupt finances. However, one should not be surprised if the date is further shifted to 1 January.

The first budget of independent India was announced in November because India gained Independence in August. R K Shanmukham Chetty presented the first budget of India on 26 November 1947. C D Deshmukh presented it on 23 May 1952. It kept moving between February-end and the last week of May for some subsequent years. During 1959-61 and 1963-64, including the interim budget for 1962-63, Morarji Desai, as the Union Finance Minister, presented every budget on his birthday, 29 February.

Briefcase Replaced by the Indian *Bahi-Khata*

The Union Finance Minister, Nirmala Sitharaman, surprised one and all when, instead of carrying the budget papers in a leather briefcase, she carried them in the traditional *bahi-khata* wrapped in red silk cloth. The year 2019, thus, marked the renunciation of one more colonial legacy.

Traditionally, Indian businessmen maintained their accounts in *bahi-khatas*, which were the records of their revenue and expenditure. 'I thought it is high time we moved on from the British hangover to do something on our own. And well, easier for me to carry too', Sitharaman said, justifying her decision[13].

The briefcase was a remnant of the British legacy and an extension of the 'Gladstone box' used in British budget presentations. Since then, the Finance Ministers have been using briefcases to carry budget papers.

But the *bahi-khata* existed for only two years (2019-20) as digital India got the upper hand. The Finance Minister chose to wrap up the digital tablet in red silk, carrying them in *bahi-khata* form to mark the blend of old and new and used the digital tablet device to read out her budget speech.

GDP Calculation New Method

Before India switched to the Gregorian calendar, the Modi government brought a revolutionary change by switching to the internationally accepted method to calculate the Gross Domestic Product (GDP). This method was recommended by the United Nations System of National Accounts in 2008 and is an international practice.

The calculation of GDP is important since it demonstrates the economic growth of a country. It includes the total output of a country–agricultural, manufacturing, and in the sector of other services. Calculating the GDP has always been a challenge because of various intangible factors.

In 2015, the Modi government said the traditional method used to calculate the GDP was flawed and adopted a new system completely in sync with the United Nations. It was based on value addition rather than product output. This method is gross value added at a basic price. The government also changed the base year for price calculation from 2004-5 to 2011-12.

The new system was criticised by the Opposition, which alleged that it was being done to inflate the economic achievements of the Modi government. However, the real reason was the Indian economy's desire to integrate with global standards.

Another move vehemently criticised was changing the base year. However, it has been a common practice in the financial management of countries. It appreciates the changing times and economic outlook. The composition of the economy and the nature of the products decide the fixing of the base year.

While it was believed that this change would normally lead to an increase in the absolute number of the GDP, it was not true. After the change, the absolute number actually went down instead of shooting up. The Opposition skirted this observation because it did not suit their allegation.

When the government changed the base year from 2004-05 to 2011-12, it used a new data series for the organised private sector, MCA-21. It now had the data of all companies–both private and public sector units–registered with the Ministry of Corporate Affairs. Every company was given a unique 21-digit code called MCA-21. MCA-21 is an e-governance initiative that enables easy and secure access to the services of the Ministry of Corporate Affairs.

Changing the base year made calculations for the subsequent years easy, but it was still difficult to get backward calculations. To overcome this hurdle, the National Statistical Commission (NSC) used the CMIE corporate database to calculate backwards from 2010-11 as a proxy of MCA-21. Now, the issue was the difference in yardsticks. While the old method measured the total outputs of the agriculture, manufacturing sector and services, the MCA-21 was an accumulation of the balance sheets of companies and judging their performance, adjusted for inflation.

The new database covered a wider sector of the economy, covering financial institutions and regulatory departments like the Security Exchange Board of India (SEBI), the Pension Fund Regulatory and Development Authority (PFRDA), and the Insurance Regulatory and Development Authority of India (IRDAI). Local organisations and institutions are also represented in the series.

In terms of academic statistics, this method was more practical since it took into consideration more indices like consumption, employment, and the performance of enterprises and included factors that are more responsive to the market environment changing every year. It is important to note that the unorganised sector was not ignored. A survey is carried out every five years and a proxy is used in between, based on data from the organised sector.

After the first three years of adapting to the new method, there were no more economic shocks from 2019 onwards. As the economy would become more formalised with the use of the GST, this method would also prove the test of time.

Scrapping Obsolete Laws

Since coming to power in 2014, the Modi government has scrapped more than 2,000 antiquated laws and rules from the British era. Some of these laws had lost their relevance, yet they continued to be on the statutes. These laws could have been easily misused by the administration to harass people. Some other laws, or rules prevented ease of doing business and hence these needed to be eradicated for India to take a big leap.

Modi's thinking has been in line with the government policy for effective and quick governance. Liberate citizens to scale new heights. These, along with other factors, have increased India's ranking in the World Bank Ease of Doing Business from 142 in 2014 to 63 in 2020. The Union government has set the target to figure in the list of top 50 countries in ease of doing business ranking[14].

Scrapping these laws complements the philosophy of the BJP that the government should not interfere in the lives of individuals. The government is the best when it governs the least. These laws empowered the executive authorities to harass people without enhancing the cause of good governance. Even for minor offences, industrialists could be threatened with jail.

'The (outdated) laws continued from the time of the British (rule), and I roped in an entire team (to review them) because I did not want the country's businesspersons to land in jail over trivial issues. We scrapped 2,000 such laws. I have to do more, and if traders sitting here know of such a law, let me know', he said at a rally in Jamnagar in October 2022[15].

Modi took the concept of ease of doing business seriously and worked systematically to improve the ranking. He knew that foreign investment in India and a vibrant economy was linked to the ease of doing business. The Department for Promotion of Industry and Internal Trade (DPIIT) engaged with the World Bank to understand the methodology better and to study global best practices to evolve a strategy for India that eases the processes.

Modi summed up the nation's thoughts in the following way, 'Due to the circumstances which existed before, there was a time when it was asked–"Why India?". Now, after looking at the impact of the reforms that have taken place in the country, it is being asked–"Why not India?"'[16].

Some utterly ridiculous laws included dictating different shopkeepers of the same market when they could open their shops, letting shops on one side of a road or a canal stay open one day and those on the opposite side the next. Such 'odd-even' schemes were meant to prevent a large gathering that could threaten the British government. While the British paranoia had turned meaningless post-1947, the awkward rules were continued by state and city governments mindlessly.

Some rules were bizarre and archaic but survived for years, like a relic in the museum, with no relevance to the functioning of modern India.

- One such example was the Indian Motor Vehicles Act, 1914, under which a Police Inspector in Andhra Pradesh was to have well-brushed teeth, and he could be disqualified if he had a pigeon chest, knock knees, flatfeet and hammer toes. One such law said the toll tax for boats ferrying passengers across the river Ganga could not be more than two annas–a denomination no longer in use.
- Under the Indian Aircraft Act, 1934, kites were also aircraft and one needed to obtain a permit as was required for flying an aeroplane.
- Under the Indian Treasure Trove Act, 1878, one could be jailed if they found anything worth more than Rs 10 and did not report it to a revenue officer.

During the campaign for the 2014 Lok Sabha elections, Narendra Modi had promised to repeal antiquated laws and rules if the BJP came to power. It is to the credit of the Modi government to have scrapped more than 2,000 such laws and rules, whereas successive governments had removed only 1,301 such laws in 65 years.

Modi knew how to expedite the process. Instead of using ad hoc measures, he set up a committee in September 2014 under Shri R Ramanujam, Secretary to PMO, to review and identify obsolete laws. Mr V K Bhasin, former secretary in the Legislative Department, was the other member.

The two-member committee had to examine all Acts recommended to be repealed by the Committee on review of Administrative Laws appointed by the Vajpayee government in 1998. Of the 1,382 Acts recommended to be repealed, only 415 were repealed. Modi wanted the committee to adopt a focussed approach[17].

The committee submitted its report to the PMO in November and recommended the repeal of 1,741 Central Acts out of the 2,784 that existed in the statute till 15 October 2014. It also identified 150 Central Acts to be consolidated into 21 Acts to avoid multiplicity[18].

The committee recognised that too many laws lead to conferring more discretion upon the enforcing agencies. Legislation in India has followed a dictum that a statute never dies unless repealed. Hence, statutes that are years old or enacted for temporary periods have continued to exist[19].

National War Memorial (NWM):

New Culture India Gate Memorial Shifted

The British built the iconic India Gate in the nation's capital in 1931 to commemorate the casualties suffered by the Indian soldiers during the First World War and the Third Anglo-Afghan War. It served as the country's war memorial as well. However, of the 83,000 Indians who sacrificed their lives, the names of only 13,516 were etched on the walls of India Gate.

After the Bangladesh Liberation War in 1972, a platform was constructed with a black marble plinth with an inverted bayonet and rifle capped by a war helmet and surrounded by four eternal flames. This structure with flames called Amar Jawan Jyoti (Flame of the Immortal Soldier) symbolised the valour of the Indian soldiers since 1971. Every year, the Republic Day parade starts after the Prime Minister visits the Amar Jawan Jyoti. But names of soldiers who sacrificed their lives are not mentioned.

Also, ever since India became independent, brave soldiers have laid down their lives for the cause of the motherland, whether it was during the wars with China and Pakistan or operations such as counter-insurgency or the fight against terrorism. More than 26,000 soldiers have sacrificed their lives to defend the country's sovereignty and integrity.

There have been more than 100 war memorials in the country, commemorating various battlefields and sacrifices of our brave soldiers. The famous quote, 'When you go home, tell them of us and say, for your tomorrow we gave our today', is inscribed at the war cemetery at Kohima.

The Chandigarh War Memorial is a tribute to Gurkha warriors from Darjeeling who sacrificed their lives in 1947. It has the names of 8,459 soldiers who sacrificed their lives since 1947. The Kargil War Memorial on the highway between Srinagar and Leh gives tribute to the soldiers who embraced martyrdom during the Kargil War of 1999. A war memorial was inaugurated in 1999 at the famous IMA (Indian Military Academy) ground in Dehradun.

A need, however, was felt for a war memorial at the national level where citizens could visit to appreciate the bravery of our soldiers and pay them respect. India was the only country in the world to not have a war memorial. Not having one at the national level was considered a national embarrassment. The Indian Army had first proposed a National War Memorial in 1960, but the proposal was shelved after the Indo-China war. It picked up momentum after the Kargil War, fought in full view of the public, celebrating the martyrdom of our brave soldiers.

However, nothing happened despite the demand consistently being raised in the defence circles. The UPA government set up a committee of ministers in 2006 headed by the then Defence Minister, Pranab Mukherjee, to study the feasibility of this demand. The committee recommended setting up a war memorial at India Gate. The Urban Development Ministry opposed saying the India Gate area was a heritage site and should not be disturbed.

However, when the then Defence Minister, A K Antony, announced in 2012 that the bottlenecks had been cleared for constructing a war memorial, Delhi Chief Minister Sheila Dikshit opposed the move. During his 2014 Lok Sabha campaign, the NDA's Prime Ministerial candidate lambasted the Congress-led UPA for its inability to construct the war memorial.

On 7 October 2015, the Modi Cabinet passed a resolution to construct a National War Memorial befitting its status and allocated Rs 500 crore for the Memorial and the Museum, of which Rs 176 crore was for the memorial alone. The hexagonal site at India Gate was finalised, and competitive bidding was invited in 2016.

Construction of the Memorial began in 2017, and Narendra Modi inaugurated the country's first National War Memorial on 25 February 2019. Spread over 40 acres of land, the Memorial has become a living memory of the sacrifices that make the country great.

The Amar Jawan Jyoti which remains kindled 24 hours has been shifted to the War Memorial. Names of all 26,942 soldiers who sacrificed their lives for the country are inscribed on 16 walls of the Memorial, built in the form of four concentric circles, each signifying different values of the armed forces.

King George Replaced by Netaji

Adjoining the India Gate is a canopy standing on four columns housing the statue of King George V, the King of England. It was a symbol of the Raj. The Indira Gandhi government shifted it to what is now known as Delhi's Coronation Park in 1968. However, it could not be decided whether another statue should adorn the spot or it should remain empty. But this was until the Modi government came to power.

Modi announced the canopy would have the statue of Netaji Subhas Chandra Bose. On 23 January 2022, the 125th birth anniversary of Netaji, Modi unveiled a hologram of the statue, which he ultimately unveiled on 8 September 2022.

The 28-feet black granite statue was carved from a monolithic granite block weighing 280 metric tonnes. The block of jet-black granite selected for the statue was transported 1,665 km from Khammam in Telangana to New Delhi in a 100-feet-long truck with 140 wheels, specially designed for the giant granite stone[20].

Prime Minister Modi's love and respect for Netaji is well known. He had often reminded people that the Congress regime had tried to downplay Netaji's contribution to the nation for their own political design. And this was not political opportunism to score brownie points against the BJP's arch-rival. Even when he was an ordinary party worker in the 1970s, he had mentioned Netaji repeatedly in his diary entries. In 1997, he unveiled a statue of Netaji in Patan, Gujarat. He was not even a Chief Minister back then.

As the Chief Minister of Gujarat, he launched the eGram Vishwagram project on 23 January 2009 from Haripura village of Surat district. It was to honour Bose, whose decisive call for India's freedom came from Haripura in the 1938 session of the Indian National Congress, of which he was the President. Modi offered broadband connectivity to all 13,693 gram panchayats in the state. He rode a cart drawn by 51 bullocks, the way Bose had done decades ago, and proclaimed, '*Tum mujhe pasina do, main tumhen hara bhara Gujarat dunga.*' He drew from Bose's slogan, '*Tum mujhe khoon do, main tumhen aazaadi dunga.*'

In 2012, he paid tributes to Netaji on the INA Day. During the Lok Sabha election campaign in 2014, Modi touched the feet of Col Nizamuddin, a surviving INA veteran, who was 114 years old then.

Subsequently, the same year, Prime Minister Modi paid homage to the martyrs at the INA Memorial Marker in Singapore on 24 November[21].

Modi unfurled the tricolour at Delhi's Red Fort on 21 October 2018, which would be an unusual day except that the date marked the completion of 75 years of the formation of the first government of free India by the Indian National Army (INA)[22].

Later that year, Modi visited Japan and met Saichiro Misumi, a Japanese comrade of Netaji. In 2015, the Prime Minister met the Bose family and promised to declassify all secret files related to Netaji, which the Union government had held under the garb of secrecy.

A strong demand for the declassification of Netaji's secret files had gained momentum after Mission Netaji, a pressure group of researchers led by authors Anuj Dhar and Chandrachur Ghose and Malayalam television personality Sreejith Panickar, came out with astounding facts about Netaji. Anuj Dhar's book *India's Biggest Cover-Up* raised pertinent questions about Netaji's death mysteries.

Renaming Rajpath as Kartavya Path

On 8 September 2022, when Modi unveiled the statue of Netaji at the canopy at India Gate, he also inaugurated the newly named Kartavya Path (previously Rajpath). The renaming was formally adopted through a resolution by the NDMC (New Delhi Municipal Corporation) on 7 September 2022. 'Kingsway, or Rajpath, was a "symbol of slavery", and it has now been consigned to history', Modi said. 'New history has been created in the form of Kartavya Path', he added[23].

While this decision showed jettisoning the legacy of the past that inflicted mental injury, it also demonstrated the desire to create a new institution that would bring a sense of pride in people. If there is no Raj, how can this be called Rajpath? Hence, the road from Raisina Hills, which houses the Rashtrapati Bhavan, to the National Stadium via India Gate was renamed Kartavya Path to remind every ruler thet they are bound by their duty and oath to serve the people of India. There is no right by virtue of the 'Raj', but only duties, by virtue of the position one occupies.

When palanquins are on full display to showcase India's rich cultural diversity and when uniformed military and police force walk in tandem displaying their armoury, discipline and might, this is not the display of the Raj but a display of the duty that binds them together to the service of the motherland. Kartavya Path would keep inspiring generations to perform their duty.

Armed Forces Shed Colonial Legacy

As the country entered Amrit Kaal, the Prime Minister urged the defence forces to shed their colonial practices. As a part of this movement, the Indian Navy has decided to rename the designations of its various ranks, and these would be reflective of the Indian heritage when the country had a strong naval presence.

During his address at the Navy Day in Sindhudurg on 5 December 2023, Modi declared that the epaulettes of all Indian Navy (IN) officers would bear the symbol of Chhatrapati Shivaji's maritime legacy. The insignia worn by flag officers on their shoulders would be an octagonal-shaped naval crest. Shivaji was known for his maritime power, and the country must aspire to become a strong navy to safeguard the borders and ensure full exploitation of the oceanic resources. The Navy has already removed the practice of carrying batons by its personnel. This custom has followed since the British day and represents a colonial legacy. 'With the passage of time, carrying batons by naval personnel has become a norm. The symbolism of authority or power pot heated through the holding of a baton is a colonial legacy that is out of place in a transformed navy of Amrit Kaal', a communication issued by the Indian Navy said[24].

However, the Navy has allowed the ceremonial placing of batons in the offices of the head of organisational units and ceremonial handing over in offices during the change of command.

As a part of decolonising the Indian mindset, the Indian Army dropped the famous Christian Hymn with origin in Scotland and England with phrases taken from *The Bible*. From 2022 onwards, the English song *Abide with me*, played during the Beating Retreat Ceremony, was replaced with the famous Hindi song *Aye mere watan ke logon*, which commemorates Indian soldiers who died in the Sino-Indian War of 1962.

The Hindi patriotic song sung by the late Lata Mangeshkar in 1963 was written by Kavi Pradeep and composed by C Ramchandra. Undoubtedly, this song resonates better with people than *Abide with me*. It touches the emotional chord of an average Indian, reminding them of the sacrifices a soldier makes to uphold the country's sovereignty.

The hymn, written by Scottish hymn writer and poet Henry Francis Lyte in 1861 and set to tune by William Henry Monk, was introduced in the Beating Retreat Parade of the Indian Army in 1950. The practice continued till 2021.

While the Republic Day Parade takes place on 26 January to showcase the strength, diversity and unity of India, the Beating Retreat Parade takes place three days later to signify the culmination of that.

Beating Retreat is a military tradition when the troops stop fighting, rest their arms to signify withdrawal from the battlefield and return to their camps at the sound of the 'retreat'. A retreat sound asks the soldiers to go back to their barracks.

New Parliament Building

The country created history with its new Parliamentary building. This epoch-making event saw hundreds of parliamentarians marching into the new building for its first session on 19 September 2023. The building was inaugurated on 28 May 2023 amidst the chants of multi-religious prayers and rituals.

On the inaugural day, Modi placed the historic Sengol beside the Speaker's Chair as a symbol of righteousness and dharma. The Sengol was gifted to Pandit Jawaharlal Nehru by a Tamil Adheenam a day before Independence. It found its way to the Nehru Gallery of the famous Allahabad Museum. Modi retrieved the Sengol to give it a rightful place in India's temple of democracy. It laid the foundation of a new tradition and began a new culture where the parliamentarians would get inspiration from the Sengol.

Close to 20 Opposition parties, including Congress and Trinamool Congress, boycotted the inaugural ceremony. In a joint statement, the combined Opposition said there was no value in a new building when the 'soul of democracy has been sucked out from the Parliament'.

They demanded the President of India to inaugurate the new Parliament Building. They ignored that the Supreme Court had already rejected a Public Interest Litigation (PIL) making a similar demand. Their action exposed the hollowness of their fight.

While hearing the PIL on the issue, Justices J K Maheshwari and P S Narasimha asked them the reason for their petition. The petitioner called it a humiliation of the President of India and, thereby, the entire nation. The Justices then pointed out that two different State Assemblies had been inaugurated by the state Chief Ministers without inviting the Governors. What was wrong if the President was not invited, in this case?

The petitioner pointed out that the President of India was an elected post, but the Governor was an appointee of the President of India. The Judges pointed out the inauguration of the Parliament Annexe and Library building by Prime Ministers. The Apex Court rejected the PIL and called it a Publicity Interest Litigation[25].

The Opposition's arguments were frivolous since the Modi government had taken all precautions to keep the President's office above board and avoid any controversy. The tenders were floated by the CPWD (Central Public Works Department) on behalf of the Lok Sabha Secretariat.

The foundation stone was laid by the Prime Minister in December 2020. Modi took a keen interest in the construction of the new building during the three subsequent years. The construction went on uninterrupted even during the Corona period, and Modi met the workers to keep their morale up. In fact, the Parliament building is a part of the Central Vista project, which is the dream project of the Prime Minister.

The Opposition ignored that in situations where written provision does not exist, the guidance for action is provided by the convention. As pointed out by the Court, Prime Minister Indira Gandhi had inaugurated the Parliament Annexe Building in 1975. In 1987, Prime Minister Rajiv Gandhi inaugurated the Parliament Library. These two instances were cited initially by Union Urban Development Minister Hardeep Puri in his tweet on 23 May 2023. 'If your (Congress) head of government can inaugurate them, why can't our head of government do the same?', he asked.

Assam Chief Minister, Himanta Biswa Sarma, pointed out that no Governor or President of India had been invited by non-BJP governments for the inauguration of new legislative assembly buildings in the last nine years[26].

Chief Minister K Chandrashekar Rao inaugurated the new secretariat building in Hyderabad on 30 April 2023. Telangana Governor Tamilisai Soundararajan spoke about how she was not invited to the inauguration function. In November 2022, West Bengal Chief Minister Mamata Banerjee and not the Governor of the state, inaugurated the Platinum Jubilee Memorial Building at the state assembly in Kolkata.

The Congress that raised objections to Modi inaugurating the new building forgot that its leaders had crossed all limits of parliamentary expectations when Rahul Gandhi and Sonia Gandhi together laid the foundation stone of the new Vidhan Sabha Bhawan in Chhattisgarh along with the Chief Minister. They had no locus to perform this function since they had no constitutional position or role in the state government.

There are examples where Prime Ministers have inaugurated the state assembly buildings. In 2019, Prime Minister Modi inaugurated Jharkhand's new assembly building even though the State was headed by Jharkhand Mukti Morcha's Hemant Soren. In 1981, the then Prime Minister Indira Gandhi inaugurated the Maharashtra Vidhan Bhawan. Prime Minister Nehru laid the foundation stone of the Karnataka assembly or Vidhana Soudha on 13 July 1951.

In 2012, President of India Pranab Mukherjee inaugurated the Vidhana Soudha (Belagavi), where the winter session is held, on the invitation of Chief Minister Jagadish Shettar of the BJP.

The hallmark of the inauguration ceremony of the new Parliament Building was Modi's way to honour the construction workers for their hard work and dedication in building a new modern structure. 11 representative workers were presented with shawls and mementoes. A digital gallery was dedicated to 60,000 workers who worked tirelessly to convert the dream into a reality.

The state-of-the-art new building is a marvel of modern architecture. The new complex has 888 seats in the Lok Sabha chamber and 384 seats in the Rajya Sabha. Unlike the old building, it does not have a Central Hall because the Lok Sabha has been equipped to house 1,272 members.

That the old Parliament had outlived its utility and the country needed a new structure befitting the aspirations of new India was mentioned earlier, too. The then Lok Sabha Speaker Meira Kumar had proposed a new Parliament building in 2012, but it did not see the light of the day.

It will accommodate more members in case of delimitation of the constituency, and more Lok Sabha and Rajya Sabha seats are earmarked for better representation. The number and the seats for each state have been in freeze till 2026.

Delimitation follows the census. The first delimitation exercise was undertaken in 1952 following the 1951 census wherein 494 Lok Sabha seats were allotted. The next delimitation happened in 1963, following the reorganisation of states in 1956. The number of Lok Sabha seats was fixed at 522. The third exercise was undertaken in 1973 and the Lok Sabha seats were raised to 543. For a new delimitation exercise, the census has to be completed which is pending because of various reasons.

The number of people represented by each Lok Sabha member has been increasing with an increase in the population. In 1951, a member of Lok Sabha represented close to 3.54 lakh voters. It increased to 15 lakh in 2014, and 18 lakh in 2019. It is likely to be more than 2 million in 2024. The government has clarified that delimitation would take place after 2024. The new Parliament Building has enough seats to accommodate the increase in seats.

The new Parliament Building had to wait more than three months for the final touches before it could host the first session on its premises. The five-day special session of Parliament was convened from 18-22 September, of which the first day, 18 September, was the joint sitting of Parliament in the old building where leaders recollected the 75 years of long journey of India's Parliamentary history before bidding adieu to the old building to embrace the new.

The second day, 19 September, was a historic day when hundreds of parliamentarians, led by Prime Minister Modi, walked from the old building to the new one for its first formal session. The day happened to be Ganesh Chaturthi, an auspicious day in the Hindu calendar. There was a mix of curiosity and excitement, as was a competition to quickly grab a seat, for no one wanted to miss the proceedings of the inaugural session.

Modi, who talked about the contributions of various Prime Ministers and other parliamentarians in the old building, spoke of the aspirational India during his address in the new building. This building would re-energise the parliamentarians to do new things to shape the future of India for the coming centuries.

It is the dawn of the Amrit Kaal as India is moving forward with a resolve for a bright future by heading into the new Parliament edifice. It is the time to begin a new journey with renewed enthusiasm and energy, Modi said.

The new journey began by writing history in India's parliamentary democracy by reserving 33 per cent of seats for women in the Lok Sabha from 2029 onwards since this would be implemented after delimitation. The number will go up to 743 seats.

The bill to this effect was introduced on the first day of the special session, and the Lok Sabha passed the bill the next day, almost unanimously. Only two members of the All India Majlis-e-Ittehadul Muslimeen (AIMIM) opposed. The bill passed by the Lok Sabha was introduced in the Rajya Sabha on 21 September and passed the same day. The President agreed to the bill on 28 September 2023.

Central Vista Project

It would be difficult to skip the Central Vista Redevelopment Project when we have dealt with the new Parliament Building at length. The Building is part of a big project called Central Vista, which will change the India Gate and the Kartavya Path skyline without disturbing the aesthetics.

Central Vista is a 3.2 km stretch from Raisina Hills, with the President's House on it, to India Gate on the Kartavya Path. The plan is to have a Common Central Secretariat to house all ministries and other offices around this stretch and to convert the North and South Block, with the most important ministries of the government, into museums.

New offices and residences would be constructed for the Vice President of India and the Prime Minister, along with a building for the SPG (Special Protection Group). The total cost for the project is estimated at Rs 13,450 crore over four years. The cost of the entire development project is likely to touch Rs 20,000 crore.

Besides being modern, these buildings were needed because the government incurred a lot of expenditure in the upkeep of the present structure that constantly demanded repair and renovation. Also, many office premises have been hired from the private sector, leading to further drain of resources. By that count, the Central Vista, which would house many government offices, is Modi government's vision statement. These are to prepare India for the future driven by technology.

New Norm for Environment Clearance

During the ten years of UPA rule, the Environment Ministry acted more like an activist than as a responsible ministry of the Union government. Both Jairam Ramesh and Jayanthi Natarajan, who held this portfolio one after the other, opposed any idea of development on the pretext of safeguarding the environment.

Ms Natarajan imposed a notorious tax on industries called the 'Jayanthi Tax'. The Sahara diaries, called Birla-Sahara Papers, have revealed that she was among the hundreds of politicians paid for environment clearances. During his Lok Sabha campaign in 2014, Modi had referred to it as 'Jayanthi Tax'.

After the Modi government came to power, it decentralised the Environment Ministry, delegated most environment clearances to states and kept some to itself. The Ministry of Environment, Forest and Climate Change created the District Environment Impact Assessment Authority (DEIAA) for proper monitoring of sand mining.

The Modi government brought flexibility and more accountability on the issue of environmental clearance. It enacted environmental and pollution control legislation to prevent indiscriminate exploitation of natural resources and promoted the integration of environmental concerns in developmental projects. Information technology and information technology-enabled services started being used to track the mined-out minerals.

The movement of such materials and sand is now controlled through transit permits, with security features like printing on IBA-approved MICR paper, unique barcode, unique QR code, fugitive ink background, invisible ink mark, void pantograph and watermark. Information technology tools, such as barcoding and SMS, began to be employed to maintain a vigil on the mined-out material from its source to its destination[27]. The use of such technologies reduced error margins while ensuring no operative bends the law.

Project promoters were permitted to hear out panels of experts for forest clearances. The industry was spared the high cost of project-specific Corporate Social Responsibility (CSR) that the expert advisory committees used to impose on businesses. Hence, identifying land for projects became easy.

The new government told the forest and environment appraisal committees to stop insisting that 5 per cent of the project cost must be invested in CSR activities. Compensatory afforestation was introduced as a solution to maintain the ecological balance. Under the UPA regime, project proposals used to be rejected for non-compliance with CSR-related diktats.

No Interview for Non-gazetted Government Jobs

One of the most remarkable moves with a significant impact on the common man is the Modi government's decision to do away with interviews for low-ranking government jobs. The decision was announced by Modi in his *Mann ki Baat* delivered in October 2015. The decision came into effect on 1 January 2016.

It was Modi's way of ensuring people that he would not allow corruption to play any role in these job recruitments. People look for middlemen, who fleece those who have passed the written examination, in the name of influencing interviews. The poor were gradually losing trust in the system, thinking they would get the job only if they paid for it.

By doing this, Modi delivered what he promised during his 69th Independence speech in 2015. This is how he visualised the issue and why he applied this remedy,

> Brothers and sisters, one of the most corrupt areas is employment. The underprivileged aspire to get a decent job. We have seen how whenever a youth receives a call for a job interview, be it in the railways, education, or even as a clerical staff, he thinks of approaching someone for a recommendation. Even their family begins to brood over the issue. Why? This is because, in our country, employment and job depend on the interview rather than the merit. Rejected candidates are often told that they have failed in the interview. To date, I have not seen any psychologist who can assess a person based on interviewing him just for two minutes.
>
> I have been ruminating over this issue for long. Is it imperative for the underprivileged or the less-educated to appear for an interview while looking for a minor job? Can he not get any job without an interview? Is a mark sheet alone a parameter to ascertain someone's expertise and skill? Of course, in roles requiring physical fitness, the norms and system could vary. The personality and experience of a candidate matter only for the jobs at senior levels, but it is painful to see candidates even from the states of Nagaland and Mizoram rush to Mumbai to appear in exams for junior-level posts in Railways. I have to overcome this problem. I implore the state governments and my colleagues in the

government to discontinue the practice of interviewing for junior-level posts as soon as possible. Such jobs should be given based on merit. It would help in curbing corruption, which ails society and would ease their problem. It is my appeal to work towards this goal[28].

By taking this momentous decision, the Prime Minister had brought relief to crores of people who vie for government jobs. Nearly 95 per cent of 36 lakh central government employees fall under the Group D, C and B non-gazetted categories. Only 5 per cent of the total employees fall under Group A and Group B's Gazetted services, where recruitment is conducted by the Union Public Service Commission.

New Laws for Criminal Jurisprudence

On 15 August 2022, Narendra Modi took five vows, Panch Pran, and wanted every citizen to do the same. These were, in the words of the PM, 'First, move forward with bigger resolves and resolve of a "developed" India; second, erase all traces of servitude; third, be proud of our legacy; fourth, the strength of our unity and fifth, duties of citizens which include the PM and CMs.'[29] These vows are essential to transform India during the Amrit Kaal–25 years when India would complete 100 years of Independence.

One of these vows was to remove the vestiges of the past that reminded of servitude. We have already seen how the government has been working with a missionary zeal to get rid of the colonial legacy and symbols and removing laws that have been out of use. The most revolutionary step was to repeal the three laws: the Indian Penal Code 1860, the Criminal Procedure Code (1898) 1973, and the Indian Evidence Act 1872, which formed the basis of criminal jurisprudence in India.

These were replaced with the Bharatiya Nyaya Sanhita Bill, 2023, the Bhartiya Nagarik Suraksha Sanhita Bill, 2023, and the Bharatiya Sakshya Sanhita Bill, 2023, respectively. The Lok Sabha passed these bills on 20 December 2023. The Rajya Sabha passed it on the next day. The Prime Minister called it a watershed moment and the beginning of a new era. The three bills got the approval of the President of India on 25 December 2023 and became Acts.

While presenting the three bills in the Lok Sabha, Union Home Minister Amit Shah said that these would 'free the people from colonial mindset. These laws were made to strengthen and protect the British rule and their purpose was to punish, not to give justice. The new legislations would protect all the rights given to Indian citizens by the constitution, and, their purpose will not be to punish but give justice.'[30]

The new law, framed as per the Indian ethos, had placed the citizens at the centre. The changes were made after consultation with the public for four years. 'Suggestions came from 18 States, 6 Union Territories, the Supreme Court, 16 High Courts, 5 Judicial Academies, 22 Law Universities, 142 Members of Parliament, around 270 MLAs and public.' Shah was present in the 158 consultation meetings that have taken place.

The law has expanded the definition of documents to include electronic or digital records, e-mails, server logs, computers, smartphones, laptops, SMS, websites, locational evidence, mails and messages on devices. A provision has been made to digitise the entire process from filing FIR to case diary to chargesheet and judgement.

One of the most citizen-friendly steps is to make videography compulsory in case of search and seizure. Without such recording, no chargesheet shall be valid. The most revolutionary step is to start Zero FIR, enabling citizens to lodge complaint at any police station. The police will transfer the case to a relevant police station within 15 days. The police will inform the family members or the arrested individual in person or online.

The scope of the summary trial has increased. Now, crimes punishable for up to 3 years will be included in a summary trial. It will end over 40 per cent of cases in session courts. The use of forensic experts has been encouraged to take conviction to 90 per cent.

A provision for attachment of property has been added to attach the property of proclaimed offenders. Harsh punishment has been added against inter-state gangs and organised crimes.

Prison undertrial has been a big issue facing the country. The new law makes provision for bail for undertrials who have spent one-third of punishment in jail, in case convicted.

The law of sedition has been scrapped to uphold the right to freedom of expression. But crimes, such as terrorism, secession, armed insurgency, and subversive activism, separatism, challenging the unity, sovereignty and integrity of India have been well defined.

Under the new law, property lying with the police stations can be disposed of by videography and after submitting the verified copy to the court. Shah said 'a total of 313 changes have been made in this law which will bring a widespread change in our criminal justice system and anyone will be able to get justice within a maximum of 3 years.'[31]

The laws are revolutionary and are changes that every Indian would welcome. An attack on the old criminal justice system was much needed since the old system was eroding the faith of the common people in the system. Criminals could escape the system due to loopholes, and innocent people suffered. The new laws have attempted to make the police more humane and accountable.

Digital India–An IT Revolution

From latest science to latest technology, everything should be available at the tip of one's finger.
–Narendra Modi

'Digital India' is not merely a slogan to showcase India's global positioning in the world of Information Technology; it is a mechanism to strengthen the government's delivery system and empower people by rooting out corruption. Technology minimises human interface and leaves little room for manipulation.

There is hardly any aspect of India left untouched by digital technology. From placing online orders for groceries to making payments using UPI, from online banking to getting government services online, from registration of birth and death to all record-keeping about land–everything is going digital in India.

Technology is not to disrupt society but to make the lives of citizens easier. The earthen diya lighted during Diwali and other festivals co-exist with the various models of LED-powered lights that are reasonably priced, too. Digital aides have not replaced books in schools and colleges, but are making studies interesting with better explanations and more practice.

It is the new India that critics often fail to see when they try to fathom the beauty of its civilisational moorings. As Prime Minister Narendra Modi has said, the beauty of the past must blend with the advancement of modern technology for a more meaningful existence[1].

Today, India is a country driven by digital technology and is on its way to becoming the world incubator for finding digital solutions for the issues man is facing.

When the Digital India initiative was launched by the Prime Minister in July 2015, few had imagined India would begin marching to digital revolution touching every aspect of our lives. It has not only penetrated and changed the way the government functions, but it has also split over to the private lives of individuals.

Modi, however, knew about the potential and put his weight behind creating a digital infrastructure that has fuelled the Digital India dream. The entire world is appreciating India's giant stride in this field in such a short time. The World Bank has lauded the inclusive character of the digital revolution that India has witnessed and has said that there is a need for other countries to emulate this model[2].

Germany's Federal Minister for Digital and Transport, Volker Wissing, during his recent visit to Bengaluru, was all praise for India's digital payment system after he purchased groceries through UPI (Unified Payments Interface). He was there to attend a meeting of G20's Digital Ministers. The German Embassy in India said,

'One of India's success stories is digital infrastructure. UPI enables everybody to make transactions in seconds. Millions of Indians use it. Federal Minister for Digital and Transport @Wissing was able to experience the simplicity of UPI payments first hand and is very fascinated!'[3] At the G20 presidency meeting hosted in Delhi, the UPI system was showcased to all the visiting dignitaries.

The transformation from 2014, when he took oath as the Prime Minister, to 2023 has been an inspiring journey for digital India. On 15 August 2014, while delivering his first Independence Day Speech from the ramparts of the Red Fort, he emphasised the importance of digital infrastructure to empower people, outlining his vision for the shape of things to come[4]. He spoke of the Bali Summit he had attended last year and the way world leaders looked at India with awe because of its advancement in IT. The drivers are not just the big cities but also two-tier and three-tier cities, where aspiring youths are using creativity and technology to give IT-based solutions, making life easier.

'There are 100 schools in my country where children are making satellites and also aspiring to release them one day. Today thousands of tinkering labs are conceiving new scientists. Today, thousands of tinkering labs are inspiring millions of children to take up the path of science and technology.'[5]

'Some 25 to 30 years ago, the world used to think we are a land of snake charmers and black magic. But our youth has surprised the world with its IT (information technology) skills…I dream of a digital India. It was once said that railways connect India. Today I say IT connects India...I fully believe a digital India can compete with the world', he added[6].

A few days later, on 21 August, Modi launched the national Digital Literacy Mission and announced that 'a digital revolution is about to begin'. He predicted that a time would come when the common man would be able to track the government's work from his mobile phone[7]. A day before this, the Union Cabinet had already approved the digital India programme to connect all 2.5 lakh gram panchayats with broadband connectivity to promote e-governance.

An estimated Rs 1,13,000 crore was to be spent to translate this dream into reality. It was based on three key areas–digital infrastructure for use by every citizen (digital identity, mobile phone and bank account, and safe and secure cyberspace); governance and services on demand (government services available online and through mobile platforms, and electronic and cashless transaction); and digital empowerment of citizens (for keeping documents and certificates available on cloud).

Digital empowerment got a further boost when, in August 2023, the government announced the extension and expansion of the Digital India programme for another five years, with an additional outlay of Rs 14,903 crore. It would also focus on the expansion of the Computer Emergency Response Team, India (CERT-in).

'We need to build cybersecurity tools for small businesses, schools, hospitals, who have to focus on their work. Cybersecurity should be easily accessible, low cost and affordable', Union Minister for Electronics & Information Technology Ashwini Vaishnaw said[8].

Under this scheme, more than 6.25 lakh IT professionals are slated to receive upskilling and re-skilling training, and close to 2.65 lakh employees shall receive information security training. The government has decided to roll out an AI-enabled (Artificial Intelligence) translation tool called Bhashini in all 22 languages[9]. Bhashini programme has been created with the support of Microsoft and OpenAI.

Such a grand vision would not have come to fruition without exposure and experience. When Narendra Modi was the Chief Minister of Gujarat during 2001-14, he successfully experimented with using IT to make governance easier. He had realised that imagination, creativity and technology would drive the human race to ease their problems. These tools were used to bring transparency in governance, digitising land records and bringing government services to the doors of people.

It happened because he was tech-savvy and was among the first few in the BJP to embrace the inventions trying to change human behaviour. At a time when the party laughed at those who used cell phones and computers, Modi was among the few who adapted to technology and tried to use the same to better party organisation.

When he took the box of a computer to the Haryana office as the party's General Secretary in-charge for the state in the early 1990s, not many knew how to operate the hardware and integrate into the internet. Modi used technology to keep abreast with world events and to connect with the youths who were quick to use technology. Acquiring mobile phones equipped with the latest and faster processors has been Modi's habit, and it has kept him hooked to the new happenings. It also explains how he can easily connect with the youths.

Let us now try to assess some major achievements of Digital India that have changed India forever.

Digital Identity: Aadhaar Card

There would hardly be anyone in the country not having a digital identity. It was achieved through an Aadhaar card that establishes identity based on fingerprinting and iris scanning. The Aadhaar card is a 12 digit individual identification number which serves as proof of identity of an individual and proof of address. If one wants to get a passport, open a bank account or interact with the government, an Aadhaar card comes in handy. More than 135 crore people in India had Aadhaar cards by November 2022[10].

Jan Dhan Account

No one can justify why so many people in the country were outside the banking system. Even if they did not have money to save, the government could have used these accounts to send money under the government benefits paid in cash. As the biggest step in financial inclusion, Modi, at his first Independence Day speech in 2014, announced the launch of Pradhan Mantri Jan Dhan Yojana (PMJYD). It allowed a zero-balance account for the underprivileged of India who were unbanked and could not afford to keep the mandatory bank deposits.

The government launched a massive campaign to include as many people in the scheme as possible in a short time. The Prime Minister had fixed the target of 7.5 crore accounts by 26 January 2015, later revised to 10 crore. Within a month, by September 2014, over 4 crore accounts were opened[11]. As of 17 January 2015, 11.5 crore accounts were already opened, reflecting Modi marching towards his mission[12].

Falling under the nodal ministry of finance, the opening up of PMJDY accounts made its way into the *Guinness Book of World Records* for the maximum number of accounts opened in a week. The certificate from Guinness World Records said, 'Most bank accounts opened in one week as part of the Financial Inclusion Campaign is 18,096,130 and was achieved by the Department of Financial Services, Government of India.'[13]

By 9 August 2023, already more than 50 crore Jan Dhan accounts were opened.

Of these, 56 per cent of accounts belonged to women, and 67 per cent were opened in rural or semi-urban areas. The deposits in these accounts were above Rs 2.03 lakh crore. More than 5.5 crore PMJDY accounts received the DBT benefits.

The scheme gives insurance cover of Rs 1 lakh, increased to Rs 2 lakh for the accounts opened after 28 August 2018. A RuPay Credit

Card is provided to such account holders along with an overdraft facility up to Rs 10,000. These accounts are being used to send government money for various welfare schemes using DBT (Direct Benefit Transfer). Account holders are also eligible for bank loans up to Rs 5,000 after six months of opening the account.

Digital Payments and DBT

The phenomenon of digital payment is based on the Aadhaar identity of the beneficiaries of government schemes. Earlier, people often complained that most benefits sent by the Central government were pocketed by middlemen, including officials and politicians. One can recall Late Prime Minister Rajiv Gandhi's saying that out of every Rupee sent to people, only 15 paise reached them. The remaining 85 paise were pocketed by middlemen.

The introduction of IT has made it possible to check corruption on a large scale. With a click of the mouse, the money meant for alleviating poverty and other schemes for people's welfare can reach their accounts without any delay. The DBT has helped the government reach more than 900 million people through 450 central schemes. Since 2014, the government has disbursed a whopping Rs 8.22 lakh crore–close to 60 per cent of the welfare and subsidies budget of the Union government–directly to the beneficiaries' bank accounts by May 2023[14].

The number of schemes and the quantum of support increases or decreases as per the need. In 2022-23 (as of 5 Jan 2023), more than Rs 3,80,000 crore was disbursed for 310 programmes meant for 159.5 crore beneficiaries. (The same person may be a beneficiary of more than one scheme)[15]. The DBT has helped the country save USD 33 billion through plugging system leakages[16].

Digitisation has helped with the exact identification of targeted beneficiaries. As of March 2021, names of more than 9.4 crore beneficiaries were removed–names that were duplicate, fake or non-existent. It helped the government save close to Rs 2.2 lakh crore[17]. Let us try to capture this phenomenon in the words of Modi,

> Ten crore fake beneficiaries have been thrown out. These 10 crore were the people who used to take the benefits of the government schemes.

> These 10 crore were those who were never even born but government money was being sent to them. You imagine the Congress government was sending money to such a large number of fake beneficiaries which was more than the combined population of Delhi, Punjab and Haryana. If our government had not delisted these 10 crore fake names from the system, the situation could have been far worse. It was not that easy to accomplish this feat, my friends. We had to give constitutional status to Aadhaar first[18].

Imagine the amount of money wasted due to loopholes in the system and corruption. Those in administration and middlemen were benefitting, and the challenges posed by vested interest were too formidable. Money pocketed by fake beneficiaries is now being spent on the needy. Modi has practically applied his public declaration–'*Na khaunga, na khane dunga*' (Neither will I pocket public money nor let anyone do so) after assuming office in 2014[19].

Many state governments have also benefited by identifying beneficiaries using Aadhaar card and saved crores of rupees earlier spent on fake beneficiaries. The Yogi government in Uttar Pradesh launched a crackdown, identified 79 lakh fake beneficiaries and saved Rs 8,000 crore pocketed by vested interests[20]. The Haryana government saved Rs 7,900 crore by identifying 36 lakh fake or duplicate beneficiaries[21].

It needed grit and determination on the part of the Prime Minister to push DBT in as many schemes as possible. The 2019 Lok Sabha election was said to be immensely influenced by the beneficiary class which had many reasons to vote for Modi. It was the first time the poor and the marginalised section felt empowered. Modi was already acquiring the image of a messiah for the deprived.

UPI at G20

As explained earlier, one of India's biggest achievements has been popularising digital payments using UPI. Even the developed world has not been able to create such an easy payment system on a massive scale using mobile linked to the accounts of citizens. It is a Unified Payment

Interface (UPI) that links multiple bank accounts to the mobile and ensures seamless payment to other payment gateways.

The system needs smartphones to download a UPI App and register using authenticated IDs and an internet connection. The number of smartphone users in India is estimated to reach over one billion in 2023. It is estimated to reach 1.55 billion by 2040. India no longer depends on other countries to feed its mobile phone demand. More than 200 companies are manufacturing smartphones in India. Even the best brand has set up its assembly or manufacturing units here.

In India, it is a craze now. Even vegetable vendors have some form of UPI payment system as India is going increasingly cashless. Cash transactions under Rs 1 lakh can be initiated through the UPI system. Even in villages, a grocery shop accepts payment using UPI. It is one of the big success stories of Digital India. As of now, a user can make up to 20 UPI transactions in 24 hours.

Payment using UPI accounted for 75 per cent of digital transactions in the country during 2022-23. The National Payments Corporation of India (NPCI) stated in June 2023 that the UPI hit a record 9 billion (900 crore) transactions in May 2023, worth more than Rs 14 lakh crore.

A PwC India report has predicted that the number of UPI transactions in India is likely to reach 1 billion per day by 2026-27 and will account for 90 per cent of the retail digital payments in the country.

India's story is bound to produce an awe-inspiring result in other countries that are yet to trust the UPI payment system as credible. Many foreign countries such as Singapore, UAE, Nepal, Bhutan, Sri Lanka and France have accepted the UPI. Now, NRIs sitting in these countries can easily make payments using UPI for clearing utility bills of their wards in India.

India showcased its UPI payment system to global leaders at the G20 presidential summit in Delhi in September 2023. It launched the G20 India Mobile App, which provided UPI payment access to all the delegates. Since they did not have bank accounts here, the delegates were given pre-filled wallets to shop online using the UPI interface. Among those who witnessed the live demonstration were the US Secretary of the Treasury, Janet Yellen and the Prime Minister of Bangladesh, Sheikh Hasina.

The government has decided to make the UPI payment system available to all NRIs. If the host countries sign an agreement with India on the UPI payment system, like France and many others have done, people in these countries and India could initiate seamless money transactions. It is likely to create a digital payment revolution on a global scale.

UMANG:
(Unified Mobile Application for New-age Governance)

India's digital story would be incomplete without mentioning UMANG–a unique IT platform created to empower the common man by bringing together various government services within his reach. It has translated the Prime Minister's dream to make all the government services accessible on one platform.

The Ministry of Electronics and IT (MEIT) gave shape to this vision of using technology to transform the lives of citizens and improve their ease of living. Indian citizens should be able to access government services round the clock using mobile. No intermediary is needed.

Modi launched the app on 23 November 2017, with 163 services and, gradually, more than 316 government departments have been added, and more than 1,750 services have been covered[22]. This app has already won four international awards for its excellence in providing citizen-centric services.

This mobile app is useful in finding out what services are available, how to access them, and then tracking the status. For example, in the 'Mera Ration' segment, citizens can check their ration card details, commodity balance of respective months, last 6 months transaction details and locate the nearest fair-price shop within the 10 km radius to their geo-location. In the segment named 'Delhi Police', the citizens may view details of their missing mobile phone, stolen vehicle, missing person, unidentified person and dead body. Citizens can also get information on traffic advisories, alerts, and complaints.

In the segment 'Direct Benefit Transfer', citizens can apply for a new PAN Card, change/correct details on their PAN Card like name, address, DOB, father's name etc., locate a centre nearest to them, and track the application. Other significant segments include 'My Aadhaar', 'Passport Sewa', 'Digilocker' and 'Jan Aushadhi Sugam'.

It is a delight to navigate through the app and explore the available government services. The tracker is user-friendly. The fact that there are 5.60 crore registered users on UMANG and more than 386 crore downloads since its launch speaks volumes for its utility.

Welfare Measures and IT

The Modi government has launched various welfare measures that have changed the fate of the underprivileged. It is a government that cares, and I have seen the eyes of poor people light up with hope at the mention of the name 'Modi'. During my visit to the remote Pindarkon village in the Chatra district of Jharkhand, I found that Modi's name touched a deep emotional chord with the poor.

It is because the Prime Minister has ensured that no middleman is involved in sending benefits meant for the beneficiaries. We have seen how the introduction of IT helped in sending subsidies in cash to Jan Dhan Yojana Accounts of beneficiaries. Some of the schemes of immense importance fall into the same category–Ujjwala Yojana, a Housing Scheme for the poor, making toilets for the poor under the Swachh Bharat Scheme, distribution of ration, child and maternity benefits, sending money to farmers in distress, sending money for scholarships, etc.

The government has already launched the Ayushman Bharat Digital Mission (ABDM) to develop a digital health infrastructure that would capture the health indicators of every citizen. Every citizen would be provided an Ayushman Bharat Health Account (ABHA) Number, a 14-digit unique number, to access digitally stored health records. It makes diagnosis and treatment faster. Registration can be done through an Aadhaar card. More than 45 crore ABHA Numbers have already been created.

Ayushman Bharat

For underprivileged families, Ayushman Bharat or Prime Minister Jan Arogya Yojana (AB-PMJAY) was launched in 2018, and became the biggest healthcare scheme in the world. The government brought top-class health care within the reach of the common man through this free health insurance scheme. The underprivileged can now go to any hospital for free treatment, and the government would bear the cost of their treatment for up to Rs 5 lakh per family per year for secondary and tertiary care hospitalisation, covering over 12 crore families. The amount is paid digitally to the hospital, and a record is maintained. It has targeted 55 crore beneficiaries, that is almost 40 per cent of the underprivileged.

Modi has spoken many times of how an entire poor family suffers if anyone from that family suffers from any disease. The family would borrow from a source or sell whatever they had for the treatment. It has invariably led to the family falling into the debt trap. They cannot afford treatment in a good hospital since it is costly. A government estimate says that close to six crore people are pushed into poverty each year[23].

Often, the government is criticised for not caring for the health of the poor. Years of neglect of this crucial sector had made good healthcare accessible to the rich only. There are many areas in the country with no proper healthcare facilities. The Modi government has taken the issue by the horns and set up AIIMS-like institutions in almost all states. New medical colleges have come up, adding more medical seats. The target is to have at least one super speciality hospital in roughly every Lok Sabha constituency.

It will take time. It needs infrastructure, trained manpower and competent doctors to run these institutions. Until then, it is undoubtedly a noble decision to bring the best healthcare facilities within the reach of the poor by providing them with cashless health insurance benefits.

The Central government funds 60 per cent, and the respective state government gives the remaining 40 per cent of the cost. In the North East states, the share of the Centre is 90 per cent, whereas in the Union Territories, it is 100 per cent. These benefits are available at all hospitals empanelled by the government.

More than 23 crore people have received treatment under the Ayushman Bharat scheme as of June 2023. BJP leaders were so impressed with this people-friendly scheme that they wanted it to be named 'Modi Care' on the pattern of the Obama Care scheme. Late Arun Jaitley was particularly keen on renaming it and had even described it as Modi Care. However, the Prime Minister did not want the scheme in his name. Nonetheless, BJP leaders continued to use 'Modi Care' in television debates.

Ujjwala Yojana

It is yet another scheme that demonstrates that the government is compassionate and cares for the deprived. It wanted to empower poor women who cooked on firewood. The aim was to provide clean cooking gas to millions of women below the poverty line. Besides giving health benefits to the beneficiaries, it also intended environmental protection by discouraging the use of firewood.

Launched in 2016, the scheme has benefitted 9.59 crore poor women. Under the scheme, the government gives free LPG connection, including gas stove, regulator and a first refill of the cylinder. The beneficiaries are given subsidies for 12 cylinders.

The target has increased, and 75 lakh more LPG connections will be added for Ujjwala beneficiaries during the three years, from 2023-24 to 2025-26. In September 2023, the Union Cabinet decided to make it 10.35 crore. The government will release these additional numbers to benefit the poor[24].

Modi had already prepared the ground for this, considering that there was a shortage of LPG connections. He launched the 'Give It Up' campaign in March 2015 and urged the rich to give up their LPG subsidy voluntarily. The result was for all to see. Modi's words carried weight. Close to one crore people had already given up their LPG connections by March 2016. The country had 15.34 crore LPG connections by then.

The Prime Minister thanked those who had given up their subsidy, eulogised their contribution towards society and announced a scroll of honour for them. 'We value your involvement and would like to have your permission to put your name in the "Scroll of Honour" for giving up subsidy', he said.

In 2020, the subsidy on LPG gas cylinders was scrapped, except for the Ujjwala Yojana beneficiaries, who received a subsidy of Rs 200 per cylinder. In August 2023, the government reintroduced a subsidy for households at Rs 200 per cylinder for up to 12 refills in a year. It was done because of the increase in the international price of gas. The subsidy for Ujjwala beneficiaries was increased to Rs 400 per cylinder.

The scheme, aimed at providing LPG connections to the BPL

households in India, has been a path-breaking initiative in more ways than one. The direct impact of the scheme has been on reducing the health hazards caused by burning solid fuels like wood, cow dung and charcoal. According to a WHO report, the smoke inhaled by women using unclean fuel is equal to smoking 400 cigarettes in an hour. About five lakh deaths occur in India due to the use of unclean fuel[25]. Moreover, when women cook, small children with their mothers also inhale a lot of smoke and solid particles, which poses a grave hazard to their health as well.

Housing for Poor

The progress of the country would be nullified if the government cannot cater to the housing needs of the homeless. With this aim, the Modi government launched an ambitious housing scheme to provide housing to all by 2024. All the houseless people, as per the census 2011, would be provided with a pucca house that would also have water and electricity.

The number of homeless people was 17,73,040, including 9,38,348 in urban areas and 8,34,692 in rural areas. This translates into 4,49,761 houseless families. While speaking in the President's address in the Lok Sabha in 2014, when the newly constituted house met for the first time, Modi said every Indian must have a house by 2022, when the country would complete 75 years of Independence. It meant constructing 55,000 to 60,000 houses per year. The scheme Housing for All by 2022 was targeting urban areas.

A similar scheme to ensure housing for all in rural areas was launched in 2016. The scheme for rural areas finalised a target of 2.95 crore pucca houses with basic amenities. The deadline has been extended to 2024. The scheme is available to those who are homeless and also those in the category of Economically Weaker Section (EWS) and Low Income Group (LIG). Differential concessional loans are available to those who fall outside this category if they do not have a house of their own.

The ambitious Pradhan Mantri Awas Yojana-Urban (PMAY-U) is being implemented by the Ministry of Housing and Urban Affairs (MoHUA), whereas the Pradhan Mantri Awas Yojana-Gramin (PMAY-G) is being implemented by the Ministry of Rural Development.

The beneficiaries are identified by the respective state governments from the list already prepared as per the 2011 census.

The scheme is working on a federal line where the Centre contributes 60 per cent of the expenditure, and the state gives the remaining 40 per cent. In the North East, the ratio is 90:10, and for the Union Territories, the Centre takes care of the entire funding. The state governments identify the beneficiaries and create an integrated network where all facilities such as water under Jal Jeevan Mission, electricity under Saubhagya Yojana, toilets under Swachh Bharat Abhiyan, LPG connection under Ujjwala Yojana, and bank accounts under Jan Dhan Yojana are given as a package. Various provisions for providing employment are applicable for these people so that the poor do not suffer due to a lack of jobs.

The achievements have been awe-inspiring. Of the 2.95 crore houses meant for rural areas, 2.13 crore have been already built by February 2023. About 55 per cent of the target has been achieved in urban areas. The government has already announced that the target would be completed by 2024. A fresh allocation of Rs 79,590 crore was finalised in the budget for 2023-24 to meet the task faster. The government would incur more than Rs 2 lakh crore to complete the mission of Housing for All.

Housing for All scheme has empowered the poor as well as the middle class. People at least would have a house of their own and live with a sense of pride. Narendra Modi had described the scheme as a gamechanger in the fight against poverty and homelessness. Rightly so, since this is one of the basic needs. It explains the demands from states to include more people and extend the deadline. He has not only built houses for the homeless but has created a space in the heart of every beneficiary who had never imagined a house of their own.

During the COVID-19 pandemic, the media highlighted the housing crisis for migrant workers who go to big cities for work. The government has responded with affordable rental housing for the urban poor who have come as migrants and are looking for temporary accommodation.

Launched in 2023, the scheme called the **Affordable Rental Housing Scheme** (ARHC) is to be implemented under two models. In the first, the government would use the fully-funded vacant houses and convert these into one-room accommodation. In the second model, vacant land would be used to construct such houses in partnership with public or private institutions. These houses would be provided to the beneficiaries near their workplace at affordable rates.

The ARHC is a centrally sponsored scheme, and a corpus of Rs 10,000 crore has been made available by the National Housing Bank. The housing finance companies will get assistance from this corpus and finance housing facilities in designated areas.

The scheme beneficiaries must belong to the EWS or the LIG category. 'Street vendors, rickshaw pullers and other service providers, industrial workers as well as migrants working with markets or trade unions, educational or health institutions, long-term tourists or visitors to the hospitality sector and students are also covered under this scheme.'[26]

Applicants must apply online on the portal of ARHC, where each applicant can see the status of his application.

Swachh Bharat Mission

The entire nation woke up to the call of Swachh Bharat when Modi took up a broom and started cleaning a Harijan locality in Delhi. He launched the Swachh Bharat Mission (SBM) or Clean India Movement along with his cabinet colleagues on 2 October 2014, the 145th anniversary of Mahatma Gandhi. Cine actor Aamir Khan joined him on the stage along with Union Ministers Nitin Gadkari and M Venkaiah Naidu.

The high point of the launch was the walkathon in which all of them participated along with thousands of ordinary citizens, including school children dressed in immaculate whites. It was quite a spectacle when the Prime Minister walked fast-paced with people to create awareness about cleanliness–a tribute to Mahatma Gandhi, who said sanitation is more important than independence.

After launching the campaign, Modi went to a Valmiki basti in Delhi's Mandir Marg area, picked up a broom and joined dozens of *safai karamcharis* to show what he actually meant. This symbolic gesture clearly told the people that everyone should take the responsibility to clean if India had to become clean and respectful. Modi was leading by example. 'If 125 crore people resolve not to dirty our surroundings, no force on earth can come and dirty our country', he had said during his first Independence Day speech in 2014.

While launching the campaign, Modi nominated nine people as the first brand ambassadors, including Salman Khan, Sachin Tendulkar and Priyanka Chopra. These nine people had to nominate nine more persons, and the chain had to continue. Each of these people would participate in a cleanliness drive and then nominate nine more. It became instantly popular, with more and more people participating in the campaign.

Another aspect of SBM was the construction of toilets in every home so that India would become Open Defecation Free (ODF). It was quite usual to see people defecating in the open. They either did not have enough toilet facilities or were not prone to using public toilets. It was not a good sight to see anyone walking towards Railway Stations in the morning and finding people defecating near railway lines. The problem was more acute for women in rural areas where they did not have enough toilet facilities.

Modi understood the issue quite well and did not feel shy about talking about this in his first Independence Day speech in 2014. He highlighted how the unavailability of toilets was creating health problems for women who would go to defecate only in the dark. A brief quote from his first Independence Day speech would help understand his thought process,

> Brothers and Sisters, we are living in twenty-first century. Has it ever pained us that our mothers and sisters have to defecate in open? Whether dignity of women is not our collective responsibility? The poor womenfolk of the village wait for the night; until darkness descends, they can`t go out to defecate. What bodily torture they must be feeling, how many diseases that act might engender. Can't we just make arrangements for toilets for the dignity of our mothers and sisters?

And then, the Prime Minister made a big announcement,

> I want to make a beginning today itself and that is–all schools in the country should have toilets with separate toilets for girls. Only then our daughters will not be compelled to leave schools midway. Our parliamentarians utilising MPLAD fund are here. I appeal to them to

> spend it for constructing toilets in schools for a year. The government should utilise its budget on providing toilets. I call upon the corporate sector also to give priority to the provision of toilets in schools with your expenditure under Corporate Social Responsibility.

He said the task has to be completed in one year.

Under the Swachh Vidyalaya Initiative, more than 4.17 lakh toilets were constructed in 2.61 lakh government schools in one year. The task of providing a toilet to every home was also achieved, with more than 11 crore toilets built by March 2023. More than 2.23 lakh community sanitary complexes were also built[27].

By 2 October 2019, the 150th anniversary of Mahatma Gandhi, all villages, gram panchayats, districts, states and union territories in India declared themselves to be open-defecation free (ODF). More than 10 crore toilets were constructed by then.

Providing toilets to ensure all 25 crore households had access to toilets was tough. But it was still tougher to ensure that people used it properly. Many cases were reported where people were not using toilets because of cultural reasons and lack of awareness. The government launched phase II of SMB under the Department of Drinking Water and Sanitation with an outlay of Rs 1.41 lakh crore for 2020-21 to 2024-25. The focus was to sustain the ODF status and adopt more scientific solid and liquid waste management in every gram panchayat with a population of 5,000 or more. A massive awareness campaign has been launched already.

Drinking Water to every Home:
Her Ghar Nal se Jal

Providing safe drinking water to people has been a great challenge. When the task was undertaken under the Jal Jeevan Mission in 2019, only about 3.2 crore (17 per cent) rural households had tap connections for drinking water. In the last four years, 13.08 crore households (66.7 per cent) of 19.23 crore rural households have been covered.

People, particularly in rural India, suffer due to scarcity of drinking water, leading to a lot of hardship. In some places, the water available is not hygienic enough to drink. Taking water to every home through taps addressed a crucial civilisational need by providing safe and adequate drinking water.

This is how Modi launched the Mission during his address on the 73rd Independence Day in 2019,

> I declare from the Red Fort today that in the days to come, we will take forward the Jal Jeevan Mission. The central and the state governments will jointly work on this Jal Jeevan Mission. We have promised to spend more than Rs 3.50 lakh crore on this mission in the coming years.

Under the mission, every household must have a tap water connection by 2024, with an outlay of Rs 3.60 lakh crore.

The programme is community-driven, with a predominance of women so that they can plan its storage, decide on routes of pipes, manage water quality and supervise a smooth running of the system created for equitable water distribution. Local NGOs have been roped in to create awareness.

One can only imagine the mammoth task of taking tap water to distant villages in Ladakh, where water freezes at sub-zero temperatures. It needs steel determination to accomplish this. On 27 July 2022, the government accomplished a near-impossible task when tap water reached Demchok village in Leh district, at a height of 13,800 feet, where the temperature gets minus 40 degrees. The villages from Chushul to Demchok and Chumar along the LAC between China and the Ladakh region of India now have tap water.

The complexity and challenges can be imagined because equipment like pipes needed to be carried to villages that did not even have roads in the mountainous terrain. The pipes had to be insulated to withstand exposure to minus temperature, and one of the biggest tasks was to keep the supply running since water could easily freeze into ice. Hence, submersible pumps were used to keep the water flow intact.

The Jal Jeevan Mission is the largest government-funded water project in the world. The significance of this project was not lost on anyone when thousands of water workers were special guests during Narendra Modi's address to the nation on 77th Independence Day. The representatives from 25 States and Union Territories included sarpanchs, plumbers, pump operators, water meter readers, and members of Village Water and Sanitation Committees. It was Modi's way of thanking them.

Electricity in Every Home

Even after 75 years of independence, more than 18,000 villages (18,452) did not have electricity. These were mostly tribal and hilly areas, not accessible easily, and the previous governments preferred to adopt an ostrich-like attitude rather than facing the issue head-on. The World Bank had reported that India had the world's largest unelectrified population.

After Modi came to power, he realised the gravity of the situation. He said,

> Few days ago, I was asked in a meeting as to how many villages in our country don't have even a single electric pole. And, it came to my notice that even after 70 years of independence, 18,000 villages in our country don't have such a facility. What can be a bigger misfortune than this?

He then announced the target of electrifying all these villages in 1,000 days.

The promise was made in 2015, and by April 2018, the task was completed when Leisang, a tiny village in a remote area of Manipur, became the last village in India to get a power connection. Modi tweeted with satisfaction,

> 28 April 2018 will be remembered as a historic day in the development journey of India. Yesterday, we fulfilled a commitment due to which the lives of several Indians will be transformed forever! I am delighted that every single village of India now has access to electricity.

The task was not only to take electricity to every village but also to every house in the country. This task was undertaken under the Saubhagya Yojana, also known as Prime Minister Sahaj Bijli Har Ghar Yojana (Easy electricity for every home), launched in October 2017.

The task was to provide last-mile connectivity to all houses in rural and urban areas. It was the world's biggest universal electrification initiative undertaken by any government. By March 2022, close to 2.86 crore households were electrified under the scheme.

Caring for Farmers

While no government can afford to ignore the farming community since the country's economic health depends on its robust agriculture, the Modi government is known for launching the biggest scheme for sending money directly into the accounts of small and marginal farmers under the Prime Minister Kisan Samman Nidhi Yojana (PMKSNY). Close to 12 crore farmers are getting Rs 6,000 per year in 3 instalments of Rs 2,000 each.

Announced by the government in its interim budget on 1 February 2019, the scheme was launched from Gorakhpur on 24 February 2019. In January 2024, the government released its 16th instalment of the scheme. The scheme is 100 per cent funded by the Union government which has earmarked Rs 75,000 per year for the empowerment of farmers.

Ever since the Modi government came to power, it has been trying to work in the interest of the farmers. While some are direct and visible, others are in the form of subsidies. Every farmer is getting Rs 50,000 per year in various forms from the Union government. The Prime Minister has called it the 'Modi Guarantee' and not a promise since farmers are already getting it. It has come as fertiliser subsidies, procuring the produce at better prices and Kisan Samman Nidhi. The government is spending Rs 6.5 lakh crore to give a boost to the agriculture sector.

In the last nine years, the government has provided fertilisers at a much cheaper rate when compared to other countries, despite a global price increase. Modi further highlighted that farmers are getting a bag (45 kg) of urea for Rs 270, as against the price of Rs 720 in Bangladesh, Rs 800 in Pakistan, Rs 2,100 in China and Rs 3,000 in the United States. The government has spent over Rs 10 lakh crore towards fertiliser subsidies in the last nine years to ensure that farmers get crop nutrients at a reasonable price. '*Isse badi guarantee kya hoti hai?*' (What is a bigger guarantee than this?), Modi asked while addressing the 17th Indian Cooperative Congress in Delhi[28].

The Centre has tried to ensure a remunerative price for farmers and has increased procurement under the MSP. The government has provided 15 lakh crore to farmers using the procurement of food grains in the last nine years[29].

The Modi government has been making efforts to bring together the entire agricultural marketing network on one digital platform E-NAM (National Agriculture Market). It was launched in 2016 as an online trading platform to ease seamless and transparent interaction between producers and buyers. It aims to help farmers market their produce and sell where they would get the best price.

E-NAM platform network with the existing Agricultural Produce Market Committee (APMC) *mandis* to create a national market for agricultural commodities. The programme is fully funded by the Central government and implemented by the Small Farmers Agribusiness Consortium (SFAC) under the Ministry of Agriculture.

The e-NAM is a single window for all APMC-related information and services related to the commodity arrivals, quality and prices, buy and sell offers and e-payment settlement directly into the farmers' account. 'It promotes uniformity in agriculture marketing by streamlining procedures across the integrated markets, removing information asymmetry between buyers and sellers and promoting real-time price discovery based on actual demand and supply.'[30]

The government has been imparting technical expertise and money to technologically modernise APMCs and Regulated Market Committees (RMCs) to enhance their capabilities and become a part of e-NAM. After COVID-19, the e-NAM mobile platform has been enlarged by launching the Farmer Producer Organisation (FPO), whereby these FPOs can trade their produce from their collection centres without bringing the produce to the nearest APMCs.

A warehouse-based trading module was also launched in e-NAM to facilitate trade from warehouses based on e-NWR (electronic-Negotiable Warehouse Receipt).

On 14 July 2022, Platform of Platforms (POP) was launched under e-NAM. With this, the farmers could sell their produce outside their state borders. It increased their digital access to multiple markets, buyers and service providers and brought transparency in business transactions. Forty-one service providers from different platforms are covered under POP, facilitating various services in the value chain such as trading, quality checks, warehousing, fintech, market information, transportation, etc.

As of 31 March 2023, more than 1.75 crore farmers and 2.43 lakh traders had registered on e-NAM. Close to 2,575 FPOs have joined the platform, along with 1361 *mandis* of 23 States and 4 UTs[31]. The achievement of e-NAM has been stupendous. A trade worth Rs 2.50 lakh crore has already been recorded on the e-NAM platform.

Antidote to Farm Laws Withdrawal

Misguided by the vested interests, lakhs of farmers were made to believe that the three farm laws brought by the government were against their interests. They launched a year-long agitation blocking the arterial routes of Delhi and tried to present the government in the wrong light. The best intentions of the government, to give farmers the freedom to sell their produce, were jeopardised because the movement got hijacked by the ganging of the corrupt[32]. The movement had the potential to disturb Punjab, a border state. We are aware of how some Khalistani supporters had infiltrated the movement[33].

The Prime Minister did what was best in the situation. His ambition was to protect the farmers from exploitation and give them the freedom to sell their produce to the best bidder, but not at a price less than the MSP announced by the government. The idea was to bring in more private participation to enable the modernisation of agriculture and set up warehouses that would have benefitted farmers.

Modi withdrew the three farm laws enacted in September 2020. These were the Farmers' Produce Trade and Commerce (Promotion and Facilitation) Act 2020, the Farmers (Empowerment and Protection) Agreement of Price Assurance and Farm Services Act 2020, and the Essential Commodities (Amendment) Act 2020. On 19 November 2021, Modi announced the withdrawal of the three legislations and on 1 December 2021, Parliament repealed the three Acts.

In his address to the nation, Modi said, 'It was unfortunate that despite the government's intentions to strengthen and empower farmers particularly those who have small land holdings, many of them were not convinced about the benefits of the laws, and therefore, the government has decided to set in motion the process of repealing all three laws.' He stressed that the three legislations were meant to benefit the farmers, but they couldn't be convinced 'despite our best efforts'.

The Supreme Court appointed multi-member panel that looked into the farm laws in detail had found that the laws were beneficial to farmers and should not have been repealed. The report was released by Anil Jaysingh Ghanwat, President of the Swatantra Bharat Party and the Shetkari Sanghatana, a member of the committee appointed by the Chief Justice's bench of the Supreme Court in January 2021.

The report contended that 'the repeal of the three farm laws is unfair to the "silent majority" that supported the farm laws'. 'The report states that it extended invitations to 266 farmer organisations, which included those protesting at the periphery of Delhi. Out of the 266 farmer organisations to whom invitations were sent, the committee could directly interact with only 73 organisations. The report claims that out of these 73 organisations, 61 organisations (85.7 per cent) representing over 3.3 crore farmers supported the laws. Four farmers' organisations, representing 51 lakh farmers (13.3 per cent), did not support the Act. Another seven farmer organisations, representing 3.6 lakh farmers (1 per cent), supported the Acts with some suggestions for modifications.'[34] The majority of farmers' organisations concluded that the laws would help farmers sell their produce outside the APMC market and gain.

Many of the critics of the government projected it as a big loss or defeat of the government. The Opposition charged that the government had withdrawn the laws fearing electoral losses in the impending assembly elections in five states–Uttar Pradesh, Uttarakhand, Manipur, Goa and Punjab[35].

But it was not true. The BJP did not have a substantial presence in Punjab since it had already left the political ground to the Shiromani Akali Dal when the two were together. This was done to foster Hindu-Sikh unity, and the alliance has given long-term peace to the state after it was devastated by terrorism under the Congress rule.

The results of the elections that took place in February also proved the contrary. The BJP won in four of the five states, and the Aam Aadmi Party won in Punjab. As attested by the report of the Supreme Court panel, a majority of silent farmers were with the government. The election results were almost a referendum on the farm laws. Yet, the government did not push these. It was Modi's sagacity that he defused the crisis by taking a step backwards.

Those who planned the agitation were exposed after the electoral reverses of the parties opposed the BJP.

It became increasingly clear that they had intended to use the farmer agitation to bring down the BJP government in Uttar Pradesh. The agitating organisations under the Samyukt Kisan Morcha (SKM), an umbrella organisation with over 500 farmers' organisations, announced they would launch the 'Defeat BJP: Mission Uttar Pradesh' campaign. They announced holding *maha panchayat*s across the states to oppose the BJP[36].

When the mission failed and the BJP won the elections, the frustration of the farmers' protest came into the open. Yogendra Yadav, who had tried to give an ideological spine to the agitation, confessed that the agitation was political and had nothing to do with the issues.

In an interview with a TV channel immediately after the results were out, Yadav said that he and Rakesh Tikait had created a conducive 'pitch' to defeat the BJP by organising a farmers' movement, but the Opposition 'did not bowl well' to benefit from it.

'Rakesh Tikait and I toured the entire UP. But remember, we are not the players. Talking about cricket, our work was like that of the "pitch roller", we laid a conducive pitch for the fast bowlers and seamers but bowling is not our job', he stressed[37].

While these leaders must be gloating over their success in subverting the three laws, the Prime Minister was determined to liberate farmers from the clutches of the *arhatia*s and middlemen who benefitted from the produce of the farmers. Digital India made it possible. Anyone registered even in one market can operate here electronically. The farmers know the MSP that the government is giving and can sell their produce online at any APMC where they get better prices. Those setting up big warehouses can buy the produce online and stock the same to prevent wastage.

Soil Health Card

It is a path-breaking scheme that the Prime Minister borrowed from his Gujarat days and introduced for the farmers across the country. The health of the soil decides productivity, and if farmers know the components of the soil they cultivate, they can inject the essential nutrients to make the soil more productive. It would go well with the slogan–'Each drop more crop' because linked to it is the quality of the soil.

Modi launched the Soil Health Card Scheme (SHC) on 19 February 2015 from Rajasthan. To be implemented throughout the country, the SHC scheme provides farmers with a mechanism to know the nutrient status of the soil. They can know which crop would yield more. The SHC is given to farmers every two years. Digital India helps maintain records and furthers studies about the nature of the soil.

The target is to make the soil-testing facility available at the doorstep of every farmer. Youths and farmers up to 40 years old are encouraged to set up Soil Health Laboratories under the SHC scheme. 75 per cent of the cost of setting up the laboratory is funded, by either the Centre or the states where these are set up.

As of 2022-2023, 511 Static Soil Tasting Labs, 123 Mobile Soil Testing Labs, 8,811 Mini Soil Testing Labs and 2,395 Village Soil Testing Labs have been working in tandem to transform agriculture by improving soil quality. A massive awareness programme has also been launched to educate farmers on this. Around 6.45 lakh demonstrations, 93,781 farmers' trainings, and 7,425 farmers' melas have been organised[38].

Technological intervention by introducing the Geographic Information System (GIS) has been achieved in the SHC scheme, and there is an attempt to map the soil across the country by the captured test results. The QR codes are automatically generated and linked with the sample and test results on the portal. The new system has become operational since April 2023, and samples are collected through mobile application. More than 12 crore farmers have already been issued SHCs.

Doubling Farmers' Income

Doubling farmers' income is a continuous process and no government can be restricted by any deadline. What matters are the steps taken for the betterment of the farming community. And the government's efforts can be judged by assessing whether farmers have improved living conditions.

We have already seen how e-NAM and SHCs have enabled farmers to get better yields. While SHCs have enabled farmers to know what nutrients to give to the soil to get better crops, e-NAM has ensured that they do not depend on middlemen to sell their produce. They can access the *mandis* to get better rates and sell them online.

The guarantee of MSP for food grains ensures that they are not exploited. The government has not only clarified that the MSP regime is there to stay, but it has also enhanced the MSP to ensure that farmers get a rate one and a half times their production cost. The MSP for paddy (common) has been increased from Rs 1,310 per quintal in 2013-14 to Rs 2,040 per quintal in 2022-23. Similarly, the MSP for wheat has been increased from Rs 1,400 per quintal in 2013-14 to Rs 2,125 per quintal in 2022-23.

Since the launch of PM Kisan Samman Nidhi, more than 11 crore farmers are getting Rs 6,000 per annum, which amounts to more than Rs 70,000 crore. The budgetary allocation to agriculture has witnessed a substantial increase. The combined budget allocation to the Agriculture Ministry and the Ministry of Fisheries, Animal Husbandry & Dairying was Rs 30,223.88 crore. In the year 2022-23, it was Rs 1,31,612.41 crore. Such a huge investment is bound to have a cascading effect on the condition of farmers[39].

Pradhan Mantri Fasal Bima Yojana (PMFBY) was launched in 2016 to mitigate the problem of high premium rates for farmers and reduction sum insured due to capping. The Fasal Bima Yojana has been strengthened, and claims settlements have been made transparent and easy.

Institutional credit for farmers has been strengthened. From Rs 7.3 lakh crore in 2013-14, the target was increased to Rs 18.5 lakh crore in 2022-23. Concessional credit of 4 per cent given to Kisan Credit Card holders has been extended to farmers working in animal husbandry and fisheries. A special drive has been undertaken since February 2020 to provide concessional institutional credit, focussing on covering all PM-KISAN beneficiaries through Kisan Credit Cards (KCC). As of

30 December 2022, 389.33 lakh new KCC applications have been sanctioned with Rs 4,51,672 crore[40].

Promoting **micro irrigation** to cover more lands under irrigation, persuading farmers to adopt the practice of **drip irrigation** to get more crop per drop and adopting **organic farming** are some other ways the government has been trying to improve farming conditions and empower farmers.

Mann Ki Baat
Transformational Instrument

A nation is advanced in proportion as education & intelligence spread among the masses.
–Swami Vivekananda

Despite the vaccine proving to be an elixir against COVID-19, people in Dularia village of Betul (Madhya Pradesh) refused to take the jab. They did not believe that the vaccine could give protection. Many Indian villages witnessed people running away when healthcare professionals approached them.

Rajesh Hirave and Kishorilal Dhurve got to speak to Modi on Friday, 25 June 2021, when they underlined their fears that the vaccine could cause death, as mentioned in the messages they got through WhatsApp. Modi explained that the vaccine was an important tool to save lives. He said he had taken the jab, and his 100-year-old mother had taken both doses without any adverse effects. The Prime Minister asked both of them to take the vaccine and encourage others to take the same[1]. By the time Modi mentioned this in his *Mann ki Baat* on Sunday, 27 June 2021, the entire village had taken the vaccine.

In a country where people do not leave government facilities, and voting is decided based on freebies given in the electoral promises, very few would believe that more than a crore people in the country have voluntarily surrendered their subsidised gas after an appeal by the Prime Minister. Many considered it unimaginable, but Modi trusted his people.

In the sixth episode of *Mann ki Baat* on 22 March 2015, Narendra Modi called out to the countrymen that those who could afford should give up their gas subsidy to enable gas connections to reach the poor and the needy. It had a dramatic effect, and close to 30 lakh people surrendered their subsidised gas connections within six months of this appeal[2]. The figure reached 1.13 crore in March 2023[3]. In various episodes of *Mann ki Baat*, Modi has profusely thanked people for their noble acts. He has described it as a silent revolution[4].

India has always needed a leader to show people the path and guide them to their destiny. In the distant past, it was Chanakya who brought all little kingdoms together and made them fight foreign invaders under the leadership of Chandragupta Maurya. The mighty Alexander the Great could not fulfil his dream of conquering India when he came to know the strength and determination of the formidable Magadh Army.

Adi Shankaracharya, who died young, gave the narrative of India being one, culturally and geographically. He established four Maths–Jyotir Math (in Chamoli, Uttarakhand), Dwarka (Gujarat), Puri (Odisha) and Shringeri (Karnataka). He outlined the virtues of *Vedas* and re-established the supremacy of *Sanatan* Dharma.

Shivaji, the great Maratha warrior, challenged the mighty Mughal Empire that was based on the supremacy of Islam. Shivaji was all-inclusive and raised consciousness about the pride of *Sanatan* Dharma. He was an ardent advocate of Hind Swaraj, and his army gave opportunities to Muslims to fight for the cause of their motherland, thereby intending that everyone has the right to fight for the cause of their motherland. His ideology was 'Nation First' based on cultural pride, and his Swaraj was based on equality, brotherhood, and justice.

At a time when the nation was suffering due to its subjugation to British rule and the atrocities committed by the supremacist white race, there rose a monk who mesmerised the world with his philosophy rooted in the *Vedas* and his ideological clarity about the basic tenets of *Sanatan* Dharma. He was none other than Swami Vivekananda who, during his famous Chicago speech in September 1893, showed the universal brotherhood enshrined in the *Sanatan* tradition and culture. The much-needed ideological spine empowered the generations after Swami

Vivekananda to work and fight for their country. There would hardly be any youth not inspired by the philosophy of Swami Vivekananda.

Swami Vivekananda immensely inspired the father of the nation, Mahatma Gandhi. When Gandhi visited Belur Math in 1921 to mark Vivekananda's birth anniversary, he said, 'I have gone through his works very thoroughly, and after having gone through them, the love that I had for my country became a thousand-fold. I ask you, young men, not to go away empty-handed without imbibing something of the spirit of the place where Swami Vivekananda lived and died.'[5]

Gandhiji was aware of the might and brutality of the British Empire, but he had also seen the soft and humane side of the ordinary British living in London. While he used the weapon of non-violence to unite the entire country under the banner of Congress, he tried to appeal to the heart of the British rulers in India and the common British citizens in London not to indulge in barbarism and set India free. His weapon of non-violence was rooted in the *Sanatan* Dharma. His ideology of Swaraj was captured in his book *Hind Swaraj*, which the British described as seditious and banned. Gandhiji's contribution to peace and non-violence was so profound that he became an international inspiration. There is hardly a country where one would not find a statue of Gandhiji as an apostle of peace and non-violence.

The only person who can fit in this mould of inspirational leaders is Prime Minister Narendra Modi. Immensely influenced by the philosophy of Swami Vivekananda, Modi has tried to achieve greatness through his hard work and commitment to the cause of building a strong nation. Not only does he command the large support base of 140 crore Indians, he has gone out of his way to inspire crores of youths who would otherwise be uninterested in daily politicking but are keen to work for the uplift of their motherland.

Modi's words carry weight for his people, and whenever he has appealed to them to do something, people have followed him with absolute trust. For them, he cannot go wrong. Even if he does go wrong, his intention cannot be questioned. He evolved the institution of *Mann ki Baat* (Straight from the Heart) to directly interact with people, understand their pains and inspire them to do better. He does not talk of politics here but speaks like an avuncular talking to his family members about what is good and what is not.

The thrust and idea behind *Mann ki Baat* was outlined by Narendra Modi in the first episode aired on Vijayadashami, 3 October 2014. He said he wanted all citizens to work together for the country's betterment and progress. His words were, 'Let us all take our nation to the new heights…Let us all take a step forward…If you take one step, our nation takes 125 crore steps to move forward…We all need to defeat all of our inner evils and decide to start doing something good for the nation'.[6]

Modi's *Mann ki Baat* gradually evolved into an institution under which he would come on the radio on the last Sunday of every month at 11 am to talk to people based on his experience and the feedback he received from the people. Even if he would be unavailable due to his engagements, there would be a recorded version to be aired at the usual time. He has spoken on various issues and crises facing India today. He has spoken about Swachh Bharat, the need for regular use of toilets, vaccine jabs, women empowerment, drug abuse and aspirations of youths.

One of the most vital issues covered by Modi is examination stress faced by students. While this has been a recurring theme every year, the *Mann ki Baat* on 22 February 2015 highlighted his sensitivity to the crises faced by the students. Students would generally be distracted by the attraction of celebrating Holi and watching the Cricket World Cup while preparing for their board examinations, giving them a tough time to prepare for the examination amidst this din.

He gave students 13 tips to enjoy the one-time opportunity of undertaking the examination without worrying much about the results. 'Examinations are not the end of our life.' He also advised parents not to put unnecessary pressure on students by comparing them with others[7]. His book *Exam Warriors* contains inspiring thoughts for students reeling under examination stress.

Modi has used this instrument to praise the country and to apprise the younger generation of the philosophy and culture of the nation. He has guided them on how to be a good citizen and thank the COVID Warriors. He has guided parents on how not to get angry with children or pressurise them unnecessarily. He has guided parents to be equally considerate toward their daughters.

Leaders across the world have been using social media–Facebook, Twitter, Instagram and YouTube–to communicate with people. Gone are the times when they depended exclusively on public rallies or the traditional media to convey such messages.

For example, ex-US President Barack Obama relied on Facebook and Twitter (now X), whereas Donald Trump used Twitter. The UK Prime Minister Rishi Sunak uses Twitter. It helps these leaders to communicate their feelings and achievements of their respective governments.

Indian Prime Minister is way ahead of many leaders in using social media to communicate. As of March 2023, he was the second most followed world leader on Twitter, second only to Barack Obama. Since his chief ministerial days, Modi has been using social media to directly connect with his people to understand their problems and pains and provide solutions.

Former Prime Minister Atal Bihari Vajpayee, at times, used his vacation to contemplate and come up with musings about the country. His famous 'Kumarakom Musings' was his address to people from a remote Kumarakom village in Kerala[8]. He had spoken about Ayodhya and Kashmir. Ex-Prime Minister P V Narasimha Rao used books and blogs to reach people.

However, none of the world leaders have thought of using radio as a medium to communicate in the modern era, even though it has an immense reach. It does not depend on power, and battery-operated radios work even in remote areas outside the reach of the internet.

When television was not popular, and technology was still in the phase of evolution, radio acted as a bridge, and the first Prime Minister of India, Jawaharlal Nehru, and his daughter, Indira Gandhi, effectively used radio to communicate with people or to announce any major decision. Lal Bahadur Shastri used radio to appeal to the people to shun partisanship and rise to the occasion. The entire nation stood behind him whenever he said something.

One should not forget that Subhas Chandra Bose used his own radio platform Azad Hind Radio in 1942 to relay activities of the Indian National Army. People used to be glued to the radio to know the activities of Netaji. Mahatma Gandhi, too, had used radio to communicate.

Most government announcements used to come on the radio, and the BBC (British Broadcasting Corporation) gained immense popularity due to its high frequency and unique style of giving news. *Binaca Geetmala* on All India Radio (AIR) was the most coveted programme for every Indian interested in Bollywood songs. It beamed from Radio Ceylon from 1952-88 and then from 1989-94 under Vividh Bharati service of the AIR.

As television gained popularity, radio got pushed to the background. Now, FM radio has come to revive the interest in radio by providing wholesome entertainment. The proliferation of smartphones and music systems in cars has further increased the importance of FM radios. Even without the internet, the mobiles or music systems in cars would catch radio signals since all of these come with an inbuilt FM radio chip. India witnessed 1.10 billion mobile connections in early 2023. It meant 77 per cent of the total population was using mobile. Every city or town now has cars fitted with radio.

Narendra Modi understood the importance of radio long back and took measures to make it more popular. Signals have been allotted to private operators in most Indian cities to increase their reach. FM has multiplied the coverage of radio. The All India Radio (AIR), the country's premier broadcaster, has 479 stations domestically to broadcast in all 22 languages listed in the Eighth Schedule of the Indian Constitution and 179 dialects. It covers 92 per cent of the country's geographical areas and 99.19 per cent of the total population[9]. AIR's overseas wing broadcasts in 27 languages, including 16 foreign languages such as French, Chinese, Japanese, Pashto, Arabic, Tibetan and Persian[10].

Mann ki Baat is broadcast in 22 Indian languages and 29 dialects, besides 11 foreign languages, including French, Chinese, Indonesian, Tibetan, Burmese, Baluchi and Arabic. No wonder Union Minister late Arun Jaitley described it as a 'social revolution on the radio' when a book marking 50 successful episodes of the programme was released in 2019[11].

Modi had realised the effectiveness of radio when, during his visit to Himachal Pradesh in 1998, he stopped for tea at a stand-alone tea shop. The person offered sweets to him and asked him to wait for the tea. Modi asked him what the matter was–was there a celebration?

When prodded further, he cited the reason for his happiness. India had exploded the nuclear bomb, and he asked Modi to listen to the radio. Such was its impact[12].

Since the address follows an informal, conversational style, Modi needs no preparation, nor is the text a prepared one. The feedback, points and issues raised by the people through various platforms, such as mygov, Narendramodi app and toll-free number (1800-11-7800), are read by the Prime Minister during his travels to understand the feelings of the senders. He easily identifies with the person asking questions and their ambience because he has travelled all across the country during 45 years in the eyes of the public[13]. Once he decides to take up the issues, the flow is spontaneous. His ability to connect and empathise with people comes in handy.

It was difficult to think of a name for a programme of public connect. Some suggestions were sought from people through the mygov platform. Various names cropped up, such as 'PM ke Sath Rubaru', 'Varta Modiji ke Saath' and 'Modi Vani'. When these names were proposed to him, he simplified the task by saying there was not much to think of. '*Arre isme kya hai? Kaho kuchh halki fulki mann ki baatein karunga*' (Just say that it will be some light hearted talks in the programme). The programme was thus named *Mann ki Baat* (Musings Straight from the Heart). It was decided to air the programme once a month at 11 am.

When the programme beamed its 100th episode, it had already become a mass movement. History was made when it was broadcast live at the United Nations headquarters in New York. Modi described it as his spiritual journey, where the broadcast expressed the feelings of crores of Indians and ensured that he was never cut off from them[14].

'For me *Mann ki Baat* is not a programme, for me it is a matter of faith, of worship, or *Vrat*. Like when people go to worship God, they bring along a *thaal* of Prasad. For me, *Mann ki Baat* is like a *thaal* of Prasad at the feet of God in the form of *janata-janardan*, the people. *Mann ki Baat* has become a spiritual journey of my being.'[15] Such profound thoughts reflect his humility and spiritual side. Swami Vivekananda believed in the principle of 'service to man is service to God', and the Prime Minister has realised this in his spiritual journey.

Mann ki Baat has become like having a celebration every month. Modi has described it as the '*Mann ki Baat* of millions of Indians and the expression of their emotions.' It has also become one of the occasions when the high and mighty government officials such as ministers and organisational leaders of the BJP would go to remote places and listen to the *Mann ki Baat* along with the commoners. It was a way to create awareness and to get feedback from people.

To celebrate its 100th episode, the party organised gatherings at four lakh centres where party workers and common people heard Modi's musings on 30 April 2023[16]. Some venues were also set up overseas. The states of New York and New Jersey passed a resolution to honour the 100th episode of *Mann ki Baat*. 'The vital broadcast had become an effective means of communication to promote good governance and deepen democracy', said the resolutions passed by the New York and New Jersey General Assembly[17]. Closer home, the Ministry of Culture organised special programmes such as unique projection mapping at historical and archaeological sites, art exhibitions with the participation of eminent artists, and Amar Chitra Katha promised to publish 12 comic strips to showcase the heroic stories of ordinary people. The one on *Mann ki Baat* Vol 1 was released on 30 April 2023. These comic stories are inspiring examples of ordinary people who dared to dream and act and made significant contributions to society.

Mann ki Baat achieved phenomenal popularity since it touched upon issues concerning the common man. It focussed less on the government's achievements and more on giving solutions to the problems people faced in their day-to-day existence. For example, the talk focussed on championing the cause of clean India, the significance of Swadeshi and khadi, love for and the need to protect nature, fighting drug menace, examination fever and facing it boldly, the importance of Indian breed dogs, not bargaining with poor street vendors, and acknowledging creativity and innovation.

People have often given him themes to speak on. The most popular campaign changing the Indian narrative on women's empowerment is the safety of girl child. The Prime Minister has spoken several times on protecting and empowering the girl child. The most popular campaign of clicking a Selfie with daughter that touched an instant emotional chord with Modi was the brainchild of Sunil Jaglan, the village headman of a Haryana village. Modi referred to Jaglan's Selfie with Daughter campaign in the ninth episode in June 2015. He urged people to carry this campaign forward by taking a selfie with their daughter and posting it on social media with the hashtag Selfie with Daughter (#SelfieWithDaughter)[18]. People posted such images blurring the boundaries dividing the different parties. It was an innovative way to increase awareness about the importance of girl child. Twitter witnessed more than 59,000 tweets under the hashtag Selfie With Daughter by overnight[19].

One of the high points of *Mann ki Baat* was the joint participation by both Modi and US President Barack Obama. Obama was India's chief guest at the Republic Day parade on 26 January 2015. The idea that Obama and Modi should do a joint *Mann ki Baat* was floated by the Prime Minister while planning the visit. The US government acceded, and on 22 January, Modi tweeted, informing about the special *Mann ki Baat* programme on 27 January. While floating the hashtag Ask Obama Modi (#AskObamaModi), he encouraged people to actively participate by sending their questions by 25 January[20].

There was no prior briefing involved. It was a heart-to-heart discussion with the US President, where both would answer questions raised by people from both countries. Both leaders spoke about giving equal access to opportunities and bettering human existence. Issues such as climate change, poverty eradication and women's empowerment dominated the discourse.

The programme was a high point of diplomacy. Modi, during his visit to the US in September 2014, spoke about the need to repair US-India ties. The US didn't know how the Indian Prime Minister would react to being forced to roll out the red carpet for him. One can recall how the US, under the influence of vested interests, had spoiled its relations with Narendra Modi, the then Chief Minister of Gujarat. Obama's visit in January 2015 was a part of this new engagement, and *Mann ki Baat* was a way to show the humane sides of both the leaders and how people of both countries loved their bonhomie.

Another landmark was when the programme reached its 108th episode on 31 December 2023. This episode has spiritual significance since 108 is considered pious in the *Sanatan* tradition. Modi's focus was on physical and mental wellness to enable the younger people to enjoy a fulsome life. *Viksit Bharat* would benefit the young, but they must be physically fit to enjoy its benefits.

He highlighted the achievements of the last year, including those in sports, science and creativity. That India has become an innovation hub shows we are unstoppable, he said. India today is a land of hope, aspirations and confidence. But the younger generation must be fully fit and healthy to enjoy the bliss of development and participate in the growth story.

The year 2023 was celebrated as the international year of millet, boosting millet-based healthy foods. The year 2024 must focus on fitness–both physical and mental. He played an audio clip of Sadhguru Jaggi Vasudev's speech on mental illness where he said, 'Mental health must be maintained without using chemicals' and that Yoga and meditation can help do that.

He also played clips of women cricketer Harman Preet Kaur, Grand Master Vishwanathan Anand and cine star Akshay Kumar, where all of them highlighted the importance of physical and mental health.

He also talked about the health startup founded by Rishabh Malhotra from Bangalore, who has started the App *Tagda Raho* that brings back the traditional system of exercises, such as *Gada vyayam*, to keep people fit.

Mann ki Baat presents the panoramic Indian culture and celebrates the personalities that have shaped India's deep cultural tradition. We may not have heard of some of these names. For example, in the 108th episode, he referred to the social reformers Savitribai Phule and Rani Velu Nachiyar as the lighthouse that advocated women's empowerment. Rani Velu from Tamil Nadu fought against British subjugation.

Moreover, in every episode, he quotes a few names doing immense service to the nation. Thus, *Mann ki Baat* has become an encyclopaedia for those who want to understand India, its rich cultural tradition and the inspirations that guide the country even today. It inspires as well as reflects. While holding a mirror to our society, it goads people to change for the better. It may not give headlines to the media, but people wait for this programme with bated breath to listen to their Prime Minister and feel an emotional connection with realities.

The Prime Minister is a communicator par excellence. He has effectively used social media to tell his people about the government's activities and achievements. *Mann ki Baat* praises the country without delving into politics. He has never used this instrument to give a reply to his opponents. For that, he uses his political rallies. It maintains his image as a non-partisan, working for a national cause.

Various world leaders have appreciated this instrument of transformation. Tesla CEO Elon Musk acknowledged PM Modi's communication skills and said, 'Prime Minister Modi's connect with the people through his radio show and social media is simply amazing!'[21] Barack Obama, during his visit to India in 2015, lauded the format of *Mann ki Baat* and described it as 'a wonderful way to connect with the people'. 'I think it's a great idea for any leader to find ways to speak directly to the people, to bypass the filter of the media and the bureaucracy', he added[22].

Former Prime Minister of Australia Scott Morrison, while praising Modi for his leadership during the COVID-19 pandemic, also highlighted the role of *Mann ki Baat* in connecting with people. He said, 'I had a good discussion with my friend Prime Minister @ narendramodi yesterday. It was great to hear about the incredible efforts by the Indian people in the fight against COVID-19. The Indian community has shown great resilience and *Maan ki Baat* has been a great way to connect with people.'[23]

Japan's former PM, Shinzo Abe, wrote a Preface to a book on *Mann ki Baat* in 2017, in which he praised the PM's tremendous efforts, 'This book is filled with Prime Minister Modi's enthusiasm for interacting with the people of India, particularly with the youth. Talking on a one-hour radio show once a month, while addressing challenging tasks as prime minister, requires tremendous effort, and I cannot but feel his strong passion for dialogue with his people.'[24]

UNESCO Director-General Audrey Azoulay has said that *Mann ki Baat* 'is certainly one of the most celebrated, with its hundreds of millions of listeners in more than 50 languages and dialects.'[25]

Momentous Decisions

Redefining Bharat- I

Arise! Awake! And stop not till the goal is reached.
–Swami Vivekananda

Individuals in history are known for what they have done to bring change and push forward the civilisational agenda. They do something new that seeks to redefine existence. Some try to resolve past conflicts and introduce new ways to make living easy and more meaningful. The same is the measuring parameter when evaluating the performance of any government.

The Modi government is identified with taking momentous decisions or actions that will change the way the country looks at itself and prepare to face the role bestowed by destiny in the twenty-first century. One can easily identify these four decisions as

- facilitating Rama temple construction at Lord Rama's birthplace in Ayodhya,
- Scrapping Article 370 in Jammu and Kashmir,
- Law to ban Instant Triple Talaq and
- Women Reservations law.

Some other momentous decisions have been discussed in the chapter on removing vestiges of the past. Banning red beacon lights on vehicles and decisions on self-attestations would also fall into this category. This chapter discusses other decisions that have changed the way society is being transformed.

A nation bereft of its roots would suffer from an inferiority complex. The British did everything to uproot the ethos of Indian culture. We have seen how Lord Macaulay sought to create brown sahibs. The contempt that the British had for Indian culture got rubbed on these brown sahibs who developed contempt for their past practices. India gained independence in 1947, but this culture did not change. Nothing substantial was done to showcase or revive the past glory.

However, the Modi government has been different. In Prime Minister Modi, we have a person born in independent India, not held hostage by the colonial mindset. He can wear Western clothes with the same aplomb as he would wear the saffron robe or the traditional Indian outfits. The man would define the clothing and not vice-versa. Only a confident leader sure of his moorings can make such bold decisions as Modi has.

Facilitating Grand Rama Temple at Ayodhya

India had a tryst with destiny when the *Pran Pratishtha* of the beautiful idol of Lord Rama was done by Prime Minister Narendra Modi on 22 January 2024. While this was the fulfilment of a promise long overdue, it was also a celebration of the values that have defined India and the *Sanatan* Dharma.

Lord Rama is an embodiment of the finer virtues that define human existence. How to behave as a member of one's family, friend circle and society, establish dharma and defeat evil? Lord Rama is an embodiment of morality and righteousness. For Him, power is a mechanism to establish order and dharma. The concept of Suraj (Good Governance) has also emanated from *Rama Rajya*.

Throughout the day, the entire country was in a celebratory mood. Images of the Prime Minister performing the ritual, aided by RSS chief Mohan Bhagwat, Uttar Pradesh Chief Minister Yogi Adityanath and Uttar Pradesh Governor Anandiben Patel, beamed throughout the day. People brought out *jhanki*s in every nook and corner, pooling in liberal donations. At night, the city of Ayodhya was lit with earthen lamps (diya), giving it an impression of Diwali across the country.

The celebratory mood had already begun. More than 22.23 lakh earthen lamps were lighted at Ayodhya on the day of Diwali in 2023. It created a new world record as 'the largest display of oil lamps'. The record for the same in 2022 was for 15.76 lakh diyas. It began in 2017 with 51,000 oil lamps and had gone to more than 9 lakhs in 2021 when it created a world record.

Having a magnificent Rama Temple at the birthplace of Lord Rama was a dream come true for crores of Indians and for the BJP that had promised to facilitate the grand temple and put the same in its agenda since the Palanpur resolution of June 1989 when it described the Rama temple agitation as a cultural movement and committed itself to build a grand temple at the Janmabhoomi site.

This dream found fruition when Narendra Modi performed the *Bhoomi Pujan* as the *Yajman* on 5 August 2020. Until a few years ago, very few believed a resolution to the dispute existing since 1949 could be amicably found and fulfilled so soon.

The Modi government was committed to building a grand Rama temple at the disputed site, but both the party and the government knew that the solution lay in the judicial process. The evidence favoured the Hindus, but the tendency to soft-peddle controversial issues and pass the buck did not help in making a decision.

Modi was L K Advani's charioteer when the BJP launched Advani's rath yatra to create awareness about the Rama temple movement. The Vajpayee government, from 1998-2004, was bogged down by coalition compulsions. Prime Minister Narendra Modi demonstrated that he was honest and sincere in his commitment, and people voted him to power in 2014 with a thumping majority. The BJP had emerged as the party with full majority in Parliament. But the party was acutely short of numbers in the Rajya Sabha. In the 2019 elections, people gave him a much larger mandate and put a big responsibility on his shoulders for making bold decisions.

It signalled that the people wanted him to act on the core promises. The party could have taken the route of resolution that RSS chief Mohan Bhagwat spoke about. However, Modi was committed to waiting for the orders of the court and sincerely hoped justice would prevail and the wrong done to India's cultural ethos for centuries would be set right. Lord

Rama is not just a religious figure but a cultural figure who established morality and demonstrated ways to live a healthy and fulfilling life.

After the Allahabad High Court's order, leading to excavation near the Janmabhoomi site, there was no doubt that a massive temple structure existed below the Babri structure. In 2010, the court finally ruled in favour of the Rama Janmabhoomi Temple at the birth site. But it split the land three ways, and all three sides appealed to the Supreme Court to put a stay on the Allahabad Court verdict.

On 21 March 2017, the then Chief Justice of India, Justice Jagdish Singh Khehar, suggested an out-of-court settlement. On 7 August, the top court constituted a three-judge bench to hear pleas against the verdict of the Allahabad High Court. It did not lead to much movement in the matter.

Earlier, the opposing party's attempt to delay the hearing was thwarted when the court rejected Kapil Sibal's plea in December 2017 to take it up after the 2019 Lok Sabha elections since it was in the BJP's election agenda. The senior opposition leader represented the Sunni Wakf Board. They calculated that a favourable decision would help Modi. However, an adverse decision was likely to strengthen Modi's hand further. The court wanted to stay neutral and opposed being dragged into any political controversy.

Finally, on 8 March 2019, the Apex Court referred the case for mediation. This also did not lead to any conclusive result. The Supreme Court, on 1 August 2019, accepted the failure of the mediation panel. It said, 'The mediation panel conveyed that they had failed to strike a consensus among rival parties and it was time to wind up the mediation process.' The next day, the Apex Court decided on a day-to-day hearing beginning on 6 August[1]. It meant that arriving at a judgement was possible soon.

The daily hearing spilled over 40 days from 6 August to 16 October. The bench that heard the appeal included Chief Justice of India Ranjan Gogoi and four other Justices–S A Bobde, D Y Chandrachud, Ashok Bhushan, and S Abdul Nazeer.

While the Supreme Court reserved its verdict, the BJP supporters grew impatient. Although every party stressed supporting the Supreme

Court's decision, there was a palpable fear that anything could happen. Justice Ranjan Gogoi was to demit office on 17 November and it was expected that the reserved judgement would be announced before that.

Modi appealed for peace and communal harmony, asking people to respect the court's judgement, whichever way it comes. A day before the judgement, he said:

> Tomorrow the verdict of Supreme Court is coming. For last few months, hearings had been continuously held in Supreme Court and the country was looking with great attention. During this time, all sections of society made efforts to create an atmosphere of harmony which is very praiseworthy.
>
> 'The Supreme Court verdict on Ayodhya will not be a victory or defeat for anyone. I appeal to the countrymen that it should be our priority that it only strengthens India's great tradition of peace, unity and harmony.[2]

There was an attempt by the BJP to tone down the rhetoric on Ayodhya. All BJP ministers and party spokespersons were asked not to be garrulous. If the decisions came in favour of the Rama temple, there was special instruction that none should make it sound like victory. The other side, the Muslim community, should not feel hurt. It was time for a reconciliation.

It was essential since the BJP cadre felt frustrated and restless. Given a choice, they would have preferred the route of legislation. It was articulated by Mohan Bhagwat during the October 2018 Vijayadashami speech, wherein he called for an ordinance route to facilitate construction.

The party could have done this, but it was wedded to the legal route and, until it failed there was no point speaking about the other options. Modi had clarified during his Lok Sabha campaign in 2019 that he would wait for the court verdict on Ayodhya. He had reiterated the same in Parliament, too.

Closer to the judgement day, a high-security alert was sounded out by the Union Home Ministry to prevent any untoward communal flare-up. The government of Uttar Pradesh had massive security arrangements in and around Ayodhya. There was a heavy deployment of paramilitary forces, too, to take care of the contingencies.

The Apex Court pronounced its judgement on 9 November 2019. It ordered that the disputed land of 2.77 acres should be handed over to a trust to be constituted by the government for the construction of the Rama Janmabhoomi. The Court also ordered that the government should give five acres of land in another place to the other party–the Sunni Waqf Board–to build a mosque.

There was no room for any controversy since the verdict was unanimous. All shades of political opinion welcomed the judgement as it sought to bury a controversy that had divided the nation on communal lines. Imminent influencers and religious leaders also welcomed the verdict. The Muslims also appealed for peace and communal harmony. As Sri Sri Ravi Shankar said, all sides had welcomed the historic judgement. 'The judgement had brought "joy and relief" to members of both the Hindu and Muslim communities', he said[3].

It had given the Central government three months to set up the Trust and formulate its modalities. On 5 February 2020, the government announced the formation of the much-awaited Trust and was handed over 2.77 acres of land along with the 67.7-acre land around the Janmabhoomi site. It was to be a 15-member Trust under the chairmanship of Mahant Nritya Gopal Das. While nine members were permanent, six were to be nominated. Prime Minister's trusted aide, Nripendra Mishra, was nominated as the chairman of the construction committee.

The Trust worked speedily and on 5 August 2020, Prime Minister Narendra Modi performed the *Bhoomi poojan* at Ayodhya to start the construction work for the grand temple. Among those who were present included Mohan Bhagwat, Uttar Pradesh Chief Minister Yogi Adityanath, then Governor of the State, Anandiben Patel and Mahant Nritya Gopal Das.

For those trying to take the credit away from the BJP, saying it happened through a court order, a summary of the history is a must. The BJP was the first political party to formally announce its support for the Rama temple, and the party had called it a symbol of India's cultural unity.

The BJP lost four elected governments on 15 December 1992, post demolition of the disputed structure–Uttar Pradesh government led by

Kalyan Singh, Madhya Pradesh government led by Sunderlal Patwa, Himachal Pradesh government led by Shanta Kumar and Rajasthan government led by Bhairon Singh Shekhawat. The government of P V Narasimha Rao banned the RSS, the VHP and the Bajrang Dal.

While one could justify the dismissal of Kalyan Singh's government since he was the Chief Minister when the demolition took place, there was no justification for the dismissal of the other three BJP governments. It was due to hatred of the Congress for the BJP's ideology and aimed at appeasing the minorities. Even the dismissal of Kalyan Singh's government was unjust since the Chief Minister had resigned after taking moral responsibility for what happened.

The BJP has been the only party that kept in its agenda the promise to facilitate the construction of a grand Rama temple, either through a judicial process by keeping its unambiguous stand or through legislation. It was never apologetic and was clear from day one that Lord Rama could not be boxed into a religious deity. It believed that Lord Rama represented the ethos of Indian culture.

When BJP President L K Advani undertook the Rama rath yatra in 1990, he aimed to raise consciousness about the great cultural symbol and mobilise support for the Rama temple. He got massive public support. People used to touch the motorised chariot he was being driven in and worship it. The crowd used to wait for hours to get a glimpse of Advani. Narendra Modi was his charioteer during the Gujarat leg of the yatra that went up to Maharashtra. Then Chief Minister of Bihar, Lalu Prasad Yadav, arrested Advani on 23 October, leading to the fall of the fledgling V P Singh government at the Centre that survived due to the outside support from the BJP.

However, Advani's arrest failed to prevent the *kar sewaks* from reaching Ayodhya. The yatra was to culminate in Ayodhya on 30 October with *kar sewa* at the temple site. The state police under Chief Minister Mulayam Singh Yadav had made elaborate security arrangements to prevent the *kar sewaks* from reaching the Janmabhoomi site. The temple city turned into a garrison, and to control the mob, the police opened fire on innocent people on 30 October. Another clash happened on 2 November when some activists tried to resume *kar sewa*. The security forces opened fire. The number of people dying in the firing was 28, according to Mulayam Singh Yadav, and 56, according to Vajpayee.

There was no need to open fire on innocent people who had gathered at the temple to perform puja as a ritual. The police, who had ample time, could have easily managed the crowd using other measures. But the Chief Minister has already drawn the line, saying he would not allow even a bird to fly in Ayodhya. *Kar sewaks* were dragged out of the houses they took refuge in and beaten. Kothari brothers–Ram and Sharad from Kolkata– who had taken the saffron flag atop the Babri structure, were shot dead. Some accounts said they were dragged out. The police had unleashed a reign of terror.

Mulayam Singh Yadav was determined to use the occasion to bolster his image as a secular leader and a saviour of Muslims. Subsequently, he came to be known as Maulana Mulayam. If Lalu Prasad Yadav had acquired a secular image by arresting Advani, Mulayam should have done something more to gain the upper hand. Both Lalu and Mulayam, as protégé of V P Singh, were trying to carve out their own constituencies.

The landmark event in the temple movement was the *kar sewa* in 1992. The RSS, the Vishwa Hindu Parishad and the BJP had organised *kar sewa* at the temple site and lakhs of Rama Bhaktas had gathered there. They were told that *kar sewa* meant performing puja and other rituals such as bhajan and kirtan. They had permission from the Supreme Court to perform *kar sewa*.

Destroying the structure was not on the agenda of any of these organisations. The Babri structure stood as a symbol of intolerance and Islamic atrocity, and it needed to be removed, either through a judicial process or through legislation. For the latter, the BJP needed an absolute majority in both houses of Parliament. It explains different reactions from different leaders when some Hindu zealots demolished the structure on 6 December 1992.

Atal Bihari Vajpayee expressed shock at the incident and stressed that 'Rama temple would not be constructed by unfair or foul means.... It would be constructed on the basis of moral strength.'[4] L K Advani, the architect of the Rama temple movement, was shocked, too, but it was due to the failure of the BJP leadership to control the mob.

The BJP has always taken pride in its disciplined cadre, and if Advani said something that was the last word for the rank and file, he being the party's organisational man. Loudspeakers were beaming consistently, asking *kar sewaks* not to go anywhere close to the Babri structure. Clearly, the crowd had the presence of many who did not belong to the RSS-BJP. (Advani had said this to the author during an interview in 1996).

We have already seen the consequences of the demolition. It led to a long, protracted battle in the court on the role of BJP leaders and others in the demolition and also about the status of the Babri structure. Thus, the consecration of the idol of Lord Shri Rama had come after a long and conflicting journey undertaken by Rama Bhaktas.

Scrapping Article 370

Till 5 August 2019, few had imagined that any government in India would dare to scrap Article 370, which gave a special status to Jammu and Kashmir. The BJP had it in its agenda, and the commitment had an ideological basis. During the 2019 Lok Sabha elections campaign, Amit Shah declared that the BJP would scrap Article 370 if it got a majority in the Parliament[5].

However, it was easier said than done. Although the BJP got a massive majority in the Lok Sabha, the combined NDA did not have the requisite majority in the Rajya Sabha. For this, the mandate in the Rajya Sabha was a must. How the government steered the motion in the Rajya Sabha is a success of the floor management that the BJP strategists achieved.

Two front management was needed–one inside the Parliament so the motion would see smooth sailing, and another in managing the likely aftermath, the fallout in the valley and elsewhere, if and when the move is made. On 2 August 2019, the Jammu and Kashmir administration issued an advisory for those undertaking the Amarnath yatra and curtailed the yatra. The reason given was a security threat to pilgrims.

It allowed the government to order massive troop deployment in the valley. Additional troops were rushed to the valley. Close to 28,000 troops from the CRPF were rushed, in addition to the 10,000 already deployed. This was to complement the response to the security threats. Nobody was aware of the real reason[6].

It was also a follow-up of the visit of the National Security Advisor, Ajit Doval, to the valley from July 24-26. He had reviewed the security situation in the valley. He also visited the Amarnath Cave to give the impression that he was there to oversee the security situation. Schools and colleges were closed for ten days, ensuring minimal movement of civilians and all entry and exit points were manned by the CRPF. Everything looked usual, and it appeared Pakistan was upto something. The Army and the Air Force were put on high alert.

There was speculation in the political circle that the Union government may scrap Article 35A, which defined the resident status of people staying in the state and prevented outsiders from owning immovable property. Article 35A and Article 370 were already challenged in the Supreme Court, keeping the issue alive.

Jammu and Kashmir Governor Satya Pal Malik tried to scotch rumours, saying people should not believe rumours regarding the state's special status.

'A lot of rumours are spread here, do not pay any heed to them. Everything is fine, everything is normal', he said[7].

Peoples Democratic Party Chief Mehbooba Mufti had already warned that the State would not be a part of India if anything was done to change the status of Jammu and Kashmir:

'If you free Jammu and Kashmir from Article 370, you will free the state from country as well…I have said many times that Article 370 links Jammu and Kashmir with the country. When you break this bridge, India loses its legitimacy over the state. It becomes an occupational force', she said[8].

The atmosphere was charged, and anything could have happened. While the local leaders of Kashmir kept the rhetoric high, the Centre was determined to push its secret plan, which even the Governor was unaware of. When National Conference leader Omar Abdullah met him on 3 August, he told them there was nothing to worry about.

'They've gone satisfied. Whatever they expected from me I did. As far as I know, there's no inclination that something's going to happen here. I don't know about tomorrow, that's not in my hands. But till today, there's nothing to worry', he said[9]. By the morning of 5 August,

Satya Pal Malik gave his consent to the President of India to make a law for the state of Jammu and Kashmir.

Curfew and other restrictions were imposed in Srinagar and other districts as precautionary steps, and most leaders, such as Mehbooba Mufti and Omar Abdullah, were put under house arrest. Internet services were shut down to prevent miscreants from misusing it to misguide the gullible people.

Having taken precautions to prevent trouble in the state, the Union Home Minister Amit Shah, who led from the front, had undertaken every possible measure to ensure maintaining the legal niceties of such a huge move. The then Law Minister Ravi Shankar Prasad was asked to prepare a draft, and Solicitor General Tushar Mehta was also consulted. The technical requirement of getting the concurrence of Governor Satya Pal Malik to the President of India was fulfilled on 5 August.

In 2018, the Supreme Court said that Article 370 had acquired a permanent status through years of existence, making its abrogation impossible. The argument was based on the understanding that the constituent assembly of the state had ceased to exist, which would authorise the President to exercise the power to abrogate[10].

While the Article has empowered the President of India to declare that this Article shall cease to be operative from a specified date, a clause in the same Article made it subject to the recommendation of the constituent assembly. But the constituent assembly was resolved in 1957.

The Constitution (Application to Jammu and Kasmir) Order 2019 took care of this by inserting a provision saying that the expression 'Constitution Assembly of the State referred to in Clause 2' shall be read 'Legislative Assembly of the State'. Changing the expression 'Constituent Assembly' to 'Legislative Assembly' provided the solution.

On 5 August 2019, the Modi government did what appeared to be unthinkable by critics and Opposition parties. He dared and scrapped Article 370 through a Presidential order. 'President Ram Nath Kovind has exercised his power under Clause 1 of Article 370. The Presidential order has done away with sections under Article 35A, which provides special privileges to permanent residents of the state', Union Home Minister Amit Shah told the Rajya Sabha[11].

'Under Article 370 there is a provision that the President may by public notification declare that this article shall cease to be operative... from such date as he may specify...Because there is President's rule, all decisions of the Assembly will be taken by the House and we can pass the order with majority', he said while explaining the legal niceties[12].

Replying to the allegation of senior leader from Jammu and Kashmir, Ghulam Nabi Azad, that the BJP had 'murdered the constitution and democracy' by scrapping Article 370, Shah said, 'This is not the truth. Article 370 has not linked J and K to India. It has only alienated J and K from the country. Only three families have looted the state and have benefited from it. The country wants to know why Article 370 was extended for so long, why people did not benefit from reservation, why so much money was pumped into J and K but why are the people still poor? Not a second should be wasted in removing Article 370.'[13]

Besides this resolution to ratify the Presidential order abrogating Article 370, Amit Shah introduced two bills–the Jammu and Kashmir (Reorganisation) Bill, 2019 [Ref Article 3 of the Constitution of India] and the Jammu and Kashmir Reservation (2nd Amendment) Bill, 2019. The Reorganisation Bill sought to make Jammu and Kashmir a Union Territory with a Legislative Assembly and Ladakh a Union Territory without a Legislative Assembly.

The bill on reservation sought to amend the Jammu and Kashmir Reservation Act 2004 and extend the 10 per cent quota to economically weaker sections of society in J and K in jobs and educational institutions. Both the bills were passed by Rajya Sabha unanimously[14].

The Rajya Sabha passed the resolution and the two bills on the same day. There was no problem getting the same passed by the Lok Sabha because of the NDA government's absolute majority in the House. Amit Shah introduced the two resolutions on Kashmir and the two bills in the Lok Sabha the next day. His words were significant and summed up the government's sentiments,

> J and K is an inalienable part of India. There are no two versions about that...Repealing article 370 is not a historic blunder, rather it is historic step to correct this historic blunder...Parliament is the highest and fully competent body to make laws and bring resolutions

regarding a state of India including J and K...I want to assure the people of J and K that the status of State would be restored once the situation normalises[15].

The Lok Sabha passed the Reorganisation Bill with 370 members in favour and 70 against it. While the Indian National Congress (INC), Nationalist Congress Party (NCP) and the Samajwadi Party opposed the bill, it was supported by the BJP, the Shiv Sena, the Biju Janata Dal (BJD), the Telangana Rashtra Samithi (TRS, now Bharat Rashtra Samithi), the Shiromani Akali Dal (SAD), the Lok Janshakti Party (LJP), the Bahujan Samaj Party and other smaller parties. However, the resolutions were supported by 351 members and opposed by 72[16].

Although none doubted the fate of the bill in the Lok Sabha, everyone's heart beat fast in anticipation of what would happen in the Rajya Sabha. The NDA did not have a majority, and a combined opposition could have easily defeated the government's move on one pretext or the other. How Amit Shah and his team got a turnaround can be a classic study of floor management.

Shah admitted later that he was apprehensive how the Rajya Sabha would react to the government's move on Kashmir. He credited Venkaiah Naidu, the Vice President of India and Chairperson of the Rajya Sabha, for the smooth sailing of the legislation in the House on 5 August.

He said, 'While piloting the bill, there were apprehensions about how the Rajya Sabha will act when I take it there. I was hesitant as the NDA did not have a majority in the Upper House...Still I decided we will take the bill first to Rajya Sabha and after that to the Lok Sabha.'[17]

Naidu used his special powers as the Chairperson and gave the government the waiver for giving advance notice and circulation of the bill beforehand. It enabled the government to maintain the element of surprise. The chair allotted only four hours to discuss and debate and suggest amendments. It did not allow the Opposition to resolve their difference and reach a consensus.

The ruling NDA had only 107 members in the Rajya Sabha, and there was a possibility of getting defeated since the majority mark was 121 in a house of 242. Yet, the resolution got support from 125 MPs, and only 61 voted against it. Others staged a walkout. The BSP, the BJD, the YSR Congress, the TDP and the Aam Aadmi Party voted in favour. The Trinamul Congress, with 13 members, walked out, and the Janata Dal United (JDU), with six members, boycotted voting. Two members of the PDP were suspended for tearing the constitution when the government announced its decision to abrogate Article 370[18].

The President of India issued a further order on 6 August stating that Article 370 had become inoperative.

The INC termed the revocation of Article 370 a 'catastrophic step' and described it as a black day in India's constitutional history. 'India has failed Kashmir in keeping its promises', Mehbooba Mufti said. Omar Abdullah said it was a total betrayal of trust. The DMK described it as a 'murder of democracy'. Rashtriya Janata Dal (RJD) leader Manoj Jha said that 'we have opened the gates for Kashmir to turn into Palestine in five years'.

We have seen that the State had made massive preparations to handle any untoward incidents. It was to the credit of the Central government that although there were sporadic protests, no incident of violence was reported. The leaders, who could incite people, were already put under house arrest. The government showed it had the spine to act tough if it involved the country's interests.

Background of the Momentous Step

When the Modi government scrapped Article 370 on 5 August 2019, every BJP parliamentarian and worker rejoiced in the fulfilment of the wishes of its founder, Shyama Prasad Mukherjee, who had founded the Bharatiya Jana Sangh (BJS) in 1951. In fact, every patriot who believed in India's territorial integrity was happy with this move.

BJS founder Shyama Prasad Mukherjee had opposed Article 370, which gave a separate status to Jammu and Kashmir. The state was granted its own flag, along with the designation to an elected head of the state as Prime Minister (Sadr-e-Riyasat) and not Chief Minister. Moreover, anyone who wanted to enter the state from outside required permission.

Mukherjee opposed it saying, '*Ek desh mein do Vidhan, do Pradhan aur do Nishan nahi challenge.*' (A single country can't have two constitutions, two Prime Ministers and two national flags). In 1953, Mukherjee observed a hunger strike and wanted to visit Jammu and Kashmir. But, he was denied permission. Yet, he forcibly entered the state's boundary and was arrested on 11 May at Lakhanpur. He fell ill and was administered an injection, which he said his doctor had labelled unsuitable. But he was still given the injection, after which his situation deteriorated, and he got a massive heart attack the next day. He died on 23 June 1953.

The demand for an independent inquiry was rejected by Prime Minister Jawaharlal Nehru. Atal Bihari Vajpayee has described his death as a 'Nehruvian conspiracy'. Mukherjee's death has remained shrouded in mystery. Many senior party leaders believe he was assassinated.

For those unaware, the BJS, founded by Mukherjee, was the first incarnation of the BJP. The BJS merged into the Janata Party in 1977 post-Emergency but came out when its integrity was questioned on the issue of dual membership (membership of both the party and the RSS). On 4 April 1980, the new incarnation was named the Bharatiya Janata Party, the party that belonged to the people and was rooted in the cultural ethos of Bharat (India).

Contrary to the general perception created by the Congress party and other vested interests that Article 370 helped to keep Jammu and Kashmir as an integral part of India, the BJP held that it was the biggest source of alienation and separatism in the state. And the only way to achieve its full integration into the larger Indian State was to scrap this Article and usher developmental activities there.

But how would this be done, and in what way? Will the BJP be able to achieve this ever?–were some questions raised by the critics. The Vajpayee government, which stayed in power for six years from 1998-2004, did not initiate any movement towards this. Atal Bihari Vajpayee was extremely popular with the Kashmiris because of his stress on *Kashmiriyat* to find a solution for the alienation of youths. He advocated people-to-people contact between India and Pakistan and held that it would soften Pakistan and contain terrorism.

The Vajpayee government was constrained due to coalition problems. The absence of a full majority in both Houses of Parliament was a must to take any decisive step on Kashmir. The party could always argue, and indeed it did whenever the issue of implementing its core agenda was concerned. BJP leaders often pointed out that it was not a BJP government but a coalition government with its own compulsions.

The verdict in 2014 had removed these compulsions. Prime Minister Modi had understood the underlying message. The country wanted him to make bigger and bolder decisions. However, the time was spent to consolidate the economy and strengthen the country. Without strengthening the foundation, making bold decisions could be counter-productive. The much bigger mandate in 2019 had firmly established that people were with Modi and wanted him to take tough decisions.

Besides the ideological opposition, scrapping Article 370 was also grounded in Modi's new slogan of faster development. The money meant for the development of the state was being pocketed by vested interests that included politicians, bureaucrats and other actors such as the Hurriyat. Development in the state was trickling down a small funnel when it needed a deluge. The entire system of governance needed to be reworked.

Article 370 had prevented other Indians from settling in the state or becoming a subject of the state. Article 370 made provision for Article 35A, under which the state perpetrated gender discrimination with impunity. It defined permanent status of the subjects and the special rights and privileges available to them. Under this, a girl marrying outside the state would lose her status as a permanent resident and all the associated privileges.

The inequality provision and failure of the political leadership to implement human rights ensured that the Valmikis, who had once saved the state from filth, did not become permanent residents despite staying in the valley for over six decades. There was a major sanitation crisis in the Jammu city in 1957. The local sweepers had gone on a strike demanding regularisation of their jobs and a salary hike. The protest continued for months, leading to a stagnation of the municipal work. It led to several cities becoming garbage dumps.

The state government, under Prime Minister Bakshi Ghulam Mohammad, decided to get *safai karamcharis* from other states. After negotiation with the Punjab government, these workers were brought to Jammu as sweepers. More than 200 Valmiki families migrated. They were promised rehabilitation and well-being of their families. But they have not been given permanent status even after 60 years. They can be employed only as sweepers and cannot aspire to any other government job. They were not even issued SC certificates in the state, which further deprived them of any opening in the Central government.

There was a need for the people of the State to look at the Central government with trust and hope. Modi's no-nonsense approach during the 2014 floods in the valley earned him praise from the local people. He spoke to flood-affected people, monitored the situation and opened the treasury to mitigate the sufferings of the people.

In 2015, Modi announced a package of Rs 80,000 crore for the development of the state and said that India was incomplete without *Kashmiriyat*. At a rally in Srinagar, he said he would follow the Vajpayee mantra of *Kashmiriyat*, *Jamhooriyat* and *Insaniyat*.

But taking development to the state was not an easy task. He needed to dismantle terrorism infrastructure, including the fear the Hurriyat Conference had created in the valley that nothing would move without their wishes. It was they who, in alliance with their Pakistani masters, decided who would win elections. The Central government agencies exposed the financial loot that Hurriyat leaders were carrying out. The government's efforts showed that stone pelters were not self-motivated but financed by the Hurriyat money.

The security of the separatist Hurriyat leaders was withdrawn, and a clear message was sent out that the state would not bear their burden anymore. India did not need these separatists with links with Pakistan, the National Conference, or the Peoples' Democratic Party (PDP) to solve the issue of terrorism. It was a different government and had demonstrated that if Pakistan attacked Uri, India would teach a lesson by destroying terrorist camps through surgical strikes (2016). Similarly, if Pakistan would do a Pulwama in 2019, India, after a few days, would do an air surgical strike at Balakot to destroy the terrorist's hideouts.

The BJP had even tried stabilising the state by forging an alliance government with its ideological adversary–the PDP, which had a soft corner for militants. The only assurance Modi wanted was to usher in faster development and to contain violence and terrorism. PDP Chief Mehbooba Mufti became the first woman Chief Minister of the state due to the support of the BJP. The PDP-BJP coalition government was formed in 2015.

The BJP pulled out of the government after 40 months. The alliance was unnatural, and both sides knew it. But the mandate was such that both had to work together. It was an opportunity to provide the bed-rock for Hindu-Muslim unity in the state. Both sides had to keep the controversial issues aside to further the governance agenda. It meant the PDP would not support militancy, and the BJP would not talk about scrapping Article 370.

A common minimum programme (CPM) was formulated to ensure the overall development of the state. If the government had stuck to the governance agenda and respected the sentiments of each other, it was not a difficult task. But the emotions that brought the two sides together subsided, and *realpolitik* took over. While it was difficult for the PDP to be stern with the militants, it was equally difficult for the BJP to continue with incidents of terrorism refusing to die down.

The nation cannot follow the way Burhan Wani was idolised after getting killed by the security forces. The ensuing massive protests and clashes with security forces led to further deaths. Many said that the situation was not handled properly by the state administration. Despite the restrictions, many people were allowed to participate in the procession after Wani's death. The BJP was clearly not amused. Some more incidents, such as the Kathua killing and disjointed statements of the PDP and the BJP, led to further souring of relations.

The Central government wanted to be tough against the militants and was not keen to talk to Pakistan, whereas the PDP believed in that approach. The Pulwama attack by Pakistan-based terrorists and the Union government's response had a clear message that there would be no compromise.

In politics, the BJP wanted better participation by local youths by telling them they need not depend on Abdullahs or Muftis and that they could take control of their own destinies. Governor Manoj Sinha had tried to take the administration to even the remote corners to demonstrate the human face of the Central government.

In October 2018, the state witnessed local elections, which were boycotted by both the NC and the PDP. In Srinagar municipal elections, independent candidates won 53 out of 74 wards. The Congress won 16, and the BJP won 4. One was vacant. In Jammu municipal polls, out of 75 wards, the BJP won 43, independent candidates won 18 and the Congress 14. In the Leh municipal poll, the Congress won all 13 seats.

The significant point in the elections in the valley was the victory of many independent candidates. There were new players who were young, educated and ready to shape the state's destiny. It needed a fresh look at the strategy, and if empowered adequately, it could become a significant political factor in the coming days.

In 2019, they got a test of empowerment when the government decided to transfer Rs 3,700 crore directly into the accounts of the newly elected Panchayats. While 10 per cent of the fund was for administrative purposes, the remaining 90 per cent was for the benefit of people.

Earlier, the Union government had taken the step to give more financial powers to about 40,000 elected local representatives by making a ten-fold increase in financial allocation, from Rs 10,000 to Rs 1 lakh and for the block councils from Rs 25,000 to Rs 2.5 lakh.

All these efforts created a new crop of young leaders ready to script a new Kashmir story. The Central government agencies had established that the hitherto political leadership of the state was corrupt and acted only for self-aggrandisement. It was now time to know their true face.

In 2017, Mehbooba Mufti said that if special rights and privileges of the people of Jammu and Kashmir were tinkered with, there would be no one left in the state to hold the national flag. She repeated her statement on the eve of the scrapping of Article 370. The BJP had promised during the 2019 Loka Sabha election campaign that it would scrap Article 370 if given enough strength. It did not go unchallenged, and Mehbooba Mufti issued a counter-threat, saying 'J and K's relations with India would end' if Article 370 was abrogated[19].

The Modi government had decided not to be cowed down by such threats.

Making Instant Triple Talaq Illegal

Late Jaipal Reddy had once told me when he was the Union Minister that we should avoid poking our noses in the internal matters of the minority (Muslim) community because it can lead to massive reaction. When I asked why the same approach was not adopted vis à vis the Hindus, the cryptic reply was the fear the minorities have of Hindu domination.

This ideology had governed the Indian establishment for a long time, even if something was wrong in the community practices. The approach was–not to disturb them even if they lived in the ghettos. Behind the principle of 'let reforms come from within' was the agenda of minority appeasement for votes. It did not matter much till the community voted en bloc for the Congress.

It led to the late Rajiv Gandhi's government overturning the judgement of the Supreme Court in the Shah Bano case in 1986. In April 1985, the Supreme Court decided that under Section 125 of the CrPC, Shah Bano had the right to maintenance from her husband after divorce. The community rose in revolt, terming it as interference in their personal code. There was widespread protest, and Rajiv Gandhi, who claimed to be liberal and modern, succumbed to the pressure despite a massive majority in the Lok Sabha.

The government enacted a law through parliamentary approval in 1986 called The Muslim Women (Protection of Rights on Divorce) Act 1986. It nullified the Supreme Court's judgement. As per the new Act, a Muslim woman was entitled to maintenance only during the period of iddat, or till 90 days after the divorce, as per provisions of the Shariat.

It is comparable to the Supreme Court's decision on 22 August 2017 that ruled triple talaq unconstitutional. The court banned the practice for six months and asked the Union government to make a law on this. The six-month period proved the need for law. It failed to put fear in the minds of law violators. They appeared to indulge in triple talaq's divorce with a vengeance.

Before the Supreme Court ruling, 177 triple talaq cases were registered, i.e., 22 cases a month. The statistics revealed that Muslim women suffered the most due to triple talaq[20].

The maulanas and the conservative section of the Muslim community tried their best to stop the government from going ahead with any legislation to ban the practice. Even Muslim women came on the streets to oppose the legislation. The Muslim women who came in favour of such a law were dubbed misguided and pro-BJP.

The opposition was ludicrous since it exposed the design of Muslim men to retain their supremacy in matters of marriage and divorce. The threat of triple talaq also acted as a deterrence to bring recalcitrant wives back to loyalty and subjugation. None was ready to argue – if the practice was Islamic, then why was it not prevalent in some of the prominent Muslim countries?

It is banned in many Muslim-majority countries, such as Tunisia, Algeria, Malaysia, Jordan, Egypt, Iran, Iraq, Brunei, the UAE, Indonesia, Libya, Sudan, Lebanon, Saudi Arabia, Morocco, and Kuwait. The practice is banned in Pakistan and Bangladesh, too.

Amidst chaos and debates, in less than six months of the Apex Court order, the Modi government made a decisive move to enact the legislation by introducing The Muslim Women (Protection of Rights on Marriage) Bill 2017 in the Lok Sabha on 28 December 2017 and got the approval of the House on the same day. However, it was stalled by the Rajya Sabha since the National Democratic Alliance (NDA) led by the BJP did not have a majority in that House.

Since there was a spate of cases related to triple talaq and the bill passed by the Lok Sabha was pending in the Rajya Sabha, the government took the ordinance route to stop this evil practice. The Muslim Women (Protection of Rights on Marriage) Ordinance, 2018. (Ord 7 of 2018) was promulgated on 19 September 2018. To convert the ordinance into law, a bill was moved again in the Rajya Sabha with necessary amendments. However, it could not be taken up for consideration since both Houses were adjourned.

Since the Parliament was not in session to convert the bill into law, and the ordinance that had made triple talaq void would have lapsed, The Muslim Women (Protection of Rights on Marriage) Second Ordinance, 2019. (Ord 4 of 2019) was promulgated on 21 February 2019. The Lok Sabha was dissolved on 25 May 2019, and the bill pending approval from the Rajya Sabha lapsed.

When Modi returned to power in 2019 with a bigger majority, it decided to fulfil its commitment to give justice to Muslim women. The government introduced a fresh bill in the Lok Sabha on 21 June 2019, which was passed on 25 July 2019. The bill passed by the Lok Sabha was introduced in the Rajya Sabha on 30 July and passed on the same day. President Ram Nath Kovind assented to the bill on 31 July 2019. It was notified in the Official Gazette on the same day.

It defined talaq as *Talaq-e-Biddat* or a similar form of talaq, pronounced by a Muslim man resulting in instant and irrevocable divorce, and declared all such forms of divorce, written or otherwise, to be void. Under *Talaq-e-biddat,* a Muslim man could divorce his wife by pronouncing 'talaq' thrice in one sitting. Now, no more.

The law made triple talaq a cognisable and non-bailable offence. The punishment is for three years and a fine. The law also provided for the maintenance and custody of minor children.

The BJP, under Modi, did what no other party had imagined. The agenda was to give dignity and equality to Muslim women by making divorce difficult. There are many areas of concern that the law of equality demands. It would take time, but it has begun.

Women Reservation Law (Nari Vandan Kanoon)

When parliamentarians entered the new Parliament building to hold the special session on 19 September 2023, they were stepping into the architecture of new India to create history. The building, the special inaugural session and the associated festivities made everyone's face beam with joy.

The Prime Minister made the day momentous by scripting history in women's empowerment. The government introduced the Women Reservation Bill in the Lok Sabha on 19 September 2023, and the House passed the bill on the next day with a thumping majority. The 108th Amendment bill was passed unanimously by the Rajya Sabha on 21 September. The President of India gave his approval to the bill on 29 September.

The government was giving women what was due since a long

time. The humble approach was evident in naming the bill Nari Shakti Vandan Adhiniyam, which meant it was a tribute to the tremendous power demonstrated by women in all walks of national life. They must be given opportunities to play better roles. They must be decision-makers of their own destiny.

The new law provides 33 per cent reservation for women in the Lok Sabha and the State Legislative Assemblies. There would be reservation for the Scheduled Castes and the Scheduled Tribes within the seats reserved for women. The seat reservation would be rotational and cease to exist after 15 years of implementation of this Act.

The law would come into force once the delimitation exercise is undertaken. The number of Lok Sabha members has been frozen till 2026. The delimitation would be taken up by the new government in 2024.

Providing with 33 per cent reservation to women has been on the agenda of Parliament since 1996 when former Prime Minister H D Deve Gowda introduced a bill to that effect. Sadhvi Uma Bharti was among those who had opposed the bill and demanded a sub-quota for OBC women within the quota for women. Late Prime Minister Atal Bihari Vajpayee, too, tried to push the bill but failed due to various conflicting issues.

In 1997, Sharad Yadav hogged the limelight for his intemperate comment that the women's reservation bill without a sub-quota for OBC women would mean only *par kati mahila* (women with short hair) would enter Parliament. The Rashtriya Janata Dal under Lalu Prasad Yadav and the Samajwadi Party under Mulayam Singh Yadav opposed any reservation for women without provision for a sub-quota.

The Vajpayee government could have steamrolled opposition from within the BJP, but vehement opposition from these two parties prevented its passage. Nitish Kumar of the Samata Party had also opposed the bill on the same ground. Taking any such decision could have painted the BJP as anti-OBC. The party was still battling its image of being a party of Brahmins and Banias.

The United Progressive Alliance (UPA), too, tried to push the bill but lacked the courage despite the support of the numbers. When the bill was introduced in the Rajya Sabha on 8 March 2010, Nand Kishore Yadav and Kamal Akhtar of the Samajwadi Party climbed on the table of the then Chairman Mohammad Hamid Ansari and uprooted the microphone. The RJD's Rajniti Prasad tore up a copy of the bill and threw it at the chair[21].

Mulayam Singh, while opposing the bill in 2010, said in Lok Sabha that 'The Women Reservation Bill, if passed in present format, would provoke young men to whistle in parliament.' In 2012, while opposing the bill, he said, 'Women will not benefit from the Women Reservation Bill because they are not as attractive in comparison to those from the affluent class.'[22]

Despite opposition, the bill was intensely debated in Rajya Sabha in 2010 and passed with 186 votes in favour and one in opposition. The BJP and the Left supported the bill. The Congress had the golden chance to get the bill passed in the Lok Sabha, where it had the majority, and there was complete support of both the BJP and the Left parties. However, due to differences within the UPA alliance and within the Cabinet, the government could not muster the courage to bring the bill before consideration of the Lok Sabha. Women organisations, in particular, expected that Mrs Sonia Gandhi, being Chairperson of the UPA, would force the government to take this decisive step.

Some OBC leaders within the BJP, such as Sadhvi Uma Bharti, had also done their bit to stall the bill in Parliament on the issue of reservation for the OBCs. Ms Bharti opposed even the bill brought up by the Modi government and said she would not allow it to be passed[23].

It was the sheer courage of Prime Minister Modi to convert this bill into legislation and steamroll whatever opposition there was. Since Modi comes from OBC, no one could doubt his intention or claim to be a benefactor of the OBCs. The Congress took a U–turn, saying there must be an OBC quota, but it had to support the bill in both Houses under public pressure.

Those who wanted an OBC quota within women's reservations gave spurious arguments. In Lok Sabha or State Legislative Assemblies, the constitution provides for reservation only for the Scheduled Castes, the Schedules Tribes and Anglo-Indian Communities. There is no reservation for OBC men in these Houses.

How can one give reservations to women from OBC? Even without reservation, most people winning Lok Sabha seats are from the OBCs. The same logic of number would force political parties to field women candidates from the OBCs.

It explains why the opposition of two members of the All India Majlis-E-Ittehadul Muslimeen (AIMIM), including Asaduddin Owaisi, to the bill did not hold ground. There is no provision for reservation of seats in the Lok Sabha on religious grounds. Except for these two, all 454 members in the Lok Sabha had voted to support the bill.

Women form almost half of the country's population, but their representation has been scant in legislative bodies, particularly the State Legislative Assemblies and the Lok Sabha. Although the representation has witnessed a steady increase from 5 per cent in the first Lok Sabha to 14 per cent now (17th Lok Sabha), the rate of increase has not been encouraging. The new legislation would definitely push for more representation of women.

India's ethos has been to empower women to empower families. In the Hindu pantheon, female goddesses represent strength and power, such as Goddess Durga, Kali, Saraswati or Lakshmi. Life is incomplete without women in performing major yajnas. In such a society, how can women be allowed to live a life of subjugation and play second fiddle?

The BJP constitution has already given 33 per cent reservation to women in its organisational structure, helping the party to throw up many women leaders who gained prominence in public life. The issue of proper representation of women came up when Rajnath Singh was the party President in 2006. Since 2007, the norm of 33 per cent has been maintained.

It was natural for the BJP to take up the cause of women's reservation in legislative bodies. The party has been articulating this from various forums, including various resolutions of the national executive and national council meetings.

Momentous Decisions

Redefining Bharat- II

I believe that the civilisation into which India has evolved is not to be beaten in the world. Nothing can equal the seeds sown by our ancestry. Rome went; Greece shared the same fate; the might of the Pharaohs was broken; Japan has become westernised; of China nothing can be said; but India is still, somehow or other, sound at the foundation.

–Mahatma Gandhi

Robert Morrison MacIver, the great Scottish sociologist, said culture is what we are, and civilisation is what we have. The thinking of every society is shaped by its cultural moorings. These may be reflected in the philosophical and spiritual tradition, the practices of statecraft or the various rituals that define a particular society. Adopting practices from outside one's context may not be suitable.

Many civilisations have perished because they failed to preserve their uniqueness. The trend to achieve cultural hegemony by Christianity, Communism or Islamism and their attempts to impose uniformity have destroyed other cultures. *Sanatan* tradition recognises the differences and does not believe in imposing uniformity. It explains why the modern form of structured democracy has deep roots in this country.

To preserve democracy and to maintain the uniqueness of the country, there is a need to make people realise their cultural roots. Only when they are strong in their belief system, they would be able to face or accept the onslaughts of the West. Not that everything from the West is negative, but the acquisitions of the West must be tested in the Indian context. When adopting the civilisational aspects of the West, we need to be careful that it does not impact our cultural ethos negatively.

When Hinduism was defamed due to the terror of Brahminism, the response to reform came in the form of Buddhism. The teachings of Buddhism are the same as discussed in the *Vedas*. 'Live and Let Live'–the philosophy of Jainism, another offshoot of Hinduism, preaches the same principle of respect for life embedded in the *Sanatan* tradition. When rituals and idol worship dominated daily existence, the Arya Samaj came as a response. When the British tried to demonstrate the dominance of their culture, the response came in the form of Swami Vivekananda, who propagated the beauty of *Sanatan* values enshrined in the *Vedas*.

A nation that forgets its culture is doomed. Those aware of this will always come forward to regenerate it by reviving the past to suit the present. Prime Minister Narendra Modi has been doing just that. He knows that India's progress is not related to debunking its past, but the values of our oldest culture must act as a lighthouse to the world. The whole world must benefit from the human values preached by this tradition. To live a wholesome life without hurting others is the best philosophy that can show light to humanity.

When Modi talks of India being the '*Vishwa* Guru, he refers to the deep philosophical principles that have guided people to live peacefully and realise the finer virtues of existence. These are the values that should guide science and technology. Under the able leadership of Modi, India is witnessing a cultural reawakening that would inspire every Indian.

On the importance of cultural confidence, Modi said, 'The cultural splendour of a nation is so vast only when the flag of its success is fluttering on the world stage. And, to reach the pinnacle of success, it is also necessary that the nation touches its cultural excellence, and stands proudly with its identity. That is why in the Azadi Ka Amrit Kaal, India has called for Panch Prans like "freedom from the mentality of slavery" and "pride in our heritage"'[1]. He was speaking at a function to dedicate the first phase of the Mahakal Lok project in Ujjain.

Respect for the culture and tradition means respect for the symbols defining the society's norms, customs, practices and values. Hence, the idol of Lord Rama is not merely a deity to revere as God; it embodies the values for which He stood. The various idols in various temples are not mere idols but the values by which human beings have been living. These idols and the philosophical traditions that guide reverence are cultural symbols that give meaning to existence and encourage people to do good to themselves and society. Temples have also served as meeting places for social functions, bringing the society together. Morality and law emanate from cultural beliefs and practices and make compliance easy.

Modi has defined the Grand Rama Temple in these terms. We have seen in the previous chapter the dream of having this temple at the birthplace of Lord Rama has been realised. Lord Rama represents the super consciousness of the *Sanatan* culture, preaching how to derive happiness from family life and how a King should behave with his people and family members. The moral values of Ramayana that have guided people and showed the path of dharma are enshrined in the temple of Lord Rama. When Babur destroyed the temple, he did not dismantle a structure. He meant to attack the rich culture and tradition of this country.

The Prime Minister gave the example of the destruction of the Somnath temple and its rebuilding every time it was destroyed. It is dedicated to Lord Shiva. 'Lord Shiva gives rise to development and creativity amidst annihilation and destruction. Shiva is unending, inexpressible and eternal. "Our faith in Shiva makes us aware of our existence beyond the limits of time, gives us the strength to face the challenges of time."'[2]

His words for the temple were profound and summed up his vision of India's great spiritual tradition. '"It is a symbol of the belief that truth can't be defeated by falsehood and faith can't be crushed by terror." The destructive powers, the thinking that tries to establish an empire on the basis of terror, may dominate temporarily, but its existence is never permanent, it cannot suppress humanity for a long time. This was true when some attackers were demolishing Somnath, it is equally true even today, when the world is apprehensive of such ideologies.'[3]

'Our thinking should be to learn from history to improve our present and create a new future', he said. The Bharat Jodo Andolan is not just about geographical connectivity but connectivity of thoughts, too. It is also a pledge to connect the modern India with its past. The thought of *Sabka Saath – Sabka Vikas, Sabka Vishwas–Sabka Prayas* emanates from this all-inclusive and human vision.

While the geographical unity of India may have depended on the might of the Empire that ruled over the vast territory, India achieved its cultural unity much earlier in history without depending on the existence or annihilation of an Empire. From Somnath and Nageshwara in the West to Baidyanath Dham in the East, from Baba Kedarnath in the North to Shree Rameshwaram in the South, and the 12 *Jyotirlinga*s spread over various places have served to outline our faith.

The Prime Minister highlighted the role of faith and belief systems in underscoring the unity of India. He described these as the spirit of *Ek Bharat, Shreshtha Bharat*. 'Arrangement of our four *dham*s, the concept of our *Shaktipeeth*s, the establishment of different pilgrimages in different corners of our country, this outline of our faith is actually an expression of the spirit of *Ek Bharat, Shreshtha Bharat*'[4].

Cultural India would also promote spiritual tourism since most Indian temples have a history attached to them. While talking about the decision to revive the *Ramayana,* Modi said it would apprise the followers of Lord Rama about the places He visited during his 14-year exile. It would make it more evident when we say Lord Rama is of the entire country. The same thought is behind building the Buddha Circuit, which would attract people from all over the world.

The tourism ministry is developing such tourist circuits on 15 themes under the Swadesh Darshan Scheme. Similarly, under the PRASHAD (Pilgrimage Rejuvenation and Spiritual Heritage Augmentation Drive) Scheme announced in 2014, the ministry is developing 40 prominent places of pilgrimage. It would promote religious tourism, spiritual tourism or cultural tourism since all three are linked.

Speaking on the role of spirituality in the nation's life, Modi said, 'It is the spiritual confidence of our civilisation, due to which India has remained immortal for thousands of years. As long as these centres of our faith are awakened, the consciousness of India is awakened, and the soul of India is awakened.'[5]

We have seen how the concepts of the Modi government have been shaped by his cultural moorings. Take, for example, the renaming of Rajpath as Kartavya path. *Kartavya* is the path of duty derived from the spiritual tradition of the *Bhagavad Gita.* The rulers are supposed to be guided by duties, and so are other individuals. So, the Republic Day parade on the Kartavya path is a way to tell the country that the trust put in the government to steer the country well has been upheld.

The concept of Amrit kaal for India to relaunch itself, celebrating 100 years of Independence, has a deep cultural meaning. 'Amrit Kaal originates from Vedic astrology. It's the most auspicious time to start a new work and refers to a time period when the gates to greater pleasure for humans, angels, and other creatures are opened'[6].

It began in 2022 when India completed its journey of 75 years and will culminate in its 100th year in 2047. Amrit kaal means the government will have to undertake a churning process by creating an infrastructure that would make the country the third-largest economy and help people reap the economic benefits. It needs long-term planning. If we work hard towards a vision of a developed India, the country will get Amrit (nectar of development). The Amrit kaal has been thus named as Kartavya kaal[7].

The new Parliament building has placed Sengol, a symbol of dharma and righteousness, close to the Speaker's podium. It represents fair and equitable governance and is supposed to guide the parliamentarians during the Kartayva kaal for meaningful actions to take India to its rightful place. Sengol also marks a smooth transition from one government to the other. The sceptre originated from the Chola dynasty, one of the most prominent and powerful dynasties of the Chola empire.

Modi knows that the strength of India is essentially cultural, and it has made the society tolerant, inclusive and integrated. You break this bond and you can break the country. This is what the British did. They created a wedge between Hindus and Muslims and introduced English education. That the country got divided into India and Pakistan was no coincidence.

Mahatma Gandhi firmly believed there was no need to banish religion from one's life to become secular. In fact, a person devoid of religious beliefs can be dangerous since he would be impervious to morality and can fall to any extent to further his personal interest. Hence, Gandhi was religious in his personal beliefs and secular in public life, whereas Muhammad Ali Jinnah was just the opposite.

Modi has followed the example of Mahatma Gandhi. Even though he dons a saffron robe while visiting a temple, his decisions are governed by public considerations. He may look like a sanyasi when he does the Ganga *Arti* at the ghat of Varanasi but, when meeting his Western counterparts, he is dressed meticulously in traditional Indian clothes or a Western formal outfit.

If India has to become a *Vishwa* Guru and guide the world to a righteous path, it must strengthen its basic value system. Modi understands that India needs information technology and artificial intelligence to improve living, but we also need a value system for their usage.

When he was the Chief Minister of Gujarat, Modi worked tirelessly to build the Statue of Unity at Kevadia at Sardar Sarovar Dam (Narmada District) to remind every Indian of the contribution Sardar Vallabhbhai Patel made to unite India and mark its transition into a vibrant democracy. He took contributions from iron and other metal parts of old farming equipment from every Indian village to create the massive structure that has become one of the biggest tourist places in the state.

Modi has not been reviving these temples and corridors as places of religious worship but as places of significant cultural values that promote universal brotherhood. The construction of the Rama temple in Ayodhya is one such example. One cannot imagine this country without Lord Rama and the cultural values that He propagated. He left material things for greater human values and sacrificed crucial years to uphold dharma.

The same is the case with other temples that have seen revivalism. These centres have evolved into places of spiritual and philosophical enlightenment. Each of these temples is a symbol of human values and universal brotherhood. These were established to promote meditation and spiritual enlightenment and to encourage followers to find their connection with God. They were not the symbols of hatred or promoted at the cost of others.

We have seen how Modi has been involved in building the Grand Rama Temple in Ayodhya which was inaugurated on 22 January 2024. We will see which other actions he took to push India's cultural awakening.

Kedarnath Shrine Reconstruction: Restoring Past Glory

When a massive flood devastated the Kedarnath shrine in June 2013, no one had imagined the ancient site would give a sense of pride to everyone with faith in the great cultural and religious site developed by Adi Shankaracharya.

Rebuilding the shrine and restoring its pristine glory was on the agenda of Modi even before he became the Prime Minister. As a chief minister, he had offered help to the Uttarakhand government, headed by the Congress, in rebuilding the shrine. Perhaps God had willed that he should. 'But perhaps Baba (Lord Shiva) had decided that the responsibility of doing reconstruction work at Kedarnath should be assigned to no one else but to Baba's son', he said while laying the foundation stone for five reconstruction projects in Kedarnath in October 2017.

The projects included better facilities for devotees, the construction of strong retaining walls using modern techniques, refurbishing the ghats at the two legendary rivers–Mandakini and Saraswati, and an all-weather approach road to the shrine. The Adi Shankaracharya's tomb, destroyed in the 2013 flood, was also to be reconstructed.

Modi knew that the construction of Kedarpuri (the entire ecosystem of Kedarnath) was costly, but he assured there would be no shortage of funds. 'Through the work we are doing in Kedarnath, we want to show how an ideal *Tirth Kshetra* should be, how it should be pilgrim friendly and (that) the well-being of the priests should be given importance', said Modi and invited private sector, too, to participate in the ambitious exercise.

Modi outlined his vision to combine the spirituality inherent in Kedarnath with modern activities such as adventure sports and ecotourism to encourage the youths to visit the place and know their culture. It also meant developing enough accommodation in and around the area to make the visit pleasant.

Modi has been monitoring the development either through video conferencing with those involved in the development work or through personal visits. He has been visiting Kedarnath regularly, either to inaugurate the completed projects, such as unveiling the 12-foot statue of Adi Shankaracharya in November 2021 or to lay the foundation of further reconstruction work. The ceremony was streamed live at 12 *Jyotirlingas* and four monasteries (maths) across the country.

The Prime Minister is a spiritual person. He has often resorted to his faith to strengthen his confidence and get the blessings of the deities. He had visited Kedarnath on multiple occasions to strengthen his resolve. A sadhu had predicted that if he did not become a public person, he would turn a hermit. This blend of concern for people and spirituality is often seen in his actions and words. During the 2019 Lok Sabha elections, Modi spent 15 hours in the cave of Kedarnath meditating in Dhyan Kutia.

When out of the cave on 19 May, he urged people to come out of their houses and vote in large numbers. 'Today is the final phase of the 2019 Lok Sabha elections. I urge all those voting in this phase to vote in record numbers. Your one vote will shape India's development trajectory in the years to come. I also hope first time voters vote enthusiastically. Chowkidar Narendra Modi (@narendramodi).'

The biggest project at Kedarnath is the construction of the longest ropeway on the planet, at 11,500 feet. The ropeway is being constructed under the Parvatmala Pariyojana, between Sonprayag and Kedarnath through Gaurikund, at the cost of Rs 1,200 crore. The ropeway, to be completed by the end of 2023, would considerably reduce the time travelling to the shrine.

It would take only one hour in ropeway to travel from Sonprayag to Kedarnath instead of 7 hours and 15 minutes on foot. It is 16 km on foot from Gaurikund to Kedarnath and takes about 6-7 hours, almost the whole day. From Sonprayag to Gaurikund, there is a motorable distance of 8 km. The earlier plan was to have a ropeway between Gaurikund and Kedarnath shrine. It is going to become the major attraction of the region.

Char Dham Yatra

While Kedarnath is being developed as a significant cultural and spiritual centre, it must be seen as a part of the *Char Dham* Yatra that promotes spiritual, religious and natural tourism. This yatra connects Kedarnath, Badrinath, Gangotri and Yamunotri with two-lane metalled roads.

The foundation stone for the Rs 12,000-crore-roadway project of 889 km was laid by Modi in December 2016 and named the Char Dham Mahamarg Vikas Pariyojna. The project in progress has already witnessed the construction of 601 km of all-weather roads. Char Dham Railway project is also being integrated to facilitate connectivity and easy movement. Several long bridges and tunnels would form a part of the project to ensure that the roads are safe from the vagaries of nature.

The construction is done by the Border Roads Organisation (BRO), and some of the routes in the extreme North are close to China. The Char Dham essentially connects Rishikesh, near Dehradun, with Yamunotri, Gangotri, Kedarnath and Badrinath. Thus, it comprises four stretches–Rishikesh–Yamunotri, Rishikesh–Gangotri, Rishikesh–Kedarnath and Rishikesh–Badrinath.

Yamunotri and Gangotri are the respective sources from where the rivers Yamuna and Ganga emerge from the snow-clad mountains. The Badrinath temple, devoted to Lord Vishnu, is considered one of the most important pilgrimages of the Hindus. The temple is also known for its scenic beauty since it is surrounded by snow-clad mountains. The temperature there is extremely low, too.

The temple, built by Adi Shankaracharya, has Nambudiri Brahmins as priests in both Badrinath and Kedarnath. It depicts the unity of the country and the well-thought-out strategy of Shankaracharya to demonstrate the cultural unity of the country. Adi Shankara went from Kerala to as far as Uttarakhand to establish the holy shrines of two major deities of the Hindus.

Besides being a spiritual journey, *Char Dham* would attract tourists with its natural beauty. The motorable roads would lure the tourists to get a glimpse of the Himalayas, which will be a lifetime experience.

Varanasi

Modi had made Herculean efforts to elevate the stature of the Kashi Vishwanath temple at Varanasi and convert Varanasi into a modern cultural centre. The travel time from the airport to the city is much less than before, and the airport matches any other modern airport in the country.

While nothing much can be done to change the narrow lanes and by-lanes since it is how the city has lived through ancient times, the look of a modern city is visible as one comes out of these congested lanes to the arterial roads. The city has immensely benefitted from being represented by the Prime Minister.

Modi knows the best way to make the city accessible to tourists and pilgrims is by improving its connectivity. Varanasi now has intermodal connectivity with various highways of international standards and waterways, besides the airport and railway station. The length of the platform at Varanasi railway station has been increased to 600 metres to accommodate long trains and new platforms have been added, besides making the station tourist-friendly by providing escalators.

All four railway stations in the Varanasi district have been developed to take care of tourists. Manduadih railway station has been renamed Banaras and made into a world-class, airport-style railway station with all modern facilities, including spacious waiting areas, food court, AC retiring rooms and dormitories. The architectural beauty of the place reflects the cultural ethos of Kashi's faith.

Varanasi became the fulcrum of waterways when Modi inaugurated the country's first multi modal inland waterways terminal in November 2018. He received the country's first container cargo transported through inland waterways, shipped from Kolkata. With this, Varanasi got linked to Haldia port through waterways transport.

The viability of the project was tested when Union Minister Nitin Gadkari flagged off two vessels from Varanasi–MV Joy Basudev and MV VV Giri–carrying assembled Maruti cars and construction materials, respectively. While announcing the ambitious plan to make the 1,620 km stretch between Varanasi and Haldia navigable for big vessels, he said that navigable rivers would bring immense benefits to Uttar Pradesh.

In January 2013, Modi flagged off the world's longest river cruise, MV Ganga Vilas, which would cover 3,200 km across 27 river systems in five states and Bangladesh in 51 days. The cruise has a capacity of 36 tourists and is running booked for the next two years. The cruise route will start from Varanasi and meander through Patna, Sahibganj, Kolkata, Dhaka, Guwahati, and finally reach Dibrugarh in Assam.

Varanasi is marked with better connectivity of roads, too. The Varanasi-Ranchi-Kolkata Expressway, costing Rs 23,500 crore, will run parallel to the Grand Trunk Road. It will cover a distance of 610 km and reduce the travel time between the end destinations by almost half. It is expected to be complete by 2027. The six-lane Prayagraj-Varanasi project on National Highway-19 has already been inaugurated.

Ring Road has also been constructed around the city connected to the highways so that most vehicles take the bypass route. New flyovers have come up, allowing decongestion of the city and better movement of vehicles. Now, Varanasi is connected with international standard roads with Lucknow, Azamgarh, Gorakhpur and Ayodhya.

The ghats of Varanasi on river Ganga add beauty to the flowing rivers. These riverfront steps lead to the banks of the river Ganga. The city has 84 ghats, but a new ghat, Namo ghat, with recreational facilities, has also come up, adding to the beauty of the riverfront. These ghats serve for bathing and worship purposes.

Of these ghats, Raja Harishchandra and Manikarnika are of great religious sanctity and are used for cremation. Modi inaugurated major projects for renovating these two ghats associated with the death rituals of the Hindus. It is believed that people who get cremated here attain salvation and overcome the cycle of birth and death. Eco-friendly crematoriums are also being constructed to ensure efficient consumption of firewood.

The ghats look much cleaner and neat now and add to the beauty of spiritualism associated with the river Ganga, the ghats and more than 10,000 temples dotting the city's landscape. Varanasi is often referred to as the city of temples, and various estimates put the number of temples at 23,000. Assi Ghat, Khidkiya Ghat, renamed as Namo Ghat, and the Dashashwamedh Ghat, adjoining the Kashi Vishwanath temple, known for Ganga *arti*, have become major attractions for tourists.

Floating jetties have become another major attraction for tourists in Varanasi. At the Namo ghat, the jetty will have two bath pools, one each for ladies and gents, to enable them to dip in the Ganga without drowning. These pools will be 4-5 feet deep and have steel rods to help the pilgrims dip in the river. The jetty will also have changing rooms. Such a jetty is already available at Dashashwamedh Ghat, which had begun as a pilot project. Other ghats are also likely to get this facility since every visitor to the city wants to take a dip in the river Ganga.

The most remarkable development that has changed the landscape of the eastern side of the river Ganga opposite the ghats is the establishment of Tent City along the 5 km long bank. Around 200 modern tents with luxurious facilities, including air-conditioners, are set up for six months (October to June) every year when the Ganga recedes and are dismantled when the river floods.

The Prime Minister inaugurated the first tent city in January 2023. It is a massive operation since it involves setting up a mini-city with clubs, pools, watch points, eating points, cruise and darshan at the Kashi Vishwanath temple. Light music is played for tourists while they get the facility of yoga classes. People have to approach the Tent city via boats from other ghats.

If cricket defines India's new culture today, nothing would be more welcome than having a cricket stadium in town. Modi laid the foundation of a 30,000-capacity international stadium in the city in September 2023. It is expected to be completed by 2025 and will give opportunity to youths to hone their cricketing skills. There will be nine practice pitches, too.

Kashi Vishwanath Temple

Mark Twain, in his book *Following the Equator: A Journey Around the World*, describes Banaras (Kashi) as a legend and older than history. He said, 'Benares is older than history, older than tradition, older even than legend, and looks twice as old as all of them put together.'

Talking about the city is essentially talking about Kashi Vishwanath temple, which is the fulcrum of the city's brush with ancient history. Whoever has gone to Banaras gets a similar experience. There is a limit to modernising the city because the by-lanes and lanes associated with the temple town have existed since time immemorial.

Yet, it was possible to modernise the city without tampering with its culture or the religiosity associated with the place. The existing temple complex could be modernised to address the demand for clean surroundings, accommodating more people. With an ever-increasing population, the big rush to the temple can be channelised without compromising its spirituality. On the contrary, cleanliness adds to the beauty and serenity of the place.

Nobody thought the temple would get such a modern and attractive ambience. The Rudraksh Convention Centre can accommodate 1,200 people at a time. The 20-foot wide corridor links the temple (Mandir Chowk) to the river Ganga. The access now is much easier from the riverside as well. Built over 5.5 lakh square feet, the corridor had brought fresh breath and open space to the temple complex, surrounded by buildings on three sides.

Those who have not visited the temple earlier cannot fathom the mammoth task it was to uplift and improve the temple complex. The congesting lanes and by-lanes have merged into the corridor. When Modi launched the Kashi Vishwanath Corridor project in March 2019, few had imagined that the task would be achieved so fast.

Many houses had to be destroyed, and ancient temples shifted to give the place the grandeur it deserved. Litigation and conflict were bound to happen. People have been living there for generations. Negotiating to purchase the old buildings, demolishing them, removing the rubble from the narrow lanes and rehabilitating the displaced people was quite a task. The razing work was manual so that the temple structure did not suffer damage.

Also, there was a problem in retaining the old culture while creating a modern complex. To add to the mammoth task was the COVID-19 pandemic that impacted crucial two years.

Over 300 buildings were purchased and demolished to create the temple corridor. The demolition led to a recovery of at least 40 ancient temples. Close to 1,111 people were rehabilitated. A transparent mechanism for paying compensation was devised. It was the blessings of Vishwanath that everything happened smoothly. Close to Rs 390 crore was spent on the purchase of buildings, and about Rs 100 crore was spent on rehabilitation. Some people came out of their homes willingly, while others needed persuasion to sacrifice their personal interest in the cause of the larger design.

The mega facelift project, built across 5,50,000 square feet, comprises 24 buildings that include an emporium, a museum, a sacred kitchen, a Vedic library, a centre to store ancient scriptures, a city gallery, and a food court–all built around the temple that serves as one of the nerve centres of the Hindu faith, attracting seven million pilgrims annually.

It has re-established the symbiotic link the temple had with the river Ganga in ancient times. The approach was disturbed due to various encroachments. Now, anyone can get on a boat and reach the magnificent new entrance to the temple complex, Ganga Dwar, via entry points from the Lalita Ghat and Jalasen Ghat. Pilgrims and tourists have started opting for this route since approaching the temple is now easier from the riverside.

The 300-metre-long Kashi Vishwanath Corridor and the renovated temple complex have given a boost to religious tourism in Varanasi. Many experts have described it as a jackpot for the tourism industry. Between 20 and 30 lakh tourists have visited the city every month, as per the latest data in 2023. Also, usually, an estimated 1 lakh pilgrims visit the temple daily, which doubles during the peak season. In the year following the inauguration by Modi in 2021, the temple was visited by 7.35 crore devotees. Also, the temple received donations of Rs 100 crore.

Varanasi has definitely come on the map of any foreign tourist visiting India. The city has emerged as a holiday destination for many who want to combine nature and spiritualism. The boatmen are happy to get more passengers than earlier since people prefer to reach the temple using the water route. They also get a glimpse of the ancient and legendary Manikarnika Ghat. People believe that those who get cremated at this ghat overcome the cycle of birth and death and get moksha.

The renovation of the temple and expansion and modernisation of Varanasi have given a boost to the city's economy. The hospitality sector has witnessed a rapid expansion, and the demand for new hotels has increased manifold. Local vendors have witnessed a surge in the demand for their goods, and real estate prices have sky-rocketed.

Senior journalist Dilip Singh is a regular visitor to the city. After his visit in 2023, he was astonished at the beauty of the Tent City on the Ganga. The city has undergone a complete transformation where the ancient structures have been blended nicely with modern aesthetics. The overhead wires have gone underground in most areas, adding to the beauty of the city. Modi should be given full marks for reviving the city's glory and bringing it to the global tourism map.

Ujjain Temple Renovation

Ujjain's Mahakaleshwar temple is another significant destination for pilgrims. People worship Mahakal for a long life and prevention of untimely death. It is believed that by the blessings of Lord Shiva, one can overcome the fear of death by visiting the temple. Ujjain is one of the four locations where Kumbh Mela is organised every 12 years. Lord Shiva is considered the God of Time and Death.

When Narendra Modi inaugurated the first phase of the Mahakaleshwar Temple Corridor Development Project in October 2022, he also spoke about his cultural vision for the country. He said that India was breaking off the shackles of colonial mentality by reclaiming its place as a world leader, and this leadership will pave the way for world peace.

While describing the new corridor as 'extraordinary and unbelievable', he said, 'This Mahakal will encourage India's tradition and culture and give it new life…Where there is innovation, there will be renovation… In this period of Independence, India's glory was being reconstructed.'

'The pride of our culture centres, which are centres of spiritual consciousness, is being restored across the country with the help of Swadesh Darshan and PRASHAD Yojana. This grand Mahakal Lok is also ready to welcome the future with the glory of the past', he said.

He spoke about the cultural significance of Jyotirlingas. 'I believe, this development of our Jyotirlingas is the development of India's spiritual light, the development of India's knowledge and philosophy. This cultural philosophy of India is once again reaching the summit and getting ready to guide the world', he said.

While talking about the importance of spirituality in the nation's life, he elaborated, 'It is the spiritual confidence of our civilisation, due to which India has remained immortal for thousands of years. As long as these centres of our faith are awakened, the consciousness of India is awakened, and the soul of India is awakened.'

The Prime Minister recalled how invaders, like Iltutmish, tried to destroy the energy of Ujjain. Efforts were made in the past to exploit India, but the country's cultural consciousness did not allow subjugation. He quoted, 'What will death do to us in the shelter of Mahakal Shiva?... India was revived, then rose again from the energy of these authentic centres of faith. Today once again, in the Azadi Ka Amrit Mahotsav, Amar Avantika is proclaiming the cultural immortality of India.'

Such a profound thought and clear vision about the cultural awakening of India came from Modi to match the serenity, vastitude and spirituality of the Mahakal Temple after the completion of the first phase. The earlier temple complex was spread over 3,03,545 square feet, but now it is spread over 21,77,540 square feet. The expansion will finally include the 18,29,200 square feet of Rudrasagar lake, making the extended corridor 50,57,200 square feet.

The first phase included construction development and renovation near the Char Dham Mandir, Nutan school complex, Ganesh school complex, 900-metre long corridor, theme park, Rudrasagar Ghat and Food court.

The second phase that would be completed in 2028 includes renovation work and construction activities at Maharajwada School Bhavan to transform it into a dharmsala, linking of Rudrasagar and Shipra rivers, beautification of the front lake area, construction of multi-level parking with a capacity of about 500 cars, and development of a 210-meter suspension bridge over Rudrasagar.

The Mahakal Lok Corridor, one of the longest for any temple in India, surrounds the Rudrasagar Lake, which is also being revamped as a part of the development project. Two grand gateways–Nandi Dwar and Pinaki Dwar–have been constructed at the starting point of the corridor. The corridor has 108 intricately carved sandstone pillars, gushing fountains and a running panel of more than 50 murals depicting stories from the Shiva Purana.

The inauguration was telecast live in 40 countries of the world. And the message of the Prime Minister was loud and clear for those who wanted to understand Indian values. 'India is reclaiming its glory by renovating the places of its pride, honour and legacy', he stressed and expressed confidence that the country, as well as humanity, would reap its benefits. 'With the blessings of Mahakal, the grandeur of India will create new possibilities of development in the world and the divinity of India will pave the way for a peaceful world.'[8]

Somnath Temple and Ambaji Temple

Temple renovation, as a part of cultural reawakening, is also undertaken in Somnath temple and Ambaji temple in Gujarat. Sardar Vallabhbhai Patel had undertaken the revival of the temple in 1947, describing the reconstruction as holy and urging everyone to participate. The renovation was completed in 1951 after his death.

The task of the modern makeover was undertaken by Prime Minister Modi, who laid the foundation in August 2021 for multiple projects in Somnath. It included the inauguration of Somnath Promenade, Somnath Exhibition Centre, and the reconstructed temple precinct of Old Somnath. He also laid the foundation stone of Parvati Temple.

Developed under the PRASHAD scheme, the Somnath Promenade along the sea is 1.48 km long and has been built at the cost of Rs 47 crore. It has added to the beauty of the temple complex and has become a major tourist attraction. It has helped prevent coastal erosion, giving the pilgrims a beautiful view of the sea surrounding the Somnath temple.

The reconstructed temple precinct of Old (Juna) Somnath has been completed at the cost of Rs 3.5 crore. This temple is also known as Ahilyabai temple since it was built by Ahilyabai, the queen of Indore when it lay in ruins.

The exhibition centre, which has become a major attraction, displays exhibits of Old Somnath temple that was destroyed. Besides spiritualism, one would have a brush with history and get a sense of the barbaric culture that defiled and destroyed the temple.

Modi reminded people of this brutal memory from history when he recalled how the temple was attacked by invaders and Muslim rulers, and how it was reconstructed, strengthening the belief in goodness[9].

Ambaji Temple

In September 2022, Modi laid the foundation for a broad gauge line to connect the Taranga Hill-Ambaji-Abu Road which is expected to benefit lakhs of pilgrims visiting the *Shaktipeeth* of Ambaji. Though the British had decided to build this line in 1930, it could not see the light of the day. Modi dusted off the past files and converted the dream of this railway line into a reality. The broad gauge of about 116 km would be built under the PRASHAD scheme and would be completed by 2026-27.

Pilgrimage facilities are being developed at Ambaji temple to enhance the spiritual experience. It includes eco-friendly modes of transport, parking facilities, toilets, cloakrooms, resting rooms, craft market etc. The idea is to attract new tourists and make them stay there.

Kailash Manasarovar

Not many in the country would be aware of the Adi Kailash temple in Pithoragarh district of Uttarakhand. About 3 km away are Gauri Kund and Adi Kailash. It is believed that Lord Shiva had rested here while going to his abode in Mount Kailash. Some even say that it was the original abode of Lord Shiva till he shifted place.

This place is considered as important as Mount Kailash, and pilgrims need Chinese government permission to visit the sacred place known as lord Shiva's abode. But to reach Adi Kailash, they only need an inner permit from the Uttarakhand government, which is available online.

This place shot into prominence when Narendra Modi visited the place in October 2023 and performed an elaborate puja ritual in a traditional outfit. Since then, tourists and pilgrims have started visiting the place in large numbers. There is a blacktopped motorable road up to Jolingkong, after which there is a 3 km trek to Parvathi Kund.

Creating Easy Route to Kailash Manasarovar Yatra

The government has already constructed a metalled road along one stretch of the Kailash Manasarovar Yatra from Daruchula to Lipulekh along the India-China borders. The construction of the 80 km stretch has been completed and opened to the public. Lipulekh is considered the gateway to Kailash Manasarovar, which is about 97 km of trek in inhospitable conditions.

This route will make the yatra to Kailash Manasarovar easier since pilgrims can use the road to reach the end road destination in India at Lipulekh. If one takes the Sikkim-Nathula Pass route and if we calculate the distance from Delhi, it involves a flight to Bagdogra (1,115 km) followed by a 1,665 km journey by road (of which only 175 km falls in India). It is followed by a 43 km trek. The other route usually taken by pilgrims was through Nepal.

To visit Kailash Manasarovar in Tibet, the pilgrims need the permission of the Chinese government. The yatra, considered holy for Hindus, has not resumed since 2019 due to various factors, such as COVID-19 and the ongoing tension with China along the borders.

The Modi government, however, is making provision for having a full view of Mount Kailash without going to either Nepal or China. It has been done by constructing roads along the India-China borders in the most difficult terrain, where temperature goes down to as low as -5 ° C. The BRO that has constructed the road at a very high altitude is in the process of developing the Kailash viewpoint.

It is sure to emerge as a major pilgrimage and tourist attraction. The Kailash viewpoint at the end of Lipulekh Pass, 4 Km away from China borders, and the Old Lipulekh Peak would give a complete view of Mount Kailash and the Manasarovar Lake. The breathtaking images of the holy abode of Lord Shiva will be captured from this new pilgrimage site. Lipulekh Pass is a 6.5 km stretch from KmVN Huts (Kumaon Mandal Vikas Nigam Limited) in Pithoragarh district. There would be a steep climb of 1.8 km on a snowy terrain to reach the Old Lipulekh Peak at about 19,000 feet.

In any case, one is not allowed to climb Mount Kailash and can only do a parikrama of the mountain which is 54 km around it. People can either trek this parikrama or use a horse or personal helpers. In earlier days, those who could not undertake the arduous journey to Mount Kailash could have darshan of Mount Kailash from the Old Lipulekh Peak.

Kartarpur Sahib Corridor

When irrational boundaries were created between India and Pakistan in 1947, one of the holiest places for the Sikhs went to Pakistan even though a majority of Sikhs stayed on the Indian side of the divided Punjab.

Even after Independence, Sikhs continued to visit Kartarpur Sahib, where Guru Nanak Dev, the founder of Sikhism, had breathed his last. The visits continued informally without interruptions till the Jassar Bridge was destroyed by the Pakistani military during the 1965 Indo-Pak war.

Sikhs longing to visit the Gurdwara Darbar Sahib had to take a visa from Pakistan and travel to Lahore, undertaking a journey of 125 km. The physical distance of the Gurdwara from the Indian side of the Indo-Pak border is only 4.7 km and is visible through the naked eye from a raised platform meant for the purpose. Kartarpur was founded by Guru Nanak, who spent his last days there.

The foundation stone to connect this distance by a corridor was laid on the Indian side by Vice President of India, M Venkaiah Naidu, in 2018. Pakistani Prime Minister Imran Khan did the same from the Pakistani side. The corridor, called Kartarpur Sahib Corridor, renamed as Sri Guru Nanak Devji Marg, was constructed within a year, by November 2019.

The memorandum of understanding between India and Pakistan for a visa-free entry in the corridor was signed in October 2019 and was valid for five years. This MoU will be renewed in 2024. The Corridor is a four-lane road covering a distance of 4.1 km on the Indian side from Gurdwara Dera Baba Nanak to the Indo-Pak border and 4.5 km from this border to Gurdwara Darbar Sahib (Kartar Sahib) in Pakistan's Narowal district.

A massive Check-Point Terminal has been constructed to ensure safe and hassle-free entry of pilgrims. Only Indians are allowed to use this corridor, which has been built to connect the two Gurdwaras. The registration formalities are completed by the Indian side.

It was the vision of late Prime Minister Atal Bihari Vajpayee, and Modi undertook to complete the task. Vajpayee had spoken to the then Prime Minister of Pakistan, Nawaz Sharif, in 1998 and again, during the Lahore Bus Yatra in 1999. The Kargil War derailed the momentum. The United Progressive Alliance (UPA) government did not achieve any headway.

It was a historic occasion when Modi flagged off the first batch of pilgrims to Kartarpur in November 2019. The Corridor promised cultural unity between the two countries and many existing possibilities between India and Pakistan. Modi thanked Imran Khan for agreeing to open the corridor. His vision was clear when he recalled the fall of the Berlin Wall that had divided East Germany and West Germany.

The opening of the corridor coincided with the celebration of the 550th year of Guru Nanak's birth anniversary. The government had already decided to celebrate Nanak's birth anniversary across the country to popularise his ideas of universal brotherhood. The corridor was closed during the COVID-19 pandemic but was reopened in 2021.

Temple in Abu Dhabi

When one is sincere in spreading the message of universal brotherhood and peace, others complement by respecting the culture they represent. This is what happened when Modi visited the UAE in 2015. It was historic as it was the first visit by any Indian Prime Minister to the UAE in 34 years.

During the visit in August 2015, the ruler of Abu Dhabi, Sheikh Mohammed bin Zayed Al Nahyan (MBZ) gifted Modi a 17-acre land for constructing a grand Hindu temple and its complex. Modi described it as 'a great step' and thanked him for this gesture.

With this, MBZ fulfilled the long due demand of the Hindus staying in Abu Dhabi that they be allowed to have a temple. Dubai has two temples and one Gurdwara, but Abu Dhabi had none. The significance of the temple was lost on no one. Modi described it as, 'This temple will not be only unique in terms of architecture and splendour, but will also give a message of "*Vasudhaiva Kutumbakam*" (the world is one family) to people across the world.'

'I am pretty confident that once this temple comes up, it will be a beacon not only of Indian culture here but also the UAE's own spirit of tolerance that celebrates diversity and enables all community the space to practice their religion, culture, identity and language', Indian Ambassador to the UAE, Navdeep Singh Suri, said.

In February 2018, Modi inaugurated the project for constructing the grand Hindu temple and described it as a symbol of universal brotherhood and a 'catalytic agent' of humanity and harmony that would reflect India's identity.

While addressing the Indian diaspora in Abu Dhabi, he pointed out that the UAE was home to about 3 million Indians, and thanked the ruler of Abu Dhabi for making their stay hospitable. The temple complex devoted to BAPS (Bochasanwasi Shri Akshar Purushottam Swaminarayan Sanstha) also houses cultural complexes and spiritual centres.

Union Minister Dharmendra Pradhan visited the construction site and took stock of the situation. The grand temple, with all its architectural beauty, would be inaugurated in 2024.

But many wonder how it is possible to have such a traditional grand temple in Abu Dhabi. The moment and sentiments are captured best in the words of Brahmaviharidas Swami, the head of the BAPS in Abu Dhabi.

'Even now many are wondering how it is possible that a temple is coming up in Abu Dhabi. Almost a 1,000 sensible people told me that it is impossible to build a traditional stone temple in Abu Dhabi. The only essence, comfort and energy that we banked upon were the prayers of Pramukh Swami Maharaj in 1997', he said at a BAPS function in Ahmedabad.

> As we walked to the ruler and our Prime Minister, we were wondering what would happen. We placed two plans before them. First was to create a mandir (temple) like a normal building, put the 'murtis' (an image of a deity) inside and do worship like a Hari mandir and the other plan was to create a stunning traditional stone mandir that captures 10,000 years of Indian art and culture. When two plans were presented, with all generosity Sheikh Mohammed bin Zayed Al Nahyan, he chose the traditional mandir, the first such mandir in the history of human civilisation.

He wanted the Swami Narayan temple to replicate the grandeur and magnificence of the original temple in India since he appreciated the values associated with these temples. These are not symbols of supremacy but symbols that showcase the finer values and wisdom associated with spiritual enlightenment. It would encourage seekers to know more about its existence and promote brotherhood.

India's External Affairs Minister, Dr S Jaishankar, has described this temple as a story of 'heart and mind'.

> The Abu Dhabi temple story was referred to as a miracle. It is. It is also diplomacy and relationships, a story of hearts and minds, and a story of the generosity of kings. But ultimately, it is the result of divine Providence. Abu Dhabi's temple is one miracle, and the second will happen in Bahrain. This is something greater than a miracle. This temple was the dream and prediction of Pramukh Swami Maharaj. BAPS temples are being built across the world, including in Paris, South Africa, Thailand and elsewhere.[10]

India and the UAE have been great trade partners. It is the third-largest trade partner after the United States and China. This grand gesture of the ruler of Abu Dhabi is certainly going to forge better cultural ties between the UAE countries and India. The UAE has already supported India's permanent membership in the United Nations Security Council.

Renovation of Krishna Temple and Construction of a BAPS Temple in Bahrain

On 1 February 2022, Indian Prime Minister Narendra Modi announced that the Kingdom of Bahrain's Crown Prince and Prime Minister, HRH Prince Salman bin Hamad Al Khalifa, had allocated land to build a Swami Narayan Hindu Temple in Bahrain along the patterns of Abu Dhabi.

'Had a warm conversation with HRH Prince Salman bin Hamad Al Khalifa, Crown Prince and Prime Minister of Bahrain. Thanked him for the Kingdom's attention to the needs of the Indian community, including the recent decision on land allotment for the Swami Narayan temple', Modi said in one of his tweets.

Bahrain already has a Krishna temple, whose redevelopment plan worth USD 4.2 million was launched by Modi during his visit to Bahrain's capital city in August 2019. This 200-year-old temple complex is getting a facelift, and new facilities, such as marriage halls, are being added to convert it into a Hindu wedding destination.

Yoga

When the world celebrates International Yoga Day on 21 June, it also remembers India and its great cultural significance. It is not a mere exercise that drives people to come on the streets and practice Yoga; it is the inherent beauty of a system evolved in ancient India by sages to give humans a mechanism for a wholesome living.

Yoga cannot make one a muscular man but can facilitate an exercise routine where the body and the mind are perfectly aligned. If the mind is healthy, the body would be healthy, too, and hence, Yogic exercise focus on meditation and looking inward. Physical fitness and mental peace are the two essentials for spiritual enlightenment.

One cannot separate Yoga from India's culture. Indian sages have been trying to find ways to equip people with the art of living. Yoga recognises that every body part is interlinked, and these parts, like the parts of a machine, need regular exercise to give maximum output. It acts as a cure for diseases by treating metabolism through exercises. Most respiratory disorders can be treated with Yoga. It also helps in treating neurological disorders.

By promoting Yoga, India has been trying to give the world an elixir for a better living. Most Yogic exercises have already been researched, and their effectiveness verified. It would be foolish to reject it only because it evolves from the *Sanatan* tradition.

Modi would be remembered for popularising Yoga on a global platform. He had proposed celebrating Yoga Day at the UN General Assembly in September 2014. During his speech, he advocated Yoga as a holistic approach to health. 'Yoga is an invaluable gift of our ancient tradition. Yoga embodies unity of mind and body; thought and action; restraint and fulfilment; harmony between man and nature; a holistic approach to health and well-being. It is not about exercise but to discover the sense of oneness with yourself, the world and the nature. By changing our lifestyle and creating consciousness, it can help us deal with climate change', he said[11].

Modi's proposal that 21 June be declared the International Day for Yoga got massive support from all 93 members when the UN passed its resolution numbered 69/131 on 11 December 2014. The proposal was co-sponsored by 175 countries. In one stroke and without using guile or force, Modi established the supremacy of India's cultural and spiritual traditions[12]. It is the first time a resolution has been adopted in such a short span of three months. Also, the resolution had the highest number of co-sponsors ever.

On 21 June, the world celebrated Yoga Day and Modi took the lead, practising yoga at the Kartavya Path in Delhi. The event made it into the Guinness World Record–first for the most number of people participating in a single yoga session at a single venue and second for the most nationalities (84) participating in a Yoga session in 2015.

Modi led the ninth International Yoga Day in 2023 at the UN Headquarters in New York, where he had gone on an official visit. The theme was 'Yoga for Vasudhaiva Kutumbakam', which means the world is one family. It was to spread universal brotherhood. Now, every year Yoga Day adopts a different theme.

The diamond city of Surat created a world record with 1.53 lakh people participating in Yoga in one place. People participated at Y junctions of roads of length 10.5 km. It broke the previous record held by Rajasthan in 2018, where 1,00,984 people participated in the Yoga Day celebration at one place in Kota, where Yoga guru Ramdev conducted the yogic asanas[13].

Vishwa Guru

When India talks about attaining the position of *Vishwa* Guru, it refers to its intention to enrich the world with India's rich cultural heritage. Making lives better, caring for each other and raising environmental awareness are all ingrained in India's cultural past and its associated rituals. Indian culture is rich in variety, depth and philosophies that abhor exclusiveness and promote multi-culturalism. This is why many world leaders have praised India's syncretic culture and the way people co-exist without creating problems for anyone.

Momentous Decisions

Redefining Bharat- III

And, infrastructure is not just about creating capital assets and generating long-term return on investment. It is not about the numbers. It is not about the money. It is about people. It is about providing them high quality, dependable, and sustainable services in an equitable manner. People must be at the heart of any infrastructure growth story.

–Narendra Modi

Building Infrastructure for Modern India

Every Indian going to China returns mesmerised by the massive infrastructure the country has built to prepare itself for the future. The usual cryptic comment is that we are no match for China. However, Prime Minister Narendra Modi has made it possible for us Indians to confidently say that we can compete. India's standoff with China on the borders has forced Indians to turn inward and realise their strength.

India has already overtaken China in terms of population, and to get the democratic dividends of being the youngest population, the country must plan well. Without a matching response, the country would fail to catch up with the opportunities provided by the ageing population of China and by the other developed countries.

Modi's success story emanates from his acute understanding of the situation and determined efforts to ensure the opportunity was not lost. His vision and capabilities to make bold decisions are redefining the new India, where the youths are seemingly more confident in taking risks. Modi has always stressed that the government must plan for India for the coming 25 years. There is a need to understand the demands and aspirations that would shape the future society. He plans to make India the third-largest economy and bring it into the category of developed nations within 25 years[1]. That is why Amrit Kaal is Kartavya Kaal for everyone, where every Indian has to work hard to realise this dream.

We have already seen how digital infrastructure has been launched to provide high-speed internet to every citizen. These have been expanding the economic activities and opening new employment opportunities, as explained in the chapter on Digital India. The government has been making a record investment in developing a massive physical infrastructure on land, water and air to boost private entrepreneurship.

According to Modi, infrastructure development is the driving force of the country's economy. He asserted that India will achieve its target of becoming a developed nation by 2047. The Asian Infrastructure Investment Bank (AIIB) Vice President (Investment Operations) and Chief Investment Officer, Dr D J Pandian, has underlined that India's infrastructure requirement is 'unimaginable'. He hailed PM Modi for the infrastructure push[2]. Modi has been trying to mobilise resources to expand infrastructure in roads, railways, waterways and airways.

The achievements of the two terms in office are no less. The statistics prove that the pace has picked up in priority areas. For example, nearly 3.75 lakh km of new roads have been built in the villages, the length of national highways has increased from 90,000 km to 1.46 lakh Km, and the length of four-lane national highways has increased 2.5 times. The length of the high-speed corridor has increased from 500 km to 4,000 km.

Also, the number of airports has doubled from 74 to 149. The cargo-handling capacity at major ports of the country has doubled, and the number of broadband users has increased 14 times. Nearly 2 lakh village panchayats of the country have been connected with optical fibre, and more than 4 lakh common service centres have opened in villages.

The metro facility, earlier limited to only 5 cities, has now expanded to 20 cities. More than 25,000 km of railway tracks have been laid. Indian Railways is going to be 100 per cent electrified soon. More than 1,300 railway stations are being transformed under Amrit Bharat

Station Scheme. Close to 10,000 Km of gas pipeline has been laid in the country to provide gas through metered pipes[3].

We will make a detailed analysis of these developments in this chapter. But let us first try to understand what Modi has done to plug the loopholes in the system. A thoughtful Prime Minister, which he is, he has launched the Gati Shakti scheme for coordination and effective implementation of all the infrastructure investments.

Gati Shakti Scheme or Masterplan

It is a game-changing decision since it will save a lot of time otherwise wasted in getting clearances from the various connected ministries, and real-time project evaluation would be done regularly.

Modi understood India needed a never-before kind of infrastructural push to prepare itself for the coming years. With this aspiration, the government decided to spend more than Rs 100 lakh crore in the coming years. All the major infrastructural projects have been brought under the Gati Shakti Masterplan launched in October 2021.

The Gati Shakti masterplan would coordinate infrastructural needs in seven prominent areas called seven engines– 1. Railways 2. Roads 3. Ports 4. Waterways 5. Airports 6. Mass Transport 7. Logistics Infrastructure. The digital monitoring system under the Gati Shakti Scheme will coordinate all the ministries and state governments to ensure multimodal connectivity without time or cost overruns.

It would not be wrong to describe Gati Shakti as a digital platform to bring together 16 ministries, including Railways and Roadways, for better coordination and implementation of the various infrastructure projects.

On India's 75th Independence Day (2021), Modi announced that he would launch Gati Shakti to ensure the government's plan to spend Rs 100 lakh crore was executed most efficiently. After two months of the announcement, Gati Shakti rolled out on 13 October.

The scheme was in Prime Minister Modi's thought process, and he had spoken about it in his Independence Day speeches in 2019 and 2020. It takes time to develop an integrated system to ensure that such a massive exercise is carried out in the most planned manner to avoid delay and cost overruns–something that ails most government projects. There has been a 20 per cent cost overrun and a three-year time overrun in government infrastructure projects. A lot of money would be saved if these were reduced.

Mahatma Gandhi spoke of trusteeship. It means those in power over government resources must spend it in a way that is not wasted, and every penny must be accounted for. The government money, collected from people as taxes, must be spent judiciously to maximise its benefits to society. This thought has been guiding the vision of the prime minister.

It intends to take the country away from ad hoc measures and enforce better resource planning and management, better integration of efforts of all nodal departments and efficiency in government spending.

If we asked anyone on the street about his thoughts on the government, he would use words such as 'inefficient', 'slow', 'tardy', etc. The work goes at a snail's pace, without any accountability, and it appears that the government is doing a favour while undertaking any work. Even after years, the signage of 'Work in Progress' refuses to go.

Even in the capital Delhi, roads and bridges are perpetually under repair or construction, causing a lot of inconvenience and despair to the common man. Why can't the government set its house in order, and give a definite timeline to remove the uncertainty?

To work on the economies of scale, the country must plan big and for the long term. The infrastructure must be planned for at least the upcoming 25 years so that the roads are not perpetually under construction, building bridges does not take years, and big projects do not get delayed due to lack of environmental clearance.

Gati Shakti would change this image by bringing in pace and efficiency. It would be done by breaking the silos in which various departments of the government work disjointedly. Since the government is one, all its departments must work in perfect coordination, guided by unified action towards a common goal. The Prime Minister has always spoken against the practice of various government departments working in silos. Therefore, the new buzzword in the Modi government that propels Gati Shakti is 'break the silos' for better governance.

Modi has aptly said, 'Just as we have been successful in taking the government facilities in the country to the right beneficiary faster with the power of the JAM trinity–Jan Dhan-Aadhaar-Mobile–Gati Shakti will do the same work in the field of infrastructure. It is coming up with a holistic vision from infrastructure planning to execution.'[4] Needless to say, the introduction of JAM has helped the government save Rs 2.75 lakh crore that used to be lost due to various leakages in the delivery system.

The situation worsens when one government department fights another in the courts. 'Sometimes, two departments of the same government confront each other in court to settle disputes by paying money to lawyers. This is not a healthy situation. It needs to change. And the way to do it is to sit together and in detail, under a broad vision, think about the roles each department needs to play and what results we can bring', Modi had said[5].

The infrastructure projects of the ministries and state governments, such as Bharatmala, Sagar Mala, inland waterways, dry/land ports, UDAN, various economic zones and product-specific clusters, defence corridors, electronic parks, industrial corridors, and agri zones, will be covered under the Gati Shakti Scheme.

A government must optimally respond to modern needs to stay relevant. It cannot lag technologically or in terms of equipment or use of modern IT tools while launching any project. It needs to attract the best minds and help to integrate government efforts through the use of technology. The master plan will use these tools for coordinated infrastructure planning. Digitisation will ensure timely clearances, flagging of issues and better project monitoring.

India needs better connectivity, where roads, rails and ports are symbiotically interlinked. If the cost of transportation is high, the product or produce would also become costly and non-competitive. Similarly, the national highways must be connected to state highways, and state highways to inner city roads and rural roads for complete road connectivity. With better planning, optical fibres and gas pipelines can be laid when road construction is in progress and not after the construction. Similarly, why should railways not be better connected with ports if exports and imports have to become lucrative?

It would help an investor make a much better business plan. For example, while setting up a fertiliser plan, one needs to know if the site has road/rail and communication connectivity. The availability of gas supply would further decide the viability of the plant. Integrated planning would ensure the country has many infrastructure sites that promote growth centres. Also, it would make gas pipelines and communication connectivity easily available to the common man at an affordable price.

The government would create the best infrastructure to promote economic activities since the cost of capital and infrastructure is huge. The government, however, would not run the business. Private players would invest, run their businesses and pay for the government-provided services. They would be able to operate at their maximum potential and maximise profit. The government's kitty would increase as business activities increase, and enable better spending on health, education and other needs of the society. Digital administration would ensure self-governance while the government would have minimal structure, thereby saving a lot on wasteful government expenses.

The multi-modal connectivity will facilitate the movement of people, goods and services from one mode of transport to another. It will achieve last-mile connectivity and reduce travel time. The logistics cost, which is very high at 13 per cent, would go down to international standards of 8 per cent.

Roadways

India has the second-largest road network in the world. The entire road network, including national highways, state highways and other roads, runs into 66.71 lakh km[6]. The national highways play a significant role by providing speed and better connectivity with various state roads. These may be described as the major arteries of the country's economy. It is estimated that close to 87 per cent of passenger traffic and 60 per cent of freight is borne by roadways[7].

Modi would be credited with strengthening these arterial roads by adding 54,858 km of new roads in the last nine years. The length of the highways increased from 91,287 Km in 2014 to 1,46,145 km by November 2023[8]. But, national highways still constitute only two per cent of all the roads, whereas state highways are a percentage more. It means there is a massive need for a further increase to match the infrastructural needs of the coming generation.

The Vajpayee government, during 1998-2004, understood the importance of improving road infrastructure. Hence, the country witnessed a massive road expansion in the four-laning of existing national highways and six-laning of selected major national highways. Vajpayee also worked hard to build rural road connectivity through pucca roads.

He strongly argued that road infrastructure would kickstart the dwindling Indian economy and provide employment to people. He gave the vision of Golden Quadrilateral and the North-South and East-West Corridor. Because of his vision of national infrastructure and development, India celebrates his birth anniversary on 25 December as Good Governance Day. When the BJP-led NDA Government demitted office in 2004, the economy was strong, with a GDP growth of above 8 per cent and inflation at a low of 4 per cent with a foreign exchange reserve of 113 Billion USD (end of March 2004). It was a milestone for India[9].

The national highways witnessed massive expansion under the Vajpayee government. It increased from 49,585 km in 1999 to 65,569 km in 2004. It means close to 16,000 km of national highways were constructed during the NDA regime of 1998-2004. The average speed of road construction during the Vajpayee government was 11-12 km per day, a remarkable improvement from the UPA average (2004-2014) of 5-7.5 km per day.

The Modi government has both speed and scale. Close to 55,000 km of national highways were added in 9 years. The speed was 28.3 km per day, 2.5 times more than the speed during the Vajpayee era[10]. It means Nitin Gadkari, Minister for Road, Transport and Highways, had a determined leadership to acquire further speed. The speed has been increased to 38 km or more per day to reach the target of 2 lakh km of national highways by 2025[11].

The most remarkable road projects have been the Bharatmala Pariyojana and the Sagar Mala Pariyojana. The Bharatmala Pariyojana involves constructing and developing a massive road network to decongest the movement of passenger and goods traffic on critical roads, connect more towns with top-class roads, construct roads in border areas and construct roads that would link to ports. It is a centrally-funded project that includes developing economic corridors and feeder routes, including connecting with the Golden Quadrilateral and the North-South and East-West Corridors.

It includes creating a network of tunnels, bridges, elevated corridors, flyovers, overpasses, interchanges, bypasses, ring roads etc., to reduce distance and increase speed. One key example that has already been built, to much appreciation of people, is the Delhi-Mumbai Express Highway (1,350 km) passing through the Delhi outskirts. The stretch up to Vadodara is already completed. The eight-lane road is a delight to drive on.

The Delhi-Meerut expressway is a 96 km long, 14-lane expressway that makes human imagination possible. It has succeeded in expanding and bringing the NCR closer. Meerut can now be reached within an hour. The roads appear to be putting garland around the map of Bharat (India), hence the name Bharatmala.

India is now known for its highly developed roads that make connectivity possible and speed up economic activities. Anyone driving on these roads is impressed by their quality, ease and majestic ambience.

Every Indian would be proud to know that India's focus on improving roadways has received worldwide recognition. Japanese Prime Minister Fumio Kishida, during his visit to India in 2022, described India as 'one of the most ambitious in the world'. In 2021, US Secretary of State Antony Blinken visited India and described road development as proof of India's commitment to infrastructural development and economic growth. World Bank president David Malpass described it as 'a model for other developing countries'.

Sagar Mala Pariyojana (meaning garland of the ocean) aims at port-led development where better connectivity of roads and ports is to be achieved for a faster movement of goods for sea shipments and vice-versa. It would make complete use of India's seashore and inland waterways. Approximately 95 per cent of our merchandise trade passes through seaports.

A total investment of USD 140 billion (as of 2023) is allotted to set up new mega ports, modernise existing ports, develop 14 Coastal Economic Zones (CEZs) and Coastal Economic Units (CEUs), strengthen connectivity of ports via international heavy goods motorable roads and railways, and develop multi-modal logistics parks[12].

As per the Sagar Mala National Perspective Plan released in 2016 at the Maritime India Summit, the project will boost India's merchandise exports to USD 110 billion by 2025 and create about one crore new jobs, including 40 lakh in direct employment[13].

The Sagar Mala project was approved by the Modi government on 25 March 2015, whereby it was decided to prepare a comprehensive plan to develop India's vast coastline of 7,500 km and 14,500 km of navigable inland waterways. It includes the development of an economic corridor of 9,000 km along the coastline, the construction of feeder routes or inter-corridor connecting roads of 6,000 km, the construction of 5,000 km of a national corridor, and the construction of other roads to achieve better inter-connectivity with ports.

Since most freight is carried via roads and railways, it is essential to connect these with modern ports that can handle volumes and reduce the waiting time. The more you wait, the more you lose in business. Waterways are the cheapest means of communication, and better and smart connectivity with ports can enhance trade manifold.

The total cost of constructing 34,800 km of roads in the first phase of Sagar Mala is Rs 5,35,000 crore. It is funded through cess, tolls and additional allocation of resources by the Central government and private investment. The programme would cover all the 577 projects linked to Sagar Mala with an expenditure of more than 8 lakh crore by 2035[14].

At the Maritime India Summit in March 2021, Narendra Modi announced that India would invest USD 82 billion in port projects by 2035. He envisioned the Sagarmala-Sagar Tat Samriddhi Yojana and released the Maritime India Vision 2030. Under the Sagar Tat Samriddhi Yojana, 1,049 projects have been identified, with an estimated expenditure of Rs 3,62,229 crore[15].

A marvel of road infrastructure is the Mumbai Trans Harbour Link Bridge, officially named Atal Bihari Vajpayee Trans Harbour

Link, inaugurated by Modi on 12 January 2024. This 21.8 km, six-lane, elevated highway bridge on the sea connects Mumbai with Navi Mumbai and reduces two hours of travel time to 20 minutes. The world's 12th longest bridge has been constructed for Rs 17,840 crore[16]. The foundation stone was laid on 24 December 2016, and the construction began in April 2018.

Waterways

Developing waterways means focussing on both inland waterways and the sea that connects India through its coastline. Shipping cargo from West Bengal to Chennai through the sea would be easier. The same goes for cargo from Kolkata to Gujarat via roads or railways.

Once, India was a maritime power. The kingdoms of the southern part of India, such as the Cholas and the Pandyas, successfully ventured into the territories of Southeast Asia for its promotion of trade and culture. Shivaji was known for his power to control the sea routes. He had built sea forts to defend the shores and control the coastlines. He had built a fleet of 50 ships that employed 10,000 sailors[17].

With the advent of the Dutch and the British, India has shown how sea power can help control territories and promote trade. With a vast coastline, India has immense potential to emerge as a significant naval power, not only in terms of defence but also in terms of trade and commerce.

It is possible only by caring for the developing ports and linking ports to roads and railways so that the movement of goods would be faster. Even now, most trading is carried out through the sea routes. About 70 per cent of India's total trade is seaborne, happening through 13 major and 205 minor ports[18].

However, it is too less compared to the vast coastline we have of 7,500 km, making it one of the largest exclusive economic zones. It has a much greater potential. But, the need was to understand the importance of seas and develop backwards and forward integration of ports through better coordination and hassle-free movement of goods and services.

The need was to strengthen the entire maritime ecosystem to enable its full potential, not only for trading but also for a blue economy where the country could optimally utilise the natural resources in the seas without endangering the environment.

In 2020, Modi renamed the Ministry of Shipping as the Ministry of Ports, Shipping and Waterways, to work towards this task and to prevent the officials from working in silos. 'With a change in name, there will be more clarity in work', Modi said[19].

We have seen how the government focussed on the Sagar Mala project for p ort-led development, where each port would be connected to the mainland via roads and railways. We have seen how economic corridors are being constructed along the coastline to facilitate industrial activities, movement of goods and warehousing.

The Modi regime has witnessed the evolution of inland waterways as an alternative mode of transportation. Since 2014, the government has invested Rs 5,200 crore, which is 200 per cent more than the investment made in 28 years before the Modi regime[20]. Inland waterways are clean, efficient and economical.

The government passed the National Waterways Act, 2016, which identified and declared 111 inland waterways as National Waterways with a total length of 20,275 km spread over 24 states. The inland waterways have the potential to share the burden of road and rail in terms of freight. The government has announced its plan to operationalise at least 23 waterways by 2030. It has identified 400 investable projects with an investment potential of Rs 2.25 lakh crore[21]. The country would have an investment of Rs 35,000 crore by 2047 to create a network of inland waterways[22].

A multimodal transport system would ensure the same cargo is handled by roadways, railways and waterways, without the need to load-unload from one carrier to another.

Railways

Usually, I do not take the railway because of a busy schedule. It was after almost 10 years that I visited the New Delhi railway station in September 2023, to pick up a friend coming from Chandigarh. I had to wait an hour and thought of strolling on the railway platform. I was stunned by the cleanliness. The tracks were dry, and the station looked much like an airport. I did miss the traditional *kulhad* tea, but it was compensated by the catering places giving a variety of food at a reasonable price.

Indian Railways has witnessed a historic transformation that cannot be missed. The railway stations are relatively cleaner and equipped with wi-fi and LED lights. While it is a unique experience to travel by train because of the introduction of the indigenously-built, fast-moving Vande Bharat trains, the utility of trains as goods carriers has also multiplied.

India had demonstrated its determination to become the first Green Railway in the world by converting all engines into electric engines with zero per cent carbon emission. Approximately 90 per cent of the broad-gauge routes have been electrified. As of June 2023, around 59,096 route Km of the total 65,350 km of broad-gauge line have been electrified. India's target is to electrify the entire stretch of 1,28,305 km of track length, of which 1,02,831 km is running track length, by 2030[23].

A comparative study would help us understand the speed with which the government is working to modernise railways. Close to 20,000 route km rail lines were electrified in the first 70 years of Independence. More than 37,000 route km have been electrified within just nine years, from 2014-23 (till July 2023). The end of this year will see a hundred per cent electrification of the broad-gauge route. Other aspects, such as installing solar lights, and solar cells for power lighting in running trains and replacing old equipment with zero-emission equipment, are slated to be completed by 2030.

One of the most remarkable achievements of the Modi government is the introduction of the fast-moving Vande Bharat trains. Similar to the Shatabdi Express, these trains cover a daily distance of 10 hours to link two cities. As of now, 34 Semi high-speed trains are running as Vande Bharat. They are distinguished by their colour, design and amenities. These trains are equipped with world-class facilities and top safety measures, including the revolutionary *Kavach* technology. These trains make travelling fast, convenient and safe.

The trains are named Vande Bharat to acknowledge the indigenous manufacture–made in India by Indian engineers. Initially, the idea of foreign collaboration was mooted, but the Integral Coach Factory,

Cochin, made it possible at half the cost demanded by foreign players. The Modi government plans to run 400 such trains by 2025, and the budget for 2022-23 has made provision for this, demonstrating the seriousness[24]. Under Vision 2047, the Railways would run 4,500 Vande Bharat trains by 2047[25].

The first train commenced operations on 15 January 2019, covering the distance from Delhi to Varanasi via Kanpur and Prayagraj. Soon, sleeper coaches will also be introduced. The government is also introducing non-AC Vande Bharat trains to make it affordable for the common man.

The first time Modi got a presentation by the Railway Ministry, he spoke about the need for station development, a railway university, faster and cleaner trains and the introduction of new and improved technologies. The Railway University Project, called Gati Shakti Vishwavidyalaya, was established in Vadodara in 2018. The need for speed was already taken care of by the Vande Bharat trains. The introduction of *Kavach*–the anti-collision technology–developed in India is the hallmark of train safety.

Modernisation of railway platforms is going on with breathtaking speed. The country faced a critical issue, not only in terms of the look and comfort but also sanitation. Managing 13,169 passenger trains daily, covering 7,325 railway stations and carrying more than 24 million passengers every day is not a joke.

A crucial complaint by railway passengers has been the lack of hygienic toilets. This complaint does not come from passengers travelling by aeroplane because the aircraft use dry toilets, with a combination of chemical decomposition of excreta and a vacuum flush system. It is now realised that railway journeys would be more pleasant if toilets were clean.

As is the case, sanitation has been a priority of the government. The government experimented by replacing traditional toilets that left the tracks dirty with bio-toilets. It installed 2,58,906 bio-toilets in all long-distance trains. Also, aircraft-style toilets have been introduced in 73,078 coaches.

It has significantly helped in reducing filth and corrosion on the tracks. Earlier, around 2,74,000 litres of human excreta and waste littered railway tracks. It is expected to save a lot of money spent on maintenance, which amounts to Rs 400 crore yearly[26]. It will also save water. It explains why the New Delhi railway station looked clean when I visited it in September 2023.

The government is trying to introduce new bio-toilets equipped with automatic hygiene and odour control systems, touch-free water taps and sensor-powered soap dispensers. Special care has been taken to ensure these are not stolen. The doorways and gangways have also been improved.

These toilets have been introduced in the Rajdhani trains, followed by express and mail trains. The estimated cost of each toilet is Rs 2.5 lakh, and the government has ordered the installation of these toilets in 6,000 coaches every year.

Another defining feature in the facelift of the railways has been the modernisation of all railway stations to give them modern facilities, such as lounges, waiting areas, shopping malls, eateries, landscaping etc., much like airports. In some cases, the government has adopted PPP mode to increase the participation of private players. It includes a multimodal integration of railway stations with the cities.

Equipping railway stations with newer facilities to give world-class experience to visitors and passengers has been a dream, which was difficult to realise due to bureaucratic bottlenecks and pending clearances. Establishing the Gati Shakti Directorate has ensured faster clearances with no time and cost overruns.

During the Amrit Kaal period (75 years of Independence to 100 years), 1,309 railway stations would be modernised, under the Amrit Bharat Station Scheme launched by Modi on 6 August 2023. Of these, the first 508 train stations across 27 states and union territories would be on priority, with an investment of Rs 24,470 crores. These stations desperately need a complete overhaul to make them fit for the coming generation.

A study by the Railway Ministry says that passenger traffic would increase by manifold, and close to 80 billion people would use railways by 2030 instead of the current 8 billion[27]. It means capacity expansion to carry the load and to tackle the high-tech, fast-moving trains.

Many eyebrows were raised when the Modi government merged the Railway Budget into the General Budget and abolished the practice of a separate budget for the Railways in 2017. Modi had ended a practice of 92 years. Some critics remarked that it would lead to a deterioration of the Indian Railways.

They believed that the practice started in 1924, had its own merits. But they failed to understand that the new government was laying the foundation for a new tradition that would steer India towards a new course and be able to match up to the expectations.

A massive expansion of railways needs massive funding and gross budgetary support to become world-class. The merger would help the presentation of a unified budget. The merger facilitates better planning and coordination for multimodal transportation. It offers more elbow room to the Ministry of Finance for better allocation of resources during the mid-year review. The actions have shown that the decision has brought the railways on the right track.

Freight: Understanding the revolutionary changes in Indian Railways under Modi would not be possible unless one understands the movement of goods by trains, commonly called freight. Railways form the backbone of the economy. A robust movement of goods indicates a healthy economy. An increase in demand for more racks means an increase in economic activities.

As statistics would show, 5,04,601 racks operated in 2022-23. It was an all-time high figure. The Prime Minister tweeted on this landmark, 'Encouraging numbers, indicating our strides in logistics and economic momentum.'[28] The freight revenue in April 2023 was Rs 13,893 crore, compared to Rs 13,011 in April 2022. There was a growth of 7 per cent.

It was possible due to the railways improving the ease of doing business by giving competitive rates and better facilities, thereby attracting business from both conventional and non-conventional sources. The introduction of information technology and transparency in operations has also increased trust.

The biggest change, however, is the construction of dedicated freight corridors for a faster and more efficient movement of goods across the country. These corridors are a network of broad-gauge railway lines exclusively meant for the goods trains. The Dedicated Freight Corridor Corporation of India (DFCCI) manages these corridors.

But for the promptness with which the railways ensured freight movement across the country, the COVID-19 crisis would have multiplied manifold. Have we ever wondered why there was no food crisis despite the national lockdown?

The reason is the Indian Railways that continued to function uninterrupted. The average freight movement speed had increased from 20-25 kmph to 40-45 kmph, but during the COVID-19 pandemic, it could run even faster, at 90 kmph, since passenger movement was almost zero and the tracks were empty. Most movements happened at night and did not allow any shortage of essential commodities.

Three Railway Corridors

The country will witness one of the biggest expansions of railways in the coming years. In its Interim Budget for 2024-25 the Modi government announced the implementation of three Railway Corridors: (i) energy, mineral, and cement corridors, (ii) port connectivity corridors, and (iii) high traffic density corridors[29].

It will ease the transportation of minerals and cement from one part of the country to another, within a short time and at a reasonable cost. Better connectivity to ports will boost exports and bring down the logistics cost. For areas with high-density passengers, a special corridor is planned to decongest and maintain service and speed.

The government has already increased the capital expenditure from about Rs 10 lakh crore to Rs 11 lakh crore. The corridors would be financed with this money and implemented under the Gati Shakti Scheme.

Bullet Trains

The railway story would not be complete without a brief mention of the introduction of fast Bullet Trains, which has caught the imagination of travellers. After removing the bottlenecks in implementing such a massive project, India's first Bullet Train that would run between Ahmedabad and Mumbai would be completed in 2026.

The ambitious project was launched in 2017, jointly by Modi

and his Japanese counterpart, the late Shinzo Abe. Modi outlined his vision in the following words, 'To grow one needs to expand his dreams and decide his strength to achieve that. It's new India which has to fly high…Bullet train is a project that will provide pace to development. Along with new technology it will also bring results faster.'[30] The project was to be completed in 2022 at an estimated cost of Rs 1.10 lakh crore.

Shinzo Abe laid the foundation stone for the project and described it as an extension of the strong bond between the two countries and a symbol of a new India. Japan promised a loan of Rs 88,000 crore at an interest of 0.1 per cent. Abe had said, 'I hope to enjoy the beauty of India through the windows of bullet train when I come to India in a few years.' He did not live to realise this dream, but millions of Indians would be able to realise this dream. When completed, the train would cover a distance of 508 km in two hours, and the project would cost Rs 2 lakh crore.

Due to a time overrun in land acquisition in Maharashtra, the COVID-19 pandemic and the delay in the finalisation of the contracts, it took five and a half years for land acquisition and award of the contract. The National High Speed Rail Corporation Limited (NHSRCL) is now operating the project in full gear. Formed as a Special Purpose Vehicle, the NHSRCL was incorporated in 2016 to finance, construct, maintain and manage the High-Speed Rail Corridor in India. There was equity participation by the Ministry of Railways and the Maharashtra and Gujarat state government. In fact, 100 per cent land acquisition and 100 per cent contracts have been awarded. A marvel under this project is the construction of a 7 km underwater sea tunnel.

Many countries, such as France, Japan and China, have been using bullet trains for many years for daily commutes. India plans to have such bullet trains between Delhi and Mumbai, Mumbai and Chennai, and Mumbai and Kolkata. It would offer the most eco-friendly mode of transport to people.

Airways: Journey from *Hawai* Chappal to *Hawai Jahaz*

The biggest challenge facing airways is making air travel affordable for the common people, encouraging them to travel by air and reducing dependence on the already overburdened railways. The twin challenges have been improving air connectivity between Indian cities and encouraging people to use it by making it more affordable and competitive.

When the Prime Minister launched the UDAN (Ude Desh ka Aam Nagrik) Scheme at Shimla and the Nanded-Hyderabad and Kadapa-Hyderabad sectors on 27 April 2017, he fuelled a revolution in the aviation sector to connect smaller cities other than metropolitan cities and bring air travel within the reach of the common man.

The policy paper in 2015 said that India had the potential to become the third-largest aviation market in the world if the 30 crore middle-class population would use airways at least once a year. This number has become increased now, and the UDAN scheme has been trying to fulfil this dream.

While launching this unique initiative, Modi said that the aviation sector was no longer the domain of the select few, 'The aviation sector in India holds opportunities. The lives of the middle class are transforming, and their aspirations are increasing. Given the right chance, they can do wonders.'

Addressing the Parivartan rally in Shimla, Modi spoke about his aviation dream. 'I want to see a common man wearing a chappal on the ground to ride a plane. UDAN is for people who want to travel long distances at cheaper prices. To fly under UDAN, one will be required to spend Rs 6 per km. This will be cheaper than the taxis.'[31]

UDAN is a first-of-its-kind scheme in the world. Under this scheme, 70 domestic airports would be connected through affordable flights. The airfare has been capped at Rs 2,500 for a one-hour journey of 500 km on fixed-wing aircraft and a 30-minute journey on helicopters.

These would include 27 fully-served, 12 under-served and 31 unserved airports. Of these, 17 airports are in the North, 12 in the East, 6 in the North-East, 11 in the South and 24 in the West regions. The scheme will be reviewed after 10 years of operation.

The scheme has shown great potential. Although flights have commenced on only 475 of the 1,154 allotted routes, the response has been encouraging. In 2018, about 2,63,000 passengers had travelled under this scheme. In 2023, this number had reached the figure of one crore. A delay in the land allocation by state governments, time taken to modernise airports, unavailability of aircraft etc., have slowed down the process, but the government is determined to make air travel affordable and safe.

Imagine the traffic this scheme would get once fully operational. The government is trying to plug the loopholes and rectify the problems to encourage larger participation. The entire process will be streamlined by 2026. The traffic would increase significantly in four years by which the scheme will be fully functional. The more than 8 billion train trips per year in the country are slated to get converted into over 1 billion flying trips. Experts predict it will happen by 2040[32].

Lifeline UDAN services during the COVID-19 pandemic emerged as a saviour. It operated 588 flights to transport essential medical supplies to various regional centres and saved lives. Small aircraft and helicopters were deployed for faster distribution of vaccines in far-flung areas.

A significant achievement in the airways sector is the expansion of airports across the country. In 2014, India had only 74 airports. In 2023, the number went up to 149. It includes 30 international airports and 107 domestic airports. The plan is to build second airports in the populated cities to decongest the traffic. 6 such airports are to be constructed by 2030, 15 by 2040 and more than 30 by 2047[33]. By 2047, Indian aviation is expected to grow at a pace that would support an economy of 20 trillion USD[34].

Aligned with the UDAN scheme, the plan for airport expansion has worked well. The number of aircraft has increased from about 400 in 2014 to 723 in 2023. To cope with the increasing traffic, Digi Yatra has been launched for domestic passengers. It ensures seamless, hassle-free and health-risk-free entry of passengers. The government plans to extend this facility, currently available in seven major airports, to other airports, as well.

Such a massive task was not possible without private participation. The role had to change from being a regulator to a facilitator, along with a change in mindset. The Airports Authority of India, which operates airports, has decided to increase its managerial role and provide services such as air traffic management and navigating and handling operations, leaving running airports to the private sector.

The privatisation of airports had started much earlier. The Cochin

International Airport was privatised in 1994 and became operational in 1998. However, the Vajpayee government gave it a spurt in 1998 when it decided to privatise the Delhi and Mumbai airports. In September 2003, the NDA government, under Vajpayee, cleared the proposal and evolved a process for joint venture participation. The idea of creating world-class airports was shaped, and the government was to look after its security and air-traffic control.

The UPA government, which came to power in 2004, realised the benefits of the decision and continued with the process. Finally, Delhi and Mumbai airports were privatised in 2006. In 2013, the UPA tried to push airport privatisation but could not succeed. Even tenders were floated for privatising six airports–Chennai, Kolkata, Ahmedabad, Jaipur, Lucknow and Guwahati–but these could not fructify.

The process, started primarily by the Vajpayee government, was given a push by the Modi government since the BJP had the ideological belief that the government must withdraw. The Modi government had faced stiff opposition to its decision to privatise and had to put on hold its decision in 2015 amidst widespread protests[35].

While the decision to privatise four airports–Kolkata, Ahmedabad, Jaipur and Chennai–was dropped, a decision was taken for private participation in the organisation and management of Ahmedabad and Jaipur airports on a pilot basis.

A major privatisation decision was taken in 2018 when bids were floated for privatising six airports–Ahmedabad, Jaipur, Lucknow, Guwahati, Trivandrum and Mangalore. In February 2019, all the airports were given to the Adani Group, who won the bidding. It happened under the Atmanirbhar Bharat Abhiyaan[36].

In 2023, the government announced the list of 25 airports to be privatised by 2025. The decision was taken in December 2022. It will be done under the PPP mode, and one big airport will be clubbed with a smaller one to maintain parity.

The decision has helped the government mop up additional resources needed for augmenting infrastructure for India in future. The Civil Aviation Ministry is looking forward to mobilising Rs 20,000 crore through asset monetisation.

Air India Privatisation: The biggest decision of the Modi government has been to privatise Air India–the national carrier with the logo of Maharaja in a welcoming gesture. Many emotions are attached to the airline since it was the only national airline.

Sadly, the airline had become chronically sick and loss-making. Any organisation unable to cope with the changing realities would die out. The same happened with Air India, and the government needed to spend Rs 100 crore yearly to keep it running.

While it enjoyed its pride in a closed economy because of government monopoly, it started bleeding once private players entered the aviation sector and gave attractive offers to consumers. The system in the government takes time to change, adversely affecting the manoeuvrability and efficacy in operation. Finally, the airline started running into losses.

It was then forced to run at taxpayers' money. The situation could not have gone for long with many private players entering the business of running aircraft. The issue was how long the government could fund a loss-making operation.

All experts and decision-makers knew that the airline would need privatisation to survive in a competitive world, but no one was ready to take the bull by the horns since there was prestige associated with having a national carrier, and the move could hurt politically. Also, there was the issue of managing workers who feared retrenchment. However, the biggest issue was finding the right buyer.

Although the decision to privatise was taken during Modi's first tenure as the Prime Minister, the renewed and stronger mandate in 2019 ratified his desire to privatise the loss-making Public Sector Undertakings (PSUs). Modi could make any decision, and people would know it was taken in the best interest of the country. In his last tenure, Modi had justified the decision to sell Air India and other loss-making PSUs. That it could not be sold was a matter of timing and process. He stressed that the government had taken all the decisions with utmost sincerity[37].

When the Secretary of the Department of Investment and Public Asset Management (DIPAM), Tuhin Kanta Pandey, announced that 'Talace Pvt Ltd won the bid to own 100 per cent of government stake in

Air India', it was a moment of triumph for the TATA Group since the airline was going back to from where it had begun in 1932. Talace is a wholly-owned subsidiary of TATA Sons.

The public also heaved a sigh of relief since TATA is one of the most trusted brands in the country. It was an assurance that the airlines would run well and the employees would be taken care of without any compromise on patriotism.

The reserve price for the bid was kept at Rs 12,906 crore, and the debt was Rs 15,300 crore. The TATA won the bid by quoting Rs 18,000 crore. The deal included a 100 per cent stake in Air India and the low-fare unit Air India Express, along with a 50 per cent holding in the ground-handling company AISATS. The transaction excludes non-core assets, including land and buildings, valued at Rs 14,718 crore. This is to be transferred to the Union government's Air India Asset Holding Limited (AIAHL)[38].

Air India is on its way to recovery with an improvement in its market share. It has already placed orders for 470 planes to increase its fleet. It is on a hiring spree to spruce up its manpower. The new excitement in the aviation sector is hard to miss.

Privatisation of PSUs

When the Prime Minister said that the government has no business to be in business, he articulated the BJP's philosophy regarding privatising the government undertakings. It is the government's responsibility to support and facilitate business, and there is no need for the government to run the business itself–Narendra Modi said in a webinar on privatisation organised by the DIPAM in February 2021[39].

The government should focus on the welfare of people and project development, he said, further adding that 'when the government monetises, that space is filled by private sector bringing in investment and best global practices'. Sick PSUs burden the economy and should not be run merely because of legacy.

Since Prime Minister P V Narasimha Rao opened the economy in the 1990s and championed a larger role for the private sector, it was accepted that there was no going back from liberalisation. During the Vajpayee era, it gained momentum when Atal Bihari Vajpayee announced a gradual disinvestment of PSUs in non-strategic sectors.

The UPA government, under Prime Minister Dr Manmohan Singh, could not go back since Singh was the architect of privatisation under Narasimha Rao. However, due to a lack of ideological commitment and pressure from the Left parties, the government kept toying between restructuring, disinvestment and privatisation.

The country was waiting for Modi to take the task forward. He was convinced that the loss-making PSUs must be divested to allow private sector participation. He had successfully experimented with this when he was the Chief Minister of Gujarat and knew that the Nehruvian description of these as temples of modern India must be dismantled to suit the needs of the rapidly changing society.

This is how Modi gave a strong justification, 'There was probably a rationale for setting up PSUs when they were originally established, but this was no longer the case in many areas. So, for instance, though Telecommunications remains a strategic sector in even the new definition, setting up an MTNL probably made sense when there were no private firms supplying telecom services, as the number of private sector telecom providers rose, the need for an MTNL came down dramatically.'

Several PSUs had become a burden over time because of recurring losses whose funding would have drained the state of further resources. Stressing that the poor have the first right over the government resources, he pointed out that money could be rather spent on building new schools, roads and hospitals.

It was not a case of selling the family silver. The monetisation of assets was to create more infrastructure to enable businesses to grow and empower youths to work in shaping their destiny. If not privatised, these PSUs were likely to close down since there was a limit beyond which the government would not fund because of pressing demands on the resources for the expansion of facilities.

This ideological clarity led to the formation of the DIPAM in 2016, two years after Modi came to power. Announcing the decisions, the then Finance Minister Arun Jaitley clarified that disinvestment was not limited merely to strategic sales or dilution of government stake but also to monetise assets owned by PSUs, such as land, manufacturing units etc. The job of identification of Central PSUs for strategic sale was to be done by the Niti Aayog in place of the Disinvestment Commission. It set the ball rolling for further clarity in approach.

In February 2021, the government announced an Atmanirbhar package for strategic and non-strategic sectors that evolved a clear-cut road map. It included the disinvestment of Air India, Shipping Corporation of India, IDBI Bank, privatisation of two PSUs and one General Insurance Company, IPO of LIC, and setting up a Special Purpose Vehicle to monetise the idle land owned by the PSUs. The government decided to mobilise Rs 1,75,000 crore by the end of 2021-22.

The government clarified that the presence of the PSUs in the following strategic sectors would be minimal:

I. Atomic energy, Space and Defence
II. Transport and Telecommunications
III. Power, Petroleum, Coal and other minerals
IV. Banking, Insurance and financial services

In the non-strategic sector, these PSUs were to be either privatised or closed[40].

The biggest step was to launch the IPO of LIC in 2022 to mop up the additional resources. A miniscule 3.5 per cent of the total share was offered and the government could mobilise Rs 21,000 crore. Such is the brand, trust of people and market[41].

As of now, the government is not privatising the LIC but for how long is difficult to say. Many private insurers have come into the market offering better services and quick claim disbursal. There will be a strong argument against privatisation if the business can compete and run profitably. But can it be competitive and efficient in days to come and meet the challenges from new players?

The trend to privatise emanates from the need to finance the infrastructure and welfare measures that would add to productivity. Another option is to incur debt, but that would be counter-productive in the long run. So is the case with banks. After mergers and consolidation of banks, the government has already decided to have a fresh look at its banking privatisation strategy. Better revenue collections through taxes, including the GST and the banking, improving upon its performance have given a breathing space.

Setting the Golden Bird Free

To combat corruption, it is the sacred duty of the government towards its people.
–Narendra Modi

The bird of the Indian economy came out of the cage of enslavement and soared high into the sky. We have seen how the Modi government achieved an economic turnaround despite unsurmountable challenges. What we see as the larger picture would not have been possible if Modi had not taken decisive steps to send the right message to those trying to subvert the system. They believed that after the initial big talk about tackling corruption and black money, the government would return to easy ways. The Prime Minister has been working on a mission–to remove the fetters and defang the economy from the clutches of vested interests by creating a level playing field. Removing corruption by creating better institutions is the Modi Guarantee.

Demonetisation: Decisive Attack on Black Money

Call it a surgical strike against black money or Operation Clean up, the entire country was shocked beyond disbelief when Prime Minister Narendra Modi announced the demonetisation of Rs 500 and Rs 1000 at 8 pm on 8 October 2016. Those who had stacked their black money in these denominations came on the verge of a collapse, and those who did not have unaccounted money rejoiced at the momentous decision.

The big divide between the honest and the corrupt surfaced, where the poor thought that every rich person driving a flashy car had black money. Many instances were reported where poor people booed the rich and banged their cars.

In one stroke, Modi strengthened the trust of the honest people. They used to sulk when people with ill-gotten money flourished without being caught. All their money was reduced to dust now. They could deposit the money in the bank, but they knew every penny would need to be accounted for. All such notes were to be deposited in banks till 30 December 2016.

Fuel pumps, government hospitals, railways, airline bookings, state government-recognised dairies, ration stores and crematoriums were allowed to take these notes till 2 December. These special concessions ensured that life was not disrupted. The Prime Minister announced such exceptions only for 72 hours, which was subsequently extended till 24 November to avoid causing inconvenience to people.

Citing an example from the economic grouping of BRICS countries (Brazil, Russia, India, China and South Africa) that aspired to become a big economic bloc, Modi said the 'I' in BRICS was shaking. But, within two and a half years, India has registered its presence as a bright spot in the global economy. '*Mool* mantra in the journey of *vikas* is *sabka sath sabka vikas*. Empowering the poor has been the motto of this government', he said in his historic speech on 8 November 2016[1].

Let us reproduce every significant word spoken that night at 8.15 pm:

> The evil of corruption has been spread by certain sections of society for their selfish interest. They have ignored the poor and cornered benefits. Some people have misused their office for personal gain. On the other hand, honest people have fought against this evil. Crores of common men and women have lived lives of integrity. We hear about poor auto-rickshaw drivers returning gold ornaments left in the vehicles to their rightful owners. We hear about taxi drivers who take pains to locate the owners of cell phones left behind. We hear of vegetable vendors who return excess money given by customers.
>
> There comes a time in the history of a country's development when a need is felt for a strong and decisive step. For years, this country has

felt that corruption, black money and terrorism are festering sores, holding us back in the race towards development.

> Terrorism is a frightening threat. So many have lost their lives because of it. But have you ever thought about how these terrorists get their money? Enemies from across the border run their operations using fake currency notes. This has been going on for years. Many times, those using fake five hundred and thousand Rupee notes have been caught and many such notes have been seized.
>
> Brothers and sisters, On the one hand is the problem of terrorism; on the other is the challenge posed by corruption and black money. We began our battle against corruption by setting up an SIT headed by a retired Supreme Court judge, immediately upon taking office[2].

He listed the various measures that the government had taken to curb black money and, finally, announced:

> To break the grip of corruption and black money, we have decided that the five hundred rupee and thousand rupee currency notes presently in use will no longer be legal tender from midnight tonight, that is 8 November 2016. This means that these notes will not be acceptable for transactions from midnight onwards. The five hundred and thousand Rupee notes hoarded by anti-national and anti-social elements will become just worthless pieces of paper. The rights and the interests of honest, hard-working people will be fully protected. Let me assure you that notes of one hundred, fifty, twenty, ten, five, two and one rupee and all coins will remain legal tender and will not be affected.

He gave a 50-day window to people for depositing notes of such denominations in banks or post offices. He also assured them there was no need to panic since the money would remain theirs. However, due to new currency coming into circulation, there would be a check on withdrawals. 'There will be a limit of Rs 10,000 per day and Rs 20,000 per week. This limit will be increased in the coming days.'

Modi said he knew there would be difficulties and appealed to common people to stay firm and resolute:

> So, in this fight against corruption, black money, fake notes and terrorism, in this movement for purifying our country, will our people not put up with difficulties for some days? I have full confidence that every citizen will stand up and participate in this "*mahayagna*". My dear countrymen, after the festivity of Diwali, now join the nation and extend your hand in this *Imandaari ka Utsav*, this *Pramanikta ka Parv*, this celebration of integrity, this festival of credibility.

These inspiring words were enough to motivate every citizen to support their Prime Minister and his vision.

Not many were aware of this decision, not even Finance Minister Arun Jaitley or RBI Governor Urjit Patel. They came to know of the move only during the Board meeting of the RBI in the North Block at 5.30 pm. The Ministers in the Modi Cabinet came to know when briefed about the decision an hour before the announcement. They were not allowed to carry mobile phones to prevent leakage of information.

'When I went to the cabinet meeting, I had no idea such a big move would be announced. The finance minister winked at me and smirked. That's when I realised something is on', Union Minister Piyush Goyal revealed a month later[3].

The official agenda of the meeting was innocuous–MoUs between India and Japan. Ministers were called to the meeting venue from 6.45 pm to 9 pm. Modi left the cabinet meeting in the middle to meet President Pranab Mukherjee to brief him about the decision[4].

Secrecy was the key to such a decision since leakage of information could have allowed hoarders of black money to transfer these to safe destinations within no time. Modi addressed the nation[5]:

> Secrecy was essential for this action. It is only now, as I speak to you, that various agencies like banks, post offices, railways, hospitals and others are being informed. The Reserve Bank, banks and post offices have to make many arrangements at very short notice. Obviously, time will be needed. Therefore, all banks will be closed to the public on 9th

> November. This may cause some hardship to you. I have full faith that banks and post offices will successfully carry out this great task of national importance. However, I appeal to all of you to help the banks and post offices to meet this challenge with poise and determination.

The RBI started printing Rs 2000 notes at least three months before the demonetisation. In reply to an RTI query, it was informed that the printing of Rs 2000 notes began on 22 August 2016, while the printing of the new Rs 500 notes began on 23 November 2016[6].

It means some people may have been aware of the new notes being printed, but no one knew it was in anticipation of the note ban since the government might have wanted to introduce a new currency.

The chest containing the new Rs 2000 notes reached the banks on the night of 8 November to mitigate the suffering. People could queue up and get their old notes exchanged for immediate needs. The Prime Minister knew about the problems arising and had prepared thc public for this:

> Time and again, I have seen that when the average citizen has to choose between accepting dishonesty and bearing inconvenience, they always choose to put up with inconvenience. They will not support dishonesty...let us ignore the temporary hardship; let us join this festival of integrity and credibility; let us enable coming generations to live their lives with dignity; let us fight corruption and black money; let us ensure that the nation's wealth benefits the poor; let us enable law-abiding citizens to get their due share[7].

On the issue of who knew about the demonetisation decision, it can be safely concluded that while there was speculation within the bureaucratic and political circle about the possibilities, no one knew for sure about the actual decision and the timing. In November 2016, Union Minister Piyush Goyal said in Rajya Sabha, 'The Board of Governors of RBI took the decision, Cabinet approved it and Modiji announced it.'[8] What Goyal said was the process dutifully followed by the government.

History of Demonetisation

Demonetisation is not new for India. Nor was Narendra Modi the first one to do so. The country witnessed it earlier, in 1946 when the currency notes of Rs 500, 1,000 and 10,000 were taken out of circulation. These were brought back into circulation in 1954 only to be banned finally in 1978.

It was a decision taken by the British government in the context of the Second World War amidst the fear of hoarding and black marketing. It was done in consultation with the then RBI Governor Chintaman Dwarkanath Deshmukh.

Other countries, such as France and Belgium, had taken a similar step, and hence, it could be considered a response to the global situation. These notes were reintroduced in 1954.

The Wanchoo Committee (1971) on tax reforms described black money as a cancer in society. It said 'black money is like a cancerous growth in the country's economy which, if not checked in time, is sure to lead to its ruination.'[9] The Committee said that black money and tax evasion had a 'pernicious effect on the moral fibre of our society'. It puts a premium on dishonesty and shatters the faith of the common man in the 'dignity of honest labour and virtuous living'[10].

The Wanchoo Committee recommended demonetisation as a way to deal with black money. Indira Gandhi was the Prime Minister, and Mr Y B Chavan was the Union Finance Minister. When Chavan took the idea to Mrs Gandhi, she dreaded and said, 'Chavanji, are no more elections to be fought by the Congress Party?'[11]

But the Janata Party government that came to power after opposing the Emergency dared to take the bull by the horns and declared demonetisation in 1978. It was easy for the new government since it had come to power on the issue of fighting corruption and black money. There was widespread appreciation when Prime Minister Morarji Desai announced demonetisation on 16 January 1978. The currency notes of Rs 1,000, 5,000 and 10,000 had become invalid.

An ordinance was promulgated, and the decision was announced in the 9 am news bulletin. The then RBI Governor I G Patel was not in its favour since he believed most black money was held in land, gold and Dollars. 'Thinking that black money is stashed away under mattresses or suitcases is naive', I G Patel reflected in his autobiography *Glimpses of Indian Economic Policy: An Insider's View*[12]. The then Finance Minister H M Patel termed it 'not worthwhile' as he believed it would cause a lot of hardship to the common man. He stressed the urgent need to address the factors leading to the generation of black money–high tax rates, controls and corruption[13].

The efforts did not yield much since only a small percentage, 0.6 per cent, of notes, was held in such high denominations. The banks and the government held around 45 per cent of these notes, and 85.6 per cent of Rs 145.42 crore held in high denominations came to the RBI for conversion into the new currency[14].

The situation was starkly different in 2016 when Narendra Modi announced demonetisation. First, the high denomination notes were in use and comprised 86 per cent of the currency in circulation[15]. The new Prime Minister had promised stringent steps to tackle black money. His credibility demanded drastic action.

Immediately after coming to power, the government demonstrated its determination by setting up an SIT to probe black money in foreign accounts held by Indians. The Supreme Court asked the government on 1 May to set up, within three weeks, an SIT on black money stashed abroad. The deadline ended on 22 May. An extension of a week was given on the plea of the Centre.

The new Prime Minister took the oath of office on 26 May 2024. The first decision of the first Cabinet of the new government was to set up an SIT following the court orders. The government could have easily bought more time and made a fresh assessment of the situation before setting up the SIT. Its speed and decisiveness demonstrated its earnestness to tackle the issue. Modi earned a lot of appreciation for this.

To comprehend this momentous decision of demonetisation, one must not forget that the new government had come to power with a decisive majority, and Narendra Modi had already emerged as a crusader against corruption and a champion of development. The economic success in Gujarat and three victories in a row have established him as a person of vision, grit and determination, dedicated to doing something good for the country.

Coinciding with Modi's third victory in Gujarat in 2012 was the Anna movement against corruption, launched in 2011. Dr Manmohan Singh's government was defamed because of corruption of some of its ministers. India Against Corruption (IAC), led by Kisan Baburao Hazare (popularly called Anna Hazare), the Bharat Swabhiman movement under Swami Ramdev, and the Rashtriya Swabhiman Andolan led by K N Govindacharya had together launched a movement against corruption. The echo of these efforts was heard in seminars all across the country. The IAC-led movement had made life difficult for those in power. It appeared as if the middle class had risen in revolt.

An offshoot of the Anna movement was the Arvind Kejriwal-led Aam Aadmi Party, which gained traction even as Kejriwal sidelined most leaders of the Anna movement one by one. In the process, Kejriwal lost the opportunity to capitalise on the gains of the movement. While his supporters wanted him to be the Chief Minister of Delhi, they trusted only one man when it came to the post of the Prime Minister. And he was Narendra Modi. Kejriwal, in the initial days, refused to criticise Modi fearing that his supporters would get upset[16].

The public looked for those who could give solutions, but they also wanted to try Kejriwal at a lower level. Modi passed the fire test, emerging as a successful leader in finding solutions. He had introduced IT to ease life and bring in transparency and had vowed to fight corruption. His idea of India, which would be etched in golden words for those who want to know what ideals India should represent, caught the imagination of people.

Various Estimates on Black Money

Various estimates of black money circulated in the media and private circles. Some credible individuals and organisations came out with their calculations. The UPA government, in March 2011, asked three organisations, namely the National Institute of Public Finance and Policy (NIPFP), the National Council of Applied Economic Research (NCAER) and the National Institute of Financial Management (NIFM), to study and find out the extent of India's black money both inside the country and abroad[17].

The Report was submitted to the government during 2014-15. The Report was submitted before the Standing Committee of Parliament but not made public due to its sensitive nature. Some newspaper reports said that the NIPFP estimated the extent of black money to be 72 per cent of the GDP, while the NCAER put the figure at 71-79 per cent of the GDP. The third think-tank gave a different figure, saying it was only 10 per cent of the GDP[18].

In 2010, the Global Financial Integrity (GFI), working in the field of tax havens, said that the cumulative value of illicit assets held by Indians was estimated to be USD 487 Billion by 2008[19]. This report of GFI was authored by former IMF Economist Dev Kar. It was close to 30 per cent of the then GDP of India.

A BJP report released by the party's then Prime Ministerial candidate L K Advani in April 2009 estimated the unaccounted Indian money in Swiss bank at Rs 25 lakh crore. It was based on the assessment by the Washington-based GFI. The BJP task force report was prepared by S Gurumurthy, Ajit Doval, Prof R Vaidyanathan and Mahesh Jethmalani. A statement released by Advani on 29 March 2009 put this figure varyingly between Rs 25 lakh crore and Rs 70 lakh crore[20].

Advani said that even if India got one-third of the tax on this black money of Rs 25 lakh crore, the country could build 2000 Super Speciality Bed hospitals in all 626 districts[21].

Yoga Guru and founder of Bharat Swabhiman Trust (Andolan), Swami Ramdev, had estimated the figure of black money stashed in foreign banks at Rs 500 lakh crore. At the individual level, S Gurumurthy, Dr Subramanian Swamy and K N Govindacharya focussed exclusively on corruption in the Congress and launched a nationwide agitation against corruption. Dr Jayaprakash Narayan of the Lok Satta added his intellectual might to the movement[22]. The big rally at Ramlila Maidan organised by the BSA was attended by more than 100 NGOs and noted activists such as Anna Hazare, Kiran Bedi, Arvind Kejriwal, Ram Jethmalani, K N Govindacharya, Dr Subramanian Swamy and others[23].

All these efforts led to India witnessing an unprecedented anti-corruption movement that gave rise to Indian Against Corruption under Anna Hazare in 2011. It launched an agitation through fast-unto-death at

Jantar Mantar on 5 April 2011. The entire middle class appeared agitated at the extent of corruption that prevailed during the UPA regime.

The major corruption cases in the headlines included the Adarsh Housing Society Scam, Radia Tape controversy, Aircel-Maxis case, CWG scam, 2G scam, Coalgate (Coal allocation scam), Cash for Vote scam, Satyam controversy and AugustaWestland Chopper scam.

At the inauguration of the first Interpol global programme on anti-corruption and asset recovery in February 2012, the Director of the Central Bureau of Investigation (CBI), India's premier investigation agency, A P Singh, said that Indians had illegal money amounting to USD 500 Billion (around Rs 24.5 lakh crore) in foreign tax havens[24].

Proffered Solutions

Many individuals and organisations gave various estimates of black money, but none could be authentic. The momentum continued even when the country neared Lok Sabha elections. All the organisations and leading influencers wanted the government coming to power to give solutions to the issue of black money.

Ramdev suggested the withdrawal of Rs 500 and 1000 notes from circulation. Since more than 80 crore people managed to live on Rs 20 per day, there was no need for high denomination notes, he said, adding that withdrawal of such notes would check hawala, black money and bribery[25]. He prescribed the death sentence as a punishment for corruption, something along the patterns of China.

S Gurumurthy had been consistently advocating demonetisation as a way to weed out black money. He termed it 'a surefire way'. In an article in the *Indian Express*, 'Demonetisation: A Surefire Way to Flush Out Black Money', he argued that black money was used for illegal activities such as tax evasion, money laundering and terrorism. Demonetisation would also favour financial inclusion, he argued. He described it as inevitable given the prevailing economic situation[26].

Explaining the situation, he said, 'If the high denomination notes constituted 34 per cent of the total economy in 2004, it went up to 79 per cent in the next six years and touched 86 per cent in 2014.'

In monetary terms, he said:

> What has grown from Rs 1.4 lakh crore (High Denomination Notes) in 2000 to Rs 14.6 lakh crore now would have increased to Rs 30 lakh crore in the next five years, by which time no government could have intervened unless it is willing to pull down the economy. Even otherwise, the economy would have collapsed on its own eventually. So demonetisation is a hedge against a crisis which might collapse the economy eventually[27].

In an interview with Doordarshan News, he said that more than 87 per cent of money in circulation was of high denominations. He strongly advocated demonetisation as a way to deal with the situation[28].

When Modi was the Chief Minister of Gujarat, he advocated demonetisation of Rs 500 and 1000 as a solution to root out black money. Discussing the economy of Gujarat, he spoke about the Indian economy in general and suggested demonetisation as a way out[29].

One name that has cropped up as someone who may have suggested demonetisation to Modi is Anil Bokil, who met Chief Minister Modi in July 2013. He ran a financial think-tank named ArthaKranti from Pune and claimed that he was the one who gave a five-step proposal to Modi, one of which was the demonetisation of high-value notes[30].

It is difficult to say whose idea prevailed. Modi has been an active listener if someone approaches him with a solution. Many people, like Bokil, must have met him and helped frame the idea. Many experts had suggested demonetisation as a probable way to tackle black money. And, as explained by Gurumurthy, the situation was precarious, and no one was ready to discuss it and bring it to the national agenda.

The crux of demonetisation was the decision itself and the way it came as a surprise. It was like the Vajpayee government exploding the nuclear bomb in Pokhran on 11 May 1998. No one knew about the decision, though many spoke about the need and the possibilities.

Demonetisation Goals

As announced by the Prime Minister on 16 November 2023, the decision aimed to–break the grip of corruption and black money, make India a cashless economy, and continue the fight against terrorism and counterfeit currency. The then RBI Governor Urjit Patel said it would encourage people to go cashless and adopt digital transactions. He attested to the objectives outlined by the Prime Minister and said that the steps were well-planned[31].

The then Economic Affairs Secretary and member of the 15th Finance Commission, Shaktikanta Das, added that 'domestic savings lying idle at home will be flowing back into the banking system so that the banks can use that money to give loans at lower interest rates'[32].

The then Finance Minister, the late Arun Jaitley, during his budget speech in 2017, justified demonetisation, terming it as a bold and decisive strike in a series of measures to arrive at a bigger, cleaner and real GDP[33]. 'The real objective of demonetisation was cash-less economy, digitisation, increased tax base and crackdown on black money. In the long run, there will be more formalisation of the economy due to demonetisation', he said at a press conference when the RBI released figures of cash that came back to the system[34].

The RBI announced in 2017 that 99.3 per cent of the high denomination notes had returned to the banks, amounting to Rs 15.31 lakh crore, 10,720 crore less than what was in circulation[35]. At the start of the demonetisation decision, the RBI had put the share of total high denomination notes at 86.4 per cent. Of this 86.4 per cent, 99.3 per cent returned to the RBI.

Disruption and Opposition Tirade

The Opposition questioned the decision of demonetisation since most of the unaccounted currency had returned to the system. What was the need for such an exercise that disrupted the life of the nation without giving anything in return?

Congress leader Mallikarjun Kharge has described it as the 'biggest destroyer of livelihoods and small businesses', and demanded a white paper on the decision. He claimed that the move 'killed aspirations and plunged India's growth'[36].

It was true that life was disrupted. It is also true that people came on the streets and queued up day after day at banks and ATMs to get their old notes exchanged. It is also true that people had problems purchasing raw materials for their production since earlier it happened in cash.

But they endured because they trusted their leader. Many felt they were participating in the cleansing process the country was witnessing. And the Prime Minister was aware of their daily struggle. In his *Mann ki Baat* in November 2016, he acknowledged the difficulties of people and thanked them for actively participating in the cleaning process.

He pointed out to them the intensity of the massive step,

> Across the country, central government, state governments, all units of the local self-government institutions, one lakh thirty thousand bank branches, lakhs of bank employees, over one and a half lakh post offices, over a lakh Bank-Mitras are relentlessly at work, day and night, with complete dedication. In the midst of immense and varied stress, all these individuals are working hard, maintaining a calm and composed demeanour, taking it as a Yagya of Service to the Nation, an attempt towards a great transformation[37].

Demonstrating its concern for the situation, the government responded to the needs of the people and showed flexibility in decision-making. The exigencies of the situation demanded fresh calibration, which was duly given. On the day of the announcement, the government allowed an exchange of only Rs 4,000 per day per person. On November 13, this limit was raised to Rs 4,500 and reduced to Rs 2,000 on 17 November. From 24 November onwards, the exchange stopped, and only deposits were allowed in banks.

From 19 December, there was a limit of Rs 5,000 per day per person on depositing old currency. If people wanted to deposit more, they had to explain the delayed deposit. From 30 December 2016, only the RBI could accept old notes. Even the RBI refused to accept deposits of old notes after 31 March 2017.

A similar calibrated response came in the case of withdrawals. Initially, the withdrawal limit from an ATM was Rs 2,000. The withdrawal limit from a bank was Rs 20,000 per week, with a daily limit of Rs 10,000 (8 November). On 13 November, the cash withdrawal limit from recalibrated ATMs was Rs 2,500. The weekly withdrawal limit was raised to Rs 24,000. On 30 November, the RBI put a limit of Rs 10,000 per month on each Jan Dhan Account.

From 30 January, the cash withdrawal limit on current accounts was removed to facilitate business transactions. From 20 February, the cash withdrawal limit on the savings account was relaxed to Rs 50,000 per day. From 13 March 2017 onwards, the government removed limitation on ATM withdrawals.

The detailed changes in the rules showed that the government was alive to the situation. The limitations on deposits and withdrawals were imposed to control the flow of money and ease transactions. The government wanted the business to pick up fast and return to normal situation hence, the withdrawal restrictions were removed from the current accounts first.

The government also shielded the poor people from getting duped or misguided by vested interests by putting a cap on withdrawals from the Jan Dhan accounts. There were instances where people deposited cash in the Jan Dhan accounts of the poor people in anticipation of getting it back later and subverting the system. However, the opposition interpreted such dynamic reactions from the government as a lack of proper planning before finalising the decisive move. But no government could have calculated each and every move in a situation where it had to fight vested interests and to protect the honest.

Congress leader Rahul Gandhi tried his best to complicate the issues and create confusion rather than appreciate the honest intention or genuineness of the move. He even visited an ATM centre in Delhi and Mumbai to make an impression about anger and mismanagement. However, he did not have many takers. When a person with high-security visits the ATMs, he becomes a centre of curiosity. Few people believed that he had gone there to empathise. Rahul Gandhi even criticised the government for some deaths that occurred while people stood in queue. He exaggerated and alleged that around 100 deaths occurred due to people standing in the queue for the withdrawals or deposits of notes in the banks or ATMs[38].

The government figure puts the deaths at a lower number. On 19 December 2018, Arun Jaitley claimed in the Rajya Sabha that the total number of deaths was four, of which three were state bank officials and one was a customer. Moreover, the government paid compensation to the family members of the deceased[39].

The death figures may have been more than what the government record shows. In reality, it is too far-fetched to link such deaths to demonetisation. People were standing in long queues. Some may have died due to heart strokes or the ailments they were already suffering from. There are many instances where people celebrated demonetisation, and even senior citizens did not complain. The hardship was only for 50 days, as the Prime Minister had informed.

If such irresponsible accusations for political gains become the norm, the government can be held responsible for every non-natural death in the country. But the credit goes to the people who bore the sacrifice with fortitude.

There are times when the benefits far outweigh the expectations. The intended aspirations get clouded due to other windfalls. Normally, when policy-makers take a decision, they have experience from the past to understand the present, but they do not have any retrospective understanding. When 86 per cent of high denomination notes were in circulation, it is natural that invalidating these notes would bring black money into the market.

It is often said that demonetisation has no benefit since it is based on the premise that all black money is in cash. Most people may have stashed their black money in real estate, gold or any tangible investment that the system cannot detect. Hence, many economists have criticised demonetisation on this ground. It would be naïve to assume that Narendra Modi was unaware of this.

Modi declared that the fight was against the ills of corruption inflicted on society in the last 70 years. The feedback and suggestions that Modi got from people for his *Mann ki Baat* after demonetisation wanted him to elaborate further on the fight against corruption. And the Prime Minister was more than keen to satisfy their curiosity. He said it would take at least 50 days for the situation to normalise.

He asserted that the decision was taken in the best national interest. The challenge was whether 125 crore people would succeed in their resolve to fight corruption. He described it as a test by fire and said the country would come out as gold[40].

Modi's resolve was to deliver the India of everyone's dreams.

Delivering a speech in Goa five days after the decisive step, he silenced his critics with his unilateral declaration:

'*Maine sirf pachas din mange hai… December 30 tak mujhe mauka dijiye…Agar December 30 ke baad, koi meri kami rehjaye, koi meri galti nikal jaye, koi meri galat irada nikal jaye, aap jis chaurahe main mujhe khada karenge, main khada hokarke desh jo saza karega, wo saza bhugatne ke liye taiyyar hoon.*' (I have only asked for 50 days. Give me time till 30 December. After that, if any fault is found in my intentions or my actions, I am willing to suffer any punishment given by the country)[41].

He declared many projects in the pipeline to check corruption, including action against *benami* property. He pointed out that although a law against *benami* property was passed in 1988, it was not notified. It was hint to denote that he knew demonetisation alone was not enough. But demonetisation sent a strong message–the decisive fight against corruption had begun.

Many critics questioned the move when 99.3 per cent of the high denomination note returned to the RBI, saying the efforts were futile and wasteful. Let us look at some facts. One indisputable argument is not everything that came into the banking system was white. Now, each Rupee had an address and hence, accountability.

Modi's justification would satisfy critics:

> No one can deny that India suffers from a huge parallel economy. Demonetisation was certainly undertaken to deliver this black economy a body blow, forcing it into the mainstream. However, it was never expected that black money would forever remain hidden and not come back into the banking system. We were, in fact, clear from the beginning that high-value notes should return to the financial system. Why else would we give the banking system so much time and options for the return of the notes? Why else would we allow acceptance of such notes through a host of avenues, ranging from petrol pumps to government dues till 15 December? Hence, a large part of the notes not returning to the banking system was never an expectation or agenda of the government[42].

Those who say the government failed to trace black money worth

Rs 3,00,000 crore are mistaken. The government never gave such an estimate, though private players and economic experts did suggest the figure. Most of the high denomination notes were indeed hoarded by big players, and there was a need to bring them into the market for the economy to grow.
It was acknowledged by the Prime Minister when he said:

> It brings back a substantial portion of the Rs 500 and Rs 1,000 notes that the RBI estimated was hoarded and kept out of the regular transactional economy by people storing them in suitcases and cupboards or under mattresses. More importantly, this has left behind a permanent financial trail. When money returns to the bank, it loses its anonymity. Every rupee leaves a trail. This changes the game as the black money that did not have an address till now has been tagged with one[43].

But what happened to those with unaccounted money when they deposited them in accounts? The government would not spare them unless they explain the source.

We now know who has it, where and when. Holders of black money may hide behind the bank accounts of others, but unlike cash holdings, they can be traced. In this game of hide and seek, they have a few days to hide, but the government has the time, mechanisms and, most importantly, the will to seek them out. More interestingly, with the existence of such trails, the identification of one culprit invariably leads to the unearthing of even larger sources and schemes of corruption. The media is replete with stories of how authorities on the trail of one set of bad elements have been led to the wrongdoings of many more[44].

The immediate fallout of demonetisation, which Gurumurthy described as positive fallout, was to the tune of Rs 4,00,000 crore if 'an average taxation of 25-30 per cent was taken into account'. It would enable the government to launch many more infrastructure projects[45].

The governmental action following demonetisation led to the recovery of thousands of crores of Rupees. In line with Modi's announcement that no one would be spared and that every money deposited would be scrutinised, the government launched Operation Clean Money in January 2017. It sought to e-verify the large cash deposits made from 9 November to 30 December–the period of demonetisation[46]. Later, it clarified that this operation had an impact on black money, widening of tax base and direct tax collection[47].

The agencies had identified 18 lakh suspects after online verification within a record time of four weeks. More than 1.75 lakh crore deposits needed investigation to trace the source of funding. The government kept investigating these accounts, holding people accountable. It announced various levels of taxation post-demonetisation to facilitate those who still held on to their deposits out of fear.

Modi announced that no one would be spared. However, his approach was more tolerant and accommodating while dealing with the common people than when he dealt with people in responsible positions who tried to subvert the system. He took action against hundreds of bank officials for their corrupt practices. All the banking heads were alerted and asked to take action against erring officials. Members from government investigative agencies posed as decoys to identify the rotten apples.

Modi did not wish to punish people as much as he was interested in bringing the black money out into the open. To achieve this, the government announced an amnesty scheme for the black money-holders, fearful of punishment from the law agencies. Towards the end of November 2016, Modi guaranteed that the tax department would not ask for the source of the funds if the depositors of unaccounted cash paid 50 per cent as tax with a quarter of their wealth instead of getting locked up for four years. Revenue Secretary Hasmukh Adhia said, 'Tax department will not ask for the source of the funds deposited in the banks…if the entire income is declared and 50 per cent tax is paid on this.'[48] The government also issued a threat that they could get a penalty of 85 per cent if they did not take advantage of the above system and were caught subsequently[49].

This disclosure scheme was different from the earlier schemes announced by various governments to trace black money and hence, was bound to be more effective. Earlier, people were asked to deposit their black money and detection and punishment were threats. But now, the money had no value, and people had the last chance to come out clean. It is intended to prevent people from using the back door of corrupt practices and risk being caught.

Modi allowed them to salvage their pride by saying that their money would be used to fund various pro-poor schemes under Prime Minister's Garib Kalyan Yojana. Within a year ie., by September 2017, around 21,000 people had disclosed Rs 4,900 crore of black money under this scheme[50].

A research paper with the Reserve Bank of India says that cash worth Rs 1.6-1.7 lakh crore was deposited in non-active accounts during the demonetisation period. Excess deposits of Rs 2.8-4.3 lakh crore accrued to the banking system[51]. Thinking about escaping the law is naïve. According to Union Minister Ashwini Vaishnaw, Rs 1.25 lakh crore of black money has been recovered[52].

The biggest fallout of demonetisation was an increasing formalisation of the economy and penetration of digitisation. The price of real estate came down substantially in major cities, such as Mumbai and Delhi, and the role of cash (unaccounted money) was reduced in high-value transactions[53]. Buying real estate had become affordable for many.

People gradually started using digital payment even for small transactions, such as buying vegetables, as seen in the chapter on digital India. The experts were questioned how Indians would survive without cash in their pockets. However, the habit has changed. Now, people hardly keep cash in their pockets. Digital India has made deep inroads in everyone's life.

Other Steps to Check Black Money

SIT on Black Money

In its first Cabinet meeting on 27 May 2014, the Modi government approved the constitution of the Special Investigation Team (SIT) to implement the decision of the Supreme Court of India. The Apex Court had asked the government to do so for the SIT to probe Indian black money stashed in foreign banks. M B Shah and Arijit Pasayat, ex-judges of the Supreme Court, were to act as Chairman and Vice-Chairperson, respectively.

Other members of the SIT included the revenue Secretary, the Directors of the Central Bureau of Investigation (CBI), the Intelligence Bureau, the Research and Analysis Wing and the Enforcement Directorate, the Chairman of the Central Board of Direct Taxes, and a Deputy Governor of the Reserve Bank of India.

Nominating names for the SIT demonstrated the Modi government's commitment towards unearthing black money. In fact, the Supreme Court appointed the SIT in July 2011. The Congress-led UPA government sat over it for three years. As rightly asked by the Prime Minister, was there anybody the UPA was trying to protect? If the BJP was not serious, it could have sought more time from the Supreme Court and the Court would have granted time since the government was new.

The SIT tried to work diligently and patiently. By 2017, some results were visible. Justice Pasayat said, 'Rs 70,000 crore of black money, including more than Rs 16,000 crore, detected after probe launched into global leaks about Indians stashing funds abroad, has been unearthed through different schemes of the government.'[54]

Treaties on Double Tax Avoidance (DTAA)

It is an instrument to prevent a person from paying taxes in two places: one, to his country of origin, and two, to the country he is working or doing business in. It means paying taxes both to the source country and the residence country. While it helps the person from paying taxes at two places, it allows the resident country to keep tabs on his account since the countries are supposed to share all information about a person's bank account. So, one cannot keep money secretly. One can earn as much and pay tax, but one cannot hide money or maintain unaccounted money.

India has signed a DTAA agreement with 94 countries, including some of the popular tax haven countries where some Indians used to hide their unaccounted money. Some were almost tax-free countries, allowing large deposits without being asked. India has not signed a DTAA with Seychelles, but it has signed a tax information exchange agreement with them[55].

The most talked about tax haven country, which many Indians preferred, was Switzerland. Their money was safe because the bankers operated through a coding system and would not share any information about individual bank accounts. The Modi government has renegotiated a new agreement under which an automatic exchange of information was activated beginning in 2018. It is no longer possible to keep money there without an address.

India has an Automatic Exchange of Information arrangement with 107 countries and shares the same with 78 countries[56]. It has become extremely difficult to stash money abroad unless it has been earned legally.

Legislation to Deal with foreign assets

People with ill-gotten wealth often purchase property in foreign lands to invest their money in these assets. The law of the country did not have enough teeth to bring these people to task. It also enabled these people to acquire citizenship in these countries and escape the law of the land of their origin.

It became a primary way to swindle money using hawala and purchase assets outside the country. Some countries would not ask for the source of the wealth if they complied with the law of the host country. After signing a treaty with some of these countries under a DTAA, as explained above, India needed a law to confiscate these assets or impose taxes and penalties on undisclosed income.

The government passed a law called The Black Money (Undisclosed Foreign Income and Assets) and Imposition of Tax Act, 2015. This Act sought to tackle black money hidden as undisclosed income and assets and to tax such illegal assets.

The Act imposed a 30 per cent tax on such undisclosed income whose value would be computed at market value prevailing at the time of discovery[57]. The Act penalises concealing foreign income and provides for criminal liability for those evading tax concerning foreign income.

The Act gave a one-time opportunity to Indian residents to declare their undisclosed foreign income or assets. For undisclosed income, the person would need to pay 30 per cent as tax and another 30 per cent as penalty. In case of non-declaration of assets or income, the penalty would be three times the value of tax evaded besides the tax of 30 per cent or 90 per cent of the value of the undisclosed assets. The Act also made provision for jail for 3-10 years for wilful evasion.

The government raised a tax demand of Rs 14,820 crore after assessing 368 cases under the black money law as on 31 May 2022, Union Finance Minister Nirmala Sitharaman said in a written reply in Lok Sabha[58]. She also informed that there were 648 disclosures of undisclosed foreign assets worth Rs 4,164 crore during the compliance window for three months after passing the law. Close to Rs 2,476 crore was collected as tax and penalty in such cases[59].

Not disclosing such foreign income or assets can attract a heavy penalty. Recently, the Mumbai Income Tax Appellate Tribunal imposed a penalty of Rs 10 lakh for each year where there was no declaration in the Schedule FA of the ITR of an individual[60]. An exchange of information with foreign countries and the use of digital technology has helped the tax authorities zoom in on the assets of non-complying individuals.

The Fugitive Economic Offenders Act, 2018

There are many instances when an economic offender has run away from India after committing economic crimes and has found refuge in other countries. They have escaped the law with legal proceedings against them in the courts. They have already bought property in a foreign land and can easily get citizenship in such countries, leading a luxurious life with ill-gotten money. Many countries grant citizenship based on investment and give them their protective umbrella unless they are proven economic offenders in some other countries.

While no country would deny citizenship based on their criteria, none of them would like to have criminals as their citizens. But unless they are declared 'criminals' by their country of origin, no legal action is possible against them. While general laws were needed to deal with such a situation, even specific laws were not there to deal with the property of these people who also had to be declared fugitives.

In 2017-2018, the number of fraud cases reported by banks increased from 4,500 cases a year in the past 10 years to 5,835. Due to such frauds, the country's financial institutions suffered a staggering loss of Rs 40,000 crore. As per the Ministry of External Affairs, over 30 people accused of economic fraud with proceedings against them in courts absconded from the country and sought refuge abroad. It also includes high profile individuals such as Vijay Mallya, Nirav Modi and Mehul Choksi[61].

To deal with the situation and because of international covenants that exist, the Modi government enacted The Fugitive Economic Offenders Act 2018, which made a provision 'to deter economic offenders from evading the process of Indian law by remaining outside the jurisdiction of Indian courts, thereby preserving the sanctity of the rule of law in India'[62].

The Act authorised the Director or any other officer not below the rank of Deputy Director to apply in the Special Court to get economic offenders declared an FEO. The reason for such an action needed to be recorded in writing, backed by documentary evidence. Also, the Director or Deputy Director has the authority to confiscate the property of such individuals. However, the Act would apply only in cases where the offence is of Rs 100 crore or more.

The Special Court has the authority to judge a person as an FEO, after which the authorities may confiscate their property if it is *benami* or illegal, even if the assets are abroad. All rights over such properties shall stay with the Union government.

India has been strongly arguing that all countries must cooperate to bring the economic offenders to justice. At a working group meeting of G20 in Delhi recently, India called upon all the G-20 Nations to adopt multilateral action for faster extradition of fugitive economic offenders and recovery of assets[63].

After implementing the Act, the ED booked 19 people, of which 10 were declared FEOs. The list included Vijay Mallya, too. They were involved in a fraud of Rs 40,000 crore. Of these, four have been extradited to India.

As of July 2023, assets amounting to Rs 15,113.02 crore have been confiscated under the PMLA and restituted to public sector banks. Also, assets worth Rs 873.75 crore have been confiscated under FEOA relating to these economic offenders[64].

When Vijay Mallya was declared an FEO in 2019, he approached the Mumbai High Court against the FEO proceedings and sought a stay. However, the court refused. Mallya is facing extradition proceedings in the UK. His days are numbered since extradition is likely anytime because of the emerging consensus among countries that a fugitive should not be allowed to misuse the legal system of a country to save himself from prosecution in his home country[65].

Both Mallya and Nirav Modi, who have defrauded Indian banks, are facing a tough time because of India's consistent pressure on the UK government to extradite both of them to face the Indian legal system where they have committed the crime.

'The British always complain that the moment we have a meeting, the first question PM Modi asks is, where are Vijay Mallya and Nirav Modi?', Senior advocate Harish Salve said while talking about the pressure on the UK government on the issue of extradition[66].

Benami Transactions (Prohibition) Amendment Act 2016

To save taxes, invest ill-gotten money in undisclosed assets and escape the law, some people often held *benami* property. It means a person keeps the property in the name of someone else who may or may not be aware of such transactions. It is entirely financed by the person called the beneficial owner. The person in whose name the property has been purchased is called *benamidar*. There have been some instances where people have bought property in the name of their servants.

During demonetisation, critics said the move would not work since only about 5 per cent of black money was in cash. They pointed out that most of the black money was in assets[67]. Modi said he knew where people kept their black money and would soon wage a war against all forms of black money. The new Act of 2016, which made a lot of changes to the old Act of 1988, intended just that. It sought to attack black money and money laundering.

Because of the criminal liability in the new Act, it cannot be applied with retrospective effect, but it has brought the fear of the law in people. Steps, such as digitisation of records, would help the authorities track all transactions and keep an eye on people trying to dispose of old *benami* property. The new Act would take care of any future transaction. Any person indulging in a *benami* transaction can be jailed for 1 to 7 years, besides a fine of up to 25 per cent of the market value of the property.

Due to loopholes in the old Benami Act of 1988, nothing much was accomplished. The New Act of 2016 plugged those loopholes by detailing the characteristics of a *benami* property. It added 72 sections, gave a detailed description and set up an authority for trying such cases.

Till July 2022, the Income Tax department had attached property worth Rs 18,400 crore under the new Benami Prohibition Act. Under the amended law, notices were issued in 3,175 cases amounting to Rs 19,222 crore. Provisional attachments amounting to Rs 18,401 crore were also made in 2,967 cases[68].

Simplification of Tax Procedures

One of the reasons people try to hide their income is high taxation and unclear procedures, which also lead to a generation of black money. Reducing the taxes and simplifying the process would encourage honest taxpayers to be more tax-compliant. It can be described as an incentive for people to follow the tax laws. These are particularly helpful for small businesses.

New Tax Rate for Domestic Companies

From the financial year 2019-20, a new provision was added to the Income Tax Act that gave domestic companies the option to pay Income Tax at the rate of 22 per cent, subject to the condition that they will not avail of any exemption or incentive. After including cess and surcharge, the effective tax rate for such companies came to 25.17 per cent. Also, such companies shall not be required to pay the Minimum Alternate Tax (MAT).

To encourage manufacturing under the Make in India label, the government allowed any new domestic company incorporated on or after 1 October 2019 to pay Income Tax at the rate of 15 per cent. This benefit is available only to those companies which do not avail any exemption/incentive and commence their production on or before 31 March 2023. Including surcharge and cess, the effective rate came to 17.01 per cent. Also, such companies shall not be required to pay the Minimum Alternate Tax.

Transparent Taxation–Honouring the Honest

To provide a seamless, painless and faceless tax regime, the Prime Minister launched a platform called Transparent Taxation–Honouring the Honest in 2020. Since only 1.5 crore people out of the 130 crore paid taxes, Modi urged that more and more people should pay the taxes to build an *Atmanirbhar Bharat*. It was in line with the government's philosophy of 'Banking the Unbanked, Securing the Unsecured, Funding the Unfunded and Honouring the Honest'[69].

Under the new taxation regime, taxpayers would get faceless scrutiny and faceless appeal where the assessing officer would not know the person he is assessing and the person to assess would not be decided by the human interface. So would be the case with appeals. It would enable a hassle-free interaction with the tax authorities and leave no room for corruption. A structural change was needed to give primacy to honest citizens. The tax structure inherited from the British needed fundamental reforms. Although incremental changes were made in the taxation regime, they did not change the fundamental character. It was crucial to change the compliance-out-of-fear into compliance-out-of-trust-and-easy-procedures.

The department has moved from doubting a taxpayer to trusting him. The department now extends the courtesy that is due to him. The Vivad Se Vishwas scheme has ensured that most cases were settled outside the court. Moreover, the department can go to the High Court only in cases involving Rs 1 crore or more. For approaching the Supreme Court, the limit is Rs 2 crore. The number of cases going for scrutiny by the agency has been reduced from 0.94 per cent in 2012-13 to 0.26 per cent in 2018-19, demonstrating that the government does not work with mistrust in its people[70]. In its Interim Budget 2024, the government announced to drop all the proceedings in disputes involving amounts up to Rs 25,000, giving relief to at least a crore of small taxpayers. Those whose tax demand aggregated to Rs 25,000 up to 2009-10 and those whose amount aggregated to Rs 10,000 from 2010 to 2014-15 have a complete waiver.

While tinkering with the tax structure, such as increasing or decreasing the tax rates, is the routine exercise any government has to do, very few try to clean the system, making it transparent and accountable. The process of tax paying has become simple, and so has the system of returns. A few years ago, it was unimaginable to think that the tax department would return the excess tax deducted without hassle. You had to either catch hold of the agents operating in the market or wait for long. Now, the department processes it and sends it to one's account only by applying for additional tax returns. The waiting time of 93 days in 2013-14, but it has now come down to 10 days, Union Finance Minister Nirmala Sitharaman said while presenting the government's Interim Budget for 2024-25[71].

One Nation, One Tax: Moment of Another Tryst with Destiny

The country became independent on 15 August 1947, but it became financially independent when the Modi government decided to implement the GST. A special session of Parliament was convened on 30 June 2017, and the historic financial reform rolled out on 1 July 2017 with the passage of the 101st Amendment to the Indian constitution. It sought to create a seamless and unified market–One Country, One System, One Market.

It was a momentous occasion. Those understanding the significance of the movement towards an easy taxation system must have felt butterflies in their stomach as the GST rolled out from the Parliament's Central Hall in the presence of the then President of India, late Pranab Mukherjee, Prime Minister Narendra Modi, Finance Minister late Arun Jaitley, many Cabinet Ministers and Chief Ministers. Sadly, the Congress and the Left parties skipped the launch.

It was like liberating the Indian businesses and economy from the worst slavery. People were free, yet the movement of goods and services within the territory of India was not. These were subjected to harassment due to the existence of various legislations. It bred corruption and forced businessmen to indulge in non-transparent transactions.

The GST was to replace more than a dozen taxes that the Central and State governments imposed, including the Value Added Tax (VAT). The system had created bottlenecks due to non-transparency and empowered the officials on the state boundaries to harass the transporters. It was a sure way to stifle the economy and prevent it from growing faster than it deserved.

Before the GST, there were many taxes such as Excise, Service, VAT, CST, Entertainment, Octroi and tax on taxes. Also, there were varying rates in different states and complicated laws and procedures. One would not forget that there used to be check posts at every interstate border that had become a symbol of harassment and corruption. Jaitley pointed out that 17 transaction taxes in states and Centre and 23 cesses would be subsumed in the GST. Harassment of a person filing Tax returns was to end, and he now needed to file only one return.

Narendra Modi described it as a 'good and simple tax' which will end the harassment of traders and small businesses while integrating India into one market with one tax rate. He said that 'being fair and transparent, the GST will end generation of black money and corruption and promote new governance culture that will end harassment at the hand of tax officials.'

Jaitley said that rolling out the GST 'will ease inflation, make tax avoidance difficult and boost GDP growth'. The implementation of the landmark unified tax should be seen as the beginning of a new journey that will expand the country's economic horizon, he argued while defending the legislation in Parliament.

Pranab Mukherjee, who had piloted the bill to this effect as the Finance Minister under the UPA regime in March 2011, described the transition as a new era in taxation, achieved due to the maturity and wisdom of India's democracy. Rightly so since it had taken years to evolve a political consensus.

He beautifully articulated this maturity, 'This consensus took not only time but also effort to build. The effort came from persons across the political spectrum who set aside narrow partisan considerations and put the nation's interests first. It is a tribute to the maturity and wisdom of India's democracy.'

Everyone knew implementing the GST was not going to be easy. While Mukherjee said the disruption was bound to be there since people would take time to adjust to the new ways, Modi said there would be teething troubles adapting to the regime. 'Even eyes have to adjust for a couple of days when a sight-corrective spectacles are worn', he added.

While describing the GST as the biggest and most ambitious tax and economic reform in its history, Jaitley said, 'The old India was economically fragmented. New India will create one tax, one market, one nation. It will be in India where Centre and states work together towards the common goal of shared prosperity.'

The significance of the new tax regime left no one doubting why it was another tryst-with-destiny moment for India. He outlined the government's vision, 'Not only will India write a new destiny, the new tax regime would also strengthen federalism…While enacting the GST, neither the states nor the Centre gave up their sovereignty. They have pooled their sovereignty to make joint decisions in indirect taxation.'

While the rollout decision looked easy, achieving a consensus between the Centre and the states was difficult. The states were at different stages of economic development; some were economically rich and some poor. They had varying activities and sources of revenue. They could also frame the indirect tax policies to generate resources. The experiment of implementing VAT was unsuccessful, and the GST promised uncertainties. The states feared losing revenue under the new regime and their sovereignty.

These fears had prevented major tax reforms contemplated by the then Vajpayee government when it implemented the VAT. But Vajpayee knew that a unified tax structure was needed. In 2000, he set up a high-powered panel to design the right GST model in the Indian context. Vajpayee's Economic Advisory Council, which included three former RBI governors–I G Patel, Bimal Jalan, and C Rangarajan–had proposed a single common Goods and Services Tax.

The UPA government under Dr Manmohan Singh decided in 2006 that the GST would roll out in 2010. However, the government could not implement it due to its failure to address the issues raised by some state governments. Failing to implement cost the government a whopping Rs 12 lakh crore, at the rate of Rs 1.5 lakh crore per year, according to the senior Congress leader Veerappa Moily as he blamed the BJP for not allowing the rollout[72].

It is true that the BJP-ruled states, including Gujarat under Chief Minister Narendra Modi, had opposed the proposal. However, there were many concerns, including financial losses to states, the mechanism of dispute resolution and products under the GST. The Congress-led UDF government in Kerala and Congress-ruled Maharashtra and Haryana had opposed the UPA-proposed GST, fearing a loss of revenue. Odisha and Tamil Nadu, not ruled by the BJP, had also opposed. The new GST under

Modi had addressed most of these issues and brought a consensus to set it rolling. The Congress's criticism was a critique of its own incapabilities.

The NDA tried to assuage the states by creating the platform of the GST council to provide an institutional mechanism for the expression of their concerns and for making decisions. The Central government also assured the states a guaranteed money flow with a minimum growth of 14 per cent per year for five years over their revenues.

The functioning of the GST has proved to be successful. Although the decisions have not been unanimous, the Council has arrived at decisions through consensus, except in one case. The GST decision on the lottery was taken through voting, whereas all 1,200 decisions taken at the 52 meetings till October 2023 have been through consensus.

There were many hiccups, such as fixing slabs on different products, changing them as per the market response and streamlining an IT process to ease the calculation of GST filing. There was opposition from businessmen also since a shift to the new system meant adopting a new process of compliance and additional expenditure. Gradually, people saw the benefits of the GST as it simplified the processes, and the results were there for all to see.

After six years of implementation, the GST has emerged as a major success story. The functioning of the GST has proved that the Centre and the states working with the spirit of cooperative federalism have risen above their differences for the good of the country.

The number of GST registrations as of 2023 was 1.4 crore, leading to increasing formalisation of the economy and the resultant increase in revenue. In fact, the GST is proving to be the game-changer for the Indian economy, which has already become the world's fifth-largest economy and aspires to become an economy of 5 trillion USD.

The numbers are envious. The GST collection for eight months from August 2017 to March 2018 was Rs 7.19 lakh crore. It touched Rs 18.10 lakh crore in 2022-23. For the quarter ending 31 January 2024, the GST collection was Rs 1,72,129 crore. During the April 2023-January 2024 period, cumulative gross GST collection was Rs 16.69 lakh crore against Rs 14.96 lakh crore during April 2022-January 2023. This was a growth of 11.6 per cent[73].

The GST process is getting further simplified with feedback from the market. Many untapped markets still deal in cash despite having a GST number. Better monitoring and simplification would increase voluntary compliance. The smaller businesses find it tough to comply, but they can pay a fixed rate on their turnover with no paperwork. E-way bills and E-invoicing have helped prevent tax evasion.

As the economy gets increasingly formalised, the size of the economy would increase further, and the government would have more resources to rationalise tax slabs and invest the money in infrastructure and welfare measures. Further reduction of tax slabs may increase compliance.

Also, the issue of bringing petroleum and alcohol under the GST would need finalisation. Since the states are already getting more revenue in their share after introducing the GST, the proclivity to keep these two should be reduced.

Insolvency and Bankruptcy Code Amendment Act 2016

One of the big-ticket reforms of the Modi government to bring the economy back on track is this law enacted in 2016. Banks give loans to companies or individuals to carry out business and add to the economy of the country. If the business performs well, it employs people, pays taxes to the government, and adds to the overall increase in the economy. Since the loans carry reasonable interest, they become a source of earning for the banks.

But what happens if, after taking these loans, the businesses do not perform and suffer losses? What will happen to the debt taken from the banks? How will the company clear the debt and pay regular interest instalments? The banks will not make a profit, and their lending capacity will be seriously compromised. It will have a cascading effect on the economy.

If the borrower fails to repay the principal and interest continuously or for 90 days, the standard asset of the bank, which was the loan, becomes a non-performing asset (NPA). The NPAs of banks as a percentage of the total increased from 2.3 per cent in 2008 to 9.3 per cent in 2017[74].

Such defaults happen at times due to mismanagement or ill intentions of individuals running the businesses. At times it happens due to the market conditions. Most of these loans were given during the year 2000 when the economy was booming, and no one anticipated a sudden slowdown. The global economic crisis since 2008 led to the market decline. At times, the banks gave more loans by restructuring so that the borrowers could service the loan, but it did not help and added up to the NPAs.

According to the RBI data, gross advances of Public Sector Banks (PSBs) increased from 18,19,074 crore in 2008 to Rs 52,15,920 crore in 2014. However, not all advances were NPAs. After a transparent recognition of stressed assets as NPAs, gross NPAs of PSBs rose from Rs 2,79,016 crore as of 31 March 2015 to Rs 8,95,601 crore as of 31 March 2018[75].

The Asset Quality Review for a clean and transparent bank balance sheet to show the condition of the banking system revealed high incidences of NPAs. The government adopted the strategy of 4R–Recognition, Resolution, Recapitalisation and Reforms, and the NPAs declined by Rs 89,189 crore as on 31 March 2019[76].

The primary reasons for a spurt in the NPAs have been aggressive lending practices, wilful default, loan frauds, corruption in some cases, and economic slowdown. The period highlighted the financial fraud by individuals who swindled the borrowed money into other activities. In some cases, loans were given on business propositions and without adequate collaterals. This observation came from the Comptroller and Auditor General of India (CAG), who pointed out this blatant violation of the banking norm for high-value lending[77].

There were laws to deal with situations when the assets become stressed. These included the Companies Act of 1956, the Sick Industrial Companies Act of 1985, the Securitisation and Reconstruction of Financial Assets and Enforcement of Security Interest Act (SARFAESI) for security enforcement, and the Recovery of Debts Due to Banks and Financial Institutions Act, 1993 (RDDBFI) for debt recovery by banks and financial institutions.

Despite these laws, recovering assets was an extremely cumbersome and time-consuming process. There was a need to improve financial discipline and make the process of recovering bad loans easy and faster. As a response, the Insolvency and Bankruptcy Code Amendment Act 2016 came into force from 1 December 2016 onwards.

The Parliamentary Committee paid due diligence after the Bankruptcy Legislative Reforms Committee submitted the draft of the new bankruptcy law as mandated by the government. Arun Jaitley introduced the draft bill in the 16th Lok Sabha as Insolvency and Bankruptcy Code 2015. The bill was sent to a Joint Parliamentary Committee that studied the bill in detail. The JPC recommendations were incorporated in a new draft bill passed by the Lok Sabha and Rajya Sabha in May 2016.

The IBC provided a time-bound 180-day recovery process for the insolvent accounts. The creditors, presided over by an insolvency professional, had to decide whether to restructure the loan or to recover the outstanding by selling the defaulter's assets.

The Code set up a ten-member Insolvency and Bankruptcy Board of India, representing the government and the RBI, to act as a regulator and oversee the insolvency proceedings across the country. The law made a provision for licensed professionals to control the debtor's assets during their insolvency proceedings.

The IBC set up two Tribunals–The National Company Law Tribunal (NCLT) to adjudicate for Companies and Limited Liability Partnership firms and the Debt Recovery Tribunal (DRT) for individuals and partnerships.

The process may be initiated by either the creditors or the debtors. In the case of companies, the original Act said the process would have to be completed within 180 days, which can be extended by another 90 days if the creditors agree. An amendment was made to the Act in 2019, which increased the resolution time to 330 days. The Act witnessed many amendments to respond to the changing demands to maintain efficiency and compliance.

The Credit Rating agency CRISIL has calculated that 'the IBC has helped to resolve Rs 3.16 lakh crore of debt that was stuck in 808 cases in the past seven years. The creditors on an average realised 32 per cent of the admitted claims and 169 per cent of the liquidation money.'[78]

The IBC had proved to be a more effective instrument for debt recovery than any of the existing ones. Other institutions, such as DRT, SARFAESI Act and Lok Adalat, have an average recovery rate of 2-20 per cent, the CRISIL said. The IBC has some positive fallout on the existing cases as settlement is resolving matters. Cases for more than Rs 9 lakh crore of filed debt have been settled before appearing before the IBC for admission. The IBC has been acting as a deterrence.

The banking system of the country must maintain its financial health to maintain the overall financial health of the country. With enough liquidity and confidence in the market, the banks can finance businesses in genuine need of funds. Union Minister Piyush Goyal rightly called the IBC a game-changing initiative of the government. It has brought about a shift in the attitudes of lenders and borrowers. While acting as an effective deterrent against unscrupulous borrowers, it has empowered banks with the tools to follow due diligence and the resultant confidence about recovery[79].

Production Linked Incentive

The government cannot and should not be in business, but it can create an atmosphere where more and more businessmen think of making manufacturing competitive. They must adopt international standards, compete with the world and earn revenue and respect by exporting better products into the international market.

India's vision of an *Atmanirbhar Bharat* would be incomplete unless its products are the best in the world. Gone are the times when Indian goods used to be manufactured under Licence Permit Raj for consumption in the Indian market. They never thought of the boundaries beyond India. Now they have to compete since the world has become increasingly globalised.

Through the PLI scheme, the government sought to invite foreign investors to set up their manufacturing units in India and promote the Indian industries to expand their capacity and improve quality. The aims were employment generation, export promotion and import substitution.

With these aspirations, the government launched the PLI scheme in March 2020 for three specific sectors–Mobile and allied Component Manufacturing, Electrical Component Manufacturing, and Medical Devices. In November 2020, Modi extended the scheme to 10 more sectors. It came in the context of the COVID-19 pandemic when the government concluded that manufacturing under the label Make in India must get a decisive push to increase the size of the economy and to meet the demands in the global market.

Modi outlined his vision under the PLI in the following words:

> Why should every district not be an exporter of India? Why should not every country import from India and every corner of the country? Why shouldn't there be all kinds of products for export? You may have also noticed an obvious difference between the earlier and existing schemes. Earlier, industrial incentives used to be the provision of an open-ended input-based subsidy. Now it has been made performance-based through a competitive process. Bringing 13 sectors under the ambit of this scheme for the first time reflects our commitment.[80]

Modi has been trying to transform the slogan of 'Make in India: Make for the World' into reality through the PLI scheme. The budget of 2021 made a provision of Rs 1.97 lakh crore to incentivise production in 14 sectors over five years beginning 2021-22. It includes sectors such as automobiles, steel, IT hardware, food products, textiles and solar energy. As explained by the Prime Minister at a webinar

> An average of 5 per cent of production is given as incentive. That is, production worth about 520 billion dollars is estimated in the next five years in India only through the PLI scheme. It is also estimated that the workforce in the sectors for which the PLI is planned will be almost doubled. The PLI scheme is going to have a huge impact in employment creation. Besides the benefit from production and exports, the industry will also reap advantages due to increase in demand following the rise in income, i.e., double the profit.'[81]

The results after two years have not failed the expectations. In February 2024, Union Finance Minister Nirmala Sitharaman told the Lok Sabha that manufacturing locations were coming up in 24 states and more than 150 districts. 'Rs 1.07 lakh crore worth of investment has been committed by private sector under the PLI Schemes. Over 7 lakh job opportunities, both direct and indirect, have already been created. Exports worth Rs 3.40 lakh crore are happening. Rs 8.7 lakh crore worth production and sales are happening. 176 MSMEs are selected as direct beneficiaries of the PLI Scheme'[82].

For decades, India has struggled with promoting world-class manufacturing at economies of scale to meet. Manufacturing must pick up pace for the economy to grow fast. But, this was not happening mainly because Indian traders found it easier to buy cheap goods from China and sell them in the Indian market. Our MSMEs suffered as a result.

India's standoff with China and the global lack of trust in China's expansionist design have forced multinational corporations to look for better avenues. During the COVID-19 crisis, India demonstrated to the world its own capabilities. Modi has showcased India at the world level by talking about its strengths and opportunities. In most parts of the world, India is a trusted name.

Without losing time, Modi had worked hard to make investment in India a big opportunity by giving attractive financial terms and ease of doing business. And it is to the credit of the government that foreign investment is coming in all sectors of the economy and not just a few sectors, such as IT or real estate. India is now on the path to becoming the manufacturing capital of the world.

The Journey from Fragile Five to Top Five

Reform, Perform and Transform.
–Narendra Modi

With a GDP of USD 3.75 Trillion (2023), India has become the fifth-largest economy in the world. In three years, i.e. by 2027, it is expected to be a USD 5 trillion economy. By 2030, India is poised to become the third-largest economy in the world by reaching a mark of USD 10 trillion. By 2047, when India completes 100 years of Independence, the country will be a USD 30 trillion economy.

When the Modi government came to power in 2014, India was the tenth-largest economy in the world, with a GDP of USD 2 trillion. By the end of 2021, India had overtaken the United Kingdom to become the fifth-largest economy in the world. By 2022, India had an economy of USD 3.5 trillion. The IMF (International Monetary Fund) says that India, with USD 4.1 trillion, will continue to hold its fifth position in the world in 2024, with the US on top (USD 28 trillion), followed by China (USD 18.6 trillion), Germany (USD 4.7 trillion), and Japan (4.3 trillion)[1].

In 2014, the economy was not in a good state. The GDP growth, which denotes the health of the economy, had slumped to 6 per cent, and inflation was high at 10 per cent. And there were no signs of recovery. Foreign Investors had clubbed India in the group of Fragile Five economies along with Brazil, Indonesia, Turkey and South Africa[2].

When Morgan Stanley placed India in the Fragile Five in 2013, the Indian economy was marked by 'weak fundamentals' such as low growth, high inflation, high external deficit, and impaired public finances. While pointing to this rating, the white paper of the Modi government brought out in February 2024 observed, 'The fact that the economy could only grow from being the 12th largest in 2004 to the 10th largest merely exposed the short-lived, qualitatively inferior and unsustainable nature of the high growth experienced between 2005 and 2012.'[3]

The question raised by the white paper should prick our conscience to find out if India had lost all ten years to revive the economy and bring it a few notches up. The Modi government has rightly pointed out that the legacy of the NDA government under Vajpayee, which had left a robust economy, was frittered away by an irresponsible government that came to power in 2004.

India worked hard under Modi. While inflation came under control, a reduced fiscal deficit and stable currency made India a favourable destination for investment.

In its fresh assessment of the Indian economy in early 2017, the IMF described India as a 'bright spot' in the global landscape. It described India as 'one of the fastest growing emerging market economies' and predicted that a key to stronger growth would be maintaining the reform momentum. It appreciated the fiscal consolidation attempted by the new government and the attempt to implement the Goods and Services Tax (GST). It appreciated the 6.6 per cent growth despite demonetisation of high currency notes and predicted that India would grow 7.2 per cent in 2017[4].

The IMF was concerned with the sorry state of the banking system, which struggled due to large NPAs that reduced its capacity to lend further loans. Demonetisation had disrupted economic activities since most transactions for smaller businesses happened in cash, and the digital payment system had not picked up momentum. The IMF lauded financial inclusion by opening crores of bank accounts for the poor and halving poverty in the country.

The IMF has been constantly rating the Indian economy as a bright spot. When even the most developed world economies witnessed a massive reduction in growth, India continued to witness impressive growth. India witnessed 6.8 per cent growth in 2022, and the momentum has continued to hover around 7 per cent.

Let us try to understand India's growth story by contextualising it in the global economy. In October 2022, the projected global growth was predicted to slow from 6 per cent in 2021 to 3.2 per cent in 2022 and 2.7 per cent in 2023. It was a significant slowdown. On the contrary, India witnessed 9.05 per cent growth in 2021, after a negative growth of -5.83 per cent in 2020 post the COVID-19 lockdown. In 2022, it witnessed 7 per cent growth[5]. The growth in real GDP during 2023-24 was estimated at 7.3 per cent compared to 7.2 per cent in 2022-23[6]. The growth is likely to be more than 7 per cent in the coming years.

These statistics prove that India witnessed steady economic growth, which was very impressive compared to other countries. And it has happened despite the setback of the COVID-19 pandemic and the Ukraine War, which sought to disrupt the supply chains.

With the country moving enthusiastically on the trajectory of innovation, expansion and growth, the economic indicators look strong. Emanating this confidence while presenting the Interim Budget 2024, Union Finance Minister Nirmala Sitharaman described GDP as meaning 'Governance, Development and Performance' and said, 'There is macroeconomic stability, investments are robust, economy is doing well, people are doing well, with greater aspirations for future, average real income has increased by 50 per cent, inflation is moderate, people are getting empowered to pursue their aspirations, there is effective and timely delivery of programmes and large projects.'[7]

Besides these, the strength of the economy lies in the gradual acceptance of the GST as beneficial for people, and the rise in GST collection shows an increase in economic activities. The DBT of Rs 34 lakh crore and financial inclusion through Jan Dhan Accounts have brought more than 25 crore people out of poverty. The poor have free subsidised gas and shelter under the PM Awas Yojana. In case they fall ill, the Ayushman Bharat Yojana comes to their rescue, providing the best healthcare within reach. They need not to worry about food since they get a free ration under the PM Garib Kalyan Yojana. Education for their children is free. Moreover, they have electric connections and potable tap water.

Now, the vast population outside the production side of the economy can aspire to improve their living conditions and become a crucial part of the economy. Under the Mudra scheme, they can contact any bank for collateral-free loans for small businesses, shops or self-employment. The government guarantees for their loans. Over 30 crore loanees under the Mudra scheme are women, and the default rate is negligible.

The government is already working to massively develop infrastructure in all areas of economic activity, whether production, transport or trade. Various linkages are established through multi-modal links to bring the logistics cost at par with the world. Developing skills is emphasised, and avenues for education are increased by opening new engineering and medical colleges, besides allowing foreign universities to open in India. The number of universities has increased from 676 in 2014 to 1,168 by the end of 2023.

While every district would have a hospital, some would offer medical education. The number of medical colleges has increased from 387 in 2014 to 706 by 2023 end, and there is a remarkable increment of seats in medical education from 51,348 to 1,08,940[8]. There was already a shortage of MBBS doctors, so this would prepare the country to tackle the health needs better.

The country is poised for a big takeoff, and reaching the goal of more than 7 per cent growth should not be a problem. The base given by the Make in India and PLI scheme would increase the size of manufacturing. The services sector is already doing well and would get a further push as it gets more organised under a liberalised regime.

The Indian economy has shown resilience to domestic and international shocks. Also, the growth is boosted by a diversified production basket independent of products or commodities. All sectors of the economy are witnessing growth–agriculture, industry and services. It is also attributable to a diversified trade basket and a broad range of trading partners. It means that a slowdown in one of its partner countries would not affect it much, and would be balanced by better growth in other parts of the world.

There was a time when most contributions to the economy came from agriculture, while industry and services lagged. It meant dependence on the vagaries of nature where adverse agricultural yield would also impact the demand in other sectors. The recent trends have shown that the share of agriculture in the Indian economy has come down from 35 per cent in 1990-91 to 15 per cent in 2022-23.

It does not mean agriculture production has declined. On the contrary, it has continued growing at 4.6 per cent per annum during the last six years. The decline in the share of agriculture came due to the expansion of other sectors[9]. The government spending on agriculture has been phenomenal, which ensured that agriculture maintained its productivity and kept improving further.

On average, the Union government has been spending Rs 6.5 lakh crore every year on agriculture and farmers. Every farmer gets Rs 50,000 per year under various schemes, including Rs 6,000 cash directly in their account[10]. In the last nine years, the government has spent Rs 15 lakh crore in procuring grains and other produce under the Minimum Support Price (MSP).

During the same period, the expenditure on the fertiliser subsidy has been Rs 10 lakh crore to ensure that the farmers gets essential nutrients for their crops at a reasonable price, even though the prices have gone up globally. Indian farmers get a bag of urea at Rs 270. The comparable price is Rs 720 in Bangladesh, Rs 800 in Pakistan, Rs 2,100 in China and Rs 3,000 in the United States[11]. Under PM Kisan Samman Nidhi, the government spends close to Rs 75,000 crore per year to send Rs 6,000 per year, in three instalments, directly into their account as income support.

The government has taken various measures to make agriculture productive, including promoting bio-fertilisers and drip irrigation, soil health cards to know the health of the soil, easy loans to Kisan Card holders, and better irrigation facilities. We have already seen efforts of the government to create an e-market to give farmers better returns and promote storage infrastructure.

Since the productivity of Indian agriculture is lesser than other developed countries, adopting modern agricultural techniques would increase production and reduce costs. For example, rice productivity per hectare in China is 6.7 tonnes, against India's 2.4 tonnes. For wheat, the productivity in India is 3 tonnes compared to 5 tonnes in China. The government is trying to bridge this gap by addressing the issue of fragmentation of holdings and lack of awareness about modern agriculture equipment.

Can India Feed the World?

The war between Russia and Ukraine–two major wheat exporters accounting for one-third of global wheat sales–led to a global food crisis. They also account for 55 per cent of the global annual sunflower oil exports and 17 per cent of maize and barley. When the world faced a food crisis, one question that came to mind was–can India feed the world?

In 2022, Prime Minister Modi told US President Joe Biden that India could supply food grains to the world to meet the crisis if the WTO allowed. 'The world is facing a new problem now; the food stock of the world is getting empty, I was talking to the US President, and he also raised this issue. I suggested that if WTO permits, India is ready to supply food stock to the world from tomorrow', PM Modi said[12]. Following this, Piyush Goyal tweeted: 'Our farmers have ensured our granaries overflow and we are ready to serve the world…India has sufficient stock to feed its people and also assist its neighbours and vulnerable nations.'[13]

India produced 135.75 million tonnes of rice in 2022-23. The production has witnessed a steady increase over the last many years. Considering the country needs 100-plus million tonnes to feed its own population, the country will still have a surplus to export. The same was with wheat, where the production was 110.55 million tonnes, and the domestic consumption was 100-plus million tonnes. With adequate storage and better productivity, India can feed many parts of the world.

India is one of the largest agricultural product exporters in the world. During 2021-22, the country recorded agriculture exports worth USD 49.6 billion, which was USD 41.3 billion in 2020-21. In 2022-23, it was USD 53 billion, showing a positive trend. 'We expect this number to grow in current year despite restrictions imposed on rice, wheat and sugar', Piyush Goyal said[14]. These restrictions kept the domestic prices of these produce in check.

The global rice market is 51 million tonnes[15]. One-third is already being met by India[16]. The demand is expected to grow manifold. In Sub-

Saharan Africa, the rice import is expected to increase by 90 per cent. India has a huge opportunity.

India has a potential in agriculture. In most parts of the world, less than 25 per cent of a country's land is under agriculture. In China, it is only 11 per cent, whereas it is 17.24 per cent in the United States. India has more than 50 per cent of its land under cultivation[17]. In terms of numbers, India has the largest arable land in the world at 179.8 million hectares, followed by the United States (167.8 Million) and China (165.2), as per the data released by the US Geological Survey[18]. However, it is also true that only about 55 per cent of the arable land has access to irrigation.

It means there is scope for expanding Indian agriculture by leaps and bounds. If more and more land is brought under targeted cultivation and adequate irrigation facilities are provided, it would be easy to achieve the economies of scale needed to become a significant food bowl of the world.

The Modi government has been making Herculean efforts to provide irrigated water to every field. The Pradhan Mantri Krishi Sinchayee Yojana (PMKSY) was approved in 2021 for 2021-26 with an outlay of Rs 93,068 crore. Under the Accelerated Irrigation Benefit Programme (AIBP), 13.88 lakh hectares would be brought under irrigation during the target period. AIBP also focussed on completing 60 ongoing projects under command area development to cover an additional land of 30.23 hectares[19].

Industry and Manufacturing

In 2014, the country's manufacturing sector required a leader who could provide them with better infrastructure, stable finances, and an end to bureaucratic red tape that led to time and cost overrun. We have already seen how the efforts of the government improved India's ranking in the ease of doing business from 142 in 2014 to 63 in 2022. It was impossible without a strong determination to change the business environment. Investors would not come unless they found it easy to do business in India due to compliance burden, fast-tracking of clearances, taxes and insolvency. The government reduced 39,000 compliances. More than 3,500 provisions have been decriminalised. In September 2021, the government launched India's National Single Window System

(NSWS), a digital platform for investors for approvals and clearances. It got more than 4 lakh visitors by January 2023[20].

The successive governments dealt with the idea of giving a push to industries, but comprehensive efforts to create the infrastructure were needed since a big takeoff was missing. The closed economy did not push competition. When reforms happened in 1991, the country witnessed unprecedented corruption. Not much was invested in core areas and the Indian industry was not ambitious to invest in technological upgradation essential for manufacturing better products.

The Vajpayee government, from 1998-2004, invested in infrastructure, such as roads, transport, ports and telecommunications, and the impact was visible when the UPA government came to power. However, the UPA failed to keep the momentum, leading to gloom.

Modi's initiatives must be seen in the context of providing a massive dependable infrastructure that would prepare the country for a big takeoff. The government worked with both scale and speed. Overall expenditure and the capital expenditure increased from Rs 5.6 lakh in 2015 to Rs 18.6 lakh crore in the 2024 budget estimate[21]. We have also seen how massive expenditure has been planned through the Gati Scheme to prepare the country for the next century.

Industrial development is not possible unless the MSME and ancillary industries get symbiotic links with big industries that plan to work on economies of scale and manufacture world-class products. The first major initiative was Modi launching the Make in India campaign in 2015. It sought to 'facilitate investment, foster innovation, enhance skill development, protect intellectual property and build best in class manufacturing infrastructure.'[22]

It identified 25 sectors in manufacturing, infrastructure and service activities. The government opened FDI in Defence, Production, Construction and Railway infrastructure. The government promoted its role from a regulator to a facilitator. It advocated its role as a collaborator and partnered with industrialists to foster growth and development. The secretaries of the government, other important functionaries and industry leaders came together on one platform in December 2014 to discuss the action plan to raise the contribution of manufacturing to

GDP to 25 per cent. The government also introduced the PLI scheme to promote manufacturing, and the industrial landscape started changing as a result of this.

It is the same strategy that Modi had adopted as the Chief Minister of Gujarat when he asked his officials to treat businessmen with respect and created special vehicles for faster clearance of projects. After establishing a reliable system that emanated trust, he invited foreign investors to invest in Gujarat. We already know how Gujarat embarked on the path of development under his leadership[23].

Foreign business organisations were also invited to invest and benefit from the economic opportunities. Key sectors, such as Railways, Defence, Insurance and Medical Devices, were also opened to FDI. These measures led to achievements and created hopes for a better India–more empowered and confident, giving goosebumps to those who want to translate dreams into reality.

Make in India was launched with the symbol of a lion on a prowl made of cogs. The strength and confidence of the lion, i.e. India, would attract the companies to invest in India. Modi described the logo as a symbol of 'manufacturing, strength and national pride…Make in India is not a slogan or a brand, but a new national movement'. He described the FDI as 'First Develop India' and said that 'for foreigners, it is an opportunity'.

He outlined his vision of the Make in India campaign while launching the lion logo in front of more than 500 top executives in the country. He said, 'The Make in India campaign aims at turning the country into a global manufacturing hub by smoothening business processes and attracting foreign companies to set up factories in India and invest in the country's infrastructure. The focus is on creating jobs and helping the "poor reach the middle class faster"'.[24]

Before 2014, there were only two mobile manufacturing companies in India. By 2021, there were more than 200 manufacturing units in the country. About 80 per cent of mobiles in India were imported from China, and export was almost nil. Now, 99.9 per cent of mobiles are manufactured in India[25].

All the leading international brands, including Apple and Samsung, have opened their manufacturing units in India. Samsung has opened the world's largest manufacturing unit in India, and Apple, which manufactures iPhones, has also started its manufacturing unit in India. Companies like Oppo, Vivo, Xiaomi, and Lava have established their presence in a big way. The Indian mobile company is estimated to be employing 1.2 million direct or indirect jobs, which would increase further in the coming years[26].

Talking about the remarkable surge witnessed by the Indian mobile industry, Union Minister Ashwini Vaishnaw said it had recorded a substantial presence with the production of USD 44 billion today from a negligible presence in 2014, of which handsets worth USD 11 billion were exported. With a magnitude of Indian electronics manufacturing worth 8.5 lakh crore, India has already become the second-largest manufacturing nation in the world[27].

Semiconductor Ambition

A country cannot become an IT giant unless it has semiconductor capabilities. Self-reliance in nano-technology is the key to self-reliance when modern life depends on technology. This feeling intensified during the COVID-19 pandemic. Also, there was a crisis of microchips, which made India increasingly realise its dependence on semiconductor manufacturers of the world. About 70 per cent of manufacturing lies in South Korea, Taiwan and China. The US came after Japan. So far as India is concerned, it imports around 95 per cent of its semiconductors mainly from China, Taiwan, South Korea and Singapore.

The demand of the Indian domestic industry for smartphones, automobiles using Artificial Intelligence, medical equipment, and industrial and consumer electronics is slated to grow manifold. India can use the domestic demand to set up semiconductor manufacturing units and meet the global demand. The Indian semiconductor industry is projected to achieve a market value of USD 55 billion by 2026.

With these aspirations, India has already launched an ambitious plan to become a semiconductor power. It has already committed USD 10 billion to push forward the India Semiconductor Mission (ISM). The Mission statement describes the plan as 'a specialised and independent

Business Division within the Digital India Corporation that aims to build a vibrant semiconductor and display ecosystem to enable India's emergence as a global hub for electronics manufacturing and design'[28].

The global chips market was pegged at USD 600 billion in 2021. It is estimated to grow to USD 1 trillion by 2030. The Indian semiconductor industry is expected to achieve a market value of USD 55 billion. Once the semiconductor echosystem is in place, India will be able to cater to the global demand for semiconductors.

Renewable Energy Focus

The growing population of India would need energy. The resultant increase in energy consumption would put pressure on availability and pose a challenge to meet the demand using clean energy. It means increasing focus on renewable energy. India's target is to meet net zero carbon emissions by 2070. India aims to generate 500 gigawatts (GW) of installed renewable energy capacity by 2030.

India is the third-largest producer of renewable energy, with 40 per cent of its installed electricity capacity coming from non-fossil fuel sources. The focus has been on capacity expansion in the manufacture of solar cells. The government has devised policies, such as curtailing PV imports, and incentives, such as PLI, to encourage local manufacturers under the Make in India campaign.

In the initial stage of setting up solar plants, there was heavy dependence on the photovoltaics imported from China. Now, the situation is changing fast. The government has brought out an attractive scheme for OEM manufacturers. By 2026, India is expected to become self-sufficient in this sector, with its capacity expected to reach 110 GW. After that, it will be able to cater to the export demand as well.

The government's decision to set up solar rooftop generating capacity on 1 crore houses is further likely to boost this sector, besides adding to the energy capacity and reducing dependence on traditional power for daily use. It is likely to fuel a solar revolution[29].

India exported solar cells and modules worth Rs 8,400 crore in FY23, a 364 per cent increase over the export of Rs 1,819 crore in FY22[30]. The top buyer was the United States. With India leading the International Solar Alliance of 118 countries, quality production of equipment to tap solar energy would be in great demand.

Startup Ecosystem

Modi's biggest contribution is to push a new culture of startup ecosystem in India. More and more youngsters prefer to work with startups than to settle in relatively safe and well-paying jobs at big multinational corporations. Learning, innovation and participation in giving solutions have become more important than a secured job. Aryan, a 20-something-year-old, having completed his Engineering degree from BITS Pilani, had many lucrative offers but he chose to join a Logistics solution startup in Bangalore for a much lesser remuneration. When asked why, he said he wanted to learn and not become a cog in a machine.

Like him, many people, exceptional in their field, want to lap up the new opportunities the vibrant India is providing. The focus is on becoming a part of the solution-givers. It has given a big push to develop new young entrepreneurs who are confident and ready to embark on a new journey. The government's role here is that of a facilitator and guide.

The change in the mindset reflects the initiatives of the Modi government. The Prime Minister launched the Startup India campaign on 16 January 2016 to build a strong ecosystem for nurturing innovation and encouraging private investment. The government earmarked Rs 10,000 crore for funding startups and relaxed compliances, including tax concessions, to promote business.

Before the Modi government came to power, the country had only 350 startups. As per data from the Department for Promotion of Industry and Internal Trade (DPIIT), India has 1,19,623 startups registered with it. Of these, 58,436 were women startups[31]. The startups have been spread over 763 districts, showing the innovation-fuelled small towns and remote districts in Tier II and Tier III cities[32]. Registration with DPIIT entitles one to many facilities, including easy seed funding from the government, tax exemptions, easy trademark registration at a 50 per cent rebate, patent registration at an 80 per cent rebate and an easy compliance window.

As of December 2023, startups had given 12.42 lakh direct jobs[33], besides opening avenues for many more through indirect linkages. Of these startups, 113 (till January 2023) are Unicorns, with a valuation of a minimum of USD 1 billion. The combined worth of all Unicorns is more than USD 350 billion. By 2026, the number of startups is likely to grow to 250, with a valuation of USD 1.5 trillion[34].

India, as of today, has the third-largest startup ecosystem after the United States and China. Some of these startups are Zomato, Ola, Physics Wallah, MobiKwik, Blinkit, Groww, PharmEasy, Digit Insurance, Cars24, Unacademy, PhonePe, Nykaa, Lenskart, Dream11, Udaan, Policybazaar, Flipkart, MakeMyTrip etc.

Mudra Loan

The Prime Minister launched this small loan scheme for small and micro enterprises on 8 April 2015. Mudra stands for Micro Units Development & Refinance Agency Ltd., a financial institution set up by the government for developing and refinancing micro-unit enterprises.

Loans from Rs 50,000 to Rs 10 Lakhs were disbursed to the needy through RRBs, Commercial Banks, Small Finance Banks, MFIs and NBFCs. The loans were described as Shishu, Kishore and Tarun, depending on the quantum of the loan, and signified the growth stage, development and funding needs of the beneficiary enterprises. Loans up to Rs 50,000 were categorised as Shishu, from Rs 50,000 to Rs 5 lakh as Kishore and from Rs 5 lakh to 10 lakh as Tarun.

The Mudra loan can be availed by non-corporate and non-farm small and micro enterprises for various purposes that can lead to income generation and employment creation in manufacturing, services, retail and agriculture and allied activities. 'As on 24 November 2023, more than 44.46 crore loans amounting to Rs 26.12 lakh crore have been sanctioned to the borrowers under the Scheme.'[35] Around 69 per cent of the beneficiaries were women.

These loans were small loans given to street vendors and self-help groups of people who wanted to be self-employed by doing small businesses in the manufacturing or services sector. With no such facility, they depended on private loans, which came at a very high interest and often caught people in a debt trap. The loans under the Mudra are without collateral and processing fees.

The Mudra scheme was a demonstration of the trust the Prime Minister had in his people. Instead of giving them benefits, empower them with concessional credits. Once they stand on their own, they will pay back. As per the RBI norms, the Mudra loan is being given at a deregulated rate decided by the financial institutions. It can come anywhere between 8 to 13 per cent.

That the borrowers are women shows that they are considered financially more prudent and would not indulge in wasteful expenditure. The government guarantees these loans through the Credit Guarantee Fund for Micro Units (CGFMU) to encourage the banks to liberally extend these loans to eligible borrowers. The banks can extend the tenure of repayment if needed.

Union Finance Minister Nirmala Sitharaman lauded the Mudra scheme in the following words: 'The growth of MSMEs has contributed massively to the "Make in India" programme as strong domestic MSMEs lead to increased indigenous production both for domestic markets as well as for exports. The PMMY scheme has helped in the generation of large-scale employment opportunities at the grassroots level and also has proved to be a game changer while boosting the Indian economy.'[36]

The NPA of Mudra loan was only 2.62 per cent on 31 March 2023[37], which shows that the scheme has been highly successful. It has helped create many self-employed persons and their integration into the formal economy.

Services

The service sector is India's fastest and largest growing sector in the economy. Usually, a country moves from agriculture to manufacturing before the service sector. India has defied this trend. The service sector has been contributing to more than 50 per cent of the GDP, providing jobs to 30.07 per cent of the population.

This sector will witness massive growth given the government's unprecedented expenditure on infrastructure such as roads, railways, airways, ports and waterways. The investment will undoubtedly promote manufacturing. But it will also facilitate faster movement of goods and services, help achieve better multi-modal transport integration, reduce logistics costs and promote tourism.

Union Minister Piyush Goyal touched the right chord when he spoke about the dependence of manufacturing and service sectors on one another, 'The two sectors need to work together as without services, manufacturing cannot succeed and without manufacturing, services cannot grow.'[38] The government understands the importance of the rapidly growing service sector. It will create jobs and help the government achieve its target of USD 5 trillion. 'It has the potential to contribute USD 3 trillion out of this', he said.

The Prime Minister has identified 12 focus areas to enhance capacity building in the service sector. These are IT & ITeS, Tourism and Hospitality, Medical Value Travel, Transport and Logistics, Accounting and Finance, Audio Visual, Legal, Communication, Construction and Related Engineering, Environmental, Financial and Education.

The government's investment in digital India has made good governance possible by introducing information technology. Under the digital India expansion, more than 2.5 lakh panchayats are linked with broadband services. It will lead to further expansion of IT-enabled services. Most Unicorns are using ITeS to promote their business. UPI-enabled services and payment gateways were not possible without the digital push.

The investment in cultural and spiritual tourism has made India a big attraction for tourists from across the world who want to experience the country's diversified flora and fauna, rivers, mountains and seas. Tourism in India has picked up after the COVID-19 pandemic. The investment in Bharatmala and Sagar Mala roads has made travel easy and exciting for nature tourists. The attractive beaches on the coastline are big attractions. More than 1,500 startups are working in the field of travel and tourism. The Prime Minister is an articulate promoter of tourism and never misses any opportunity to sing praises for the beauty of India, its rich cultural tradition and its abundance of infrastructure, which makes tourism attractive. While addressing a meeting of G20's Tourism Ministers, he pointed out that 'India's efforts in the tourism sector are centred on preserving its rich heritage while creating a world-class infrastructure for tourism…In the last nine years, we have placed special emphasis on developing the entire ecosystem of tourism in the country.'[39]

'Be it Music or Food, Arts or Culture, the diversity of India is truly majestic…From the high Himalayas to dense forests, dry deserts to beautiful beaches, adventure sports to meditation retreats, India has something for everyone', he pointed out[40]. Recently, the Prime Minister visited Lakshadweep and promoted tourism by sharing a picture of him sitting in an armchair on the beach. In this pitch of Vocal for Local, he encouraged people to explore the beautiful island, which could match any other similar destination. Earlier, Modi had promoted destination wedding in India, asking those who go abroad for destination weddings to wed in the beautiful locales of India.

The government launched the Incredible India 2.0 campaign in September 2017. It was a marked shift from the earlier one as it took over the digital and social media sphere, from generic to specific. The campaign focussed on niche tourism, such as yoga, wellness, luxury, cuisine and wildlife. The transformative experience is highlighted through autobiographies of travellers with the tagline 'Find the Incredible You'. The campaign won the Pacific Asia Travel Association (PATA) Gold Award for 2019.

To promote tourism, the government has allowed 100 per cent FDI in the tourism industry following the automatic route. Also, 100 per cent FDI is allowed for projects such as developing exquisite hotels, resorts, and recreational facilities. FDI of USD 17.02 billion had come between 2000 and 2023 in hotel and tourism[41].

The travel and tourism industry contributed USD 178 billion to India's GDP in 2021. In 2017, before COVID-19 struck, we had more than 10 million foreign tourists, generating a foreign exchange earning of more than USD 27.31 billion[42]. In 2022, foreign exchange earning was USD 16.92 billion as the arrival of foreign tourists picked up. There was a growth of more than 92 per cent in 2021[43].

India has the best medical infrastructure to promote medical tourism, where foreign tourists get world-class treatment at an internationally competitive price. India is promoting super-speciality hospitals in many cities. It has also been promoting traditional healing methods as a part of medical tourism. The 22 All India Institute of Medical Sciences (AIIMS) focus on the Heal in India mission to transform the country into a global medical tourism hub. These high-quality hospitals with strict quality control will cater 'not only to domestic patients but also patients from abroad seeking quality medical treatment at affordable cost.'[44]

Medical tourism in India has a huge growth potential. In 2022, around 2 million tourists from 78 countries visited India for medical wellness and IVF treatment, generating USD 6 billion. It is expected to reach USD 30 billion by 2026[45]. It will push growth in the hospitality sector as well.

The construction sector is expected to reach USD 1.4 trillion by 2025. By 2030, close to 600 million people (60 crore) are likely to live in cities, accounting for 70 per cent of GDP. It would create a demand for an additional 25 million mid-range and affordable houses. The construction sector, including infrastructure, is expected to employ 100 million people, including skilled workers, by 2030.

The expenditure incurred by the government to construct 11 high-speed corridors and strengthen road, railway and airport networks would fall in the construction industry sector. It will increase the demand for steel, cement and labour, both skilled and unskilled. The decision of the government to spend Rs 10 lakh crore on infrastructure in the budget of 2023 and increasing it in the Interim Budget of 2024-25 will push this further.

One of the biggest achievements of the government has been expanding the air network to bring air travel within the reach of the common man. One should not be surprised to find crowded airports, with people standing in long queues, waiting to enter the airport. It shows affordability has increased. We have seen how Modi has tried to popularise air travel through the UDAN scheme.

Indian aviation contributed roughly 5 per cent to the GDP and provided 4 million jobs (2023). India is one of the fastest-growing civil aviation markets in the world, with air passenger traffic growing by 11 per cent every year. The number of domestic air passengers is expected to be

300 million in 2030, from 153 million in 2023. The number of airports will increase from 149 to 200. Despite such an intensity, the aviation penetration would be only 10-15 per cent, leaving a scope for massive expansion[46]. Union Minister Jyotiraditya Scindia pointed out that the fleet size has grown from 400 to 700 and would be 2000 in the next decade[47].

The infrastructural investment in railways has followed the dictum 'hungry for cargo'. The ease of doing business and customer-centric approach have helped the railways to attract additional freight. In 2022-23, it achieved the highest-ever freight loading of 1512 MT. The infrastructure aims to target 45 per cent of the freight and contribute 1.5 per cent to the GDP[48].

Foreign Direct Investment

FDI inflows of a country demonstrates its economic health. Foreign companies and governments buy stakes in the companies of host countries, anticipating good returns. It links the economies of the country in the long run, leading to technological upgradation and competitiveness where domestic companies cannot afford expansion due to the lack of investment or access to modern technology.

That India has become an important destination for foreign investors shows that the country is going up. The total FDI inflows in India in 2022-23 was USD 70.97 billion. The investors' confidence has increased after the stable Modi government came to power in 2014. The increasing ease of doing business and easing of FDI norms have made the country attractive to foreign investors. In 2012-13, the FDI inflow was USD 22 billion. In 2014-15, FDI inflow increased to USD 45.15 billion, which further increased to USD 60.22 billion in 2016-17. During 2021-22, the country received the highest FDI inflow of USD 83.57 billion.

All sectors of the economy have attracted FDI, which means less vulnerability and prospect of growth in all the sectors such as pharmaceuticals, automobiles, textiles, railways, airways, banking and insurance, telecommunication, etc. The total FDI inflow in the last 23 years has been USD 919 billion. Of this, the inflow in the last nine years was USD 595.25 billion, almost 65 per cent of the total of 23 years[49].

Foreign Exchange Reserve

In March 2014, India's foreign exchange reserve was USD 304.2 billion. By the end of December 2023, the reserve stood at USD 620.441 billion. It is enough to give import cover for 10.2 months.

It will ensure that the Rupee will be stable against the Dollar and the country's currency will be stable for the next five to six years despite the current account deficit and trade deficit[50].

The situation is bound to improve further with Indian goods becoming more competitive due to the acquisition of technology and expansion. The government's focus on import substitution and the buoyancy in exports would ease the pressure on foreign exchange, strengthening the economy.

Guarding the Borders

Preparing for Two Plus Front War

Faith is of no evil in absence of strength. Faith and strength, both are essential to accomplish any great work.

–Sardar Vallabhbhai Patel

A government's key assessment parameter would be how it has tackled internal and external security threats, its responses to threats from outside and a long-term vision to keep the defence forces ready for any eventuality. It means an agile defence force equipped with the best technology. Finally, it is the men handling the machine who are the key factors hence, their motivation level is crucial.

The nine years of the Modi government have demonstrated that there would be no compromise on the country's dignity as a peace-loving and democratic nation. We will extend the hand of friendship, but it should not be seen as a sign of weakness. Beneath the velvet gloves is the steely determination to punish those responsible for making the country bleed.

When Pakistan-backed terrorists attacked India's army headquarters at Uri in Jammu and Kashmir (18 September 2016), India launched a demonstrable surgical strike ten days later on 28 September to destroy the terrorist hideouts in Pakistan. When the terrorists attacked CRPF's moving convoys in Pathankot on 14 February 2019 killing 46 personnel, India launched air strikes on terrorist training camps in Balakot on 26 February 2019. Pakistan did not know how to respond to the new India that would not let things go unpunished.

Fearing major strikes, Pakistan had to return Wing Commander Abhinandan Varthaman, who had descended on Pakistani territory after destroying a Pakistani fighter aircraft (27 February) trying to enter the Indian airspace. Pakistanis captured Abhinandan but returned him to India within 60 hours.

It is comparable to what they did to Captain Saurabh Kalia, whom they had captured when he was on routine patrolling along the Kargil borders in May 1999. He was tortured and killed by the Pakistanis, and his dead body was returned to India. The post-mortem report revealed that Captain Kalia and his men were subjected to cigarette burns, and their eardrums were pierced with hot rods. They had many broken teeth and bones, fractured skulls, eyes punctured before being removed, cut lips, chipped noses, and amputated limbs[1]. It was barbarism of the worst kind.

There was a potent threat that if Abhinandan was not returned, India could launch an all-out war against Pakistan, and it was this fear that forced Pakistan to behave. The government officials in Pakistan feared that India was preparing to attack Pakistan[2]. With most countries standing firmly behind India, Pakistan could not look anywhere for support.

The Abhinandan episode demonstrated that India would go to any extent to safeguard its people. The might of the defence forces were not just for the show. It was used effectively to rescue the Indians stranded in the war-torn zone of Yemen in 2015. The Indian armed forces had launched Operation Raahat to evacuate Indian nationals and others stranded in Yemen. Around 6,000 people, including more than 1,900 foreign nationals, were evacuated.

The continuous bombing at multiple locations in Yemen by Saudi Arabia had made any rescue operation non-feasible. The evacuation of Indian civilians looked next to impossible. Modi spoke to Saudi King Mohammed bin Salman, who was gracious enough to honour the friendship by allowing a ceasefire of two hours from 9 am to 11 am for one week.

Foreign Affairs Minister Sushma Swaraj, who was coordinating the rescue operation, then spoke to Yemenis to open their port in Aden and airport in Sanaa to evacuate the civilians to Djibouti during the same time. 'Yemenese (sic) told me they will do anything for the Indians', Swaraj recounted talking about the execution of the rescue operation[3]. MoS for External Affairs, Gen V K Singh, was in charge of this operation, and he supervised the operation on the field.

The Indian Air Force launched a similar mission called Operation Sankat Mochan in 2016 to rescue Indians stranded in South Sudan during the civil war in Sudan. The Air force deployed two C17 Globemasters to evacuate. During the Ukraine crisis in 2022, Operation Ganga was launched to evacuate more than 15,000 Indians, mostly students. The significance of the Indian flag was witnessed globally when even Pakistani and Turkish students used Indian flags to cross various checkpoints in Ukraine and get to safety[4]. The heart of every Indian swelled with pride.

Strengthening the Defence Forces

A country like India needs a strong military force, more so because of its two hostile neighbours–Pakistan and China–who have proved to be untrusted and wily. Despite working in the human spirit, India's size and its forward stride in development have become an eyesore to many parts of the world.

There has always been a comparison between the two countries separated from each other in 1947, yet starkly different in their governance ethics. While one is under military dictatorship with an economy that is on the verge of collapse, the other is democratic despite huge differences among people and the lands they inhabit. With China, there is a comparison that despite being not as developed as China, India has democracy and human values to cheer up for. The whole world recognises how democracy is thriving in India in tandem with development.

For these reasons alone, the Indian rulers needed to maintain a strong military equipped with modern weapons. The first attempt at gaining strength came from Atal Bihari Vajpayee, who tested the nuclear bomb and declared India to be a nuclear power. It was to warn the world not to mess with India, which would do everything to safeguard its interests. During the Vajpayee government, India surprised the world by winning the war against Pakistan in Kargil. The bravery of young Indian soldiers has been etched in the military history of the world.

When the Modi government came to power, many issues were being discussed at the level of top military, which was not good for the morale of the forces. General V K Singh, the then chief of the Army Staff, accused another General of trying to bribe him, but the political leaders took no action[5]. A situation of conspiracy and mistrust had emerged among the top brass. The icing on the cake of chaos was the report that the Indian defence force was ill-equipped to deal with any emergency.

General Singh had written a letter to the Prime Minister in 2012 alerting him about the critical status of the defence forces and the country's lack of preparedness. There was an ammunition shortage that compromised the Army's capabilities to manoeuvre. The Comptroller and Auditor General of India found that in 2012, the army had only about 10 per cent of the total 84 per cent of the ammunition used by Artillery guns and tanks. In 2011 and 2013, almost 65 per cent of the weapons had only 10 days of reserve[6].

The CAG pointed out that the Indian Army was using obsolete artillery, the technology of World War 2 and the 1970s. The acquisition of new weapons, a part of the 10th Army plan of 2002-07, had not materialised. On the Indian Navy, the CAG said it lacked competitiveness in the sea[7]. The Parliamentary Standing Committee on Defence had sounded a similar warning about the shortage of ammunition.

Going by the rulebook, the Army is supposed to maintain a war wastage reserve of 40 days. Because of the perpetual shortfall, in 1999, the Army decided to have a minimum acceptable risk level (MARL) of stocks for at least 20 days.

The Indian Air Force wanted a squadron strength of 42, but it had only 32 fighting squadrons. It created operational difficulties, and Defence Minister Manohar Parikkar had flagged the issue to Prime Minister Modi. There are 16-18 aircraft in one squadron. The Rafale deal with France had got stuck, and the much talked about indigenously manufactured Tejas aircraft had not yet passed the battle-readiness test.

Under Modi: The Rafale Deal

Buying Rafale fighter aircraft from France was the only big decision of the Modi government after coming to power. Although negotiations with the French company began during the regime of the United Progressive government from 2012 onwards, orders could not be placed since terms of sales were not finalised. Then Defence Minister A K Antony declared that aircraft purchase orders could not be placed due to budgetary constraints. The cost of 126 Rafale aircraft was Rs 60,000 crore[8].

There were also procedural problems, as was deciding the lowest bidder. The tender for the deal was floated in 2006, and in 2008, the decision to buy 126 Rafale was announced when French President Nicolas Sarkozy visited India to grace the Republic Day parade as the chief guest. Out of 126, only 18 were to be bought from France, and the rest, 108, were to be manufactured in India. However, the deal got stuck due to massive irregularities reported widely in the media. The anti-corruption Anna movement had come around the same time and the UPA government had been completely defamed.

Narendra Modi picked up the old thread and realised that buying fighter aircraft was critical for strengthening the Air Force, and there was scope for negotiating a fresh deal. During his visit to France in April 2015, he declared that India had decided to acquire 36 fully equipped Rafale from France, describing it as a 'critical operational necessity'. Subsequently, the government withdrew the tender of the 126 aircraft and began negotiations for 36 aircraft. India and France signed an MoU for this acquisition, and in May 2026, the two sides arrived at a figure of Euro 7.87 billion or Rs 58,891 crore. In January 2016, India and France inked a deal whereby France would deliver the first fighter aircraft in 36 months and the rest over 66 months.

It is clear that the priority was to get the fighter planes as quickly as possible. It was easy to take it off the shelf from France rather than keeping the deal hanging in procedural problems to bring these under Make in India. It also explains why the number of aircraft was reduced to 36, which was enough for the critical need to secure the borders.

Soon after taking over his office in 2019, Air Chief Marshal RKS Bhadauria described the induction of the Rafale as a 'game changer'.

Dassault Aviation manufactured Rafale is a 4.5 generation aircraft with a radar-evading stealth profile. It can perform numerous roles such as air dominance, interdiction, aerial recce, precision long-range strike and carry multiple weapons.

On 8 October 2019, Defence Minister Rajnath Singh received India's first Rafale aircraft in France and described it as a historic day. France could meet its deadline, and all 36 aircraft were delivered to India by December 2022.

Many experts would attest that Rafale has strengthened the Indian Air Force and enhanced its capabilities manifold. However, the Opposition Congress, backed by other Opposition parties, tried to create controversy over the deal, saying it was overpriced, and alleged that the government got into some underhand dealing. The Opposition ignored that it was a government-to-government deal and was done to speed up the deal. His charges did not hold ground in front of people who trusted Modi and his integrity, and the public voted him back to power with a thumping majority. The Supreme Court that examined the deal rejected the plea of wrong-doing and gave a clean chit to the government while dismissing the petitions seeking a court-monitored probe into the deal. 'There was no occasion to doubt the decision-making process in the deal', the court held[9]. Later, the Apex Court rejected all the review petitions as well.

In 2019, after examining the price negotiations and procedures, the Apex Court upheld that 'the reworked Rafale deal for purchase of 36 fighters was indeed a better buy'. The Comptroller and Auditor General of India (CAG), too, had attested later that the Modi government's Rafale deal was a much better deal for the country[10].

Tejas Induction

One of the Opposition charges in the Rafale deal held that the government had ignored the indigenous defence organisation Hindustan Aeronautical Limited (HAL). They held that the government had ignored HAL in a deal HAL should have seen through. Now, reports have come that HAL-manufactured aircraft would have been costlier, and Dassault Aviation was not guaranteeing the delivery timeline.

Former Air Force Chief, Air Chief Marshal A Y Tipnis has admitted that manufacturing Rafales in India was challenging for the HAL, even if not impossible. 'The fact is the HAL has not performed to the level it could have. It promises more than it can deliver and quality of work has been substandard in many cases. It has also backtracked on its promises.'[11]

The HAL needed a complete overhaul and a change in its mindset and preparedness for a country that could not compromise on timely delivery of technology. The flagship of Defence Aviation, HAL needed to improve its efficiency and lead technological upgradation. The Atmanirbhar Bharat campaign, launched by Modi through Make in India, would not succeed unless defence indigenisation kept pace. There was no way HAL could have been ignored or undermined in such a situation.

HAL's turnover in 2014-15 was Rs 15,480 crore. Over 2,000 items were produced indigenously, saving Rs 100 crore. Its turnover was Rs 16,524 crore in 2015-16, and the exports stood at Rs 401 crore. In 2022-23, the revenue was Rs 26, 500 crore, representing an 8 per cent growth over the previous year's revenue of Rs 24,620 crore.

Describing the growth, CMD of HAL said, 'Despite the challenges of supply chain disruptions due to geo-political situations, the company could achieve the targeted growth in the top line. This was possible with the increased thrust on indigenisation and with the available inventory.'[12] HAL is targeting double-digit growth from 2024 onwards.

The Congress and other parties had described the HAL as sick because of Modi's decision on Rafale. The organisation gave a big slap to this thinking by multiplying its revenue and standing up to the task of strengthening defence. Union Minister Rajeev Chandrasekhar pointed out that HAL has become a Rs 1.35 lakh crore company under the leadership of Modi[13]. The shares of the HAL have gone up by five times since 2013.

The HAL achieved a landmark when the Prime Minister inaugurated the country's largest Helicopter manufacturing unit in Tumakuru in Karnataka in February 2023. He laid the foundation for this dream indigenisation project in 2016.

'HAL's new factory and growing prowess is exposing several old lies, and those who made the false allegations. Reality is speaking. The very same HAL is making modern Tejas (fighter jets) and strengthening India's self-reliance in the defence sector', Modi said at the inauguration ceremony.

The Greenfield Helicopter Factory spread across 615 acres of land, plans to meet all helicopter requirements of the country. More than 1,000 helicopters, ranging from 3-15 tonnes, will be manufactured over 20 years, generating a revenue of Rs 4 lakh crore. It will save the revenue spent on imports, encourage local industries and create an ecosystem that would generate business and employment[14].

Another landmark for HAL came during Modi's visit to the United States in June 2023. GE Aerospace, the world leader in aircraft engine and avionics, inked a deal with HAL to jointly produce India's indigenous fighter aircraft Mk-II Tejas. Modi had gone to the US at the invitation of US President Joe Biden. An older version of GE Engine F 404 is already powering Tejas I, but the more advanced LCA needed the F414 version. The HAL procured eight F414 Engines for the development programme of Tejas Mark II.

The deal was possible because the US and India have come closer and have reached an agreement for defence cooperation. In 2016, Washington designated India as a 'major defence partner'. India's military purchases from the US had crossed USD 20 billion in 2020.

A moment of pride was when the Prime Minister took a 30-minute sortie of the 4.5 generation aircraft and was immensely impressed by the capabilities of the aircraft. He became the first PM to ride an indigenously developed fighter plane.

After his ride in November 2023 during his visit to the HAL in Bangalore, his instant comment on Twitter was: 'Successfully completed a sortie on the Tejas. The experience was incredibly enriching, significantly bolstering my confidence in our country's indigenous capabilities, and leaving me with a renewed sense of pride and optimism about our national potential.'[15]

The sortie with a trained fighter pilot showed the Prime Minister's confidence in indigenous capabilities and the progress made by HAL towards being *Atmanirbhar Bharat*. In another tweet, he said: 'Flying in Tejas today, I can say with immense pride that due to our hard work and dedication, we are no less than anyone in the world in the field of self-reliance. Heartiest congratulations to the Indian Air Force, DRDO and HAL as well as all Indians.'

In fact, the HAL has led India's Atmanirbhar Bharat campaign and helped indigenise the Indian Air Force. However, there has been an inordinate delay in making it a part of the force. The project to build the Light Combat Aircraft (LCA) Tejas got approval in 1994. It took its first sortie in 2001. Going by the norm, it should have been inducted into the Air Force by 2008-09. As Manas Bihari Verma, the scientist supervising Tejas as its project head during the experimental years, said, there may be some obscurantist forces trying to delay the project to import some foreign aircraft[16]. It took 33 long years for Tejas to become fully operational.

Adversity often brings opportunities. It was the case of Tejas, too, which suffered due to the sanctions on imports the developed world had imposed on India post-Pokhran II. The project needed to import 50 critical components to make the aircraft flight-worthy. Later, these were developed indigenously, Verma pointed out.

Not much was spent on Research and Development (R and D), and HAL was satisfied with the assembly work of major critical equipment. Narendra Modi provided the much-needed inspiration through the Make in India pitch and Atmanirbhar Bharat.

A change in focus also brought about a shift in the thinking, which was reflected in strengthening research, linking organisational goals with startup culture to create a manufacturing ecosystem, bringing structural changes within the organisation to make it more efficient and opening up a marketing and business wing to showcase the products in the international market.

The HAL realised that not pushing its product adequately made it lose an opportunity to sell Tejas to Malaysia even as a much inferior aircraft from South Korea clinched the deal. It set up a new commercial and marketing wing for such situations. This wing is expected to specialise in meeting international queries and promoting HAL's products globally. It is also setting up a marketing office in Kuala Lumpur to market its products in South East Asia.

As of 2020, HAL had made a combined expenditure of Rs 6,783 crore in the last five years on R and D. In 2023, it decided to spend Rs 2,000 core on R and D[17]. More investment in research means more opportunities for indigenisation and better integration with the vast pool of talent available in the country.

The HAL already has Rs 84,000 crore worth of orders for aircraft supply, including 83 LCA Tejas Mark-1A, which would be inducted in the Air Force. The IAF would have 40 LCA, over 180 LCA Mark-1A and at least 120 LCA Mark-2 fighter planes in the next 15 years. It would gradually phase out the MIG series. The decision to place orders for 100 more Tejas Mark-1A has been made already.

More than 16 countries, including the United States, have shown interest in buying a more lethal version of the current–Tejas Mark-2 from the HAL. The Cabinet Committee on Security (CCS) has already given its nod to produce LCA Mark-2, which would fill the critical gap and eventually replace MIG 29, Mirage 2000 and Jaguar Fleet. It is slated to lead to collaboration with private players to ramp up production to meet the global demand. The HAL would lead and coordinate[18].

Make in India

The government has taken various initiatives to incentivise manufacturing under the Make in India campaign. The biggest impact is visible in the defence sector, where two defence corridors–one in Uttar Pradesh and the other in Tamil Nadu–were established in 2018 and 2019, respectively. The corridor in Uttar Pradesh crossed through six locations–Agra, Aligarh, Chitrakoot, Jhansi, Kanpur and Lucknow. Similarly, the one in Tamil Nadu crossed through five locations–Chennai, Coimbatore, Hosur, Salem and Tiruchirappalli.

Adequate infrastructure was created in these areas to promote Make in India through the participation of both the public and private sectors in small and medium industries and to boost defence production. It would, in turn, help reduce imports in defence and boost exports.

The impact was for all to see. India's defence export had reached an all-time high, surging from Rs 680 crore in 2013-14 to Rs 16,000 crore in 2022-23. The target is to reach Rs 35,000 crore by 2024-25[19].

Talking about the possibilities, Union Defence Minister Rajnath Singh said:

> The country's defence sector has scaled greater heights due to the reforms taken by the government in the past few years. We have created a conducive ecosystem for exports and FDI with focus on manufacturing products indigenously…The Ministry of Defence has set a target of achieving a turnover of Rs 1.75 lakh crore in aerospace and defence goods and services by 2024, including exports of Rs 35,000 crore[20].

Exports include Akash missiles, Brahmos, Pinaka and Dornier-228, thermal imagers, 155mm Advanced Towed Artillery Guns (ATAGs), Radars, Simulators, Body Armours, Mine Protected Vehicles, etc. There is also an increasing demand for Light Combat Helicopters, Aircraft Carriers and Light Combat Aircraft (LCA) Tejas.

India's defence exports have catered to the needs of countries such as Sri Lanka, Bangladesh, Myanmar, Nepal, Vietnam, Indonesia, Malaysia, the Philippines, Thailand, UAE, Saudi Arabia, Egypt, Israel, Russia, France, the United Kingdom and the United States of America.

Significant progress has been made in manufacturing bullet-proof jackets. Gone are the days when the DRDL (Defence Research Development Laboratory) had developed an indigenous jacket that could not be used since it weighed 25 kg and was uncomfortable to wear.

After intensive research, in 2023, India and DRDO developed the world's lightest bullet-proof jacket weighing 9 kg. These jackets are high in demand internationally. Besides meeting the demands of the Indian defence forces, India is exporting these jackets to more than 100 countries[21].

Many private players are participating in defence production, trying to make the products globally competitive. Some of these include Tata, Mahindra, Reliance, Adani, L and T India, Kalyani Group, Hinduja Group, Alpha Design Technologies, Punj Lloyd, etc.

The indigenous defence production suffered because the country laid stress on importing rather than investing in research and design. The motive behind the previous dispensation is anybody's guess. While India is importing critical equipment such as Rafale, Missile Defence

Systems and Drones for safeguarding borders, most of the other demand is fulfilled locally.

Even when India decided to purchase AK 203 Rifles, it also manufactured them through a transfer of technology mechanism. The Indian Army has already purchased 70,000 of these highly sophisticated rifles from Russia and is to manufacture another six lakhs indigenously in collaboration with Russia over 128 months. So is the case with other big defence deals, such as submarines from Germany, with the first few to be produced in Germany together with Indian private players and others in India.

The government has tried to bolster defence and safeguard borders without talking much about defence spending. Modern weaponry and agile soldiers ensure that the borders cannot be violated. The nation is prepared for a 'Two and a half front war', Chief of the Defence Staff, General Bipin Rawat, thundered in 2017[22].

The country secured its air borders from both Pakistan and China using the Russian S-400 missile system. Three squadrons have been deployed along the borders. Two more squadrons will further boost the air defence. It is the world's most lethal Modern Long-Range Surface-to-Air Missile (MLR SAM).

This Surface-to-Air Missile is capable of intercepting and destroying aerial targets, such as aircraft, drones, cruise missiles and ballistic missiles. It has a range of 400 km and an altitude of 30 km, engaging 36 targets simultaneously.

Another landmark in the air defence system is Project Kusha, which aims to develop a long-range air defence system by 2028-29. Developed by the DRDO, it would rival the S-400 and would be capable of destroying enemy targets such as cruise missiles, stealth fighters and drones.

Revamp of Ordinance Review Board

A decisive step towards defence modernisation was revamping the 200-year-old Ordinance Review Board, which operates 41 ordinance factories spread all over India. They focussed on the production of ammunition and defence equipment. The government accepted the proposal to restructure ORB and created seven corporate entities in 2021.

It was in tune with Modi's philosophy of reform, perform and transform. The seven entities would work like any corporate sector to maximise competitiveness and cost-efficiency. It was to make India move faster towards *Atmanirbhar Bharat.* The reform was suggested about two decades ago.

These seven entities were–ammunition and explosives group, vehicles group, weapons and equipment group, troop comfort items group, ancillary group, optoelectronics group and parachute group. The nomenclature suggests their areas of activity.

There were serious complaints against the ORF on various fronts, and the ordinance factories had become synonymous with poor-quality products, inordinate delays and outdated technology. The production cost was too high because of the high employee cost.

An internal assessment by the army mentioned that 'faulty ammunition and armament supplied by the OFB caused army casualties and bled the exchequer...In the last six years, 403 accidents occurred resulting in the deaths of 27 soldiers and a loss of Rs 960 crore.'[23]

Major Defence Acquisition

On 16 February 2024, the Defence Acquisition Council (DAC) cleared capital acquisitions worth Rs 84,560 crore to strengthen the Armed Forces and the Indian Coast Guard. It focussed on defence purchases from Indian vendors. The DAC amended the Defence Acquisition Procedure of 2020 to promote the procurement of advanced technologies from startups and MSMEs.

Proposals include new generation Anti-Tank Mines, Air Defence Tactical Control Radar, Heavy Weight Torpedoes, Medium Range Maritime Reconnaissance and Multi-Mission Maritime Aircraft, Flight Refueller Aircraft and Software Defined Radios[24].

Strengthening the Navy

The Indian Navy has cleared the way for acquiring 31 predator drones from the United States. It will bolster India's surveillance and reconnaissance capabilities on the seas. The USD 4 Billion contract includes associated weapons essential for operational deployment[25].

These drones are equipped with strike missiles and can engage enemy targets with high precision. It will empower the Navy in various roles, including anti-submarine warfare, anti-surface warfare, electronic warfare and expeditionary missions.

By 2047, as India completes its centenary, the Navy will be completely self-reliant. The Indian Navy has plans to acquire a fleet strength of 200 warships by 2027, from the 150 at present. Comparatively, China has 355 warships.

The giant step was taken when the Navy commissioned its biggest warship, the indigenously built aircraft carrier Vikrant. In December, the powerful warship Stealth Destroyer, Mormugao, submarine INS Vagir were commissioned. They have significantly augmented sea denial and sea control capabilities on the high seas. The Indian Navy has acquired the strength to challenge any naval power in the Indian Ocean.

A significant development has been the launch of the anti-submarine warfare ship Arnala, which will replace Abhay-class anti-submarine warfare ships. The Arnala ships are more powerful and are the Indian Navy's first anti-submarine warfare ship. It is designed to undertake anti-submarine operations in coastal waters. Orders for eight such warships have been placed with the Garden Reach Shipbuilders and Engineers in Kolkata.

India now has 17 submarines, including 4 German HDW, 7 Russian Kilo-class, 5 Kalvari class French Scorpenes and 1 Indian nuclear-powered submarine Arihant.

On 3 February 2024, the Navy commissioned survey vessel INS Sandhayak at the Naval Dockyard in Visakhapatnam. Rajnath Singh said the new ship would help 'further strengthen India's role as a superpower in the Indo-Pacific region', highlighting the role of the Indian Navy in strengthening maritime security.

He highlighted the role India needs to play as a promoter of world peace, and the purpose was its growing power to ensure a rule-based world order. 'Our aim is to stop illegal and unregulated fishing in the Indian Ocean and Indo-Pacific region. The Navy is stopping narcotics and human trafficking in this region. It is committed not only to stopping piracy but also making this entire region peaceful and prosperous', he asserted[26].

The navy protects civilian vessels passing through the Indian Ocean and the Arabian Sea. It has already been thwarting piracy attempts and saving sailors. 'The Indian Navy is facilitating safe trade in the Indian Ocean region while ensuring peace and prosperity. Many defence experts are calling this the rise of a superpower. This is our culture, to protect everyone', the defence minister said[27].

The Indian Navy would get more firepower by getting the 26 Rafale Marine Fighter Jets for which deals have already been finalised. The deal under the government-to-government contract would cost India Rs 50,000 crore. It includes 22 single-seat jets and 4 twin-seat trainers, with weapons, simulators, spares, crew training and logistics support[28]. These deadly fighter planes would strengthen the fire capabilities of INA Vikrant and INS Vikramaditya.

Creating the Institution of the CDS

The requirement for the position of a Chief of Defence Staff was felt during the wars with China and Pakistan. The issue cropped up every time experts talked of better integration between the forces. In 1999, the Kargil Review Committee under K Subrahmanyam recommended creating the CDS. In 2001, the Group of Ministers, which studied the recommendations, suggested setting up the institution of the CSC. The deliberations failed to culminate into a decision until 2017 when the Cabinet Committee on Security took up the issue.

During his Independence Day speech on 15 August 2019, the Prime Minister announced the creation of the position of the CDS. Subsequently, a committee was formed under the National Security Advisor, comprising other members such as the Cabinet Secretary, the Defence Secretary and the Chairman of the Chief of Staff Committee (C-COSC) to activate the decision. On 24 December 2019, the CCS formally established the post of Chief of Defence Staff.

The position was created to improve coordination, tri-service effectiveness and overall integration of the combat capabilities of the Indian armed forces. The CDS was also assigned the task of prioritising capital expenditure among the tri-services and overall defence planning. General Bipin Rawat became the first CDS on 1 January 2020.

Modi described the institution as carrying forward the task of modernising the armed forces and meeting the hopes and aspirations of every Indian. 'For long the country was debating the appointment of Chief of Defence Staff, but no decision could be taken. This decision is the symbol of the self-confidence of a new India.'[29]

The CCS had also approved creating the Department of Military Affairs. Under the new arrangement, any work related to Military Affairs is to be done only by the Department of Military Affairs whereas, the Department of Defence will deal with issues related to the country's defence.

The new department was shaped as a truly integrated department to achieve better results through effective coordination between the Armed Forces and the Civil Services. It is intended to facilitate inter-service integration and better civilian-military coordination. It also aimed at strengthening the process of Joint Planning, Operations and Procurement, thereby making the Armed Forces more effective and efficient[30].

Following the philosophy of *Atmanirbhar Bharat*, the new Department of Military Affairs (DMA) released the first indigenisation list of 101 items in August 2020 and the second indigenisation list of 108 items in May 2021. The items in these lists can be procured only from indigenous industries.

The CDS and the DMA are working hard to achieve better integration of the three services to enhance military capabilities. The procedures are being worked out to integrate Defence Planning, Procurement and Operations and to rationalise optimum utilisation of available resources.

One Rank One Pension (OROP)

The issue of One Rank One Pay (OROP) has been in the limelight ever since the army veterans started demanding parity in the pension of retired defence personnel. A demand was raised that a soldier retiring in the same rank and with the same length of service should get the same pension irrespective of the year of retirement.

The Koshyari Committee Report (2011), which looked into the issue of OROP, defined a 'uniform pension be paid to the armed forces personnel retiring in the same rank with the same length of service irrespective of their date of retirement and any future enhancements in the rate of pension to be automatically passed on to the past pensioners'.

The demand existed since the 1970s. Political parties gave lip service but did not have the sincerity to implement the concept. The outgoing UPA government hurriedly accepted the OROP in 2014 due to election compulsions, and on 1 February 2014, it announced the OROP but had no clue how to go about it. It allocated a meagre sum of Rs 500 crore. That it was an election stunt was obvious since the UPA in 2009 said that 'there are administrative, technical and financial difficulties in implementing OROP and it is for these reasons that the present government took some time to fulfil its promise'.

It was clear that the UPA had worked under pressure from Modi, who expressed his determination to implement OROP immediately after coming to power. During a rally of army veterans in Rewari on 15 September, two days after the BJP's official declaration that he would be the party's Prime Ministerial candidate for the 2014 Lok Sabha polls, Modi had thundered that the OROP was a justified demand and sought a white paper on the issue[31].

'Today I publicly demand from the Government of India on behalf of the army men and ex-service men of this country, to publish a white paper on the status of "one rank, one pension" scheme.' If Atal Bihari Vajpayee had returned to power in 2004, he would have resolved the issue, he added.

Naturally, after coming to power Modi started finding ways to implement his promises. Modi has always respected army men and their sacrifices for the country. The time has come to show that he cared. But it was not as easy as said. There were lots of bureaucratic hurdles. Many experts declared it was impossible to implement OROP, and Modi would not bite the bullet.

Modi knew the complications, the resistance from particular interests and the financial burden this would put on the exchequer. One such issue was delving deep into the records, identifying the beneficiaries of old pension schemes and bringing them at par. It involved computational problems. However, the demand from the army could not be made subservient to other issues.

On 5 September 2015, Prime Minister Modi announced the historic decision to implement the OROP. 'For four decades, the issue of One Rank One Pension has been left unaddressed. Men who give their lives to the nation have been asking for OROP, and there is nothing more important than maintaining the dignity of these men', he said. It was to be implemented from the back date of 1 July 2014. The pension would be re-fixed every five years, based on the pension of those retiring in 2013.

He announced paying the arrears in four half-yearly instalments. However, all the family pensioners, including those receiving Special/ Liberalised family pension and Gallantry award winners, were to be paid arrears in one instalment.

It meant an expenditure of Rs 10,925.11 crore in payment of arrears and an annual expenditure of Rs 7,488.7 crore[32]. The first instalment, amounting to Rs 2,861 crore, was already paid to 15.91 lakh pensioners by 31 March 2016. In the first five years, approximately Rs 42,740.28 crore was disbursed to 20,60,220 Defence Forces and family pensioners[33]. A total of approximately Rs 70,000 crore has been deposited in the bank account of beneficiaries, the Prime Minister pointed out[34].

Addressing a rally in Rewari on 17 February 2024, Modi reminded people of his promises on the OROP and the fulfilment of the promise after he came to power. He said Rewari saw the promise and also the fulfilment as it was Modi *ki* guarantee. Rewari was the first witness to Modi guarantee.

Agniveers or Fire Warriors

Modi has always tried to give solutions, and in one stroke he resolves many issues. The country has been debating whether formal military training should be made compulsory for every citizen in anticipation of a disciplined citizenry and to provide the country with a well-trained human pool, which can come in handy during a national emergency.

Some of the countries such as Russia, China, Iran, South Korea, North Korea, Israel, Brazil and Sweden have compulsory military training for citizens. Some also have conscripted soldiers. India adopted the policy of having a professional army recruited through the voluntary will of the people. The policy has withstood till now.

However, with fast-changing developments where artificial intelligence and air power play a major role, two issues have cropped up among policy-makers–whether there is a need for expanding foot soldiers matching the population? How to keep a decisive edge in the military without compromising on the basics? Above all, how to maintain a balance where professional soldiers are not outnumbered by the staff supposed to support the front warriors?

The idea of Agniveers (Fire Warriors) can be further appreciated when we try to understand how it is practised in the United States. The US started a short-term enlisted programme in 2003, offering the option of enlistment for eight years, of which two years would be spent in active duty, four years in Active Guard/Reserves, and the last two years in Inactive Reserves. The US military was also allowed other short-term enlistment schemes ranging from two to four/six years. In shorter enlistment, little training is required, but jobs involving complexity require more rigorous training and, hence, longer enlistment. Some jobs in the Navy even have an enlistment programme of five years.

As early as 2022, the US started a new two-year enlistment programme under which recruits would spend only two years after basic and advanced training on active duty. They would be required to spend an additional two years on a part-time basis in the Army Reserve, during which they would be attached to a local unit[35].

India has tried to strike a balance by providing youths an opportunity to spend four years of their lives, when they are the most active physically and mentally, to join the military and serve the country. The age group is 17.5 to 21 years, as practised in advanced countries, too. Also, many promising youths do not wish to commit themselves full-time to the army, though they may lap it up if the duration is less. It would increase the potential to catch the most agile in this age group.

And by the time other people in their age group are still toying with the idea of what to do in life, these Agniveers–matured, robust, disciplined and organised–would be ready to take on the world on their terms. From among those who would want to continue in the army, only 25 per cent would be taken in regular jobs for 15 more years. The rest would be recruited in para-military forces and the State and Central Police force.

When these Agniveers come out of their army period, they would get a handsome amount of Rs 11.71 lakh, and they can start any business since banks would be more than keen to give them loans under various government schemes. During the duration of the enlistment, they would get a non-contributory insurance of Rs 48 lakh. Their salary has been fixed at Rs 30,000 monthly, which would go up to Rs 40,000. One-third of the same would create an Agniveer corpus with a matching amount from the government.

The Agnipath scheme to recruit Agniveers from both sexes for all ranks below the officers was launched on 15 June 2022. It announced the recruitment of more than 40,000 Agniveers in the army and 3,000 each in the Navy and the Air Force. The qualification was Class 10, 12 or ITI.

Naturally, the scheme intends to bring down the age profile of the armed forces by about 4-5 years, make the army more agile by giving options and making available a vast pool of talent for any emergency.

As is the case in the country, even the best schemes get criticised for political reasons. Opposition parties opposed the scheme, raising many questions and creating confusion among youths who took the army as an employment opportunity. People came on the streets and blocked roads and traffic, burnt trains and anarchy was let loose at many places in Bihar and Uttar Pradesh.

The government explained that the Agniveers had nothing to fear since most would get absorbed in other uniform services. Many industrialists came forward, saying that the Agniveers would be given preference over others in recruitment to these organisations after completing their tenure.

With the kind of training these Agniveers would receive in the army, they would be coveted by the para-military forces and the police all over the country. Imagine the kind of discipline this would bring in these people who would be possible recruits for other responsible jobs in government and private sector.

Some people challenged the Agniveer recruitment on one plea or the other, but the Delhi High Court rejected those petitions and upheld the policy of the Central government. The Supreme Court upheld the decision of the High Court.

Those arguing against the scheme based on job or recruitment forgot the basic tenet that the army is an opportunity to serve the country, and any recruitment must serve the interest of the motherland. The recruitment, therefore, must be seen in the context of the need to strengthen national security. The main aim is to win the war and have people accordingly. Agniveer is expected to bring a transformational change.

The massive response to recruitment rallies across the country was a slap on the face of those who opposed it. Rather than demotivating youths, the scheme got a massive response. Short-term military training, training in firearms and the thrill of adventure often motivate youths. Seeing the unprecedented response, which was often unmanageable, the government tweaked the recruitment process under which every candidate now is first supposed to sit for a competitive examination. Only those who qualify would undergo a test at the recruitment rally and then a medical test. Beginning in 2023, the first Common Entrance Examination (CEE) was organised in 375 centres spread over 176 pan locations.

Modi Makes Friends Worldwide

Be it the First World War or the Second World War, India never attacked other countries. We never attacked any country for conquering their territory. But our brave soldiers fought for others and sacrificed their lives in both the Wars. And, the world must recognise this.
–Narendra Modi

Narendra Modi was highly popular even when he was the BJP's Prime Ministerial candidate in 2013 and had launched his election campaign. His swearing-in ceremony on 26 May 2014 was sure to attract international attention. Here was a man born in independent India and keen to make a new beginning to rightfully claim its place in the new world order–a place that was due to the second-largest population in the world united by geography and culture.

India bled when Partition was enforced, and Pakistan was created on religious grounds. India was a statement of how different people with different ideologies and faiths existed harmoniously in the cultural mosaic. While formal democracy was adopted as the form of government, India has always been democratic. Only the form of democracy was different.

In Modi, the country saw a leader personifying India's cultural values. He would cultivate friends in the best interest of the country and not allow personal prejudices to overshadow his actions. The time had come to pick up the thread from another great son of India, Atal Bihari Vajpayee, who showed what a statesman he was when he undertook the bus to Lahore to build bridges with Pakistan. Alas! Pakistan failed to respond and did a Kargil at its own peril.

Modi idolises Swami Vivekananda for understanding India's cultural and spiritual journey and for spiritual upliftment and linking with the world. But he is also a follower of Shivaji. Behind the velvet handshake or warm embrace is the steely determination to strengthen India. If you are a friend, the relationship will be of trust and complementarity. If it is enmity, the country will do everything to get justice and make the rule of law prevail. India is not a bully, but it won't tolerate a bully either.

In Modi's own words, his way of dealing with 'our neighbours is to be constructive and cooperative when required and, equally, to be firm and steadfast when needed. Both on initiatives and challenges, one can see the difference with the past.'[1]

Modi wanted to give peace a chance to prevail. He wanted to begin a new chapter for lasting peace and prosperity in the immediate neighbourhood. He has often repeated both India and Pakistan should work jointly for the common good. He has always tried to make a distinction between the people of Pakistan and the establishment that has been using terrorism as a state policy.

It is with these thoughts that Modi invited leaders of all countries of the SAARC (South Asian Association for Regional Cooperation) to his swearing-in ceremony organised at the forecourts of the Rashtrapati Bhavan. Among those who attended included Afghanistan's President Hamid Karzai; Bhutan's Prime Minister Tshering Tobgay; Maldives' President Abdulla Yameen Abdul Gayoom; Nepal's Prime Minister Sushil Koirala, Sri Lanka's President Mahinda Rajapaksa and Prime Minister of Pakistan Nawaz Sharif. Bangladesh's Prime Minister, Sheikh Hasina, could not attend due to her prior engagement, but the country was represented by Speaker of *Jatiya Sangsad,* Shirin Sharmin Chaudhury. Mauritius' Prime Minister Navin Ramgoolam was also invited.

There was a genuine jubilation across India. The entire world was watching the big event with keen interest. Here was a man who had overcome all odds and opposition to get elected to the top post. There was also curiosity and apprehension since vested interests had tried to malign Modi's image as being partial. How he would treat the Pakistani

Prime Minister was the main agenda of the media since the relationship between the two countries had dipped low.

During his election campaign, Modi had demonstrated his determination to establish peace. He talked about Hindu-Muslim unity and invited both India and Pakistan to launch a combined fight against poverty. He had offered India's full economic cooperation but had warned against continuing the policy of exporting terrorism to India.

Modi did not see the country with the binaries of Hindus and Muslims. At the Hunkar rally in Patna in October 2013, he said, 'Hindu poor should be fighting the poverty in their community instead of Muslims just as the poor among Muslims should be fighting their poverty rather than Hindus.' He stressed that 'Hindus and Muslims needed to unite for the sake of growth.'[2]

He had a one-to-one interaction with all the leaders who had come for the swearing-in ceremony and tried to build a relationship of trust. Personal interaction with world leaders often helps them to understand each other, which is crucial for the benefits to flow both ways. Modi has charmed world leaders with his warmth and genuine affection.

The transition–from an authentic victory in 2014 to a sweeping victory in 2019–was achieved with hard work and commitment to the nation. He demonstrated that he was a strong leader and could set aside protocols to cultivate friends. While crossing over Pakistani airspace during his return journey from Afghanistan, he visited Nawaz Sharif's ancestral village, Raiwind, near Lahore, in 2015 to join the marriage celebration of his granddaughter. It happened suddenly when he called Nawaz Sharif to wish him on his birthday Sharif gave an impromptu invite, and Modi landed there, extending a hand of friendship. However, the gesture to cultivate friendship was not a sign of weakness. There have been times when he warned Pakistan to stop supporting terrorism and urged it to work towards peace.

However, Pakistan did not take Modi's hands of friendship seriously. Pakistan's Uri and Pulwama attacks met India's surgical strike and Balakot attack. Pakistan captured Wing Commander Abhinandan Varthaman, only to release him immediately, fearing another retaliation from India.

Since then India has learnt to live without bothering about Pakistan.

It has also managed to ensure that the world does not look at India with the binary of India-Pakistan. Occasional statements here and there about Pakistan and terrorism are the only things between India and Pakistan at a bilateral level.

Taming the Dragon

Modi has earned fame and accolades worldwide. Whoever he met during his international visits became his friend. His warm hugs and earnestness to give solutions made him endearing. He even offered a friendly hand to China to increase regional prosperity, but China, known for its expansionist designs, tried to alter the boundary at Doklam.

Ever since the China-India standoff in Doklam in 2017, the relationship between the two has not been good. India has rebuffed the Chinese expansionism. In June 2020, violent clashes occurred in the Galwan Valley. Colonel Bikkumalla Santosh Babu's bravery on the front and fist-to-fist fight at the borders at Doklam gave a bloody nose to the Chinese.

India witnessed the martyrdom of 20 of its soldiers. However, these soldiers demonstrated that the Chinese soldiers were no match for their unparalleled professionalism. Before dying, these soldiers inflicted heavy casualties on China, and twice as many Chinese soldiers were killed.

Many rounds of talks have taken place between the military commanders of both sides for disengagement. Aware of unpredictable China and its expansionist design, India has bolstered its military presence along the borders. China has reportedly deployed more than 50,000 troops, and India is matching up to the same.

It is a different India under Modi. China had not expected such a response. Usually, Indian leaders would prefer to be low-key while dealing with China. Modi has asserted on many platforms that the world of territorial expansion is over, and countries should learn to acquire prosperity through mutual economic cooperation. India does not mince words when condemning China's aggressive stance on the borders. Defence Secretary Giridhar Aramane recently described China as a 'bully' and thanked the United States for the intelligence support to India on the standoff.

India's determination to boldly face the bully was obvious in the tenor of Aramane's statement at the second INDUS-X defence summit with US Indo-Pacific Command Chief Admiral John C Aquilino in February 2024. He said,

> India is giving a face off to our neighbour in almost all the fronts we have with them, wherever there is a mountain pass, we are stationed there... and wherever there is a road we have to be there. So that way we are there standing against a bully in a very determined fashion.[3]

Earlier, there used to be a lurking fear of China. Under Modi, the military has realised its strength. While the whole world is watching the long standoff between India and China, India has successfully built its equations with Vietnam, the Philippines and Japan–the three neighbours of China upset with Chinese expansionism. Taiwan, too, is unhappy with Chinese aggression. Narendra Modi has also made the whole world realise the double-speak of China.

While the standoff continues, Modi has taken all steps to strengthen the military in all its wings. Today, India is many times stronger than it was in 2014. Modi also knows that none of the countries would come to India's rescue, and any threat must be fought on its own strength. The talk of international law or world order is for those who have power.

Modi is not an ordinary Prime Minister. He is the master of ceremonies wherever he visits. He has established an emotional chord with the Indian diaspora during his foreign visits. The diaspora is keen to give him a rousing reception. The cheering by the crowd and the respect he enjoys among people of Indian origin would make any leader envious of his popularity.

Ever since he became the Prime Minister, he has visited more than 72 countries and has established a one-to-one rapport with their leaders. It also includes visits to countries wielding immense power and influence on the world stage. He had visited the United States eight times, France seven times, Germany six times, the UK thrice and Australia twice. He has good equations with G7 developed countries.

One would not forget the historic reception, much like a rock star, which he received at New York's Madison Square in September 2014. The reception was a testimony to the chemistry Modi has with the Indian diaspora. Non-resident Indians had flown from places in the United States to get a glimpse of Modi at the grand reception. It announced to the world that India had arrived.

Those keeping track of the events would remember that when the US had denied a visa to Modi as Gujarat's Chief Minister under the influence of vested interests in India, the Indians retaliated by making him address the Indian diaspora in 18 US cities through video conferencing in May 2013[4].

After Modi became the Prime Minister, the US did not know how it would react. But Modi had buried the hatchet to cultivate a good relationship with the US even if his supporters were having a moment of triumph. US President Barack Obama appeared too keen to please Modi. The high point was the joint editorial they wrote for *The Washington Post* in which the central theme was 'Forward together we go–*chalein saath saath*'. Modi also wrote an independent editorial for the *Wall Street Journal*, highlighting the importance of India-US relations.

That the two world leaders had struck the right chord was visible when Obama visited India in 2015 and became India's chief guest at the Republic Day Parade. He became the first US President to do so. The bonhomie between the two was evident. While Modi addressed him as 'my friend Barack', Obama expressed the desire to wear a Modi kurta.

The US welcome to Modi reached another high point in his September 2019 visit. The reception he got at 'Howdy Modi' (Howdy means 'How do you Do') at the community summit at NRG Stadium, Houston (Texas) was unparalleled for any world leader. The then-US President Donald Trump was overwhelmed by the response and, ushered by Modi, they together took an unplanned lap of honour. The bonhomie between Modi and Trump or between a rising India and the US could not be missed by anyone. Trump had likened Modi's popularity to the King of Pop, Elvis Presley.

Modi's critics concluded that his equation with Trump would not allow easy relationship with the new US President, Joe Biden, who succeeded Trump in 2021. However, they were in for a big shock as Indo-US relations kept scaling new heights. It is despite the jarring notes that came due to US expectations on the Ukraine crisis and India's independent stand vis-à-vis Russia. However, the reality of India being the largest democracy, the dynamism of Modi and the need to contain China have brought the US back on track with India. India has clarified that it would not indulge in bloc politics and would continue to have an independent relationship with other countries.

The rousing reception was repeated and outperformed at Modi's next historic visit to the US in 2023. The four-day meeting was marked with a ceremonial welcome, bilateral meetings with US President Joe Biden, Modi's address to the joint session of the US Congress, and interaction with CEOs of top business corporations. Another high point was Modi leading a yoga session at the UN Headquarters in New York to mark the 9th International Day of Yoga, in which people from more than 180 countries participated[5].

Despite not liking India's decision to import oil and continue its military ties with Russia, the US has understood that a strong India is needed for a new global order. The US has realised India's defence needs and its trust in Russia as a friend. On the contrary, the good equation that Modi enjoys with Russian President Vladimir Putin allows the world to open backdoor diplomacy with Russia.

It explains the rousing reception Narendra Modi got in the US under Joe Biden in June 2023. After a one-to-one meeting during the State visit, they both released a joint statement stating that the two countries were 'among the closest partners in the world', and of a 'new level of trust and understanding'.

Biden went the extra mile beyond protocol to add a personal touch. He hosted a State-dinner, and both he and his wife, Jill Biden, engaged with Modi at multiple events. They even hosted a private meal for the Indian Prime Minister, a rare honour.

The visit was marked by his address to the joint sitting of US Congress on 22 June. It was the second time he addressed the US Parliament, the first being in 2016. Modi spoke amidst clapping by US senators, 'In the past few years, there have been many advances in AI–Artificial Intelligence. At the same time, there have been even more momentous developments in another AI–America and India', Modi said while describing Indo-US ties[6].

Biden had already acknowledged the popularity of Modi. On the sidelines of the meeting of QUAD in Tokyo in 2023, Biden is quoted as having told Modi playfully, 'You are causing me a real problem. Next month we have a dinner for you in Washington. Everyone in the country wants to come. I have run out of tickets. You think I am kidding? Ask my team. I am getting phone calls from people I have never heard of before. Everyone from movie stars to relatives. You are too popular.'[7] Biden and Modi hugged each other at the G7 meeting in Hiroshima (before QUAD), and the warmth was evident.

The new evolving equation between the US and India was evident when India's HAL signed an agreement with GE of the US for joint production of Aerospaces' F414 fighter-plane engines in India.

United Kingdom

His visit to the United Kingdom in November 2015 will be remembered for his historic reception at the famous Wembley Stadium in London, where more than 60,000 people gathered to listen to him. The then-Prime Minister of the UK, David Cameron, made a prophetic declaration while introducing Modi to the crowd. 'Team India, team UK–together we are a winning combination.' As the crowd cheered, he said it would not be long before there was a British Indian Prime Minister in Downing Street.

After seven years, in October 2022, a British-born person of Indian origin, Rishi Sunak, became the Prime Minister of the UK. He also became the first Hindu to hold the post. Sunak has never made any efforts to hide his being a Hindu. Modi and Sunak hit an instant chord for bettering India-UK relations.

France

India and France have been all-weather friends and this relationship has further strengthened under Modi. His visit to France, Germany and Canada in 2015 was remarkable. Together, India and France formed the International Solar Alliance to boost non-conventional source of energy and save the world. Both countries have decided to set up a Solar Academy in Senegal to promote solar energy.

India signed defence deals with France for purchasing 36 Rafale jets for the Indian Air Force and three submarines for the Navy, besides an agreement for defence technology cooperation. France agreed to cooperate in the Make in India mission. India had described Rafale as a critical operational necessity, and France proved to be a true friend by delivering the first batch of five Rafale aircraft in July 2020, two months after the Chinese aggression in the Galwan Valley.

Another defence cooperation for 26 Rafale jets for the Indian Navy and three submarines was signed with France during Modi's visit to Paris in July 2023. Modi has already built a personal rapport with French President Emmanuel Jean-Michel Frédéric Macron. France has always supported India's strong claim for a permanent seat at the UN Security Council.

During his visit to India on 26 January 2024, Macron and Modi decided to have an India-France Defence Industrial Roadmap to take the bilateral relationship to a new level. It included a defence space partnership for satellite launches and an industrial partnership between Tata Advance System Limited (TASL) and Airbus for setting up an assembly line for producing H125 helicopters. France and India will celebrate 2026 as the India-France Year of Innovation[8].

France has already taken the initiative to start the IMEC (India, Middle East Europe Economic Corridor), a corridor connecting India to Europe via the Middle East. To shape this corridor of multi-modal connectivity, Macron has already appointed Gérard Mestrallet as the envoy to prepare the groundwork to kickstart the project. France aims to organise a meeting of the IMEC members in two months[9].

Canada

Canada is India's ninth-largest trading partner and the two share old ties. Both countries have signed an agreement for strategic tie-ups such as nuclear cooperation, Extradition Treaty, Mutual Legal Assistance Treaty, Agreement on Patents, Agreement on Cooperation in Agriculture, Agreement on Science and Technology and Environment Cooperation, and MoU on Energy cooperation. Recently, the relationship came under strain due to the differing perceptions of the two countries on certain individuals and organisations operating from Canada.

But the parameters of bilateral relations are still strong. The two are already discussing cooperation in areas of electric vehicles, cyber systems, quantum technology, green hydrogen fuel, deep sea mining, and affordable healthcare, including pharmaceuticals and biomedical instrumentation. Around 23 lakh Indian diaspora staying in Canada will always help the two countries to come together for better bilateral ties[10].

Germany

India and Germany have shared good trade relations. Modi visited Germany in April 2015. Together with German Chancellor Angela Merkel, he inaugurated the world's largest industrial fare in Hanover. He also unveiled the statue of Mahatma Gandhi there. Modi said that Indian Lions and German Eagles were great partners.

Germany lost on the fighter jet deal to France but emerged as a strong contender to build six non-nuclear military submarines for India, costing Rs 43,000 Crore. The prestigious project called P-751 India (India Submarine Acquisition Project) is one of the biggest Make in India programmes to be manufactured in India in collaboration with strategic partners[11].

Australia

Modi became the first Indian Prime Minister to address a joint sitting of both houses of Parliament (Federal Parliament) in Australia on his three-day visit to the country in November 2014. Two months before this, Australian Prime Minister Tony Abbott had visited India. The bilateral meeting was preceded by the meeting of the G20 in Brisbane. The focus was economic and strategic cooperation.

After nine years, when he visited Australia again in 2023, he was welcomed like a hero. The Indian diaspora had made elaborate arrangements to welcome him at the Qudos Bank Arena Stadium in Sydney. He was welcomed amidst Vedic chants. Thousands of people constantly clapped during his hour-long speech and showed the new dimension of soft power that India had become. Modi had already become a popular global leader. The Australian Prime Minister, Anthony Albanese, who assumed office in 2022, was clearly bowled over by the rockstar welcome that the Indian Prime Minister received.

'The last time I saw someone on this stage was Bruce Springsteen and he did not get the welcome that Prime Minister Modi has got.... Prime minister Modi is the boss', Antony Albanese said, acknowledging the huge popularity Modi enjoyed[12].

Russia

The Indian Prime Minister has cultivated new and trusted friends, but not at the cost of old ones. Russia and Putin are good friends, and India has shored up its defence using trusted Russian technology. Both countries have worked together on defence, oil, nuclear energy and space exploration. Russia is already supplying an S-400 missile defence system that would not allow an enemy aircraft or missile to penetrate Indian space at a distance of up to 400 km.

Like a tried and trusted friend, India has always supported Russia. It did not vote against Russian aggression against Ukraine, even as it advocated communication as a means of resolution. Time and again, Narendra Modi has declared that the era of war is over and dialogue is the only way to resolve conflict. When the UN demanded that Russia should reverse its annexation of Ukraine, India abstained from voting. It abstained even when a UN resolution condemned the Russian invasion of Ukraine.

India refused to join the West and Europe in imposing sanctions on Russia and continued to work on bilateral terms, including importing oil from Russia under a separate arrangement even when the US and other countries disliked it.

Rather than isolating, the Indian Prime Minister believes in engaging with Russia more intensely. Putin calls him a true friend of Russia. They share a wonderful relationship of mutual trust. The US, the West and Europe have started respecting the Indian position. Now they know whom to approach if they want to reach Putin.

QUAD

The way Modi has built a circle of friends in the Pacific is laudable. The QUAD (Quadrilateral Security Dialogue), a strategic alliance of Australia, Japan, the US and India, is significant for the Pacific. At the ASEAN summit in Manila in 2017, leaders of these countries decided to revive the grouping to counter China's growing assertiveness in the Pacific. Shinzo Abe of Japan, Malcolm Turnbull of Australia, Donald Trump of the US and Narendra Modi took the decision.

South East Asia

India has strengthened its links with the Southeast Asian countries, particularly Vietnam, the Philippines and Indonesia. Narendra Modi has transformed the 'Look East' policy to 'Act East'. He has made personal efforts to strengthen this friendship. En route to China for the G20 summit in September 2016, he visited Vietnam for two days. It was the first visit by an Indian Prime Minister in 15 years.

India and Vietnam are already into strategic defence deals. India is cooperating with Vietnam in the exploration of oil and natural gas. Vietnam, with its old cultural links with India, is a champion of free navigation and maritime security.

During Modi's visit, India and Vietnam signed twelve agreements. The relationship was upgraded from a strategic partnership to a comprehensive strategic partnership. It opened new possibilities. The visit focussed on enhanced defence cooperation, which is significant since India, too, has a strategic interest in the South China Sea.

Narendra Modi visited Manila in 2017 to attend a meeting of the ASEAN-India summit and a summit of East Asia. The South China Sea dispute dominated the deliberations on the first day of the summit, showing the sensitivity of ASEAN countries against the aggressive designs of China. Addressing a gathering of the Indian community, Modi sent out his message saying India has never taken anything from anyone.

Modi said that his visit to the Philippines commencing tomorrow for attending the India-ASEAN summit 'symbolises the country's commitment to deepening ties with the ASEAN member states and the Indo-Pacific region as part of the "act east policy"'.[13]

The Indian Prime Minister visited Bali (Indonesia) in November 2022 to attend the 17th meeting of the G20 Summit at the invitation of Indonesian President Joko Widodo. The top highlight of the meeting was Indonesia handing over the G20 Presidency to India, effective from 1 December 2022.

Modi said, 'India will assume the G20 Presidency for the coming year. Our agenda will be inclusive, ambitious, decisive and action-oriented. We will work to realise all aspects of our vision of "One Earth, One Family, One Future".'

The G20 comprises 19 countries–Argentina, Australia, Brazil, Canada, China, France, Germany, India, Indonesia, Italy, Japan, South Korea, Mexico, Russia, Saudi Arabia, South Africa, Turkey, the UK, the USA and the European Union (EU). Together, they account for over 80 per cent of the global GDP, 75 per cent of international trade and two-thirds of the world population.

Immediate Neighbours

Ever since becoming the Prime Minister of India, Narendra Modi has demonstrated his neighbour-first approach. He knows that neighbours cannot be changed, and it is essential to have good relations with them. The old boundary dispute with Bangladesh has been resolved through the exchange of enclaves.

'Sometimes we wonder if there can be solutions to problems with neighbours...There was a land dispute with Bangladesh since that country was born in 1971. Since then, the question was pending. One issue was about water sharing, another about demarcation of boundary in the sea and third about land boundary', Modi pointed out while addressing a gathering of the Indian diaspora in Brussels in May 2016[14].

'You would be happy to know that after our government came, without firing any bullet, without any fight, by just sitting with Bangladesh, the border dispute was ended…Whoever had to come to India, they came, whoever had to go to Bangladesh they went, the border was demarcated and now fencing work is going on there. The disease of infiltration will also end and both countries will live peacefully and happily. Water dispute has also been resolved', he told the gathering.

The historic agreement for exchanging enclaves with Bangladesh was achieved in 2015 and was signed in Dhaka between Modi and Bangladesh Prime Minister Sheikh Hasina on 6 June 2015. Under the land boundary agreement that was pending for the last 41 years, the disputes over 162 enclaves were amicably settled. Both countries pledged to root out terrorism, and India gave a USD 2 billion line of credit.

Modi visited Dhaka again in 2021 when three major events coincided–the Golden Jubilee of Independence of Bangladesh; the birth centenary of Sheikh Mujibur Rahman, the father of the nation of Bangladesh; and 50 years of establishment of diplomatic relations between India and Bangladesh. During the visit, Modi awarded the Gandhi Peace Prize for 2020 to Sheikh Mujibur Rahman and the award was received by his daughters, Sheikh Hasina and Sheikh Rehana. It was the first time that the award was given posthumously. Both countries decided on a joint celebration of the bilateral relations, and India announced the establishment of a Bangabandhu Chair at Delhi University. India also announced 1000 Suborno Jayanti scholarships for Bangladeshi students pursuing courses in India.

The high point of the meeting was Modi's visit to Jeshoreshwari temple in Shyamnagar of Satkhira district and to the birthplace of the Matua gurus, Harichand and Guruchand, in Orakandi.

Modi's love and respect for India's immediate Himalayan neighbours was evident when he visited Bhutan in June 2014. It was Modi's first visit outside India, and the way people lined up on both sides of the road in Thimphu demonstrated their love for India. The visit was also a manifestation of Modi's neighbourhood-first policy.

'India is associated with the progress and happiness of Bhutan and will continue to do so. The two countries are made for each other. The colour of our passports may vary, but our heritage and values remain the same', he said during a royal banquet. He described Bhutan as his first foreign visit as a 'natural choice'.

His second visit to Bhutan was in 2019 when he inaugurated the building of the Supreme Court constructed with India's help. Ten MoUs were signed between the two countries, including Telecom, Space, Education and Power. Modi said, 'India is honoured to have a friend and a neighbour like Bhutan and India is honoured to be a part of the development of Bhutan.'

Modi visited Nepal in August 2014, and it was after 17 years that an Indian Prime Minister had visited the country. The visit intended to recognise and further the cultural and historical ties between the two countries and reaffirm India's commitment to Nepal. People-to-people relations have been quite good, but some recent events showed that the Himalayan country was comfortable with India's approach to some issues.

'This is the land of Sita and Janak, Nepal-India relations are as old as the Himalayas and the Ganga', Modi said during his visit. Before he embarked on the visit, he underlined the significance of the chemistry between the two countries. 'My visit reflects our shared heritage of nature, history, culture, spiritualism and religion. It highlights the high priority that my government attaches to our relations with Nepal and our determination to take our relationship to an entirely new level.'[15]

While addressing the Nepalese Parliament, Modi announced Rs 10,000 crore as concessional credit to Nepal. He proposed a HIT formula for development where H means Highways, I means I-ways, and T means Transways. 'These three combined together would pave the way for rapid development of the country and India wants to give this gift at the earliest', he said[16].

The high point of the visit was the love and affection people showered on him. They swarmed the streets of Kathmandu to welcome Modi. He visited the Pashupatinath Temple in a traditional Hindu outfit. Both Modi's attire and his devotion were discussed in the media.

His second visit happened the same year in November to participate in the 18th SAARC summit. The bilateral meetings and the response Modi got from people there indicated that Modi has established a rapport that India and Nepal had never seen. Doubts were replaced with trust and platitudes with actions.

India handed over a modern trauma centre to Nepal and a multi-purpose helicopter to the Nepalese army. Various agreements were signed for India's participation in furthering the development of Nepal. Modi clarified to everyone that India was a trusted neighbour and friend. A bus service was started between the two countries and named Pashupatinath Express.

Modi visited Nepal five times, and the last was in May 2022. He visited Lumbini, the birthplace of Lord Buddha, and laid the foundation of the Buddhist Culture and Heritage Centre.

Afghanistan

Modi's attempt to create a special equation with the neighbouring countries would be incomplete without discussing Afghanistan. India has been an active player in trying to bring peace and stability to Afghanistan, particularly in the context of the US pullout.

At the G20 summit, Modi had expressed India's concerns for Afghanistan, and the focus was on preventing the Afghani territory from becoming a source of radicalisation and terrorism. Modi also stressed the need for urgent and unhindered humanitarian assistance to Afghan citizens.

He had visited Afghanistan twice, once in December 2015 and again in June 2016. Along with Afghanistan President Ashraf Ghani, he inaugurated the new Afghan Parliament in Kabul, built by India in 2015. India has been involved in many construction projects in Afghanistan.

Taliban's takeover of the country on 15 August 2021 by overthrowing the Ghani government disrupted the bilateral ties even as India kept talking of humanitarian assistance for Afghan citizens. India established a backdoor diplomacy with Taliban next year in the interest of peace and resumed diplomatic operations. India has been working hard to resume the unfinished projects in Afghanistan.

The development partnership exists in more than five hundred projects spread across each of the 34 provinces in critical areas such as power, water supply, road connectivity, healthcare, education, agriculture and capacity building. Students from Afghanistan are also given an opportunity to study in India.

Sri Lanka

Sri Lanka has been India's consistent friend, and Modi visited the country thrice–in 2015, 2017 and 2019. Despite being a close-door neighbour, Sri Lanka had to wait nearly three decades for the Indian Prime Minister to visit. In the meantime, Sri Lanka moved closer to China. Modi has been trying to correct this balance and re-establish Indian influence over Sri Lanka based on friendship and trust.

He advised the Sri Lankan government to establish democracy, as per the mandate of the 13th Amendment. The amendment, following the Sri Lankan-India Accord of 1987, provided for holding elections to provincial councils. India tried stabilising the Sri Lankan economy through a currency swap agreement between the RBI and the Central Bank of Sri Lanka. Both countries have signed agreements on energy cooperation.

Sri Lanka suffered from a financial crisis in 2021-22, with the government officially declaring it the worst economic crisis in the last 73 years. A food emergency was declared in August 2021. It was due to mismanagement and the COVID-19 Pandemic, which adversely affected the tourism revenue. The financial crisis was catastrophic, and there was a severe paucity of foreign exchange reserves.

'A friend in need is a friend indeed'–proving the adage, India provided financial help and humanitarian assistance to Sri Lanka worth USD 4 billion, making it the first creditor nation to offer financial assurance to kickstart the IMF process. Since mid-March 2022, India has given over 2.7 lakh metric tonnes of diesel and petrol, besides 40,000 tonnes of rice.

Sri Lankan President Ranil Wickremesinghe thanked India profusely during his address to Parliament's ceremonial sitting in August 2022. He said, 'I wish to specially mention the assistance provided by India, our closest neighbour, in our efforts of economic revitalisation.... The Government of India under the leadership of Prime Minister Modi has given us a breath of life. On behalf of my people and that of my own, I convey our gratitude to Prime Minister Modi, the government and people of India.'[17]

Speaker of the Sri Lankan Parliament, Mahinda Yapa Abeywardena, expressed gratitude for 'trustworthy friend' India for saving Sri Lanka and preventing a 'bloodbath' during its unprecedented economic crisis last year. 'Not a single nation has extended that kind of assistance to Colombo as done by New Delhi', he added[18]. The relations of the past were repaired, and both friends realised that geographical neighbours cannot be ignored.

The Arab World

In the outer concentric circle of India's immediate neighbours lies the Arab world, which cannot be ignored, and India's relationship with these countries must be healthy, based on mutually beneficial engagement. Modi visited this region six times–in 2015, 2018, 2019, 2022, 2023 and 2024. India hosts the largest Muslim population in the world and has a right to speak on their behalf more than any other country. Also, it gives tremendous leverage to India in the Arab world.

Modi delinked religion and argued for relations to be guided by geo-political realities. The old ties of this world with India were based on this understanding. Modi has invested a lot of time in cultivating the leaders of Arab countries, and the equation is such that he can call them up anytime with ease. It came in handy when, for example, during the Yamen crisis, both Saudi Arabia and Yemen cooperated with the Indian evacuation efforts.

He strengthened India's relations with countries like Qatar, UAE, Saudi Arabia, Bahrain, Jordan and others without compromising its relationship with Israel. India enjoys a unique position where both sides trust India's commitment to peace and neutrality while dealing with issues. Modi became the first Indian Prime Minister to visit Palestine and receive its highest civilian award[19].

More than 9 million Indians, or around 30 per cent of Indians abroad, live in Arab countries for a living. About 57 per cent of India's total foreign remittances come from the Gulf countries. The region also accounts for India's two-thirds of crude oil supplies. In the last eight years, the relationship has metamorphosed into strategic areas of defence cooperation, counter-terrorism, cyber-security, organised crime and piracy.

The newfound trust has brought a new buoyancy. The Arab world is also becoming a big investor in Indian businesses. In 2022-23, the UAE emerged as the fourth largest investor, with an investment of USD 3.35 billion. It jumped three times over from its investment of USD 1.03 billion in 2021-22. The UAE has already committed to investing USD 75 billion in India. It would come in areas of infrastructure and renewable energy[20]. Saudi Arabia has already committed to invest USD100 billion in Indian projects. The new economic corridor IMEC was not possible without the full cooperation of Saudi Arabia and the UAE.

The newfound friendship was also evident in the new BAPS Swami

Narayan Temple founded in Abu Dhabi as a symbol of India's cultural pride. Modi inaugurated the temple in February 2024. He described the temple as a symbol of shared heritage, marking a golden chapter in the UAE's history of human civilisation. He thanked Sheikh Mohammed bin Zayed, referring to him as 'brother'[21]. 'The Government of UAE has not only won the hearts of Indians living in UAE, but also of all 140 crore Indians', he added[22].

Operation Raahat would not have been possible unless Modi had a personal equation with the leaders of both countries. More than 4,000 Indians and other citizens were rescued from the war-torn Yemen. Gen V K Singh, who supervised the operation, was lauded by the Prime Minister, who said, 'I believe this is the first time in the world that a government minister has stood on the battlefield like a soldier to do this work...I salute General V K Singh.'

Narendra Modi has emerged as a tall leader in the global order based on his commitment to peace and happiness. His sincerity of purpose and the ability to deliver have been acknowledged and appreciated. The entire world watched how India, under Modi, gave the elixir of life, the vaccine for COVID-19. It happened when the developed world was trying to resolve their crisis at home. Modi gave vaccines to some of the foreign countries free of cost and saved millions of lives.

By December 2022, India has supplied 282 million doses of vaccine to 101 countries and two UN entities under the Vaccine Maitri programme. WHO chief Tedros Adhanom Ghebreyesus lauded Modi's commitment to supporting vaccine equity and sharing the COVID-19 vaccine with other countries in times of need.

The respect and popularity Modi enjoys was evident when Prime Minister of Papua New Guinea, James Marape, touched the feet of Prime Minister Narendra Modi during his visit to the island country on 21 May 2023. This traditional respect is hardly seen in international relations.

The Most Popular Global Leader

Modi's governance experience and global vision have made him the most popular leader in the world. His views on every issue of global importance are considered noteworthy. Whether it is global warming, fighting terrorism or securing the seas for everyone equally, Modi plays a significant role. No matter where he went during his visits, he has always impressed the world with his global vision of peace and unity.

Various rating agencies rated him as the world's most popular leader. As early as February 2024, Modi emerged as the most popular global leader with 78 per cent approval ratings, leaving behind US President Joe Biden and UK Prime Minister Rishi Sunak. This is as per a survey conducted by a US-based global decision intelligence agency, Morning Consult. The survey was conducted from 30 January to 5 February[23]. In December 2023, the same agency rated him as the world's most popular leader with an approval rating of 76 per cent.

While heaping praise on Modi as the most popular global leader, Mukesh Ambani, chairman of Reliance Industries, tried to sum up the reason for the Prime Minister's popularity. He said, 'My friends abroad ask me, "What is the meaning of the slogan that millions of Indians are chanting–Modi *hai to Mumkin Hai*?" I tell them, "It means, India's Prime Minister makes the impossible possible with his vision, determination and execution!" They agree, and they also say, "Modi *hai to mumkin hai*!"'[24]

Modi *ki* Guarantee

When I talk about the guarantee, I bind myself to it.
It doesn't let me sleep. It propels me to work harder.
It leads me to give my everything to the people of the country.
–Narendra Modi

I have seen the eyes of poor people glimmer with hope on hearing the name Modi. Years of neglect and hopelessness surrounding their daily existence have forced them to reconcile to their fate and pray that their next life, if at all, will be better. Prime Minister Modi has transformed this thinking by taking the government to them and empowering them to change their destiny in this life itself.

I had a chance visit to Pindarkom village in the Gidhaur subdivision of Chatra district in Jharkhand. It is a Naxal-affected place, which is not connected by any pucca road. I was surprised to see public toilets there, along with electricity and water. Though people suffered due to a lack of employment opportunities, they were happy with the government and how it cared for them. While talking to them, I realised that the name 'Modi' has transformed all barriers and has become synonymous with hope for the poor and the downtrodden. The images have been etched in my memory like a permanent mark.

Modi has been working hard to provide the Indian citizens with what is due to them. Citizens are not merely those who are wealthy or powerful or form a part of the middle class. A huge section of the population is living a life of poverty, and the government need to hold their hands like an indulgent parent, enabling them to come to par with others. If they are poor, it is not their fault. It shows that successive governments have not cared enough for them, or enabled them to live a life of dignity.

Modi has said he spends sleepless nights thinking of completing the last-mile delivery for the needy. It is a promise that he has made to himself to work for the poor and the deprived. And it sums up Modi *ki* Guarantee. It means rectifying the system that leaked to the extent that only 15 paisa out of the 100 reached the beneficiaries. It meant putting checks and balances in place to make the existing structure foolproof so that the middlemen who pocketed the benefits were at bay. Modi's efforts have ensured that more than 25 crore people have come above the poverty line in the last 10 years.

Some economists often argue that the massive expenditure on providing free ration and other benefits to people leaves little room for increasing capital expenditure. The government has allayed this fear by increasing capital expenditure, even if it means raising the fiscal deficit by a few points. However, investing in infrastructure without considering human resources would lead to lopsided economic growth.

Handholding people to empower them and make them a part of the larger economy will be beneficial in the long run. If the basic needs of people, like housing, health, education and food, are taken care of, they would be encouraged to improve their conditions by focusing on upskilling and earning more. They would send their children to school and demand better education rather than sending them to work for petty jobs to supplement the family income.

Modi is taking these guarantees to people through Viksit Bharat Sankalp Yatra and encouraging those still outside the system to avail the benefits of the various government schemes meant for them. Many people lack awareness, and it would be the best opportunity to help them enlist without hassle. Modi launched the Yatra from the Khunti district of Jharkhand on 15 November 2023, on the birth anniversary of Bhagwan Birsa Munda, celebrated as the Janjatiya Gaurav Divas. The launch venue was significant since it wanted to give justice to tribals and other deprived sections of society that were left out. The aim was to achieve 100 per cent saturation[1].

Five specially designed IEC (Information, Education and Communication) vans, carrying the messages of the government's flagship programme moved into various tribal helmets. Similar programmes were organised in 68 districts in the country with significant tribal population. It has been one of the largest outreach programmes of the government that aimed to cover more than 2.55 lakh gram panchayats and over 3,600 urban local bodies by January 2024.

It also gave opportunities to the Prime Minister to interact with the beneficiaries and know their problems and experiences. The government agencies got an opportunity to enlist people for various programmes. By the beginning of January 2024, more than 1.64 crore citizens received Ayushman Bharat Health Coverage, and over 9.47 lakh enrolled under the PM Ujjwala Yojana. More than 27.31 lakh young people volunteered to join the MY Bharat scheme, under which they get a chance to participate in the development of the country and assume leadership roles.

The Modi *Ki* Guarantee theme was an experiment during the assembly elections in five states in November 2023–Rajasthan, Madhya Pradesh, Telangana, Chhattisgarh, and Mizoram. Amidst the prediction of doom, the BJP registered an impressive victory in the Hindu heartland. What seemed to have worked for the BJP was Modi's hectic campaign and the Modi *ki* Guarantee on making the lives of people better. The BJP then decided to use this slogan and its meaning for people in the Lok Sabha campaign as well. What is often called Modi magic is the outcome of this guarantee to the electorate and their trust in the Prime Minister.

To understand the need and focus of this Viksit Bharat Sankalp Yatra to spread the message about Modi *ki* Guarantee, it is necessary to consider how Modi has empowered crores of people to make them part of the larger national narrative. It is the Modi Guarantee translated into action which has been discussed elaborately in our chapter on welfare measures. A brief reference here would be in order.

Some of Modi's targets were–to take drinking water through a pipe to every home (her ghar nal se jal), to give regular power and subsidised gas connection for cooking, an assured healthcare plan for the poor through Ayushman Bharat for a health emergency, free foodgrains and cereals to 80 crore people, and money directly into their account for the various government benefits they are entitled to.

Let us look at some of these benefits that are reaching the beneficiaries without fail. Giving a free ration to 81.35 crore people free of cost under Pradhan Mantri Garib Kalyan Anna Yojana (PMGKAY) will cost about Rs 2 lakh crore per year. This scheme has been extended for another five years, beginning 1 January 2024. This food and nutritional security will cost Rs 11.80 crore in five years. The free ration would be distributed uniformly through a network of over 5 lakh Fair Price Shops. Modi guarantees that no one will sleep hungry or suffer due to a lack of nutrition.

When Modi launched the Jal Jeevan Mission in 2019, only 3.23 crore rural households had tap water connections. More than 14 crore households were added in the last five years. This is an example of Modi's guarantee which has ensured tapped water even in the remote areas of Ladakh, where temperature goes down to minus degrees and water freezes. The Prime Minister promised housing for the poor, and more than 4 crore houses are being constructed to meet this target.

In 2014, 18,452 villages in India were without electricity, and the Prime Minister promised every village electricity within 1,000 days. On 28 April 2018, as Leisang, the tiny hamlet in Manipur, connected to the grid, it became the last of the Indian villages to get a power connection. It was exactly 998 days after his promise. He described it as a historic day in the development journey of India[2]. When Modi makes a promise, he creates the necessary institutions to deliver it.

The Saubhagya scheme (Pradhan Mantri Sahaj Bijli Har Ghar Yojana), launched in 2017 to provide electricity to every willing household completed its task by reporting 100 per cent electrification on 31 March 2021. Including 2.81 crore households that got electricity under the scheme, a total of 2.86 crore households have been electrified[3].

Apart from shelter, food, drinking water and electricity, Modi's guarantee ensures free or subsidised gas connection to BPL families in the name of women. More than 10 crore women have already received gas connections under the scheme.

The biggest Modi guarantee is health insurance for every poor family under Ayushman Bharat, through which any family member can get free, best-quality treatment of up to Rs 5 lakhs every year. This scheme has given a safety net to 55 crore individuals or 12 crore families.

Everyone in the country has affordable quality medicine through PM Jan Aushadhi Kendras. In 2014, there were only 80 such Kendras. Under the relaunched Pradhan Mantri Bharatiya Janaushadhi Pariyojana Kendra (PMBJK), 10,000 such Kendras are functioning in the country's 785 districts, selling medicine worth Rs 1,000 crore by the end of 2023. People saved up to Rs 5,000 crore, which they would have otherwise spent on medicine. The Modi guarantee is to take the number of Jan Aushadhi Kendras to 25,000[4].

Close to 1,963 medicines and 293 surgical devices dealing with cardiovascular, anti-cancers, anti-diabetics, anti-infectives, anti-allergic, gastrointestinal medicines, nutraceuticals, etc. are being supplied under the scheme. Five warehouses are providing backup, and 36 distributors are working in the background to keep the system running. Ayurvedic products have been added to boost immunity.

Besides these, there are targeted benefits for special categories such as farmers, women and youths. Farmers are getting income support of Rs 6,000 per year in three equal instalments. Considering there are more than 11 crore beneficiaries under this scheme, the Modi guarantee ensures that this amount, totalling Rs 70,000 crore, reaches the account of beneficiaries every year.

Modi's guarantee adequately focuses on agriculture and farmers. It begins with buying farm produce under MSP (Minimum Support Price) to make agriculture more productive by adopting modern technology and organic manures. The budget for agriculture today stands at Rs 1.27 lakh crore, a three-fold increase over the budget of 2014-15. The government has empowered farmers through liberal credits, hassle-free and liberal crop insurance and soil health cards, besides providing them with essential nutrients for the soil. The government has encouraged farmers to become entrepreneurs, and more than 7,000 vibrant startups have emerged in agriculture and its allied activities[5]. Modi is trying to prevent the exploitation of farmers at the hands of the middlemen by creating an e-NAM platform where they can know the best prices for their produce and sell these instantly.

Modi has also emerged as a champion of women's rights. The beneficiary account holders in most of his schemes are women. It goes well with his understanding that when you empower a woman, you empower the whole family. He wants every Indian to treat women with dignity and not take them as weak or inferior. They are the pivots of his developmental programmes, which he called women-led growth.

When the government opened 51.8 crore accounts under the scheme, more than 28 crores of these belonged to women. More than 37.76 crore people have taken Mudra loans, amounting to Rs 20.43 lakh crore. Of these, 69 per cent of beneficiaries are women.

A unique initiative is the launch of the Lakhpati Didi Yojana under a skill development programme through which more than 3 crore *lakhpati didis* (millionaire girls) will emerge in various Self-Help Groups (SHGs). Launched on 15 August 2023, the scheme envisages interest-free loans to women and focussed skill development so they can earn at least Rs 1 lakh per year for their families[6]. Under the livelihood improvement programme, one should not be surprised to find women using drones to sprinkle fertilisers on standing crops.

Modi's guarantee for women will ensure them one-third of reservations in the Lok Sabha and legislative assemblies. Women's reservation has become a reality since the law Nari Shakti Vandan Adhiniyam was enacted. However, implementing the law will take more time since both census and delimitation are pending. The new Parliament building has enough sitting capacity to accommodate new members.

The focus on rural sanitation, menstrual hygiene management, and initiatives like Beti Bachao, Beti Padhao extend Modi's guarantee to better the lives of women.

For the younger people in the adult generation, enumerable opportunities have opened up due to easily accessible non-collateral loans under the Mudra Yojana. They can start their own business, and pay the loan gradually, for which the government has given the guarantee. Under Stand-up India Yojana, a higher dimension loan is possible, and preference is given to women and candidates from the SCs and the STs.

The youths have the guarantee that they will get the best opportunities to innovate and excel. They can no longer say that the system is not supporting their desire to experiment. Because of Modi's focus on encouraging local talents, more youths want to become a part of the startup ecosystem after professional degrees. Around 10,000 Atal Tinkering Labs are functioning in the country to encourage and handhold youths to start their own enterprises. It is no wonder that India has the third-largest startup ecosystem in the world.

There is Modi's guarantee for the taxpayers and the middle class for better infrastructure so that they can enjoy the rewards of their hard-earned money. There are better roads to drive, better and affordable air travel, good and sanitised railway travel and overall improvement in the situation because of the expanding market. The system is on track. Transparency and full accountability of the government would continue.

Modi guarantees that the country's economy will grow to USD 5 trillion, and India will become the third-largest economy soon. Modi guarantees that inflation will be under check as will be the prices of essential commodities. Thorough planning and buffer stock with dynamic decision-making ensures that the prices of essential commodities are under check.

People are already experiencing Digital India advancement as promised by the Prime Minister. Digital India infrastructure is being planned to prepare the country for artificial intelligence. The government has already decided to provide more than 2,50,000 panchayats and more than 6,00,000 villages with broadband connectivity. It will bring a digital revolution on an unprecedented scale.

Modi's Viksit Bharat campaign is to empower people so that the country gets ready for the larger vision to help India develop by 2047 when it will celebrate 100 years of Independence. An elaborate quote from that interview he gave to India Today would help us understand this better:

> If you observe closely, there is a historic parallel to the times we are living in. A hundred years ago, there was optimism about gaining freedom. From 1922 to the period up to 1947, everyone wanted to contribute towards the freedom movement. Some contributed by

spinning khadi, some by taking part in various movements, people contributed in whatever way they could. The next 25 years are crucial for the nation. I see a similar optimism among the people to make India a developed country by the time we celebrate 100 years of independence. This energy is my driving force. *Hum GYAN pe dhyaan denge, GYAN ko sammaan denge, toh Viksit Bharat banega.* (If we focus on knowledge and respect it, we will become a developed nation) *GYAN* means G for *Garib,* Y for *Yuva,* A for *Annadata*, N for *Narishakti*. India has a demographic advantage. This advantage must be converted to productivity and economic growth[7].

Ashtalakshmi

Assimilating North East

Relationships are based on four principles: respect, understanding, acceptance and appreciation.
–Mahatma Gandhi

In the words of Amit Shah, when Modi became the Prime Minister, he said that 'the development of India lies in the development of North East'. This inclusive thinking was missing under various Delhi establishments, and the North East suffered due to neglect or lopsided thinking.

Many people from the North East have a different experience since people in other parts of India consider them foreigners because of their different racial stock. Their experiences were not good when they joined as a student or an employee in this part of the country. Being Western in their dressing and liberal in their thinking, they are often mistaken and assaulted.

Since people in other parts of India treat people from the North East differently, they do not get opportunities to interact and integrate with the mainstream. It has often led to alienation. One should not get offended when one hears a person from the North East saying 'India does not treat us well'. Rather than feeling hurt, there is a need to figure out why the states of the North East have suffered due to neglect. Why people from Delhi have often ignored them even though these are border states and mean so much for the country's security and development?

A sincere effort to build bridges with people was made under the regime of Atal Bihari Vajpayee, who used to say that the seven states should not be seen as a problem but as an opportunity for growth and economic development. He set up the DONER (Department of Development of North Eastern Region) in September 2001, focusing on integrating all works of various ministries for the development of the North East. The DONER was turned into a full-fledged ministry in May 2004 for infrastructural development of the region. In 2002, the government included Sikkim in the NEC as the eighth member state and fulfilled a longstanding demand of Sikkim.

Vajpayee was a visionary who, under the 'Look East' Policy, wanted to link northeastern states with countries of the Association of South East Asian Nations (ASEAN) and write the story of economic prosperity. He tried to resolve conflicts and write development chapters of the neglected regions. Vajpayee announced a special development package for the North East and gave a 28-point programme to address issues concerning the power sector, border trade, horticulture, rural infrastructure, roads and air links, medical education, health services, Industrial Training Institutes, Information Technology, border fencing and upgrading police infrastructure.

Between 1998-99 and 2002-03, the NDA government released over Rs 44,000 crore for the North East. The Vajpayee government has also decided to allocate 10 per cent of the budget of all Union Ministries and departments to the North East. It also created a pool of non-lapsable funds.

Dr Manmohan Singh, who followed Vajpayee, gave the North Eastern Region Vision of 2020 released in 2008. Projects were given, but there were time and cost overruns. Many big-ticket projects that the UPA government launched in the North East could not be completed. Many projects on developing border roads suffered due to a lack of environmental clearance.

Most projects waited for completion by the Modi government, for example, the country's longest river bridge over river Lohit that connects Assam and Arunachal Pradesh. Modi inaugurated the Rs 2,056 crore, 9.15 km long strategic bridge in May 2017. The feasibility study of the bridge began in 2004, but the UPA could not complete the project in time[1].

Modi was determined to carry forward the vision of Vajpayee by picking up the threads from there and translating the vision into action with his determination and speed. He also decided to translate the North Eastern Region Vision 2020 into a reality by launching infrastructural development on an unprecedented scale.

His love for the North East and his missionary zeal to ensure the development of the region made him visit it at least 60 times in the last 9 years. Following his instructions, members of his council of ministers visited the region around 400 times. No other Prime Minister or the council of ministers had worked so hard for the region.

The result is a miraculous transformation of the region and North East being cited all over as the Modi government's development model. While inaugurating the Purvodaya conclave, showcasing the transformation, the Union Minister Dr Jitendra Singh said that the transformation resulted from massive expenditure and work at double the speed[2].

The change is also visible in reduced violence and returning peace. The government has already resolved thc Bodoland issuc. Mccting the longstanding demand of the people there, the AFSPA (Armed Forces Special Powers Act) has been removed, except from some parts of Assam and Manipur. While talking about the security situation in the North East, Home Minister Amit Shah said that in the ten years from 2004-14, 11,121 violent incidents happened in the North East, and it declined by 73 per cent to 3,114 from 2014-23. Deaths among security forces dropped by 71 per cent from 458 to 132, while deaths of civilians declined by 86 per cent, Shah added[3].

While talking about insurgency, he pointed out that more than 8,900 militants had surrendered, eschewed violence and joined the mainstream. It has also brought down the incidents of insurgency. 'The North East, which was struggling with various problem caused by ethnic, linguistic, border and extremist groups, also got the beginning of a fresh and durable era of peace in these 10 years.'[4] He described the last 10 years as the golden era for the North East.

Modi is the biggest messenger of peace in the region. He pointed out how conflict and insurgency have been replaced by lasting peace and how states are trying to resolve boundary disputes through peaceful dialogue. Addressing a rally in February 2024, he pointed out that more than 10 agreements on peace have been signed[5].

The Modi government has taken proactive measures to reduce the distance between Delhi and these states and worked hard to integrate them better with people from other parts of India. To sensitise the public towards the people from the North East and to control crime against them in the national capital, Delhi police, under the Union government, decided to recruit members from the North East in its force. In 2018, it decided to induct 391 male candidates and 189 female candidates[6]. It is expected to make people from the North East experience a more compassionate Delhi since whatever happens in Delhi has repercussions in the respective states. The government has also been advising other states to recruit people from the North East, particularly in the police forces in metropolitan areas.

The government has also made punishment harsher by up to five years if someone calls a person from the North East 'chinki', an offensive term often used by people from other parts of the country to slur people from the North East. The pride of place at the 75th Republic Day Parade in 2024 was the all-women contingent of Delhi police, and it was adjudged the best. Around 80 per cent of the participants were women from the North East[7].

The Prime Minister knows that only the language of development can override conflict. People from the North East must feel that Delhi cares for them. The roads and other infrastructure facilities they witness in other states must be available in the eight states of the North East. Modi has laudably taken development to their doorstep. 'I want to see North East develop the same way as the whole world looks at East Asia', he said, outlining his vision for the North East. 'Your dream is my promise', he stressed[8].

A look at some of the statistics would testify to this. The first Software Technology Park in India was launched by Vajpayee in Assam in 2001. The second was launched 20 years later in 2021 in Kohima as the country's 61 STPI intended to boost the startup ecosystem in the region.

Under the Gross Budgetary Support (GBS) scheme, which is 10 per cent of the Union Budget, the Modi government has spent about

Rs 3.37 lakh crore in the North East (from 2014-15 to 2021-22). An allocation of Rs 94,679.53 crore was further added in 2023-24[9]. As the budgetary outlay of the Centre increases, this allocation would also increase, leading to better prosperity of the region.

The DONER and the North East Council (NEC) have sanctioned 1,350 projects worth Rs 15,867 crore. During the budget for 2022-23, the government launched a 100 per cent centrally-funded scheme called the DevINE scheme for the holistic development of the region. The total allocation for four years is Rs 6,600 crore.

The Modi government is known for its speed and quality of infrastructure. Earlier, during the UP regime, the speed of the construction of national highways in the North East was 0.6 km per day. It increased to 1.5 km per day between 2014-19. Till 2013-14, the total length of national highways was 8,480 km. It increased to 15,735 km in 2022-23[10].

Since 2014, the government has spent Rs 19,855 crore on the development of new tracks besides doubling the existing metre gauge. The number of airports has increased from 9 in 2014. The number of waterways increased from 1 in 2014 to 18.

To bring the North East closer, Modi has taken steps to enhance digital connectivity. Rs 3,466 crore has been spent for this, and more than 4525 villages have 4G connectivity. On the front of electricity, more than 26.14 lakh households have electricity. All this led to an increase in the culture of entrepreneurship.

A total of 243 power projects were sanctioned under various schemes worth Rs 3,200 crore. Of these, 211 projects have been completed.

Various efforts of the government led to an increase in agriculture exports from USD 2.52 million in 2016 to USD 17.2 million in 2021-22. It resulted from an expansion of the National Bamboo Mission and the Mission on Edible Oil[11].

While the Prime Minister ensured that people from the North East get the benefits of various government schemes such as free food under the PM Garib Kalyan Yojana and free medical treatment under Ayushman Bharat, it has also emphasised the expansion of educational and sports facilities. Under the Khelo India scheme, launched in 2018,

62 sports infrastructure projects worth Rs 423.01 crore were sanctioned in 2021. The landmark was setting up the first National Sports University in Manipur at the cost of Rs 643.34 crore. Modi laid the foundation stone in March 2018.

Higher education has been another priority sector. The government has spent Rs 14,009 crore since 2014 and set up 191 new learning institutions. Under the IshanUday special scholarship scheme, the government gave yearly financial assistance to 10,000 fresh students from the region. Those pursuing a general degree or technical or professional course are entitled to a monthly stipend of Rs 5,400 to 7,800 if their annual family income is not more than Rs 4.5 lakh. From 2015-16 to 2020-21, the government spent Rs 661.1 crore to disburse scholarships to 44,000 students.

The Prime Minister refers to the eight states of the North East as Ashtalakshmi, highlighting the hidden potential of these states to become an engine of growth and an integral part of *Atmanirbhar Bharat*. Various products of this region have a unique regional stamp that promotes the concept of producing locally and marketing globally.

Moreover, a highway is being constructed to link the North East with Myanmar and Thailand and thereby with the economies of the ASEAN countries. It would facilitate trade and development and lead to the North East becoming a hub of economic activities. The 1,400 km long highway, first proposed by Vajpayee, got delayed due to problems in Myanmar. 'But it has been a very difficult project, mainly because of the situation in Myanmar. And one of our priorities today is to find ways of how to resume this project, how to unlock it, and how to make it because large parts of the project have been built', said external affairs minister S Jaishankar during his visit to Thailand in 2023[12].

Why do They Oppose Him?

Great spirits have always encountered violent opposition from mediocre minds
- Albert Einstein

One can understand the reasons behind Opposition parties opposing Narendra Modi. In competitive politics, they have to, since their survival depends on mobilising the section of the population that may have been rough-shouldered by government policies. Even for the good of the nation, you need to remove the bottlenecks and annoy many people, including the vested interests and people who seek to misuse the system for their personal benefits.

There may be many people, such as the Leftists, who oppose Modi because one cadre-based party cannot tolerate the other. Their ideology, which is borrowed, may also conflict with the ideology of the BJP, which is rooted in cultural nationalism. Nationalism, for many, is anathema and often synonymous with majoritarianism. There are some people, like the Islamists, who think that the government represents the larger Hindu population and that continuing the same would endanger their special status in the future.

We will analyse a few of these factors to understand the battle cry the Opposition Congress and other parties give every time during the elections. Sometimes, it seems the Congress does not understand the cultural ethos governing this oldest civilisation for centuries. Though ruled by the Islamic rulers for around 400 years, preceded by the Mongol attacks in the twelfth century and ruled by the British for another 200 years, India has maintained its unique cultural identity. It is neither British nor Islamic. It is *Sanatan,* governed by values that celebrate human existence. It is a way of life in daily existence.

A person wearing *janeu* (sacred thread) over his sleeve and donning makeovers to demonstrate his Hindu identity shows that he has failed to understand the moorings of the country. If you are what you are and work seriously to ameliorate the plight of the poor, you will get support. People had accepted Sonia Gandhi as their leader despite her foreign origin. There was a time when the BJP was forced to drop the issue of her foreign origin since it did not resonate with the people. The second term for the Congress in 2009 was because of the popularity of Dr Manmohan Singh, who belonged to the Sikh community that forms less than two per cent of the population. Your religious identity does not matter if you are sincere in your work.

Against this, Modi is what he is. He does not feign identity. He wears attires of different cultural traditions and celebrates diversity, but does not hide his faith to draw support, whether in India, UAE or the United Nations. People love his ways and trust his sincerity, simplicity and honesty. He is a champion of taking India's cultural values across the world to promote a perfect unison of heart and mind in the dispensation of justice. He always speaks his mind boldly for a just global order.

Earlier, the government used to change but Lutyens' Delhi always prevailed. It is better understood in the adage prevalent in Delhi, also shown in the movie *Kashmir Files,* 'They have the government but the system is ours.' Though the Vajpayee government brought many changes, it could not take the Lutyens' Delhi by the horns since there were coalition compulsions.

There used to be an unwritten law that the holy cows (important leaders) in the Opposition parties would not be touched, though the lesser minions could be sacrificed. A change of government, therefore, did not matter much as long as the pliable bureaucrats and friendly politicians would oblige by running errands for the Opposition as well. In such a vast system of government and administration, nobody would actually notice. The media would also keep these holy cows happy.

Modi's ascension changed these overnight. He had come with the promise of change and transformation and was bound by his promises. Trying to fulfil these promises, he had no option but to ride roughshod over those who had hijacked the system. The Congress and other Opposition parties are clueless on how to tackle Modi. He has no friends to influence him, though he may listen to their advice if given in the interest of the country.

Those indulging in corruption while holding power are gradually finding the noose of the law closing in on them. The government agencies have the freedom to do their job without fear. Those arrested are finding it tough to get bail because of the meticulous job of the investigative agencies. It is evident that actions are not motivated by political agenda and are backed by a foolproof and detailed investigation.

Whether it is Rahul Gandhi, Mamata Banerjee, or Lalu Prasad Yadav, the thread that unites them is the same–the fear of the law and the failure to discover ways to tackle Modi. They know Modi must be pulled down and a new government installed to tame these menacing agencies. Rahul Gandhi tried to undermine Modi's credibility outside and issued unsavoury statements criticised for being 'anti-national' and 'insulting to the country'[1]. During his visit to the UK in May 2022, Rahul Gandhi said, 'So, the deep state, the CBI, the ED, is now chewing the Indian state and eating it, much like in Pakistan'[2]. It showed his scant regard for the institutions. These institutions cannot act arbitrarily, and even if they do, the Courts are there to take care of that.

Action Against Powerful NGOs

A strong India rising firmly on the world horizon with its robust democratic institutions is an eyesore for dictators around the world. Countries and their leaders are increasingly realising that it is much safer to do business in India and run their operations from here than the uncertain future in China or other countries that thrive on dictatorship based on ideology or military strength. Naturally, these countries would try to malign India and use the fault lines to show India as a land of conflict and unrest. Our Opposition parties and vested interests are falling prey to their conspiracy[3].

Such vested interests would show India as a land of conflict and will use all assets, including gullible politicians, Non-Governmental Organisations (NGOs) and media, to show India in a bad light. No less than Prime Minister Dr Manmohan Singh had criticised foreign-backed NGOs for 'stalling the use of genetic engineering in agriculture and leading protests against the Kudankulam nuclear power plant in Tamil Nadu.'[4]

The issue figured prominently in 2020-21 when farmers started agitating against the three farm laws without showing any keenness to discuss its merits or otherwise of the issue. The government showed maturity and withdrew the legislations in the interest of national security and integration. But it is still inexplicable why Greta Thunberg and pop singer Rihanna tweeted in favour of farmers' agitation. They acted as paid assassins and became a part of the toolkit in the hands of anti-India groups. Prime Minister Modi rightly said that there was an international conspiracy to defame India.

Let us understand the ecosystem of these NGOs. Most NGOs serve an important function by taking the government policies to the last person. They act as checks on the pilferage of money and supplement the work of the government. Some big NGOs are funded by foreign institutions and players, undertaking various activities to improve lives based on their own resources. But many vested interests work under the guise of these NGOs and encourage subversive activities to jeopardise India's sovereignty.

These NGOs, funded by foreign donors, are governed by the FCRA (Foreign Currency Regulation Act). Since it involves foreign exchange, a meticulous record is required to track whether the money is clean and coming from known sources or via the hawala route or funded by questionable organisations. Also, the purpose of the money needs to be recorded to check if it was spent as per the mandate of the donor.

From 2016-17 to 2018-19, i.e. for three years, over Rs 58,000 crore was received by NGOs registered under the FCRA[5]. There are 22,400 NGOs registered under the FCRA. After coming to power, the Modi government has cancelled the registration of more than 20,000 NGOs for violating various provisions of the Act. It means these NGOs cannot receive foreign funding. Some of these NGOs are rights-based advocacy groups[6].

Although foreign funding is allowed, its source and expenditure need to be disclosed to the government. It is to ensure that the funds are not misused. Many NGOs would act as umbrella NGOs to patronise smaller NGOs through liberal funding and get them to come on the streets when it's time to oppose certain interests and push forward their own interest. This had become the standard practice by most of these NGOs. Many times, gullible people who come on the streets are not even aware of what they are protesting against.

The new FCRA Act, which came into effect on 29 September 2020, debars people from the following categories from accepting foreign funding–election candidates, editors or publishers of a newspaper, judges, government servants, members of any legislature and political parties and public servants.

Another provision of the new Act forbids the recipient of foreign funds to transfer it to another entity. Another provision of the Act has brought administrative expense from 50 per cent to 20 per cent. Moreover, an FCRA account can be opened only with the SBI.

These provisions of the new Act have tried to make the NGO regime under the FCRA more transparent and accountable. There is no bar if any NGO genuinely wants to work in the country. But they should know that they cannot work under secrecy and cannot use the money to put unnecessary pressure on the government. Opening an account with only one bank would lead to better governance and accountability.

Let us briefly analyse the activities of two world-reputed NGOs– the Amnesty and the Greenpeace. London-based Amnesty operates in the field of human rights. In 2000, it was permitted to receive foreign funding. The permission was denied subsequently, and the ED froze the account in 2018 on money laundering charges. It got a reprieve from the court. However, the accounts were sealed again since they did not have the FCRA license. Amnesty's FCRA registration was cancelled in 2010, but it replied and started operation.

To circumvent the law, Amnesty used the FDI route to get funds from the UK in four entities in India. A significant amount of this money was routed to Amnesty. Amnesty tried to bypass the FCRA by floating a company, Amnesty International India Pvt Ltd and received

FDI to fund its activities. Amnesty received money in the garb of exporting services.

'Amnesty International, UK sent Rs 51.72 crore to AIIPL in the guise of Export of Services and Foreign Direct Investment. However, there was no documentary proof for the alleged export such as invoices and copies of the agreement submitted during the investigation', a statement from the ED said[7]. Instead of answering the ED or fighting its battle, Amnesty alleged a witch-hunt and closed its operation in India on 29 September 2020. It may have imagined that as a supranational organisation, it could arm-twist India, but failed since none of its benefactors could support violating the law of the land where it operates.

Greenpeace India, working for the environment, was charged with financial fraud and false data. It was charged with underreporting foreign contributions and 'using them without government approval'. The government found that it maintained multiple accounts without informing authorities.

The Modi government stopped the foreign funding of this organisation on 9 April 2015 for six months and froze all its accounts, saying its activities prejudicially affected the country's public and economic interests in violation of the FCRA. A report from the Home Ministry said that foreign contribution was used 'to influence and lobby for the formation of government policies'[8].

The Registrar of Tamil Nadu government cancelled the registration of Greenpeace India in May 2015 over 'fraudulent conduct of business and falsification of accounts'. It directed the NGO to dissolve within a month[9].

One can imagine that these thousands of NGOs employed lakhs of people directly or indirectly, and it would not be unnatural if their anger translated into opposition. Some prominent voices against the Modi government, as heard on television debates or read in the columns of various newspapers, are those who were regular beneficiaries of the largesse of these NGOs, including fully-funded foreign tours.

Let us not forget that these NGOs had enlisted the support of Indian parliamentarians to write to Barack Obama not to give the visa to Modi. 65 parliamentarians had written a letter to Obama in 2012, asking him to continue the policy of no visa to Modi[10]. These NGOs have been actively involved in painting Modi in a bad light.

Action Against Shell Companies

The government set up a Task Force in February 2017 to prevent illegal activities such as opening shell companies to facilitate tax evasion. The Department of Financial Services, CBDT, CBEC, CBI, ED, SFIO, FIU-IND, RBI, SEBI, DG GSTI and DG-CEIB were its members.

The Task Force created three lists, namely–The Confirmed List I, which identified 16,537 companies as confirmed shell companies; The Derived List of 16,739 companies, which had 100 per cent common directorship with confirmed shell companies; and The Suspect List of 80,670 companies identified through Red Flag indicators.

Shell companies exist only in names and are often used to register fake business transactions and act as conduits for generating black money. Money circulating through the hawala route also finds a safe parking spot in these companies. Setting up the Task Force complemented the government's other efforts to fight black money.

The Registrar of the Companies (ROCs) identified and removed the names of 2,26,166 companies from its registration list. These companies had not filed their Financial Statements or Annual Returns for two or more continuous financial years. The ROC disqualified 3,09,619 directors for non-compliance of company norms[11]. Till 2021-22, names of as many as 4,32,796 companies were struck off by the ROC. The Task Force continues to identify defaulting companies to bring financial discipline.

All those people who have suffered due to this cannot believe that the country is on the path of course correction where honest taxpayers would be rewarded and those trying to subvert the system would be punished. They are influential people forming a part of the elite society. Modi has disturbed their equilibrium with the system.

Paint Modi as Anti-Muslim

Those with no single instance to prove against Modi continue to oppose him by trying to paint him as anti-Muslim. They try to weave an ideology of Hindutva for the government and its supporters and juxtapose it against Muslims. The postulation is Hindu majority support, which means being anti-Muslim. The fact is far from this. Modi has been working for the poor, and there is no discrimination based on religion or caste.

Many schemes meant for the poor have benefitted Muslims the most. They benefit from various schemes, including Ayushman Bharat Yojana, maternity benefits and housing. Danish Azad Ansari, a minister of the Yogi government in Uttar Pradesh, said that 35-40 per cent of beneficiaries of the government schemes have been backward Pasmanda Muslims or forward Muslims.

'Till 2014, only 4.5 per cent Muslims were government employees, and the figure has gone up to 10.5 per cent in the last nine years', BJP's minority cell general secretary Sufi M K Chishty claimed[12]. A comparison between figures of the NDA government from 2014-19 with the figures of the UPA government from 2009-14 demonstrates that more student from the minority community received government scholarships under the Modi government. While the number for the UPA stood at 2.94 crore for the five-year period mentioned, the corresponding figure for the NDA government was 3.14 crore[13].

The Modi government has given liberal scholarships to students from minority communities for pre-matric and higher secondary level students (Class 11 and 12). Muslims have been the biggest beneficiaries. Between 2014-15 and 2021-22, the then Union Minister for Minorities, Mukhtar Abbas Naqvi, said that a total of more than 3.36 crore pre-matric scholarships were granted to Muslim students, 53,13,905 to Christian students, 35,90,880 to Sikh students, 12,98,637 to Buddhist students and 4,58,665 to Jain students, costing Rs 9057.08 crore[14]. The scholarship was later amended and is now available only to students of classes 9 and 10. Since education up to class 8 is free and the attendance record shows that students from minorities were at par with the rest, there was no need to give overlapping schemes. The scholarship in class 9 and 10 would ensure that students continue their education and do not drop out.

A sizeable section of the male population in the Muslim community felt hurt when the government pushed the triple talaq laws to ban instant divorce. This has given justice to Muslim women, but many men considered it as an infringement on their personal law. The radicals in the community have been using this to mobilise opinion against Modi, ignoring the Supreme Court's mandate that such a law be made.

The removal of Article 370, the construction of the Rama temple at Ayodhya and the revival of other cultural symbols have become tools in the hands of Leftists, liberals, and the Congress to mobilise Muslim opinion against Modi. In their rhetoric, they ignore that the basis of each of these has nothing to do with Muslims.

Middlemen

The largest opposition to the Modi government was the farmers' agitation during 2020-21. What was the protest about when all those concerned with agriculture opined that the three laws were beneficial for the country? The agitation was backed by the middlemen, who did not want to lose control over the system.

Seeing a flicker of hope, the Leftists, Islamists and the Congress joined hands against Modi. Later events proved that the agitation intended to defeat the BJP at the assembly elections in Uttar Pradesh in 2022. The farmers' groups campaigned against the BJP but failed to prevent the party from registering an impressive win.

Another set of middlemen is hurt due to the government devising ways to reach the beneficiaries directly. One can recall how late Rajiv Gandhi admitted that only 15 paise out of a rupee reached the beneficiaries. Who were the ones pocketing the 85 per cent? They have adequate reasons to oppose the government.

The JAM trinity helped identify about 10 crore fake beneficiaries. They were getting benefits, although they did not exist in reality. These fake beneficiaries have been identified since 2014 under Operation Clean[15].

The Modi government has been trying to identify and remove them from the list. By 2023, more than 17.1 million duplicate or ineligible farmers were found benefitting from PM Kisan Samman. This alone will help save the government Rs 9000 crore[16]. In the case of MGNREGA, the government has identified and deleted 3.3 million duplicate or fake job cards.

Another scam has come to light in the case of scholarships to students. We have heard of fake registrations of students to get grants from the government. Around 53 per cent of institutions under a minority scholarship programme across the country are fake, leading to a scam of more than Rs 144 crore. The government has already ordered a CBI inquiry into this[17].

It is obvious that those who were pocketing money by subverting the system would be unhappy.

Media

Although the media landscape is changing, there are many smarting under the insult of being ignored by the Modi dispensation. Lutyens' Delhi media have often basked in the glory of being coopted by whoever has been in power. The editors of prestigious newspapers used to compete with each other to have meals with the Prime Minister. Many acquired enormous clout and became middlemen to strike deals with others.

Modi changed all of that. He decided he did not need Lutyens' media to be in power or to acquire a good image. He developed his own social media to reach people and spoke his mind regularly on the issues facing the country. Earlier, media persons used to accompany the Prime Minister on foreign tours. He stopped this practice. He never asked the media what to write and what not to write.

His adage has been, 'I will do my work and you do yours'. Despite many critics in the media, there has not been even one case of corruption or nepotism against Modi. Many people in the media are unhappy, and they privately or publicly speak against the government on issues that cannot be established as facts.

Serpents in the Gloves

Those who supported Modi anticipating their own raise are unhappy. Some prominent people were accommodated in the first term, but the co-option discontinued as the focus shifted to delivering better governance. Modi knows that it is difficult to make everyone happy. You help one person and you end up annoying a hundred others who may not get the same treatment. In such a situation, it is better to give a level playing field to everyone.

I have heard some of the hardened cadre of the BJP-RSS speaking badly about Modi in their personal conversation. When I protest and ask them to substantiate with facts, they say you will come to know of this soon. I laugh at them since the source of their frustration is their desire to raise. Also, they know that Modi would march ahead irrespective of their support.

Modi is doing everything as per the ideological commitment of the BJP for a strong nation. But if one is creating a foolproof system, one cannot have a parallel system to oblige people at the personal level. For example, if there is no interview for Class 3 and 4 posts in the Central government, the system cannot be manipulated. This is exactly what people had voted him for–transparency and accountability.

The Modi government is pragmatic and flexible. The BJP under Modi knows that it must stay in power to streamline things. Power is the biggest instrument to bring change. It cannot stress ideological steadfastness beyond a point. One slip and the hard work of years would go to waste. Every Lok Sabha or Assembly seat matters and the party calculates how to win. The BJP has realised its strength of being a cadre-based party. The superstructure is supported by the base of the cadre, most of whom have been trained in the RSS shakhas. Thus, it does not change the basic character of the party if people from outside join it. The party also cannot send an image that others are not welcome.

Acknowledgements

I extend my heartfelt gratitude to all my friends and well-wishers who consistently nudged my conscience and encouraged me to write an assessment of nine-plus years of the Modi government.

To my critics, who whispered behind my back that I was a one-book wonder and the purpose of writing the book was merely to join the BJP at a good position and further my political ambition, I express my appreciation. Your scepticism served as a reminder of the importance of integrity and authenticity in my work.

Both sides, in their own way, urged me to delve deeper into the subject and pen another book on Narendra Modi, whom I had called the Gamechanger in my earlier work *Narendra Modi the Gamechanger*. Thus, I found myself compelled to revisit the topic and examine how Narendra Modi was reshaping governance for the betterment of our nation.

I am grateful to the Bharatiya Janata Party for entrusting me with the role of spokesperson, which not only provided valuable insight into effective communication strategies but also helped crystallise the framework for this book in my mind. My tenure as spokesperson allowed me to dissect the hollow arguments of the BJP's opponents and underscore the transformative leadership of Narendra Modi.

I sincerely thank Vitasta Publishing and its Managing Director Renu Kaul Verma, my wife, for constantly egging me on to finish writing the book. I thank my younger brother, Santosh Verma, for allowing me and my research team to use his office space, and facilitating our project.

A big thank you to Varsha Koli and Surajit Dasgupta for assisting me in my research. Thank you, Ravi Ranjan Mishra, for your guidance on crucial economic decisions that enriched the content of this work.

Acknowledgement is also due to the staff of Vitasta for taking personal care in shaping the production of the book. The editor of the book, Vichitra, did a splendid job in a very short time. I thank Faiza Yameen for giving me the perspective on how Muslims were reacting to the decisions taken by the Government on issues concerning minorities.

Last but not least I express my profound gratitude to the Hon'ble Governor of Kerala, Arif Mohammad Khan, for writing the Foreword to this book. I am thankful to Shri M J Akbar, Prof Dinesh Singh, Prof Jagadesh Kumar and Maj Gen K K Singh (retd) for their kind words about this book, which have added depth and credibility to its content.

References

Understanding the Leader and His Vision

1. Verma, Sudesh (2014) *Narendra Modi–The GameChanger*. New Delhi: Vitasta Publishing.
2. NDTV (2021) *"Never Imagined...": PM Modi On Completing 20 Years In Public Office* NDTV [Online] Retrieved from: https://www.ndtv.com/india-news/pm-modi-20-years-public-service-never-imagined-pm-modi-on-completing-20-years-in-public-office-2566815 [Accessed: 1 April 2024].
3. Ibid.
4. India Today (2020) *Farmers Protest December 4: British MPs seek UK's intervention in agitation against farm laws* India Today [Online] Retrieved from: https://www.indiatoday.in/india/story/farmers-protest-delhi-haryana-punjab-noida-ghaziabad-ghazipur-border-delhi-chalo-march-traffic-live-news-updates-1746519-2020-12-04 [Accessed: 1 April 2024].

Prime Minister Modi

1. For more into the details of the Gujarat riots and what the SIT and court said, please refer: Verma, Sudesh (2014) *Narendra Modi–The GameChanger*. New Delhi: Vitasta Publishing.
2. See: Verma, Sudesh (2014) *Narendra Modi–The GameChanger*. New Delhi: Vitasta Publishing.

3. Economist.com (2013) *Narendra Modi is the world's most popular leader* The Economist [Online] Retrieved from: https://www.economist.com/asia/2023/06/15/narendra-modi-is-the-worlds-most-popular-leader [Accessed: 1 April 2024].

New Cultural Awakening, Removing Vestiges

1. India Today (2019) *A minute to acknowledge the day when India was 'educated' by Macaulay* indiatoday.in [Online] Retrieved from: https://www.indiatoday.in/education-today/gk-current-affairs/story/a-minute-to-acknowledge-the-day-when-india-was-educated-by-macaulay-1160140-2018-02-02 [Accessed: 1 April 2024].
2. Ibid.
3. Naoroji, Dadabhai (2020) *Poverty and un-British Rule in India*. London: S. Sonnenschein.
4. Al Jazeera (2018) *How Britain stole $45 trillion from India* aljazeera.com [Online] Retrieved from: https://www.aljazeera.com/opinions/2018/12/19/how-britain-stole-45-trillion-from-india [Accessed: 1 April 2024].
5. Press Information Bureau (2022) *The Prime Minister, Shri Narendra Modi addressed the nation from the ramparts of the Red Fort on the 76th Independence Day* pib.gov.in [Online] Retrieved from: https://pib.gov.in/PressReleasePage.aspx?PRID=1852024 [Accessed: 1 April 2024].
6. Press Information Bureau (2014) *PM encourages self-certification in place of affidavits and attestations to benefit the common man* pib.gov.in [Online] Retrieved from: <u>PM encourages self-certification in place of affidavits and attestations to benefit the common man</u> (pib.gov.in) [Accessed: 1 April 2024].
7. The Economic Times (2014) *PM Narendra Modi pushes for self-attestation of documents* The Economic Times [Online] Retrieved from: PM Narendra Modi pushes for self-attestation of documents - The Economic Times (indiatimes.com) [Accessed 1 April 2024].
8. Press Information Bureau (2017) *End of Red Beacons: A big blow to VIP culture* pib.gov.in [Online] Retrieved from: https://pib.gov.in/newsite/printrelease.aspx?relid=161226 [Accessed: 1 April 2024].
9. Ibid.

10. Chatterjee, Partha ed (2001) *'Development planning and the Indian state' in State and Politics in India.* New Delhi: Oxford University Press.
11. The Times of India (2016) *Scrap railway budget: Niti Aayog panel* timesofindia.indiatimes.com [Online] Retrieved from: https://timesofindia.indiatimes.com/india/scrap-railway-budget-niti-aayog-panel/articleshow/52860225.cms [Accessed: 1 April 2024].
12. *The London Gazette,* Supplement, (1921). Page 278.
13. Deccan Herald (2023) *From bahi-khata to longest speech, Sitharaman holds several budget records* deccanherald.com [Online] Retrieved from: https://www.deccanherald.com/business/union-budget/from-bahi-khata-to-longest-speech-sitharaman-holds-several-budget-records-1186075.html [Accessed: 1 April 2024].
14. Press Information Bureau (2022) *Ease of Doing Business", Department for Promotion of Industry and Internal Trade (DPIIT), Ministry of Commerce* pib.gov.in [Online] Retrieved from: chrome-extension://efaidnbmnnnibpcajpcglclefindmkaj/https://static.pib.gov.in/WriteReadData/specificdocs/documents/2022/nov/doc20221123133801.pdf [Accessed: 1 April 2024].
15. The Economic Times (2022) *My government scrapped 2,000 obsolete laws, helped improve India spot in ease of doing business list: PM Modi* economictimes.indiatimes.com [Online] Retrieved from: https://economictimes.indiatimes.com/news/politics-and-nation/my-government-scrapped-2000-obsolete-laws-helped-improve-india-spot-in-ease-of-doing-business-list-pm-modi/articleshow/94767779.cms?from=mdr [Accessed: 1 April 2024].
16. Ibid.
17. Press Information Bureau (2014) *PM sets up Committee to identify obsolete laws within three months* pib.gov.in [Online] Retrieved from: https://pib.gov.in/newsite/PrintRelease.aspx?relid=109106 [Accessed: 1 April 2024].
18. Prime Minister of India (2014) *Report of the Committee to Identify the Central Acts which are not Relevant or No Longer Needed or Required Repeal in the Present Socio-Economic Context* pmindia.gov.in [Online] Retrieved from: https://www.pmindia.gov.in/wp-content/uploads/2015/01/Extracts-of-the-Committee-of-the-Report-Vol.I-.pdf [Accessed: 1 April 2024].
19. Ibid.

20. First Post (2022) *Explained: The making of the grand Netaji Subhas Chandra Bose statue unveiled at India Gate* Firstpost [Online] Retrieved from: https://www.firstpost.com/explainers/netaji-subhas-chandra-bose-statue-india-gate-narendra-modi-kartavya-path-central-vista-delhi-11207501.html [Accessed: 1 April 2024].
21. First Post (2023) *Modi's recognition of Netaji: Change in narrative?* Firstpost [Online] Retrieved from: https://www.earshot.in/series/firstpost-explainers-news-english/modis-recognition-of-netaji-change-in-narrative--english [Accessed: 1 April 2024].
22. The Times of India (2018) *Welcome recognition for Netaji's legacy at last: How India's struggle for independence was really won* The Times of India [Online] Retrieved from: https://timesofindia.indiatimes.com/blogs/toi-edit-page/welcome-recognition-for-netajis-legacy-at-last-how-indias-struggle-for-independence-was-really-won/ [Accessed: 1 April 2024].
23. Narendra Modi (2022) *New history has been created in the form of 'Kartavya Path': PM Modi* narendramodi.in [Online] Retrieved from: https://www.narendramodi.in/text-of-prime-minister-narendra-modi-s-address-at-inauguration-of-kartavya-path-in-new-delhi-564301 [Accessed: 1 April 2024].
24. Asian News International (2023) *Indian Navy ends 'colonial legacy' of carrying batons with immediate effect* aninews.in [Online] Retrieved from: https://aninews.in/news/national/general-news/indian-navy-ends-colonial-legacy-of-carrying-batons-with-immediate-effect20230729162534/?amp=1 [Accessed: 1 April 2024].
25. Times Now (2023) *Supreme Court Rejects PIL Against Inauguration of New Parliament Building by PM Modi* timesnownews.com [Online} Retrieved from: https://www.timesnownews.com/india/supreme-court-rejects-pil-against-inauguration-of-new-parliament-building-by-pm-modi-article-100522074 [Accessed: 1 April 2024].
26. India Times (2023) *New Parliament building- no governor or President had been invited for laying the foundation stones in the last nine years-Sarma* economictimes.indiatimes.com [Online] Retrieved from: https://economictimes.indiatimes.com/news/india/new-parliament-building-no-governor-or-president-had-been-invited-for-laying-the-foundation-stones-in-the-last-nine-years-sarma/articleshow/100480547.cms?from=mdr [Accessed: 1 April 2024].

27. Press Information Bureau (2016) *Decentralization of Environmental Clearance for Sustainable sand Mining and Mining of Minor Minerals Introduced: Javadekar* Press Information Bureau [Online] Retrieved from: https://pib.gov.in/newsite/PrintRelease.aspx?relid=134689 [Accessed: 1 April 2024].
28. Prime Minister of India (2015) *PM Modi during his 69th Independence Day speech* pmindia.gov.in [Online] Retrieved from: https://www.pmindia.gov.in/en/news_updates/pms-address-to-the-nation-on-69th-independence-day/ [Accessed: 1 April 2024].
29. Zee Business (2022) *PM Narendra Modi's Panchpran - 15th August - five pledges that will make India a developed nation in 25 years* zeebiz.com [Online] Retrieved from: https://www.zeebiz.com/india/news-pm-narendra-modis-panchpran-15th-august-five-pledges-that-will-make-india-must-be-a-developed-nation-in-25-years-194205 [Accessed: 1 April 2024].
30. Press Information Bureau (2023) *Union Home Minister and Minister of Cooperation, Shri Amit Shah introduces the Bhartiya Nyaya Sanhita Bill 2023, the Bharatiya Nagarik Suraksha Sanhita Bill, 2023 and the Bharatiya Sakshya Bill, 2023 in the Lok Sabha, today* pib.gov.in [Online] Retrieved from: https://pib.gov.in/PressReleaseIframePage.aspx?PRID=1947941 [Accessed: 1 April 2024].
31. Ibid.

Digital India – An IT Revolution

1. Narendra Modi (2015) *PM's speech at the launch of Digital India Week* narendramodi.in [Online] Retrieved from: https://www.narendramodi.in/pm-s-remarks-at-the-launch-of-digital-india-week-175128 [Accessed: 1 April 2024].
2. Outlook India (2023) *World Bank Praises India's Digital Infrastructure For Its Transformative Potential* outlookindia.com [Online] Retrieved from: https://business.outlookindia.com/news/world-bank-praises-indias-digital-infrastructure-for-its-transformative-potential [Accessed: 1 April 2024].
3. Twitter 20 August 2023 @GermanyinIndia [Online] Retrieved from: https://twitter.com/GermanyinIndia/status/1693162556918210966 [Accessed: 1 April 2024].

4. Narendra Modi (2014) *PM's address to the nation on 15 August* narendramodi.in [Online] Retrieved from: https://www.narendramodi.in/pms-address-to-the-nation-on-15th-august-6461 [Accessed: 1 April 2024].
5. The Indian Express (2023) *PM Narendra Modi Independence Day speech full text* indianexpress.com [Online] Retrieved from: https://indianexpress.com/article/india/prime-minister-narendra-modi-independence-day-speech-2023-full-text-8893141/ [Accessed: 1 April 2024].
6. BBC (2014) *India: Five unusual messages from Narendra Modi's speech* bbc.com [Online] Retrieved from: https://www.bbc.com/news/world-asia-india-28799397 [Accessed: 1 April 2024].
7. The Economic Times (2014) *PM Narendra Modi says 'digital revolution is about to begin'; showcases his vision* economictimes.indiatimes.com [Online] Retrieved from: https://economictimes.indiatimes.com/news/politics-and-nation/pm-narendra-modi-says-digital-revolution-is-about-to-begin-showcases-his-vision/articleshow/40581868.cms?from=mdr [Accessed: 1 April 2024].
8. The Hindu (2023) *Digital India expansion gets ₹14,903 crore outlay* thehindu.com [Online] Retrieved from: https://www.thehindu.com/news/national/cabinet-approves-extension-of-digital-india-project-with-outlay-of-14903-crore/article67201285.ece [Accessed: 1 April 2024].
9. Ibid.
10. Money Control (2023) *Economic Survey 2023: 135.2 crore Aadhar Numbers generated till November 2022* moneycontrol.com [Online] Retrieved from: https://www.moneycontrol.com/news/business/budget/economic-survey-2023-135-2-crore-aadhaar-numbers-generated-till-november-2022-9971821.html [Accessed: 1 April 2024].
11. Bank Bazaar (2023) *PM Jan Dhan Yojana* bankbazaar.com [Online] Retrieved from: https://www.bankbazaar.com/saving-schemes/pradhan-mantri-jan-dhan-yojana.html [Accessed: 1 April 2024].
12. Narendra Modi (2015) narendramodi.in [Online].
13. Prime Minister of India (2015) *Guinness book of World Records recognises Pradhan Mantri Jan-Dhan Yojana* pmindia.gov.in [Online] Retrieved from: https://www.pmindia.gov.in/en/major_initiatives/pradhan-mantri-jan-dhan-yojana/ [Accessed: 1 April 2024].

14. National Informatics Centre (2023) *Direct Benefit Transfer – A blessing during the time of Pandemic* nic.in [Online] Retrieved from: https://www.nic.in/blogs/direct-benefit-transfer-a-blessing-during-the-time-of-pandemic/ [Accessed: 1 April 2024].
15. Money Control (2023) *Economic Survey 2023: DBT has helped transfer more than Rs. 26.5 lakh crore till date for central schemes* moneycontrol.com [Online] Retrieved from: https://www.moneycontrol.com/news/business/economic-survey-2023-dbt-has-helped-transfer-more-than-rs-26-5-lakh-crore-till-date-for-central-schemes-9975061.html [Accessed: 1 April 2024].
16. Mint (2023) *India's digital transformation offers global solutions: PM Modi* livemint.com [Online] Retrieved from: https://www.livemint.com/news/india/indias-digital-transformation-offers-global-solutions-pm-modi-11692430005129.html [Accessed: 1 April 2024].
17. Ibid.
18. Narendra Modi (2023) *For the first time in the country, the poor have got security as well as dignity: PM Modi* narendramodi.in [Online] Retrieved from: https://www.narendramodi.in/text-of-prime-minister-narendra-modi-s-address-at-republic-tv-s-conclave-569674 [Accessed: 1 April 2024].
19. Deccan Herald (2014) *Modi asserts commitment against graft* deccanherald.com [Online] Retrieved from: https://www.deccanherald.com/india/modi-asserts-commitment-against-graft-2214068 [Accessed: 1 April 2024].
20. Business World (2022) *UP Govt saves over Rs 8000 Cr with the help of UIDAI* businessworld.in [Online] Retrieved from: https://www.businessworld.in/article/UP-Govt-Saves-Over-Rs-8-000-Cr-With-The-Help-Of-UIDAI/29-09-2022-448652/ [Accessed: 1 April 2024].
21. The Statesman (2023) *DBT, Aadhaar linkage helps Haryana identify over 36 lakh duplicate beneficiaries* thestatesman.com [Online] Retrieved from: https://www.thestatesman.com/india/dbt-aadhar-linkage-helps-haryana-identify-over-36-lakh-duplicate-beneficiariesransfer-dbt-and-aadhar-card-haryana-has-saved-over-rs-1503243147.html [Accessed: 1 April 2024].
22. UMANG *Introduction to UMANG App* umang.gov.in [Online] Retrieved from: https://web.umang.gov.in/landing/aboutus [Accessed: 1 April 2024].

23. National Health Authority *Pradhan Mantri Jan Arogya Yojana (PM-JAY* nha.gov.in [Online] Retrieved from: https://nha.gov.in/PM-JAY [Accessed: 1 April 2024].
24. Press Information Bureau (2023) *75 lakh additional LPG connections to be released in 3 years* pib.gov.in [Online] Retrieved from: https://pib.gov.in/PressReleaseIframePage.aspx?PRID=1957091 [Accessed: 1 April 2024].
25. Narendra Modi (2019) *Ujjwala Ensures Health, Savings & Opportunities for the Poor* narendramodi.in [Online] Retrieved from: https://www.narendramodi.in/ujjwala-ensures-health-savings-opportunities-for-the-poor-14-march-2019-544033 [Accessed: 1 April 2024].
26. PM Modi Scheme (2024) *Affordable Rental Housing Scheme (ARHC) 2024: Online Registration & Benefits* pmmodischeme.in [Online] Retrieved from: https://pmmodischeme.in/affordable-rental-housing-scheme/ [Accessed: 1 April 2024].
27. Press Information Bureau (2023) *Over 11 crore Toilets & 2.23 lakh Community Sanitary Complexes built across All States/UTs Under Swachh Bharat Mission - Grameen* pib.gov.in [Online] Retrieved from: https://pib.gov.in/PressReleaseIframePage.aspx?PRID=1907510 [Accessed: 1 April 2024].
28. The Times of India (2023) *Every farmer getting benefit of Rs 50k per year; that's 'Modi's guarantee', not just promise: PM* timesofindia.indiatimes.com [Online] Retrieved from: https://timesofindia.indiatimes.com/india/every-farmer-getting-benefit-of-rs-50k-per-year-thats-modis-guarantee-not-just-promise-pm/articleshow/101419242.cms [Accessed: 1 April 2024].
29. Ibid.
30. Press Information Bureau (2023) *National Agriculture Market (e-NAM) One Nation One Market for Agricultural produce* pib.gov.in [Online] Retrieved from: https://static.pib.gov.in/WriteReadData/specificdocs/documents/2023/apr/doc2023414181301.pdf [Accessed: 1 April 2024].
31. Ibid.
32. The Times of India (2022) *The ugly underbelly of the 'agitation' against farm laws* timesofindia.indiatimes.com [Online] Retrieved from: https://timesofindia.indiatimes.com/blogs/seeing-the-invisible/the-ugly-underbelly-of-the-agitation-against-farm-laws/ [Accessed: 1 April 2024].

33. The Indian Express (2021) *'Khalistanis' have infiltrated farmers protest, will show IB inputs: Centre tells SC* indianexpress.com [Online] Retrieved from: https://indianexpress.com/article/india/khalistan-farmers-protest-supreme-court-7143649/ [Accessed: 1 April 2024].
34. The Wire (2022) *'Silent Majority' Supported the Three Farm Laws: SC-Appointed Committee Report* thewire.in [Online] Retrieved from: https://thewire.in/agriculture/farm-laws-supreme-court-committee-report-released#:~:text=The%20report%20claims%20that%20out,did%20not%20support%20the%20Act [Accessed: 1 April 2024].
35. The Times of India (2021) *Repeal of farm laws a face-saving tactic ahead of key polls: Sharad Pawar* timesofindia.indiatimes.com [Online] Retrieved from: https://timesofindia.indiatimes.com/city/mumbai/repeal-of-farm-laws-a-face-saving-tactic-ahead-of-key-polls-in-mumbai-pawar/articleshow/87809015.cms [Accessed: 1 April 2024].
36. The Wire (2022) *'Defeat BJP: Mission Uttar Pradesh,' Farmers to Campaign Against BJP Ahead of 2022 Polls* thewire.in [Online] Retrieved from: https://thewire.in/agriculture/defeat-bjp-mission-uttar-pradesh-farmers-to-campaign-against-bjp-ahead-of-2022-polls [Accessed: 1 April 2024].
37. OpIndia (2022) *Yogendra Yadav admits that he and Rakesh Tikait created a 'conducive pitch' to defeat BJP by organizing farmer protests but SP 'did not bowl well'* opindia.com [Online] Retrieved from: https://www.opindia.com/2022/03/yogendra-yadav-admits-that-farmer-protest-was-meant-to-defeat-bjp-in-up/ [Accessed: 1 April 2024].
38. Digital Sansad (2023) *SOIL HEALTH CARD SCHEME*, Starred Question Number 394, sansad.in [Online] Retrieved from: https://sansad.in/getFile/loksabhaquestions/annex/1711/AS394.pdf?source=pqals [Accessed: 1 April 2024].
39. Press Information Bureau (2023) *Income of Farmers* pib.gov.in [Online] Retrieved from: https://pib.gov.in/PressReleaseIframePage.aspx?PRID=1906878 [Accessed: 1 April 2024].
40. Ibid.

***Mann Ki Baat* : Transformational Instrument**

1. The Hindustan Times (2021) *Encouraged by PM Modi on Man Ki Baat, Man Takes Covid-19 Vaccine Shot* thehindustantimes.com [Online] Retrieved from: https://www.hindustantimes.com/india-news/encouraged-by-pm-modi-on-mann-ki-baat-man-takes-covid-19-vaccine-shot-101624786459914.html [Accessed: 1 April 2024].
2. Government of India (2015) *Mann Ki Baat* mygov.in [Online] Retrieved from: https://www.mygov.in/group-issue/mann-ki-baat-prime-minister%E2%80%99s-radio-programme-september-20-2015/ [Accessed: 1 April 2024].
3. Government of India (2023) *Give it UP* mopng.gov.in [Online] Retrieved from: https://mopng.gov.in/en/marketing/give-it-up [Accessed: 1 April 2024].
4. Government of India (2015) *Mann Ki Baat* mygov.in [Online] Retrieved from: https://www.mygov.in/group-issue/mann-ki-baat-prime-minister%E2%80%99s-radio-programme-september-20-2015/ [Accessed: 1 April 2024].
5. Mahatma Gandhi, *Collected Works*, Vol 22, pp 291, gandhiashramsevagram.org.
6. Akashvani AIR (2014) *Mann Ki Baat* Episode 1 [Online] Retrieved from: https://www.youtube.com/watch?v=yHHa895Qv-c [Accessed: 1 April 2024].
7. Bharatiya Janata Party (2015) *Mann Ki Baat* Episode 5 [Online] Retrieved from: https://www.youtube.com/watch?v=RC8Y7AEUuYI [Accessed: 1 April 2024].
8. Outlook (2022) *Musings From Kumarakom* outlookindia.com [Online] Retrieved from: https://www.outlookindia.com/national/musings-from-kumarakom-news-210627 [Accessed 1 April 2024].
9. Prasar Bharati *All India Radio: Profile* prasarbharati.gov.in [Online] Retrieved from: https://prasarbharati.gov.in/all-india-radio-2/ [Accessed: 1 April 2024].
10. Ibid.
11. Press Information Bureau (2019) *Shri Arun Jaitley releases the book 'Mann Ki Baat – A Social Revolution on Radio'* pib.gov.in [Online] Retrieved from: https://pib.gov.in/Pressreleaseshare.aspx?PRID=1567138 [Accessed: 1 April 2024].

12. Press Information Bureau (2018) *50th episode of Mann ki Baat, 25 October 2018,* pib.gov.in [Online] Retrieved from: https://pib.gov.in/Pressreleaseshare.aspx?PRID=1553746 [Accessed: 1 April 2024].
13. Ibid.
14. PM of India (2023) *100th episode of Mann Ki Baat* pmindia.gov.in [Online] Retrieved from: https://www.pmindia.gov.in/en/news_updates/pms-address-in-the-100th-episode-of-mann-ki-baat/ [Accessed: 1 April 2024].
15. Ibid.
16. The Indian Express (2023) *BJP plans 4-lakh venues for 100th episode of PM's 'Mann Ki Baat'* indianexpress.com [Online] Retrieved from: https://indianexpress.com/article/india/bjp-plans-4-lakh-venues-for-100th-episode-of-pms-mann-ki-baat-8581998/ [Accessed: 1 April 2024].
17. The Economic Times (2023) *New York, New Jersey issue resolutions in honour of 100th episode of Maan Ki Baat* economictimes.indiatimes.com [Online] Retrieved from: https://economictimes.indiatimes.com/news/india/new-york-new-jersey-issue-resolutions-in-honour-of-100th-episode-of-mann-ki-baat/articleshow/99884665.cms?from=mdr [Accessed: 1 April 2024].
18. BlueKraft Digital Foundation (2019) *Mann ki Baat: A Social Revolution on Radio*. New Delhi: Rupa Publishing.
19. The Times of India (2015) *Social Media Takes to Selfie With Daughter Whole-heartedly* timesofindia.com [Online] Retrieved from: https://timesofindia.indiatimes.com/india/social-media-takes-to-selfiewithdaughter-whole-heartedly/articleshow/47857629.cms [Accessed: 1 April 2024].
20. BlueKraft Digital Foundation (2019) *Mann ki Baat: A Social Revolution on Radio*. New Delhi: Rupa Publishing.
21. Money Control (2015) *Global Leaders and Influencers Praise PM Modi's Impact and Leadership* moneycontrol.com [Online] Retrieved from: https://www.moneycontrol.com/news/india/global-leaders-and-influencers-praise-pm-modis-impact-and-leadership-10839341.html [Accessed: 1 April 2024].
22. India Today (2015) *PM Modi and Obama to host 'Mann ki Baat' in a joint radio address* indiatoday.in [Online] Retrieved from: https://www.indiatoday.in/obama-in-india/story/modi-barack-obama-joit-radio-address-mann-ki-baat-236829-2015-01-21 [Accessed: 1 April 2024].

23. News 18 (2023) *Opinion | How PM Modi's Mann Ki Baat Connects Him with Citizens and Local Issues* news18.com [Online] Retrieved from: https://www.news18.com/opinion/opinion-how-pm-modis-mann-ki-baat-connects-him-with-citizens-and-local-issues-7677133.html [Accessed: 1 April 2024].
24. BlueKraft Digital Foundation (2019) *Mann ki Baat: A Social Revolution on Radio*. New Delhi: Rupa Publishing.
25. Deccan Herald (2023) *UNESCO DG features in 100th episode of 'Mann Ki Baat', asks about 'Indian way' to ensure quality education for all* deccanherald.com [Online] Retrieved from: https://www.deccanherald.com/india/unesco-dg-features-in-100th-episode-of-mann-ki-baat-asks-about-indian-way-to-ensure-quality-education-for-all-1214412.html [Accessed: 1 April 2024].

Momentous Decisions: Redefining Bharat- I

1. India Today (2019) *Ayodhya mediation has failed, says CJI. Land dispute case now to be heard by Supreme Court* indiatoday.in [Online] Retrieved from: https://www.indiatoday.in/india/story/ayodhya-mediation-failed-case-to-be-heard-by-supreme-court-1576449-2019-08-02 [Accessed: 1 April 2024].
2. *PM Modi appeals for peace and harmony before Ayodhya verdict* (2019) daijiworld.com [Online] Retrieved from: https://www.daijiworld.com/news/newsDisplay?newsID=642024 [Accessed: 1 April 2024].
3. India Today (2022) *Ayodhya verdict welcomed by one and all: Sri Sri Ravi Shankar* indiatoday.in [Online] Retrieved from: https://www.indiatoday.in/india/story/sri-sri-ravi-shankar-ayodhya-verdict-welcomed-one-all-1617875-2019-11-11 [Accessed: 1 April 2024].
4. The Times of India (2014) *Did Vajpayee have premonition about Babri masjid demolition* timesofindia.indiatimes.com [Online] Retrieved from: https://timesofindia.indiatimes.com/india/did-vajpayee-have-premonitionabout-babri-masjid-demolition/articleshow/33252774.cms [Accessed: 1 April 2024].
5. The Economic Times (2019) *Will scrap Article 370 once BJP gets majority in Parliament: Amit Shah* economictimes.indiatimes.com [Online] Retrieved from: https://economictimes.indiatimes.com/news/elections/lok-sabha/india/will-scrap-article-370-once-bjp-gets-

majority-in-parliament-amit-shah/articleshow/68956911.cms?from=mdr [Accessed: 1 April 2024].

6. India Today (2019) *Another 28,000 troops rushed to Kashmir Valley week after 10,000 were deployed* indiatoday.in [Online] Retrieved from: https://www.indiatoday.in/india/story/28-000-more-troops-deployed-in-kashmir-valley-1576280-2019-08-02 [Accessed : 1 April 2024].
7. The Indian Express (2019) *J&K Governor Satya Pal Malik: Don't pay heed to rumours on Article 35A* indianexpress.com [Online] Retrieved from: https://indianexpress.com/article/india/jk-governor-satya-pal-malik-special-status-of-state-article-35a-central-forces-elections-5863755/ [Accessed: 1 April 2024].
8. Scroll.in (2019) *J&K: Local leaders warn BJP not to scrap Article 370, ex-CM says it could 'free' state from India* scroll.in [Online] Retrieved from: https://scroll.in/latest/919410/j-k-local-leaders-warn-bjp-not-to-scrap-article-370-ex-cm-says-it-could-free-state-from-india [Accessed: 1 April 2024].
9. NDTV (2019) *Don't Know About Tomorrow But Nothing To Worry About Today: J&K Governor* ndtv.com [Online] Retrieved from: https://www.ndtv.com/india-news/jammu-and-kashmir-governor-dont-know-about-tomorrow-but-nothing-to-worry-about-today-2079962 [Accessed: 1 April 2024].
10. The Times of India (2018) *Article 370 has acquired permanent status: Supreme Court* timesofindia.indiatimes.com [Online] Retrieved from: https://timesofindia.indiatimes.com/india/article-370-has-acquired-permanent-status-supreme-court/articleshow/63603527.cms [Accessed: 1 April 2024].
11. Mint (2019) *Article 370 scrapped, Jammu & Kashmir to be carved into two Union Territories* livemint.com [Online] Retrieved from: https://www.livemint.com/news/india/jammu-kashmir-amit-shah-moves-rajya-sabha-to-scrap-article-370-1564984999538.html [Accessed: 1 April 2024].
12. Ibid.
13. Ibid.
14. Press Information bureau (2019) *Government brings Resolution to Repeal Article 370 of the Constitution* pib.gov.in [Online] Retrieved from: https://pib.gov.in/newsite/PrintRelease.aspx?relid=192487 [Accessed: 1 April 2024].

15. Press Information Bureau (2019) *Parliament approves Resolution to repeal Article 370; paves way to truly integrate J&K with Indian Union* pib.gov.in [Online] Retrieved from: https://pib.gov.in/newsite/PrintRelease.aspx?relid=192505 [Accessed: 1 April 2024].
16. The Times of India (2019) *Bill to bifurcate J&K, resolution to scrap Article 370 get Parliament nod* timesofindia.indiatimes.com [Online] Retrieved from: https://timesofindia.indiatimes.com/india/bill-to-bifurcate-jk-resolution-to-scrap-article-370-get-parliament-nod/articleshow/70556953.cms [Accessed: 1 April 2024].
17. The Times of India (2019) *Amit Shah: Sans majority, was worried about Rajya Sabha nod for J&K bill* timesofindia.indiatimes.com [Online] Retrieved from: https://timesofindia.indiatimes.com/city/chennai/shah-sans-majority-was-worried-about-rs-nod-for-jk-bill/articleshow/70635539.cms [Accessed: 1 April 2024].
18. NDTV (2019) *Already, Rajya Sabha Clears J&K As Union Territory Instead Of State* ndtv.com [Online] Retrieved from: https://www.ndtv.com/india-news/bill-to-bifurcate-jammu-and-kashmir-into-2-union-territories-passed-by-rajya-sabha-2080688 [Accessed: 1 April 2024].
19. The Times of India (2019) *J&K ties with India will end if Art 370 scrapped: Mehbooba Mufti* timesofindia.indiatimes.com [Online] Retrieved from: https://timesofindia.indiatimes.com/india/jk-ties-with-india-will-end-if-art-370-scrapped-mehbooba-mufti/articleshow/68714860.cms [Accessed: 1 April 2024].
20. India Today (2017) *Triple Talaq Bill passed: Why India needed to get rid of this social malaise* indiatoday.in [Online] Retrieved from: https://www.indiatoday.in/india/story/triple-talaq-bill-lok-sabha-supreme-court-bjp-congress-illiteracy-education-levels-marriage-act-1118069-2017-12-28 [Accessed: 1 April 2024].
21. The Indian Express (2023) *Hanging fire for 27 years: How Women Reservation Bill kept lapsing through its tumultuous journey* indianexpress.com [Online] Retrieved from: https://indianexpress.com/article/political-pulse/hanging-fire-for-27-years-how-women-reservation-bill-kept-lapsing-through-its-tumultuous-journey-8945864/ [Accessed: 1 April 2024].
22. The Times of India (2012) *Mulayam opposes Women Reservation Bill says 'our poor and rural women are not attractive'* timesofindia.indiatimes.com

[Online] Retrieved from: https://timesofindia.indiatimes.com/india/mulayam-opposes-women-reservation-bill-says-our-poor-and-rural-women-are-not-attractive/articleshow/17160615.cms [Accessed: 1 April 2024].

23. Zee News (2023) *Uma Bharti Goes Against BJP, Bats For OBC Quota Within Women's Reservation* zeenews.india.com [Online] Retrieved from: https://zeenews.india.com/india/uma-bharti-goes-against-bjp-bats-for-obc-quota-within-womens-reservaton-2666338.html [Accessed: 1 April 2024].

Momentous Decisions: Redefining Bharat- II

1. Asian News International (2022) *Necessary for nation to stand proudly with its identity to reach pinnacle of success, says PM Modi* aninews.in [Online] Retrieved from: https://www.aninews.in/news/national/general-news/necessary-for-nation-to-stand-proudly-with-its-identity-to-reach-pinnacle-of-success-says-pm-modi20221012011218/ [Accessed: 1 April 2024].
2. Press Information Bureau (2021) *Prime Minister inaugurates and lays foundation stone of multiple projects in Somnath* pib.gov.in [Online] Retrievedfrom: https://pib.gov.in/PressReleaseIframePage.aspx?PRID=1747666 [Accessed: 1 April 2024].
3. Ibid.
4. Ibid.
5. Asian News International (2022) *Necessary for nation to stand proudly with its identity to reach pinnacle of success, says PM Modi* aninews.in [Online] Retrieved from: https://www.aninews.in/news/national/general-news/necessary-for-nation-to-stand-proudly-with-its-identity-to-reach-pinnacle-of-success-says-pm-modi20221012011218/ [Accessed: 1 April 2024].
6. WION (2023) *What is Amrit kaal...* wionews.com [Online] Retrieved from: https://www.wionews.com/india-news/what-is-amrit-kaal-why-did-the-indian-fm-mention-the-term-several-times-in-her-union-budget-2023-speech-557815 [Accessed: 1 April 2024].
7. The Economic Times (2023) *Amrit Kaal has been named as Kartavya Kaal: PM Modi* economictimes.indiatimes.com [Online] Retrieved from: https://economictimes.indiatimes.com/news/india/amrit-kaal-has-been-named-as-kartavya-kaal-pm-modi/articleshow/101478517.cms?from=mdr [Accessed: 1 April 2024].

8. PM of India (2022) *PM addresses public function in Ujjain, Madhya Pradesh after dedicating Phase I of the Mahakaal Lok Project to the nation* pmindia.gov.in [Online] Retrieved from: https://www.pmindia.gov.in/en/news_updates/pm-addresses-public-function-in-ujjain-madhya-pradesh-after-dedicating-phase-i-of-the-mahakaal-lok-project-to-the-nation/ [Accessed: 1 April 2024].
9. Press Information Bureau (2021) *Prime Minister inaugurates and lays foundation stone of multiple projects in Somnath* pib.gov.in [Online] Retrieved from: https://pib.gov.in/PressReleaseIframePage.aspx?PRID=1747666 [Accessed: 1 April 2024]
10. BAPS Swaminarayan Sanstha (2023) *PSM100: BAPS Gulf Countries Day, Ahmedabad, India* baps.org [Online] Retrieved from: https://www.baps.org/News/2023/PSM100-BAPS-Gulf-Countries-Day-22968.aspx [Accessed: 1 April 2024].
11. United Nation (2023) *9th International Day of Yoga* un.org [Online] Retrieved from: https://www.un.org/en/observances/yoga-day#:~:text=Recognizing%20its%20universal%20appeal%2C%20on,many%20benefits%20of%20practicing%20yoga [Accessed: 22 April 2024].
12. Ibid.
13. The Times of India (2023) *International Day of Yoga: Surat etches its name in Guinness World Records* timesofindia.indiatimes.com [Online] Retrieved from: https://timesofindia.indiatimes.com/city/surat/diamond-city-etches-its-name-in-guinness-world-records/articleshow/101174921.cms [Accessed: 1 April 2024].

Momentous Decisions : Redefining Bharat- III

1. Hindustan Times (2024) *India to become developed nation in 25 years: Modi at Vibrant Gujarat Summit* hindustantimes.com [Online] Retrieved from: https://www.hindustantimes.com/india-news/india-developed-nation-25-years-narendra-modi-vibrant-gujarat-summit-101704871798304.html [Accessed: 1 April 2024].
2. Facebook 20 November 2021 @DDNewsLive [Online] Retrieved from: https://www.facebook.com/DDNews/photos/a.224386814404838/2112584742251693/?type=3&locale=ms_MY [Accessed: 22 April 2024].

3. Press Information Bureau (2024) *ADDRESS BY THE HON'BLE PRESIDENT OF India Smt. Droupadi Murmu to Parliament* pib.gov.in [Online] Retrieved from: https://pib.gov.in/PressReleaseIframePage.aspx?PRID=2000781 [Accessed: 1 April 2024].
4. Press Information Bureau (2021) *English rendering of PM's address at the launch of PM Gati Shakti, National Master Plan for Multi-Modal Connectivity* pib.gov.in [Online] Retrieved from: https://pib.gov.in/Pressreleaseshare.aspx?PRID=1763594 [Accessed: 1 April 2024].
5. The New Indian Express (2017) *PM expresses concern over lack of coordination among govt depts.* newindianexpress.com [Online] Retrieved from: https://www.newindianexpress.com/nation/2017/Jan/20/pm-expresses-concern-over-lack-of-coordination-among-govt-depts-1561739.html [Accessed: 1 April 2024].
6. Press Information Bureau (2024) *Year End Review 2023-Ministry of Road Transport and Highways* pib.gov.in [Online] Retrieved from: https://pib.gov.in/PressReleaseIframePage.aspx?PRID=1993425 [Accessed: 1 April 2024].
7. Ministry of Road Transport and Highways *Introduction: Ministry of Road Transport and Highways* morth.nic.in [Online] Retrieved from: https://morth.nic.in/ [Accessed: 1 April 2024].
8. Ibid.
9. India Today (2024) *Should PM Manmohan Singh relish Vajpayee government's economic legacy?* indiatoday.in [Online] Retrieved from: https://www.indiatoday.in/magazine/cover-story/story/20040531-should-manmohan-singh-relish-vajpayee-govt-economic-legacy-789941-2004-05-30 [Accessed: 1 April 2024].
10. Press Information Bureau (2024) *Year End Review 2023-Ministry of Road Transport and Highways* pib.gov.in [Online] Retrieved from: https://pib.gov.in/PressReleaseIframePage.aspx?PRID=1993425 [Accessed: 1 April 2024].
11. Economic Times (2023) *ET GBS 2023: On track to build 200k km of national highways by 2025, says Nitin Gadkari* economictimes.indiatimes.com [Online] Retrieved from: https://economictimes.indiatimes.com/news/economy/infrastructure/et-gbs-2023-on-track-to-build-200k-km-of-national-highways-by-2025-says-nitin-gadkari/articleshow/98055270.cms?from=mdr [Accessed: 22 April 2024].

12. Wikipedia *Sagarmala Project* Wikipedia.com [Online] Retrieved from: https://en.wikipedia.org/wiki/Sagar_Mala_project [Accessed: 1 April 2024].
13. Press Information Bureau (2016) *Sagarmala National Perspective Plan Released* pib.gov.in [Online] Retrieved from: https://pib.gov.in/newsite/printrelease.aspx?relid=138881 [Accessed: 1 April 2024].
14. Government of India *Overview of Sagarmala Programme* sagarmala.gov.in [Online] Retrieved from: http://sagarmala.gov.in/about-sagarmala/introduction#:~:text=Overview%20of%20Sagarmala%20Programme,required%20to%20meet%20these%20targets [Accessed: 23 April 2024].
15. *Maritime India Summit* (2021) shipmin.gov.in [Online] Retrieved from: https://shipmin.gov.in/news-events-project/maritime-india-summit-2021 [Accessed: 1 April 2024].
16. Raj Bhavan Mahrashtra (2024) *PM inaugurates, dedicates to nation and lays the foundation stone of multiple development projects worth more than Rs 12,700 crore in Navi Mumbai, Maharashtra* rajbhavan-maharashtra.gov.in [Online] Retrieved from: https://rajbhavan-maharashtra.gov.in/en/12-01-2024-pm-inaugurates-dedicates-to-nation-and-lays-the-foundation-stone-of-multiple-development-projects-worth-more-than-rs-12700-crore-in-navi-mumbai/ [Accessed: 2 April 2024].
17. India Today (2022) *How Shivaji Maharaj laid the foundation to make India a naval power* indiatoday.in [Online] Retrieved from: https://www.indiatoday.in/india/story/chhatrapati-shivaji-maharaj-indian-navy-ensign-ins-vikran-commission-naredra-modi-maratha-1995610-2022-09-02 [Accessed: 2 April 2024].
18. Nautilus Shipping (2022) *13 Major Ports in India* nautilusshipping.com [Online] Retrieved from: https://www.nautilusshipping.com/major-ports-in-india [Accessed: 2 April 2024].
19. Mint (2020) *Shipping Ministry to be renamed as Ministry of Ports, Shipping and Waterways: PM Modi* livemint.com [Online] Retrieved from: https://www.livemint.com/news/india/shipping-ministry-to-be-renamed-as-ministry-of-ports-shipping-and-waterways-pm-modi-11604846585205.html [Accessed: 2 April 2024].

20. Press Information Bureau (2023) *Inland Waterways powering the growth of India's economy* pib.gov.in [Online] Retrieved from: https://pib.gov.in/PressReleasePage.aspx?PRID=1953882 [Accessed: 2 April 2024].
21. Business Standard (2024) *India to begin 23 waterways by 2030, says PM Modi* business-standard.com [Online] Retrieved from: https://www.business-standard.com/article/economy-policy/india-to-begin-23-waterways-by-2030-says-pm-modi-121030200549_1.html [Accessed: 2 April 2024].
22. The Economic Times (2023) *Taking cargo off trucks and putting back onto ships: Modi govt's big plan to develop 23 river systems* economictimes.indiatimes.com [Online] Retrieved from: https://economictimes.indiatimes.com/industry/transportation/shipping-/-transport/taking-cargo-off-trucks-and-putting-back-onto-ships-modi-govts-big-plan-to-develop-23-river-systems-as-inland-waterways/articleshow/98427384.cms?from=mdr [Accessed: 2 April 2024].
23. The Times of India (2023) *100% electrification: How the Indian railways is adopting green mobility* timesofindia.indiatimes.com [Online] Retrieved from: https://timesofindia.indiatimes.com/blogs/voices/100-electrification-how-the-indian-railways-is-adopting-green-mobility/ [Accessed: 2 April 2024].
24. The New Indian Express (2022) *Is the target of 400 Vande Bharat trains by 2025 too fast and furious? Experts think so* newindianexpress.com [Online] Retrieved from: https://www.newindianexpress.com/nation/2022/Feb/13/is-the-target-of-400-vande-bharat-trains-by-2025-too-fast-andfurious-experts-thinkso-2419120.html [Accessed: 2 April 2024].
25. The Right News (2023) *By 2047, India will have 4,500 Vande Bharat trains running across country, Union Minister says* therightnews.in [Online] Retrieved from: https://www.therightnews.in/2023/12/08/by-2047-india-will-have-4500-vande-bharat-trains-running-across-country-union-minister-says/ [Accessed: 2 April 2024].
26. Mumbai Mirror (2021) *Bio-toilets save Rly Rs 4,00 cr a year* mumbaimirror.indiatimes.com [Online] Retrieved from: https://mumbaimirror.indiatimes.com/mumbai/other/bio-toilets-save-rly-rs-400-cr-a-year/articleshow/83269272.cms [Accessed: 2 April 2024].

27. Mint (2023) *Budget 2024: Railways to invest ₹7 tn to lay tracks over the next decade* livemint.com [Online] Retrieved from: https://www.livemint.com/news/india/budget-2024-railways-to-invest-7-tn-to-lay-tracks-over-the-next-decade-11703439309357.html [Accessed: 2 April 2024].
28. The Statesman (2023) *Rise in freight train operations indicate India's strides in logistics, economic momentum: PM Modi* thestatesman.com [Online] Retrieved from: https://www.thestatesman.com/india/rise-in-freight-train-operations-indicate-indias-strides-in-logistics-economic-momentum-pm-modi-1503179553.html [Accessed: 2 April 2024].
29. Press Information Bureau (2024) *PM GatiShakti provides big boost to planning multimodal connectivity expanding economic, social, digital infrastructure* pib.gov.in [Online] Retrieved from: https://pib.gov.in/PressReleasePage.aspx?PRID=2001784 [Accessed: 2 April 2024].
30. India Today (2017) *India's first bullet train project launched, PM Narendra Modi calls it New India's big dream* indiatoday.in [Online] Retrieved from: https://www.indiatoday.in/india/story/narendra-modi-shinzo-abe-bullet-train-project-live-updates-1044291-2017-09-14 [Accessed: 2 April 2024].
31. India Today (2017) *From hawai chappal to hawai jahaz, PM Modi wants to see a slipper-wearing commoner board a plane!* indiatoday.in [Online] Retrieved from: https://www.indiatoday.in/india/story/pm-modi-udan-scheme-modi-wants-commoner-to-wear-hawai-chappal-to-ride-plane-973935-2017-04-27 [Accessed: 2 April 2024].
32. Skift (2023) *Skift India Daily: A Billion Air Travelers Expected by 2040—How Adani Airports Is Preparing* skift.com [Online] Retrieved from: https://skift.com/2023/03/23/skift-india-daily-a-billion-air-travelers-expected-by-2040-how-adani-airports-is-preparing/ [Accessed: 2 April 2024].
33. Infra.com (2023) *Aviation ministry plans development of 6 'Twin City' airports by 2030* infra.economictimes.indiatimes.com [Online] Retrieved from: https://infra.economictimes.indiatimes.com/news/aviation/aviation-ministry-plans-development-of-6-twin-city-airports-by-2030/104273958 [Accessed: 2 April 2024].
34. Press Information Bureau (2024) *Union Minister for Civil Aviation Shri Jyotiraditya M Scindia inaugurates Asia's largest Aviation Expo-Wings India 2024* pib.gov.in [Online] Retrieved from: https://pib.gov.in/PressReleaseIframePage.aspx?PRID=1997295 [Accessed: 2 April 2024].

35. Business Standard (2015) *Decision to drop privatisation of airports was taken at PM's level* business-standard.com [Online] Retrieved from: https://www.business-standard.com/article/economy-policy/decision-to-drop-privatisation-of-airports-was-taken-at-pm-s-level-115081900733_1.html [Accessed: 2 April 2024].
36. The Times of India (2019) *Adani group wins bids to operate 5 airports for 50 years* timesofindia.indiatimes.com [Online] Retrieved from: https://timesofindia.indiatimes.com/business/india-business/adani-highest-bidder-for-five-airports-including-ahmedabad-jaipur-lucknow/articleshow/68150898.cms [Accessed: 2 April 2024].
37. The Times of India (2018) *Government has done what it had to with 'utmost sincerity' for Air India: PM Modi* economictimes.indiatimes.com [Online] Retrieved from: https://timesofindia.indiatimes.com/business/india-business/government-has-done-what-it-had-to-with-utmost-sincerity-for-air-india-pm-modi/articleshow/64827103.cms [Accessed: 2 April 2024].
38. Press Information Bureau (2021) *Government Approves Air India Disinvestment: Tatasons' SPV–Talace Pvt Ltd-Wins Bid for Air India* pib.gov.in [Online] Retrieved from: https://pib.gov.in/PressReleaseIframePage.aspx?PRID=1762146 [Accessed: 2 April 2024].
39. Press Information Bureau (2021) *PM addresses webinar on effective implementation of Budget provisions regarding Disinvestment and Asset Monetization* pib.gov.in [Online] Retrieved from: https://pib.gov.in/Pressreleaseshare.aspx?PRID=1700549 [Accessed: 2 April 2024].
40. Press Information Bureau (2021) *Policy of Strategic Disinvestment announced; Clear Roadmap for Strategic and Non-Strategic Sectors* pib.gov.in [Online] Retrieved from: https://pib.gov.in/Pressreleaseshare.aspx?PRID=1693899 [Accessed: 2 April 2024].
41. The Economic Times (2022) *LIC IPO subscribed nearly 3 times; govt raises Rs 21,000 cr* economictimes.indiatimes.com [Online] Retrieved from: https://economictimes.indiatimes.com/markets/ipos/fpos/lic-ipo-subscribed-over-2-times-so-far-issue-closes-today/articleshow/91435009.cms?from=mdr [Accessed: 2 April 2024].

Setting the Golden Bird Free

1. Press Information Bureau (2016) *Text of Prime Minister's Address to the Nation* pib.gov.in [Online] Retrieved from: https://pib.gov.in/newsite/PrintRelease.aspx?relid=153404 [Accessed: 2 April 2024].
2. Ibid.
3. The Economic Times (2017) *One year of note ban: The ultra-secret move that no one came to know for several months* economictimes.indiatimes.com [Online] Retrieved from: https://economictimes.indiatimes.com/news/politics-and-nation/one-year-of-note-ban-the-ultra-secret-move-that-no-one-came-to-know-for-several-months/articleshow/61528334.cms?from=mdr [Accessed: 2 April 2024].
4. Ibid.
5. Ibid.
6. The Economic Times (2017) *Printing of Rs 2000 note started in August 2016* economictimes.indiatimes.com [Online] Retrieved from: https://economictimes.indiatimes.com/news/economy/policy/printing-of-rs-2000-note-started-in-august-2016/articleshow/57432874.cms?from=mdr [Accessed: 2 April 2024].
7. Press Information Bureau (2016) *Text of Prime Minister's Address to the Nation* pib.gov.in [Online] Retrieved from: https://pib.gov.in/newsite/PrintRelease.aspx?relid=153404 [Accessed: 2 April 2024].
8. Tax Heal (2016) *Piyush Goyal's speech on demonetisation on 16.11.2016 in Rajya Sabha* taxheal.com [Online] Retrieved from: https://www.taxheal.com/piyush-goyals-speech-on-demonetisation-on-16-11-2016-in-rajya-sabha.html [Accessed: 2 April 2024].
9. Ranina, H P (2021) *Wanchoo Committee Report On Black Money* indianliberals.in [Online] Retrieved from: https://indianliberals.in/forum-of-free-enterprise/wanchoo-committee-report-on-black-money-h-p-ranina.pdf [Accessed: 2 April 2024].
10. Ibid.
11. Godbole, Madhav (1996) *Unfinished Innings: Recollections and Reflections of a Civil Servant* Orient BlackSwan.
12. Patel, I G (2003) *Glimpses of Indian Economic Policy: An Insider's View* Oxford India.

13. India Today (2016) *Finance Minister who imposed demonetisation in 1978 said it is not worthwhile* indiatoday.in [Online] Retrieved from: https://www.indiatoday.in/india/story/demonetisation-black-money-corruption-modi-government-finance-minister-hm-patel-353510-2016-11-23 [Accessed: 2 April 2024].
14. Kumar, Arun (2017) *Demonetization and the Black Economy* Penguin Random House India.
15. Ibid.
16. Surajit Dasgupta, founder of the Aam Aadmi Party, in an interview to the author on the Anna movement, September 2023.
17. Government of India (2012) *Black Money White Paper 2012* dor.govgt.in [Online] Retrieved from: https://www.dor.gov.in/sites/default/files/FinalBlackMoney.pdf [Accessed: 2 April 2024].
18. DNA (2019) *India's Black Money Economy estimated at 79 per cent of GDP during 2009-11* dnaindia.com [Online] Retrieved from: https://www.dnaindia.com/business/report-india-s-black-money-economy-estimated-at-79-of-gdp-during-2009-11-2724048 [Accessed: 2 April 2024].
19. Hindustan Times (2012) *Black Money: India Ranked 8 Among 150 Countries* hindustantimes.com [Online] Retrieved from: https://www.hindustantimes.com/business/black-money-india-ranked-8-among-150-countries/story-W6twLQiN4uCvF069uLPVRI.html [Accessed: 2 April 2024].
20. Bharatiya Janata Party (2009) *Statement by Shri LK Advani at press meet in Mumbai on Swiss accounts Task Force report* bjp.org [Online] Retrieved from: https://www.bjp.org/pressreleases/statement-shri-lk-advani-press-meet-mumbai-swiss-accounts-task-force-report [Accessed: 2 April 2024].
21. Ibid.
22. Opinion Express No 5 Vol 20 (2013) *United we are, divided we operate: India's fight against corruption*opinionexpress.in [Online] Retrieved from: https://opinionexpress.in/assets/magzine/_90906_2020_04_09_1599206726.pdf [Accessed: 23 April 2024].
23. Organiser (2011) *Historic rally in Delhi against corruption and black money Crusade against corruption will continue: Baba Ramdev* organiser.org [Online] Retrieved from: https://organiser.org/2011/03/13/46295/general/r95c457f9/ [Accessed: 2 April 2024].

24. The Times of India (2012) *Black Money: Indians have stashed over $500 billion in banks abroad, says CBI* economictimes.indiatimes.com [Online] Retrieved from: https://timesofindia.indiatimes.com/india/black-money-indians-have-stashed-over-500bn-in-banks-abroad-says-cbi/articleshow/11871624.cms [Accessed: 2 April 2024].
25. The Economic Times (2012) *Government only has to withdraw 500 & 1,000 notes: Baba Ramdev* economictimes.indiatimes.com [Online] Retrieved from: https://economictimes.indiatimes.com/news/politics-and-nation/government-only-has-to-withdraw-500-1000-notes-baba-ramdev/articleshow/15484696.cms?from=mdr [Accessed: 2 April 2024].
26. The New Indian Express (2016) *Note ban was an inevitable step: Gurumurthy* newindianexpress.com [Online] Retrieved from: https://www.newindianexpress.com/nation/2016/Dec/24/note-ban-was-an-inevitable-step-gurumurthy-1552563.html [Accessed: 2 April 2024].
27. Ibid.
28. DD News (2016) *War on Black Money: An Interview with S Gurumurthy* prasarbharati.gov.in/doordarshan [Online] Retrieved from: https://www.youtube.com/watch?v=0eaCr21PB6I [Accessed: 2 April 2024].
29. Counterview (2019) *Three years on, mystery surrounds as to who advised Modi on demonetization* counterview.net [Online] Retrieved from: https://www.counterview.net/2019/10/three-years-on-mystery-surrounds-as-to.html [Accessed: 2 April 2024].
30. Financial Express (2017) *Who is Anil Bokil? The man who suggested note ban to Modi* financialexpress.com [Online] Retrieved from: https://www.financialexpress.com/policy/economy-who-is-anil-bokil-the-man-who-suggested-note-ban-to-modi-923526/ [Accessed: 2 April 2024].
31. The Economic Times (2016) *RBI Governor Urjit Patel says demonetisation was well planned* economictimes.indiatimes.com [Online] Retrieved from: https://economictimes.indiatimes.com/news/economy/policy/rbis-urjit-patel-says-demonetisation-was-well-planned/articleshow/55856676.cms?from=mdr [Accessed: 2 April 2024].
32. Twitter (2017) @DasShaktikanta twitter.com [Online]
33. India Budget (2017) *Arun Jaitley's Budget Speech in Lok Sabha* indiabudget.gov.in [Online] Retrieved from: https://www.indiabudget.gov.in/budget2017-2018/ub2017-18/bs/bs.pdf [Accessed: 2 April 2024].

34. Business Today (2017) *What was the purpose of demonetisation? RBI says 99 per cent of banned Rs 500, Rs 1000 notes returned* businesstoday.in [Online] Retrieved from: https://www.businesstoday.in/latest/economy-politics/story/99-percent-of-demonetised-notes-returned-to-system-rbi-data-demonetisation-83157-2017-08-30 [Accessed: 2 April 2024].
35. Reserve Bank of India (2017) *RBI Annual Report* rbi.org.in [Online] Retrieved from: https://rbi.org.in/Scripts/AnnualReportPublications.aspx?Id=1198 [Accessed: 2 April 2024].
36. The Economic Times (2022) *Demonetisation anniversary: Congress calls it 'biggest destroyer of livelihoods', demands white paper from Modi govt* economictimes.indiatimes.com [Online] Retrieved from: https://economictimes.indiatimes.com/news/politics-and-nation/demonetisation-anniversary-congress-calls-it-biggest-destroyer-of-livelihoods-demands-white-paper-from-modi-govt/articleshow/95384117.cms?from=mdr [Accessed: 2 April 2024].
37. PMO India (2016) *Mann Ki Baat* [Online] Retrieved from: https://www.youtube.com/watch?v=kJhZIIQHeGM [Accessed: 2 April 2024].
38. Mint (2016) *Rahul Gandhi's speech on Demonetisation What Rahul Gandhi has said so far* livemint.com [Online] Retrieved from: https://www.livemint.com/Politics/OU5TOgnc9zy4LbOIRczpVK/Demonetisation-What-Rahul-Gandhi-has-said-so-far.html [Accessed: 2 April 2024].
39. CNBC TV18 (2018) *Government finally admits four persons died during demonetisation, says no study done on its impact* cnbctv18.com [Online] Retrieved from: https://www.cnbctv18.com/economy/government-finally-admits-four-persons-died-during-demonetisation-says-no-study-done-on-its-impact-1736641.htm [Accessed: 2 April 2024].
40. Narendra Modi (2017) *Mann Ki Baat* narendramodi.in [Online] Retrieved from: https://www.narendramodi.in/text-of-pm-s-mann-ki-baat-address-on-all-india-radio-on-27-november-2016--533318 [Accessed: 2 April 2024].
41. The Indian Express (2016) *PM Modi on Demonetisation: Bear Pain for 50 days, then punish me* indianexpress.com [Online] Retrieved from: https://indianexpress.com/article/india/india-news-india/demonetisation-of-rs-500-rs-1000-notes-pm-modi-bear-pain-for-50-days-then-punish-me-4373933/ [Accessed: 2 April 2024].

42. India Today (2017) *Interview of the Year: PM Narendra Modi exclusive, his first since demonetisation* indiatoday.in [Online] Retrieved from: https://www.indiatoday.in/magazine/cover-story/story/20170109-narendra-modi-black-money-demonetisation-opposition-830098-2016-12-29 [Accessed: 2 April 2024].
43. Ibid.
44. Ibid.
45. DD News (2016) *War on Black Money: An Interview with S Gurumurthy* prasarbharati.gov.in/ddnews [Online] Retrieved from: https://www.youtube.com/watch?v=0eaCr21PB6I [Accessed: 2 April 2024].
46. *Income Tax Department Launches Operation Clean Money* (2017) itgoawbunit.org [Online] Retrieved from: https://itgoawbunit.org/pdf/357221749Clean.pdf [Accessed: 2 April 2024].
47. Press Information Bureau (2017) *Impact of Demonetisation on Black Money, Widening of Tax Base and Direct Tax Collections* pib.gov.in [Online] Retrieved from: https://pib.gov.in/newsite/printrelease.aspx?relid=170405 [Accessed: 2 April 2024].
48. The Economic Times (2016) *Pay 50% tax on unaccounted deposits, or 85% if caught, says Modi Government* economictimes.indiatimes.com [Online] Retrieved from: https://economictimes.indiatimes.com/news/economy/policy/30-tax-10-penalty-and-33-surcharge-proposed-on-undisclosed-income-under-demonetisation/articleshow/55664876.cms?from=mdr [Accessed: 2 April 2024].
49. Ibid.
50. The Economic Times (2017) *21,000 people disclose 4900 crore black money under PMGKY* economictimes.indiatimes.com [Online] Retrieved from: https://economictimes.indiatimes.com/news/politics-and-nation/21000-people-disclose-rs-4900-crore-black-money-under-pmgky/articleshow/60410466.cms?from=mdr [Accessed: 2 April 2024].
51. Deccan Chronicle (2019) *Less active accounts got Rs 1.7 lakh-crore* deccanchronicle.com [Online] Retrieved from: https://www.deccanchronicle.com/business/in-other-news/120817/less-active-accounts-got-rs-17-lakh-crore.html [Accessed: 2 April 2024].
52. The Times of India (2022) *Rs 1.25 lakh crore black money recovered* timesofindia.indiatimes.com [Online] Retrieved from: https://

timesofindia.indiatimes.com/business/india-business/rs-1-25-lakh-crore-black-money-recovered-by-government-ashwini-vaishnaw/articleshow/96165365.cms [Accessed: 2 April 2024].

53. Tata Capital (2023) *The Impact of Demonetisation on real estate in India* tatacapitals.com [Online] Retrieved from: https://www.tatacapital.com/blog/loan-for-home/impact-of-demonetisation-on-real-estate-in-india/ [Accessed: 2 April 2024].
54. Business Standard (2019) *SIT on black money reveals data: Rs 70,000 Cr illegal cash detected so far* business-standard.com [Online] Retrieved from: https://www.business-standard.com/article/economy-policy/sit-on-black-money-reveals-data-rs-70-000-cr-illegal-cash-detected-so-far-117030300004_1.html [Accessed: 2 April 2024].
55. Digital Sansad (2015) Starred Question Number 92 on DTAA sansad.in [Online] Retrieved from: https://sansad.in/getFile/loksabhaquestions/annex/6/AS92.pdf?source=pqals [Accessed: 2 April 2024].
56. The Indian Express (2022) *India gets 4th set of Swiss bank account details: Significance, what happens next* indianexpress.com [Online] Retrieved from: https://indianexpress.com/article/explained/explained-economics/india-gets-4th-set-of-swiss-bank-account-details-significance-what-happens-next-8201032/ [Accessed: 2 April 2024].
57. Income Tax India (2015) *Black Money (Undisclosed Foreign Income and Assets) and Imposition of Tax Act, 2015* incometaxindia.gov.in. [Online]
58. Mint (2022) *No estimate of exact money deposited by Indian citizens, companies in Swiss banks: Nirmala Sitharaman* livemint.com [Online] Retrieved from: https://www.livemint.com/news/india/govt-raises-tax-demand-of-rs-14-820-cr-under-black-money-law-for-undisclosed-foreign-income-11658763560193.html [Accessed: 2 April 2024].
59. Ibid.
60. The EconomicTimes (2023) *Not disclosing foreign shares, investments, assets in your ITR can lead to penalty of Rs 10 lakh* economictimes.indiatimes.com [Online] Retrieved from: https://economictimes.indiatimes.com/wealth/tax/not-disclosing-foreign-shares-investments-assets-in-your-itr-can-lead-to-penalty-of-rs-10-lakh/articleshow/103983914.cms?from=mdr [Accessed: 2 April 2024].

61. Mint (2018) *Nirav Modi, Vijay Mallya, and 29 other Indian fugitives owe Rs 40,000 crore* livemint.com [Online] Retrieved from: https://www.livemint.com/Companies/2rBU4V1jumGfJguL9rdSyO/Nirav-Modi-Vijay-Mallya-and-29-other-Indian-fugitives-owe.html [Accessed: 2 April 2024].
62. Department of Economic Affairs (2018) *The Fugitive Economic Offenders Act, 2018* dea.gov.in [Online] Retrieved from: https://dea.gov.in/sites/default/files/FEO%20Act%202018_0.pdf [Accessed: 2 April 2024].
63. Press Information Bureau (2023) *1st Anti-Corruption working group meeting of G-20 nations held in Gurugram* pib.gov.in [Online] Retrieved from: https://static.pib.gov.in/WriteReadData/specificdocs/documents/2023/mar/doc2023320174001.pdf [Accessed: 2 April 2024].
64. The Economic Times (2023) *ED booked 19 people under Fugitive Economic Offenders Act* economictimes.indiatimes.com [Online] Retrieved from: https://economictimes.indiatimes.com/news/india/ed-booked-19-people-under-fugitive-economic-offenders-act/articleshow/102319919.cms?from=mdr [Accessed: 2 April 2024].
65. Business Today (2023) *'Have no intention to...': UK minister's big statement on extradition of Nirav Modi, Vijay Mallya* businesstoday.in [Online] Retrieved from: https://www.businesstoday.in/latest/world/story/have-no-intention-to-uk-ministers-big-statement-on-extradition-of-nirav-modi-vijay-mallya-393970-2023-08-13 [Accessed: 2 April 2024].
66. News 18 (2023) *PM Modi Brings Up Extradition of Vijay Mallya, Nirav Modi with UK in Every Meet: Harish Salve* news18.com [Online] Retrieved from: https://www.news18.com/india/narendra-modi-extradition-vijay-mallya-nirav-modi-harish-salve-8298247.html [Accessed: 2 April 2024].
67. Hindustan Times (2016) *Demonetisation: Could it not have been done more efficiently?* hindustantimes.com [Online] Retrieved from: https://www.hindustantimes.com/editorials/demonetisation-could-it-not-have-been-done-more-efficiently/story-DXCcFl0nmSBv4NJpiIn0xI.html [Accessed: 2 April 2024].
68. The Hindu (2022) *IT Dept attaches properties worth 18400 crore under Benami Act* thehindubusinessline.com [Online] Retrieved from: https://www.thehindubusinessline.com/economy/it-dept-attaches-properties-worth-18400-crore-under-benami-act/article66053206.ece [Accessed: 2 April 2024].

69. Embassy of India (2020) *Prime Minister Narendra Modi launches platform for "Transparent Taxation - Honouring the Honest* eoilisbon.gov.in [Online] Retrieved from: https://www.eoilisbon.gov.in/news_letter_detail/?id=65 [Accessed: 2 April 2024].
70. Ibid.
71. Business Today (2024) *Interim Budget 2024: Processing time of income tax returns slashed to just 10 days, says FM Sitharaman* businesstoday.in [Online] Retrieved from: https://www.businesstoday.in/personal-finance/tax/story/interim-budget-2024-processing-time-of-income-tax-returns-slashed-to-just-10-days-says-fm-sitharaman-415737-2024-02-01 [Accessed: 2 April 2024].
72. The Times of India (2017) *India lost Rs 12 lakh crore due to BJP's opposition to GST, says Congress leader Veerappa Moily* timesofindia.indiatimes.com [Online] Retrieved from: https://timesofindia.indiatimes.com/business/india-business/india-lost-rs-12-lakh-crore-due-to-bjps-opposition-to-gst-says-congress-leader-veerappa-moily/articleshow/57894683.cms [Accessed: 2 April 2024].
73. Press Information Bureau (2024) *At ₹1,72,129 crore, GST collections are 2nd highest ever; crosses ₹1.70 lakh crore mark for the third time in FY 2023-24* pib.gov.in [Online] Retrieved from: https://pib.gov.in/PressReleasePage.aspx?PRID=2000957 [Accessed: 2 April 2024].
74. PRS Legislative Research (2018) *Examining the rise of Non-Performing Assets in India* prsindia.org [Online] Retrieved from: https://prsindia.org/theprsblog/examining-the-rise-of-non-performing-assets-in-india [Accessed: 2 April 2024].
75. Press Information Bureau (2019) *Bank NPA: Ministry of Finance* pib.gov.in [Online] Retrieved from: https://pib.gov.in/newsite/PrintRelease.aspx?relid=190704 [Accessed: 2 April 2024].
76. Ibid.
77. Comptroller and Auditor General of India (2015) *Chapter 6: Non-performing Assets; Report by the Comptroller and Auditor General of India* cag.gov.in [Online] Retrieved from: https://cag.gov.in/uploads/download_audit_report/2017/Chapter_6_%E2%80%93_Non-performing_Assets_of_Report_No.16_of_2017_-_Performance_audit_Union_Government_Credit_Risk_Management_in_IFCI_Limited_Reports_of_Ministry_of_Finance.pdf [Accessed: 2 April 2024].

78. The Hindu (2023) *IBC recovery rates have fallen, even as average resolution time has increased: CRISIL Ratings* thehindubusinessline.com [Online] Retrieved from: https://www.thehindubusinessline.com/companies/ibc-recovery-rates-have-fallen-even-as-average-resolution-time-has-increased-crisil-ratings/article67569134.ece#:~:text=Recovery%20rates%20under%20the%20Insolvency,days%2C%20according%20to%20CRISIL%20Ratings [Accessed: 2 April 2024].
79. Hindustan Times (2021) *Piyush Goyal calls Insolvency and Bankruptcy Code 'gamechanger reform'* hindustantimes.com [Online] Retrieved from: https://www.hindustantimes.com/india-news/piyush-goyals-calls-insolvency-and-bankruptcy-code-gamechanger-reform-101637853120828.html [Accessed: 2 April 2024].
80. Narendra Modi (2021) *Make in India, make for the world: PM Modi at webinar on PLI scheme* narendramodi.in [Online] Retrieved from: https://www.narendramodi.in/text-of-prime-minister-narendra-modi-s-address-at-the-webinar-on-production-linked-incentives-scheme-554289 [Accessed: 2 April 2024].
81. Ibid.
82. Twitter (2024) @NSitharman twitter.com

The Journey from Fragile Five to Top Five

1. Forbes India (2024) *The top 10 largest economies in the world in 2024* forbesindia.com [Online] Retrieved from: https://www.forbesindia.com/article/explainers/top-10-largest-economies-in-the-world/86159/1 [Accessed: 2 April 2024].
2. Money Control (2017) *Three years of Modi Govt: India goes from 'fragile five' to 'fabulous few' in 1000 days* moneycontrol.com [Online] Retrieved from: https://www.moneycontrol.com/news/business/markets/column-3-years-of-modi-govt-india-goes-from-fragile-five-to-fabulous-few-in-1000-days-2280127.html [Accessed: 2 April 2024].
3. Department of Economic Affairs (2024) *WHITE PAPER ON THE INDIAN ECONOMY* dea.gov.in [Online] Retrieved from: https://dea.gov.in/sites/default/files/White%20Paper%20on%20the%20Indian%20Economy%20-%20February%202024.pdf [Accessed: 2 April 2024].

4. International Monetary Fund (2017) *For India, Strong Growth Persists Despite New Challenges* imf.org [Online] Retrieved from: https://www.imf.org/en/News/Articles/2017/02/21/NA022217-For-India-strong-growth-persists-despite-new-challenges [Accessed: 2 April 2024].
5. MacroTrends (2024) *India GDP Growth Rate 1961-2024* macrotrends.net [Online] Retrieved from: https://www.macrotrends.net/global-metrics/countries/IND/india/gdp-growth-rate [Accessed: 2 April 2024].
6. Press Information Bureau (2024) *FIRST ADVANCE ESTIMATES OF NATIONAL INCOME, 2023-24* pib.gov.in [Online] Retrieved from: https://pib.gov.in/PressReleaseIframePage.aspx?PRID=1993550 [Accessed: 2 April 2024].
7. The Economic Times (2024) *Budget 2024: FM Sitharaman outlines top 10 achievements of Modi government in 10 years* economictimes.indiatimes.com [Online] Retrieved from: https://economictimes.indiatimes.com/news/economy/policy/budget-2024-narendra-modi-as-pm-top-10-achievements-of-india-central-government-bharatiya-janata-party-from-2014-to-2024/articleshow/107311704.cms?from=mdr [Accessed: 2 April 2024].
8. The data have been taken from the Interim budget presented by the Modi government on 1 February 2024 and the White Paper that was subsequently brought on 8 February 2024.

9 (a). The Economic Times (2023) *Share of agriculture in India's GDP declined to 15% in FY23: Govt* economictimes.indiatimes.com [Online] Retrieved from: https://economictimes.indiatimes.com/news/economy/agriculture/share-of-agriculture-in-indias-gdp-declined-to-15-in-fy23-govt/articleshow/106124466.cms?from=mdr [Accessed: 2 April 2024].

9 (b). Press Information Bureau (2023) *Agriculture sector remains buoyant with 4.6 percent annual growth during last six years* pib.gov.in [Online] Retrieved from: https://pib.gov.in/PressReleasePage.aspx?PRID=1894900 [Accessed: 2 April 2024].

10. The Economic Times (2023) *Government spending Rs 6.5 lakh crore annually on agriculture, farmers' welfare: PM Modi* economictimes.indiatimes.com [Online] Retrieved from: https://economictimes.indiatimes.com/news/india/government-spending-rs-6-5-lakh-crore-annually-on-agriculture-farmers-welfare-pm-modi/articleshow/101413874.cms?from=mdr [Accessed: 2 April 2024].

11. Ibid.
12. NDTV (2022) *PM Modi Tells Biden "World Facing Food Shortage, India Can Help Provided...* ndtv.com [Online] Retrieved from: https://www.ndtv.com/india-news/pm-narendra-modi-tells-joe-biden-world-facing-food-shortage-india-can-help-provided-2880799 [Accessed: 2 April 2024].
13. Fortune India (2022) *Can India Be a Global Food Bowl?* fortuneindia.com [Online] Retrieved from: https://www.fortuneindia.com/long-reads/can-india-be-a-global-food-bowl/109640 [Accessed: 2 April 2024].
14. The Economic Times (2024) *India's agricultural exports to rise despite curbs on wheat, rice, sugar* economictimes.indiatimes.com [Online] Retrieved from: https://economictimes.indiatimes.com/news/economy/agriculture/indias-agricultural-exports-to-rise-despite-curbs-on-wheat-rice-sugar/articleshow/106633466.cms?from=mdr [Accessed: 2 April 2024].
15. Fortune India (2022) *Can India Be a Global Food Bowl?* fortuneindia.com [Online] Retrieved from: https://www.fortuneindia.com/long-reads/can-india-be-a-global-food-bowl/109640 [Accessed: 2 April 2024].
16. Press Information Bureau (2021) *India's rice exports rose by over 33% to 11.79 MT in first seven months of current FY, likely to surpass last FY's record over 17MT* pib.gov.in [Online] Retrieved from: https://pib.gov.in/PressReleasePage.aspx?PRID=1782368 [Accessed: 2 April 2024].
17. Trading Economics (2024) *India - Arable Land (% Of Land Area)* tradingeconomics.com [Online] Retrieved from: https://tradingeconomics.com/india/arable-land-percent-of-land-area-wb-data.html#:~:text=Arable%20land%20(%25%20of%20land%20area)%20in%20India%20was%20reported,compiled%20from%20officially%20recognized%20sources [Accessed: 2 April 2024].
18. Mint (2017) *There's more farmland in the world than was previously thought* livemint.com [Online] Retrieved from: https://www.livemint.com/Politics/aI28vAplwqEqm2LnziWU3I/Theres-more-farmland-in-the-world-than-was-previously-thoug.html [Accessed: 2 April 2024].
19. Press Information Bureau (2021) *Cabinet approves implementation of Pradhan Mantri Krishi Sinchayee Yojana for 2021-26* pib.gov.in [Online] Retrieved from: https://pib.gov.in/PressReleasePage.aspx?PRID=1781719 [Accessed: 2 April 2024].

20. INC42 (2023) *Economic Survey 2022-23: India Reduced 39,000+ Compliances For Ease Of Doing Business* inc42.com [Online] Retrieved from: https://inc42.com/buzz/economic-survey-2022-23-india-reduced-39000-compliances-ease-of-doing-business/ [Accessed: 2 April 2024].
21. Department of Economic Affairs (2024) *The Indian Economy: A Review* dea.gov.in [Online] Retrieved from: https://dea.gov.in/sites/default/files/The%20Indian%20Economy-A%20Review_Jan%202024.pdf [Accessed: 2 April 2024].
22. PM of India *Make In India* pmindia.gov.in [Online] Retrieved from: https://www.pmindia.gov.in/en/major_initiatives/make-in-india/ [Accessed: 2 April 2024].
23. Verma, Sudesh (2014) *Narendra Modi–The GameChanger*. New Delhi: Vitasta Publishing.
24. NDTV Profit (2014) *'This is the Step of a Lion': PM Modi on his Make-in-India Campaign* ndtvprofit.com [Online] Retrieved from: https://www.ndtvprofit.com/business/pm-modi-unveils-a-lion-logo-for-his-make-in-india-campaign-670682 [Accessed: 2 April 2024].
25. The Times of India (2023) *How did India become the second-largest mobile manufacturer in the world?* timesofindia.indiatimes.com [Online] Retrieved from: https://timesofindia.indiatimes.com/blogs/unheard-echoes-of-young-mind-2/how-did-india-become-the-second-largest-mobile-manufacturer- [[Accessedin-the-world/ [Accessed: 2 April 2024].
26. The Economic Times (2024) *India mobile phone manufacturing industry likely to create up to 2,50,000 jobs in next 12-16 months* economictimes.indiatimes.com [Online] Retrieved from: https://economictimes.indiatimes.com/jobs/fresher/india-mobile-phone-manufacturing-industry-likely-to-create-up-to-250000-jobs-in-next-12-16-months/articleshow/107529553.cms?from=mdr [Accessed: 2 April 2024].
27. FirstPost (2023) *India's mobile phone manufacturing at $44 billion, exports at $11 billion, says IT Minister Vaishnaw* firstpost.com [Online] Retrieved from: https://www.firstpost.com/tech/india-mobile-phone-manufacturing-at-44-billion-exports-at-11-billion-says-it-minister-vaishnaw-13438992.html [Accessed: 2 April 2024].
28. Government of India *India Semiconductor Mission* ism.gov.in [Online] Retrieved from: https://www.ism.gov.in/ [Accessed: 2 April 2024].

29. The Economic Times (2024) *Interim Budget 2024 offers free electricity to 1 crore households through rooftop solar* economictimes.indiatimes.com [Online] Retrieved from: https://economictimes.indiatimes.com/industry/renewables/interim-budget-2024-offers-free-electricity-to-1-crore-households-through-rooftop-solar/articleshow/107317621.cms?from=mdr [Accessed: 2 April 2024].
30. The Economic Times (2023) *Whopping 364 per cent jump in India's solar exports within a year* economictimes.indiatimes.com [Online] Retrieved from: https://energy.economictimes.indiatimes.com/news/renewable/tables-turning-for-indias-solar-story-exports-see-364-per-cent-sharp-increase-in-fy23/101742619 [Accessed: 2 April 2024].
31. Government of India *Introduction and 8-Year Factbook* startupindia.gov.in [Online] Retrieved from: https://www.startupindia.gov.in/content/sih/en/Prabhav-100K-Startups.html [Accessed: 2 April 2024].
32. Invest India *Startup Ecosystem in India, The Indian Unicorn Landscape* investindia.gov.in [Online] Retrieved from: https://www.investindia.gov.in/indian-unicorn-landscape [Accessed: 2 April 2024].
33. Indian Century (2024) *Celebrating 8 Years of Startup India* indiancentury.in [Online] Retrieved from: https://www.indiancentury.in/2024/01/26/celebrating-8-years-of-startup-india/ [Accessed: 2 April 2024].
34. Business Today (2024) *T V Mohandas Pai's prediction: India will be a leading global power by 2029* businesstoday.in [Online] Retrieved from: https://www.businesstoday.in/magazine/columns/story/tv-mohandas-pais-prediction-india-will-be-a-leading-global-power-by-2029-417107-2024-02-12 [Accessed: 2 April 2024].
35. Digital Sansad (2023) *Unstarred Question Number 97, 2023/ mudra shishu loans* sansad.in [Online] Retrieved from: chrome-extension://efaidnbmnnnibpcajpcglclefindmkaj/https://sansad.in/getFile/loksabhaquestions/annex/1714/AU97.pdf?source=pqals [Accessed: 2 April 2024].
36. Press Information Bureau (2023) *More than 40.82 crore loans amounting to ₹23.2 lakh crore sanctioned under Pradhan Mantri MUDRA Yojana (PMMY) since inception* pib.gov.in [Online] Retrieved from: https://pib.gov.in/PressReleaseIframePage.aspx?PRID=1914739 [Accessed: 2 April 2024].

37. Financial Express (2023) *This many Mudra loans disbursed to micro, small enterprises turned bad as of March 2023* financialexpress.com [Online] Retrieved from: https://www.financialexpress.com/business/sme-this-many-mudra-loans-to-micro-small-enterprises-turned-bad-as-of-march-2023-3203908/ [Accessed: 2 April 2024].
38. FirstPost (2023) *Service sector can help Narendra Modi govt achieve target of $5 trillion GDP: Piyush Goyal* firstpost.com [Online] Retrieved from: https://www.firstpost.com/business/service-sector-can-help-narendra-modi-govt-achieve-target-of-5-trillion-gdp-piyush-goyal-7705011.html [Accessed: 2 April 2024].
39. Narendra Modi (2023) *PM addresses G20 Tourism Ministers' Meet* narendramodi.in [Online] Retrieved from: https://www.narendramodi.in/prime-minister-narendra-modi-addresses-g20-tourism-ministers-meet-571366 [Accessed: 2 April 2024].
40. Ibid.
41. Invest India *Unlock the Marvels of Incredible India: Powerhouse of Tourism and Hospitality* investindia.gov.in [Online] Retrieved from: https://www.investindia.gov.in/sector/tourism-hospitality [Accessed: 2 April 2024].
42. Statista (2024) *Total contribution of travel and tourism to GDP in India 2013-2021* statista.com [Online] Retrieved from: https://www.statista.com/statistics/313724/total-contribution-of-travel-and-tourism-to-gdp-in-india-by-segment/ [Accessed: 2 April 2024].
43. Invest India *Unlock the Marvels of Incredible India: Powerhouse of Tourism and Hospitality* investindia.gov.in [Online] Retrieved from: https://www.investindia.gov.in/sector/tourism-hospitality [Accessed: 2 April 2024].
44. The Times of India (2023) *AIIMS-led Heal in India to boost medical tourism* timesofindia.indiatimes.com [Online] Retrieved from: https://timesofindia.indiatimes.com/city/nagpur/aiims-led-heal-in-india-to-boost-medical-tourism/articleshow/106412883.cms [Accessed: 2 April 2024].
45. Hindustan Times (2022) *Medical tourism in India: Top destinations scenarios and all you need to know* hindustantimes.com [Online] Retrieved from: https://www.hindustantimes.com/lifestyle/travel/medical-tourism-in-india-top-destinations-scenarios-and-all-you-need-to-know-101668163467932.html [Accessed: 2 April 2024].

46. The Times of India (2024) *Air passenger traffic in India expected to reach 300 million by 2030: Jyotiraditya Scindia* timesofindia.indiatimes.com [Online] Retrieved from: https://timesofindia.indiatimes.com/india/air-passenger-traffic-in-india-expected-to-reach-300-million-by-2030-jyotiraditya-scindia/articleshow/106954624.cms [Accessed: 2 April 2024].
47. Ibid.
48. Invest India (2024) *Industry Scenario: Indian Railways* investindia.gov.in [Online] Retrieved from: https://www.investindia.gov.in/sector/railways [Accessed: 2 April 2024].
49. Make In India *Foreign Direct Investment* makeinindia.com [Online] Retrieved from: https://www.makeinindia.com/policy/foreign-direct-investment [Accessed: 2 April 2024].
50. CNBC TV18 (2024) *India has enough forex reserves to keep the rupee strong for 5-6 years, says Piyush Goyal* cnbctv18.com [Online] Retrieved from: https://www.cnbctv18.com/economy/indias-forex-reserves-enough-to-keep-currency-strong-for-5-6-years-says-piyush-goyal-18521291.htm [Accessed: 2 April 2024].

Guarding the Borders: Preparing for Two Plus Front War

1. The Independent (1999) *Pakistan `tortured Indians to death'* independent.co.uk [Online] Retrieved from: https://www.independent.co.uk/news/world/pakistan-tortured-indians-to-death-1099605.html [Accessed: 3 April 2024].
2. India Today (2020) *Bajwa's legs shook, Pakistan dreaded India would attack if Abhinandan not released: Pak MP* indiatoday.in [Online] Retrieved from: https://www.indiatoday.in/india/story/pakistan-feared-india-attack-if-abhinandan-not-released-1736112-2020-10-29 [Accessed: 3 April 2024].
3. The Economic Times (2018) *Narendra Modi's call to Saudi King helped India's operation 'Rahat' in Yemen: Sushma Swaraj* economictimes.indiatimes.com [Online] Retrieved from: https://economictimes.indiatimes.com/news/politics-and-nation/narendra-modis-call-to-saudi-king-helped-indias-operation-rahat-in-yemen-sushma-swaraj/articleshow/62405284.cms?from=mdr [Accessed: 3 April 2024].

4. The Times of India (2022) *Indian tricolour came to rescue of fleeing Pakistani, Turkish students from Ukraine* timesofindia.indiatimes.com [Online] Retrieved from: https://timesofindia.indiatimes.com/india/indian-tricolour-came-to-rescue-of-fleeing-pakistani-turkish-students-from-ukraine/articleshow/89938817.cms [Accessed: 3 April 2024].
5. India Today (2012) *Army chief General V K Singh's war on India* indiatoday.in [Online] Retrieved from: https://www.indiatoday.in/magazine/cover-story/story/20120409-bribery-row-defamation-army-chief-general-singh-letter-manmohan-757927-2012-03-30 [Accessed: 3 April 2024].
6. Deccan Herald (2009) *No ammunition for artillery guns of Indian Army: The shortfall is steadily on rise since 2009* deccanherald.com [Online] Retrieved from: https://www.deccanherald.com/india/no-ammunition-artillery-guns-indian-2127681 [Accessed: 3 April 2024].
7. India Today (2012) *CAG highlighted gaps in defence in Dec 2011 but govt remained inactive: Report* indiatoday.in [Online] Retrieved from: https://indiatoday.in/india/north/story/cag-report-lack-of-defence-preparedness-98244-2012-04-05 [Accessed: 3 April 2024].
8. The Hindu (2014) *Fighter jet deal put off to next fiscal due to budget constraints: Antony* thehindubusinessline.com [Online] Retrieved from: https://www.thehindubusinessline.com/economy/policy/fighter-jet-deal-put-off-to-next-fiscal-due-to-budget-constraints-antony/article20722943.ece1 [Accessed: 3 April 2024].
9. The Economic Times (2018) *Rafale deal: SC gives clean chit, here is a brief timeline of the fighter jet case* economictimes.indiatimes.com [Online] Retrieved from: https://economictimes.indiatimes.com/news/defence/sc-gives-clean-chit-on-rafale-here-is-a-brief-timeline-of-the-fighter-jet-deal/articleshow/72050006.cms?from=mdr [Accessed: 3 April 2024].
10. The Times of India (2019) *Supreme Court's second clean chit on Rafale a big boost for PM Modi* timesofindia.indiatimes.com [Online] Retrieved from: https://timesofindia.indiatimes.com/india/supreme-courts-second-clean-chit-on-rafale-a-big-boost-for-modi/articleshow/72063722.cms [Accessed: 3 April 2024].
11. Hindustan times (2018) *HAL could have built Rafale jets in India, says former boss* hindustantimes.com [Online] Retrieved from: https://

www.hindustantimes.com/india-news/hal-could-have-built-rafale-jets-in-india-says-former-boss/story-Cr0dMhZXToq1GBIdXY97YI.html [Accessed: 3 April 2024].

12. Mint (2023) *HAL records highest-ever revenue of ₹26,500 cr for FY 22-23* livemint.com [Online] Retrieved from: https://www.livemint.com/companies/news/hal-records-highest-ever-revenue-of-rs-26-500-cr-for-fy-22-23-11680268927449.html [Accessed: 3 April 2024].
13. Business Today (2023) *Rajeev Chandrasekhar attacks Rahul Gandhi over HAL, says company became 'Rs 1.35 lakh cr company under PM Modi'* businesstoday.in [Online] Retrieved from: https://www.businesstoday.in/latest/politics/story/rajeev-chandrasekhar-attacks-rahul-gandhi-over-hal-says-company-became-rs-135-lakh-cr-company-under-pm-modi-391012-2023-07-24 [Accessed: 3 April 2024].
14. Press Information Bureau (2023) *Prime Minister dedicates to the nation HAL Helicopter Factory-India's largest-at Tumakuru, Karnataka* pib.gov.in [Online] Retrieved from: https://pib.gov.in/PressReleasePage.aspx?PRID=1896758 [Accessed: 3 April 2024].
15. X (formerly Twitter) @narendramodi (2023) twitter.com [Online] Retrieved from: https://twitter.com/narendramodi/status/1728388759161311548?lang=en [Accessed: 3 April 2024].
16. The Hindu (2016) *Pokhran-II delayed Tejas project, says former scientist* thehindu.com [Online] Retrieved from: https://www.thehindu.com/news/national/Pokhran-II-delayed-Tejas-project-says-former-scientist/article60452518.ece [Accessed: 3 April 2024].
17. PSU Watch (2023) *HAL spending over Rs 2000 crore this year on R&D: Official* psuwatch.com [Online] Retrieved from: https://psuwatch.com/defencewatch/hal-spending-over-rs-2000-crore-this-year-on-rd-official [Accessed: 3 April 2024].
18. News18 (2022) *16 Countries Interested in LCA Tejas Mk2, Efforts on to Identify Private Agencies to Speed Up Production* news18.com [Online] Retrieved from: https://www.news18.com/news/india/16-countries-interested-in-lca-tejas-mk2-efforts-on-to-identify-private-agencies-to-speed-up-production-6222199.html [Accessed: 3 April 2024].
19. First Post (2024) *BrahMos, ammo & more: A look at weapons India exports* firstpost.com [Online] Retrieved from: https://www.firstpost.

com/explainers/brahmos-missiles-ammunition-more-a-look-at-india-defence-exports-13733092.html [Accessed: 3 April 2024].

20. Press Information Bureau (2021) *Raksha Mantri Shri Rajnath Singh says, the new companies to be engines of growth for the economy and play important role in defence manufacturing ecosystem* pib.gov.in [Online] Retrieved from: https://pib.gov.in/PressReleasePage.aspx?PRID=1764148 [Accessed: 3 April 2024].
21. The Economic Times (2019) *India exporting bulletproof jackets of international standard to over 100 nations: BIS* economictimes.indiatimes.com [Online] Retrieved from: https://economictimes.indiatimes.com/news/defence/india-exporting-bulletproof-jackets-of-international-standard-to-over-100-nations-bis/articleshow/71099991.cms?from=mdr [Accessed: 3 April 2024].
22. India Today (2017) *Doklam border standoff: Will there be an India-China war?* indiatoday.in [Online] Retrieved from: https://www.indiatoday.in/magazine/cover-story/story/20170807-doklam-stand-off-india-china-dispute-will-china-go-to-war-1026539-2017-07-28 [Accessed: 3 April 2024].
23. Indian Defence Review (2021) *From OFB to Seven DPSUs* indiandefencereview.com [Online] Retrieved from: https://www.indiandefencereview.com/news/from-ofb-to-seven-dpsus/ [Accessed: 3 April 2024].
24. Press Information Bureau (2024) *Aatmanirbhar Bharat: DAC clears capital acquisition proposals worth Rs 84,560 crore to boost the capabilities of the Armed Forces & Indian Coast Guard* pib.gov.in [Online] Retrieved from: https://pib.gov.in/PressReleaseIframePage.aspx?PRID=2006552 [Accessed: 3 April 2024].
25. The Economic Times (2024) *Navy clears deal for 31 Predator Drones from US, contract signing expected in coming months* economictimes.indiatimes.com [Online] Retrieved from: https://economictimes.indiatimes.com/news/defence/navy-clears-deal-for-31-predator-drones-from-us-contract-signing-expected-in-coming-months/articleshow/107808515.cms?from=mdr [Accessed: 3 April 2024].
26. Hindustan Times (2024) *Navy adding capability to reinforce India as superpower in Indo-Pacific: Rajnath* hindustantimes.com [Online]

Retrieved from: https://www.hindustantimes.com/india-news/navy-adding-capability-to-reinforce-india-as-superpower-in-indo-pacific-rajnath-101706960493108.html [Accessed: 3 April 2024].

27. Ibid.
28. The Times of India (2023) *France submits bid for selling 26 naval Rafale fighters to India* timesofindia.indiatimes.com [Online] Retrieved from: https://timesofindia.indiatimes.com/india/france-submits-bid-for-selling-26-naval-rafale-fighters-to-india/articleshow/106162598.cms [Accessed: 3 April 2024].
29. Press Information Bureau *Chief of Defence Staff: A historic reform in Higher Defence Organisation* pib.gov.in [Online] Retrieved from: https://static.pib.gov.in/WriteReadData/specificdocs/documents/2021/oct/doc202110501.pdf [Accessed: 3 April 2024].
30. Ibid.
31. Narendra Modi (2013) *Shri Narendra Modi speech at Ex-Servicemen Rally in Rewari, Haryana: 15.09.2013* narendramodi.in [Online] Retrieved from: https://www.narendramodi.in/full-text-of-shri-narendra-modis-speech-at-ex-servicemens-rally-rewari-2798 [Accessed: 3 April 2024].
32. Press Information Bureau (2021) *One Rank One Pension* pib.gov.in [Online] Retrieved from: https://static.pib.gov.in/WriteReadData/specificdocs/documents/2021/nov/doc202111601.pdf [Accessed: 3 April 2024].
33. Ibid.
34. The Economic Times (2023) *Congress earmarked Rs 500 crore for OROP, we have given Rs 70,000 crore to ex-servicemen: PM Modi* economictimes.indiatimes.com [Online] Retrieved from: https://economictimes.indiatimes.com/news/elections/assembly-elections/madhya-pradesh-assembly-elections/congress-earmarked-rs-500-crore-for-orop-we-have-given-rs-70000-crore-to-ex-servicemen-pm-modi/articleshow/105072584.cms?from=mdr [Accessed: 3 April 2024].
35. US Army Recruiting Command (2022) *Army expands short-term enlistment options* recruiting.army.mil [Online] Retrieved from: https://recruiting.army.mil/News/Article/2925198/army-expands-short-term-enlistment-options/ [Accessed: 3 April 2024].

Modi Makes Friends Worldwide

1. Narendra Modi (2014) *Narendra Modi's Interview with Arnab Goswami of Times Now* narendramodi.in [Online] Retrieved from: https://www.youtube.com/watch?v=m3TTX2Xpsqc [Accessed: 3 April 2024].
2. India Today (2013) *Narendra Modi asks Hindus and Muslims to fight poverty together at Patna rally* indiatoday.in [Online] Retrieved from: https://www.indiatoday.in/india/east/story/narendra-modi-in-patna-hunkar-rally-bjp-215649-2013-10-26 [Accessed: 3 April 2024].
3. Indian Defence News (2024) *India Standing Against a Bully: Defence Secretary Giridhar Aramane* indiandefensenews.in [Online] Retrieved from: https://www.indiandefensenews.in/2024/02/india-standing-against-bully-defence.html [Accessed: 3 April 2024].
4. The Times of India (2013) *Modi addresses NRIs in 18 US cities via video conference* timesofindia.indiatimes.com [Online] Retrieved from: https://timesofindia.indiatimes.com/videos/news/modi-addresses-nris-in-18-us-cities-via-video-conference/videoshow/20023891.cms [Accessed: 3 April 2024].
5. India Today (2023) *Watch: PM Modi leads Yoga Day celebrations at UN HQ in New York* indiatoday.in [Online] Retrieved from: https://www.indiatoday.in/india/video/watch-pm-modi-leads-yoga-day-celebrations-at-un-hq-in-new-york-2395981-2023-06-21 [Accessed: 3 April 2024].
6. First Post (2023) *'Many advances in AI...even more in another AI–America and India': PM Modi at joint session of US Congress* firstpost.com [Online] Retrieved from: https://www.firstpost.com/world/ai-is-artificial-intelligence-and-america-and-india-pm-modi-at-joint-session-of-us-congress-12780012.html [Accessed: 3 April 2024].
7. NDTV (2023) '*You Are Causing Me A Real Problem...': Biden To PM On Upcoming US Trip* ndtv.com [Online] Retrieved from: https://www.ndtv.com/india-news/at-hiroshima-meet-joe-biden-asked-for-pm-modis-autograph-heres-why-4052866 [Accessed: 3 April 2024].
8. Ministry of External Affairs (2024) *State Visit of the President of France to India* mea.gov.in [Online] Retrieved from: https://www.mea.gov.in/incoming-visit-info.htm?1/1442/State+Visit+of+the+President+of+France+to+India+January+2526+2024 [Accessed: 22 April 2024].

9. The Economic Times (2024) *France seeks first meeting for India-to-EU infrastructure link* economictimes.indiatimes.com [Online] Retrieved from: https://economictimes.indiatimes.com/small-biz/trade/exports/insights/france-seeks-first-meeting-for-india-to-eu-infrastructure-link/articleshow/107868896.cms?from=mdr [Accessed: 3 April 2024].
10. Business Standard (2024) *India, Canada discuss collaboration in science, technology sector* business-standard.com [Online] Retrieved from: https://www.business-standard.com/india-news/india-canada-discuss-collaboration-in-science-technology-sector-124022101105_1.html [Accessed: 3 April 2024].
11. The Economic Times (2021) *Govt okays Rs 43,000 cr order to procure six submarines* economictimes.indiatimes.com [Online] Retrieved from: https://economictimes.indiatimes.com/news/defence/construction-of-six-advanced-submarines-for-indian-navy-approved/articleshow/83228961.cms?from=mdr [Accessed: 3 April 2024].
12. Hindustan Times (2023) *'PM Modi is the boss': Why Australia's Albanese mentioned Bruce Springsteen* hindustantimes.com [Online] Retrieved from: https://www.hindustantimes.com/india-news/pm-modi-is-the-boss-australias-anthony-albanese-at-event-in-sydney-101684833960763.html [Accessed: 3 April 2024].
13. The Economic Times (2017) *Philippines visit symbolises India's vow to deepen ties with ASEAN: Narendra Modi* economictimes.indiatimes.com [Online] Retrieved from: https://economictimes.indiatimes.com/news/politics-and-nation/philippines-visit-symbolises-indias-vow-to-deepen-ties-with-asean-narendra-modi/articleshow/61606600.cms?from=mdr [Accessed: 3 April 2024].
14. The New Indian Express (2016) *Some Neighbours Don't Understand that Issues Can be Resolved by Talks: PM's Veiled Dig at Pakistan* newindianexpress.com [Online] Retrieved from: https://www.newindianexpress.com/world/2016/Mar/31/some-neighbours-dont-understand-that-issues-can-be-resolved-by-talks-pms-veiled-dig-at-pakistan-918559.html [Accessed: 3 April 2024].
15. Government of India (2014) *Statement by Prime Minister prior to his departure for Nepal* mea.gov.in [Online] Retrieved from: https://www.mea.gov.in/outoging-visit-detail.htm?23806/

Statement+by+Prime+Minister+prior+to+his+departure+for+Nepal [Accessed: 3 April 2024].
16. Deccan Herald (2014) *Modi announces USD 1 bn concessional line of credit to Nepal* deccanherald.com [Online] Retrieved from: https://www.deccanherald.com/archives/modi-announces-usd-1-bn-2202545 [Accessed: 3 April 2024].
17. The Economic Times (2022) *Sri Lankan President Ranil Wickremesinghe thanks India for providing 'a breath of life' to crisis-hit island nation* economictimes.indiatimes.com [Online] Retrieved from: https://economictimes.indiatimes.com/news/india/sri-lankan-president-ranil-wickremesinghe-thanks-india-for-providing-a-breath-of-life-to-crisis-hit-island-nation/articleshow/93318253.cms?from=mdr [Accessed: 3 April 2024].
18. India Today (2023) *You saved us, prevented bloodbath: Lankan leader thanks India for help* indiatoday.in [Online] Retrieved from: https://www.indiatoday.in/world/story/you-saved-us-prevented-bloodbath-lankan-leader-thanks-india-for-help-2403877-2023-07-08 [Accessed: 3 April 2024].
19. Mint (2018) *PM Narendra Modi conferred 'Grand Collar of the State of Palestine'* livemint.com [Online] Retrieved from: https://www.livemint.com/Politics/NlhWJzNtuEemKZyRf2QxIM/PM-Narendra-Modi-conferred-Grand-Collar-of-the-State-of-Pal.html [Accessed: 3 April 2024].
20. Mint (2023) *UAE emerges as fourth largest investor in India during FY23 as FDI jumps three-folds to $3.35 billion* livemint.com [Online] Retrieved from: https://www.livemint.com/economy/uae-emerges-as-fourth-largest-investor-in-india-in-fy23-as-fdi-jumps-three-folds-to-3-35-billion-11686490190581.html [Accessed: 3 April 2024].
21. Narendra Modi (2024) *PM Modi inaugurates BAPS Hindu Mandir in Abu Dhabi, UAE* narendramodi.in [Online] Retrieved from: https://www.narendramodi.in/prime-minister-narendra-modi-inaugurates-baps-hindu-mandir-in-abu-dhabi-uae-579420 [Accessed: 3 April 2024].
22. Ibid.
23. Hindustan Times (2024) *PM Modi most popular global leader. Where are Biden, Trudeau in this list?* hindustantimes.com [Online] Retrieved

from: https://www.hindustantimes.com/india-news/pm-narendra-modi-most-popular-global-leader-where-are-biden-trudeau-in-this-list-101708599211399.html [Accessed: 3 April 2024].

24. The Times of India (2024) *PM Modi most successful Indian Prime Minister, greatest global leader, says Mukesh Ambani* timesofindia.indiatimes.com [Online] Retrieved from: https://timesofindia.indiatimes.com/india/pm-modi-most-successful-indian-prime-minister-greatest-global-leader-says-mukesh-ambani/articleshow/106696910.cms [Accessed: 3 April 2024].

Modi *ki* Guarantee

1. Press Information Bureau (2023) *Viksit Bharat Sankalp Yatra* pib.gov.in [Online] Retrieved from: https://pib.gov.in/PressReleaseIframePage.aspx?PRID=1977618 [Accessed: 3 April 2024].
2. WION (2018) *'Historic day', tweets Modi as electricity reaches all Indian villages* wionews.com [Online] Retrieved from: https://www.wionews.com/india-news/every-village-now-has-access-to-electricity-pm-modi-tweeted-as-electricity-reached-all-villages-on-saturday-133539 [Accessed: 3 April 2024].
3. Press Information Bureau (2023) *Implementation of household electrification under Saubhagya and RDSS* pib.gov.in [Online] Retrieved from: https://pib.gov.in/PressReleaseIframePage.aspx?PRID=1989801 [Accessed: 3 April 2024].
4. Press Information Bureau (2023) *Pradhan Mantri Bhartiya Janaushadhi Pariyojana achieved their target of Rs 1000 Crore in sales in FY 2023-24* pib.gov.in [Online] Retrieved from: https://pib.gov.in/PressReleaseIframePage.aspx?PRID=1988675 [Accessed: 3 April 2024].
5. Narendra Modi (2024) *Top 10 Guarantees of Prime Minister Narendra Modi* narendramodi.in [Online] Retrieved from: https://www.narendramodi.in/top-10-guarantees-of-prime-minister-narendra-modi-579804 [Accessed: 3 April 2024].
6. The Indian Express (2024) *Target for 'Lakhpati Didi' increased from 2 crore to 3 crore: What is the scheme* indianexpress.com [Online] Retrieved from: https://indianexpress.com/article/what-is/target-for-lakhpati-didi-increased-from-2-crore-to-3-crore-what-is-the-scheme-9138990/#:~:text=The%20scheme%20aims%20to%20empower,and%20skills%20for%20livelihood%20improvement. [Accessed: 3 April 2024].

7. Narendra Modi (2023) *PM Modi's interview to India Today* narendramodi.in [Online] Retrieved from: https://www.narendramodi.in/pm-modi-s-interview-to-india-today-31st-december-twenty-twenty-three-577618 [Accessed: 3 April 2024].

***Ashtalakshmi:* Assimilating North East**

1. Deccan Chronicles (2017) *NDA at 3: Modi opens longest bridge in Northeast, blames UPA for delay* deccanchronicle.com [Online] Retrieved from: https://www.deccanchronicle.com/nation/current-affairs/260517/indias-longest-bridge-delayed-by-10-years-because-of-upa-modi-in-assam.html [Accessed: 3 April 2024].
2. Press Information Bureau (2023) *Dr Jitendra Singh's visit to Assam to inaugurate PURVODAYA* pib.gov.in [Online] Retrieved from: https://pib.gov.in/PressReleaseIframePage.aspx?PRID=1936666 [Accessed: 3 April 2023].
3. Hindustan Times (2024) *'10 years under Modi govt have been golden era for Northeast', says Amit Shah* hindustantimes.com [Online] Retrieved from: https://www.hindustantimes.com/india-news/10-years-under-modi-govt-have-been-golden-era-for-northeast-says-amit-shah-101705673436529.html [Accessed: 3 April 2024].
4. Ibid.
5. Narendra Modi (2024) *The Entire North East region trusts Modi's Guarantee: PM Modi* [Online] Retrieved from: https://www.youtube.com/watch?v=0qIDATLX-8o [Accessed: 3 April 2024].
6. India Today (2018) *Why is Delhi Police hiring people from Northeast?* indiatoday.in [Online] Retrieved from: https://www.indiatoday.in/mail-today/story/why-is-delhi-police-hiring-people-from-northeast-1306134-2018-08-06 [Accessed: 3 April 2024].
7. NDTV (2024) *Delhi Police All-Women Team Wins Republic Day Best Marching Contingent Award* ndtv.com [Online] Retrieved from: https://www.ndtv.com/india-news/republic-day-parade-delhi-police-all-women-team-win-best-marching-contingent-award-4954485 [Accessed: 3 April 2024].
8. Narendra Modi (2024) *The Entire North East region trusts Modi's Guarantee: PM Modi* [Online] Retrieved from: https://www.youtube.com/watch?v=0qIDATLX-8o [Accessed: 3 April 2024].

9. Press Information Bureau (2023) *Budget Details of Ministry of Development of Northeast Region* pib.gov.in [Online] Retrieved from: https://pib.gov.in/PressReleaseIframePage.aspx?PRID=1895626 [Accessed: 3 April 2024].
10. Press Information Bureau (2023) *Dr Jitendra Singh's visit to Assam to inaugurate PURVODAYA* pib.gov.in [Online] Retrieved from: https://pib.gov.in/PressReleaseIframePage.aspx?PRID=1936666 [Accessed: 3 April 2023].
11. Ibid.
12. Mint (2023) *Modi proposes 12-point cooperation plan with ASEAN countries* livemint.com [Online] Retrieved from: https://www.livemint.com/news/india/modi-proposes-12-point-cooperation-plan-with-asean-countries-11694081412775.html [Accessed: 3 April 2024].

Why do they Oppose him?

1. The Indian Express (2023) *'Insulting India': Rahul Gandhi's remarks in US draw BJP's ire* indianexpress.com [Online] Retrieved from: https://indianexpress.com/article/india/rahul-gandhi-us-visit-bjp-insult-india-8638301/ [Accessed: 3 April 2024].
2. India Today (2023) *7 instances when Rahul Gandhi attacked Indian govt on foreign soil* indiatoday.in [Online] Retrieved from: https://www.indiatoday.in/india/story/7-instances-when-rahul-gandhi-attacked-modi-govt-on-foreign-soil-2342253-2023-03-03 [Accessed: 3 April 2024].
3. The Daily Guardian (2021) *India is fighting back doomsayers* thedailyguardian.com [Online] Retrieved from: https://thedailyguardian.com/india-is-fighting-back-doomsayers/ [Accessed: 3 April 2024].
4. The Hindu (2012) *Manmohan criticizes NGOs for protests in Kudankulam* thehindu.com [Online] Retrieved from: https://www.thehindu.com/news/national/manmohan-criticises-ngos-for-protests-in-kudankulam/article2924905.ece [Accessed: 3 April 2024].
5. Mint (2020) *Rs 58,000 cr foreign funds to NGOs in 3 years: MHA* livemint.com [Online] Retrieved from: https://www.livemint.com/news/india/rs-58-000-cr-foreign-funds-to-ngos-in-3-years-mha-11600175452018.html [Accessed: 3 April 2024].

6. First Post (2018) *FCRA licences of 20,000 NGOs cancelled: Act being used as weapon to silence organisations* firstpost.com [Online] Retrieved from: https://www.firstpost.com/india/fcra-licences-of-20000-ngos-cancelled-act-being-used-as-weapon-to-silence-organisations-3181560.html [Accessed: 3 April 2024].
7. Hindustan Times (2022) *ED attaches ₹1.54 crore in bank accounts of trust linked to Amnesty India* hindustantimes.com [Online] Retrieved from: https://www.hindustantimes.com/india-news/ed-attaches-1-54-crore-in-bank-accounts-of-trust-linked-to-amnesty-india-101665152217777.html [Accessed: 3 April 2024].
8. The Economic Times (2015) *Government blocks Greenpeace India's foreign fundings, suspends NGO's license for 6 months* economictimes.indiatimes.com [Online] Retrieved from: https://economictimes.indiatimes.com/news/politics-and-nation/government-blocks-greenpeace-indias-foreign-fundings-suspends-ngos-licence-for-6-months/articleshow/46864928.cms?from=mdr [Accessed: 3 April 2024].
9. Ibid.
10. The Economic Times (2013) *65 MPs write to Barack Obama: Don't Give Vias to Modi* economictimes.indiatimes.com [Online] Retrieved from: https://economictimes.indiatimes.com/news/politics-and-nation/65-mps-write-to-barack-obama-dont-give-visa-to-modi/articleshow/21275735.cms?from=mdr [Accessed: 3 April 2024].
11. Press Information Bureau (2018) *Task Force on Shell Companies takes pro-active and coordinated steps to check the menace of shell companies* pib.gov.in [Online] Retrieved from: https://pib.gov.in/newsite/PrintRelease.aspx?relid=179863 [Accessed: 3 April 2024].
12. NDTV (2023) *Minority Communities Benefitted Most Under Modi Government: BJP Leader* ndtv.com [Online] Retrieved from: https://www.ndtv.com/india-news/minority-communities-benefitted-most-from-welfare-schems-under-modi-govt-bjp-minority-cell-leader-4170286 [Accessed: 3 April 2024].
13. The Print (2019) *More Muslims got govt scholarships under Modi govt than during Congress-led UPA-2* theprint.in [Online] Retrieved from: https://theprint.in/india/more-muslims-govt-scholarships-modi-govt-congress-upa/308154/ [Accessed: 3 April 2024].

14. The Indian Express (2022) *Only class 9, 10 students to be considered for pre-matric scholarship scheme* indianexpress.com [Online] Retrieved from: https://indianexpress.com/article/education/only-class-9-10-students-to-be-considered-for-pre-matric-scholarship-scheme-scholarships-gov-in-8296707/ [Accessed: 3 April 2024].
15. Hindustan Times (2023) *11 crores fake names removed from gov schemes since 2014: PM Modi in MP* hindustantimes.com [Online] Retrieved from: https://www.hindustantimes.com/india-news/11-crores-fake-names-removed-from-govt-schemes-since-2014-pm-modi-in-mp-101696518746096.html [Accessed: 3 April 2024].
16. The Economic Times (2023) *Weeding out fake welfare scheme beneficiaries to help save Rs 18K cr* economictimes.co [Online] Retrieved from: https://economictimes.indiatimes.com/news/economy/policy/weeding-out-fake-welfare-scheme-beneficiaries-to-help-save-18k-cr/articleshow/104476897.cms?from=mdr [Accessed: 3 April 2024].
17. India Today (2023) *Biggest minority scholarship scam busted, 53% of institutions 'fake'. CBI to probe* indiatoday.in [Online] Retrieved from: https://www.indiatoday.in/india/story/beneficiaries-of-minority-schemes-fake-smriti-irani-orders-probe-2423647-2023-08-19 [Accessed: 3 April 2024].